by
Gene Hutmaker
and *(with some reluctance)*
Michael A. Hutmaker

"Banned in the Bronx: The Yankee Hater Memoirs: 1953-2005," by Gene Hutmaker and Michael A. Hutmaker. ISBN 1-58939-841-6.

Manufactured in the United States of America.

Life is one Big Baseball
GAME

Sometimes you strike out
&
Sometimes you hit a Home Run

BANNED in the BRONX
The Yankee Hater Memoirs 1953 – 2005

by

Gene Hutmaker
and
Michael A Hutmaker, Ed. D.

Best Wishes
Gene Hutmaker

Dedication

This book is dedicated to two of the most important women in my life.

My Mom

Stella "All-Star" (Kowalski) Hutmaker. Even though the former basketball star of the 1930's has been gone for many years I still felt her nagging, oops, I mean her guidance in completing this endeavor.

My Wife

Josephine Grace (Suppa) Hutmaker. Who motivated me by nagging, oops, I mean giving me the encouragement over the years to put my baseball knowledge to good use – and for putting up with me since 1966 (especially my Yankee hating rantings).

Acknowledgments

As I came to the end of this long and winding road I can come up with a list as long as this book of people that have inspired, encouraged, and provided me with the ground work to complete this endeavor. But no, I'll cut it short.

Most importantly I would like to give my immeasurable thanks to my wife Josephine (wait a minute she's in the dedication) and my sons, Mike and Chris – as a dad I couldn't have hoped for better offspring (except for them being Yankee die-hards – how'd I go wrong there). Although Mike is a Pinstriper, he is my collaborator making sure I restrained from my "going off on a tangent" tendencies. Chris has been a major part of my life for the past 33 years and without him this book would not be possible. Then naturally there's my dad and sister Carole Rossi, who tapped their memory banks for me for the events of the '50's and '60's.

I have to give mention to my cousin Ron Wnek, formerly of Brooklyn, who I went with to so many games in the '50's and '60's, as well as the rest of my family members for their input.

Not to be left out are my 2 million or so in-laws who I want to thank (for letting me in the family) especially pro-Met and anti-Yankee Tom and Antoniette Alessandra (Josephine's sister) who, like me, have the misfortune to have a Yankee-lover son, Frank (at least their other son, Anthony hates the Yankees).

Next I have to thank Burt Bauman, my friend who I coached with for ten years in the '80's. As a third base coach, he sent more guys home than the end of World War II. Also, Burt is a former Boys of Summer Brooklyn Dodger fan and now a Met fan and a true Yankee Hater- so naturally we hit it off. With this I am also grateful to all the South Brunswick Township residents I've met throughout my 35 years here, especially those in the South Brunswick Athletic Association (SBAA). And I cannot forget all the guys that played baseball, soccer, and basketball for me during my coaching years.

And lastly, but not least are the thousands of post office co-workers I've encountered over the years (since 1963) that I have to express my gratitude to for putting up with my endless baseball jargon. These include four that I've known for the past 24 years – Phillies fan Jim Puvel - Mets fan Jaime Ayala (a former minor league catcher who handled my Yankee tirades like he did his pitchers) - Rich Hebble, a Yankee fan liberal who wants Joe Torre to be Postmaster General (whenever The Boss axes him) - and Bill Basilone, a Yankee fan who seemingly knows more about the Pinstripers than George Steinbrenner. And I must mention Yankee fan Joe Sica (he started in the Post Office in 1964) who I've been talking baseball with for the past 40 years – Joe was a high school All-County All-Star in the early '60's who played center field like his boyhood idol Mickey Mantle.

And thanks to anyone I might have overlooked (i.e. army, school) that supplied any input in assisting me in the book that may be Banned in the Bronx.

Contents

Foreword
By Dr. Michael A. Hutmaker

What do you write in a foreword? Especially for a book that mocks your team. My father wrote over fifty years of stories with much ease (though he was a big fan of fine tuning) and I'm at a loss for words. For starters, the first question is why a Yankee fan would participate in a book that highlights some of the not so successful moments of the Bronx Bombers. The main reason, I guess is that blood is thicker than water, and in this case blood is thicker than team allegiance. Another reason is that non-Yankee fans have so little to cheer for that I figured that even they need something to look forward to. When you are on top people always aim to knock you down. The final reason was to quiet my dad. You know how a little kid is always tugging at your sleeve trying to get your attention; that was him during this process (it's not easy raising parents).

My brother, Chris, and I are lucky to have our parents (as they are lucky to have us). They basically gave us the ability to make our own choices. Even to be Yankee fans (though my mom could care less who we cheered for, but since it irked our dad, she always sided with us). Growing up with this non-believer was interesting. My father has that corny 'dad humor'. He considers himself quite the quipster, but every once in a while he comes up with a good one (that is something you'll have to decide for yourself). He truly enjoyed raising me and Chris. I guess it was because he never had a brother (my mother always said she felt like she was raising three boys). He would organize baseball, basketball, and football games with us and our friends in the neighborhood; he would even play to even up the teams. This eventually progressed to him coaching us for more than ten years. The coaching kept him away from most of his house and yard work (my mother would not buy the explanation that raking ball fields constituted yard work). He rationalized that this was part of what he called his responsibility for child development. He would coach my teams during the regular season and Chris' summer tournament teams. He was also glad when we started playing soccer and basketball. This way he was too busy with 'child development' to get to the chores. He had much success as a coach. A lot of it had to do with me and Chris being pretty good athletes, as well as most of our friends that he coached. However, one of his quirks was his superstitious nature. An example of this was how he kept the cheap sunglass industry afloat in the 1980s. Whenever he would lose a game in a frustrating manner, he would toss out those $5 sunglasses out of the car window on the way home. He reasoned that he would never lose again with those sunglasses.

The thing about my dad is that he has this uncanny ability to spit out stories, statistics and facts about baseball. It got to the point where I dubbed him "the Rainman of Baseball facts", after the Tom Cruise/Dustin Hoffman movie. The amount of baseball facts, from the well known to the minutia of who started or hit in what game of any World Series, is ridiculous. He sometimes doesn't remember where his keys are, but he can recite a starting line-up from a World Series game forty years ago. He is the baseball version of the know-it-all TV character, Cliff Claven from the TV show "CHEERS". He even threatened to write the creators of the show to put him on as Cliff's cousin (it didn't hurt that he works in the Post Office and even physically resembles the character). Speaking of TV my dad's favorite all-time program is Seinfeld, especially any episodes with a baseball connection (i.e. Steinbrenner and George Costanza); but he does not eat a Snickers candy bar with a knife and fork ala Danny Tartabull.

When people come over to the house he eventually lures them upstairs to see his "Baseball Room' (which was my old room) to show them his thousands of baseball cards, World Series programs and MacFarlane figurines (I put up 20 shelves for him as a birthday present so he can display them). Even though all of their guests see the room, I think that my mother has only been in there to turn off the lights or lower the volume on the TV. Even though he is a devout Yankee-hater, my dad does have a sense of objectivity when it comes to baseball. He tends to hate the Yankee organization rather than specific players. For instance he firmly believes that more recent Yankees, such as Munson, Gossage, Mattingly, and Guidry, should be strongly considered as members of the Hall of Fame, along with non-Yankees Minnie Minoso, Gil Hodges, and, his boyhood favorite, Ken Boyer.

So, my role in this project was to make sure my dad stayed on target with his Forrest Gump-like recollection of his 50+ year journey as a Yankee hater (in each chapter, you never know what you're going to get), throw in some Yankee highlights (Editor's Notes:) that he chose to ignore, and support his endeavor. But now that it is complete, I don't know what he will do with his free time (I guess he'll finally get to doing some of that house and yard work...you're welcome mom).

Why I Hate the Yankees

In 1976 the movie Network was nominated for the Academy Award for best picture (it lost out to Rocky). I saw it in New York City the first week it was out and what I remember from it was actor Peter Finch's classic hanging out of the window monologue "We're not going to take it anymore." Peter Finch won the Oscar for Best Actor.

Well this is how I feel about all the sports books that are out about the New York Yankees.

I am 60 years old and for over 50 years, I have been an avowed "Yankee Hater".

I'm just so tired of seeing books about the Mick, Yogi, the Babe, DiMaggio, Whitey, Rizzuto, etc. and the books 1947 & 1949. However, I did immensely enjoy "October 1964" by Dave Halberstam for its glorious conclusion. (It was the year my favorite team, the St. Louis Cardinals defeated the Yanks in the World Series).

I have two sons, both in their 30's. I raised them to make their own choices, even when picking a team to root for. They, much to my dismay, picked the Yankees. Actually, growing up in central Jersey, they root for all the area teams in all the sports including the Mets and the Phillies, - but mostly they are avid Yankee fans (my younger son, Chris, is also a Dallas Cowboy fan). They are getting tired of me complaining of all the Yankee books and challenged me to write a Yankee Hater Book.

I have decided to take up this quasi-challenge only if my older son, Mike, assisted me on completing it, basically to keep it rated PG. The following is over a 50-year period of Yankee failures with little mention of any of their success.

It should be noted that I really only "hate" the Yankee players while they're in their NY Pinstripes (i.e. Reggie Jackson was OK when he was on other teams, except '73 when as an Oakland Athletic, he clobbered the Mets in the World Series).

Something about me - most of my leisure time involves sports (dominated by baseball). I also follow college basketball and pro and college football. This book is written basically from my perspective and recollection of what happened. I did some research for some of the stats and also to clarify the hazy parts. But mostly it is from my memory.

When it comes to baseball, my memory is pretty good. I might spend two or three days a week trying to remember where I put my keys, but I can remember my first year of following baseball – 1953 when Carl "The Reading Rifle" Furillo of Brooklyn won the batting title with a .344 average by sitting out the end of the season due to injuring his hand in a fight with the Giants, thus beating out my idol Stan Musial (.337) and his Cardinal teammate Red Schoendienst (.342). My sons call me the 'Baseball Rainman' (my middle name is Raymond), but I don't watch Judge Wopner or hate K-Mart.

From 1951 – 52, I didn't know that much about baseball. It was probably early in 1951 when our neighbor, an RCA engineer, gave us a 10-inch television (the relatively new entertainment device for homes). I recall in October 1951 a bunch of people in my house hollering and screaming – it was Bobby Thomson's "Shot Heard Round the World" home run that gave the NY Giants the National League pennant over the Brooklyn Dodgers. I didn't pay it too much mind.

Prior to 1953, I also knew of baseball players because of the advertisements of cigarettes (Chesterfield, Lucky Strikes etc.) showing Joe DiMaggio, Yogi Berra, Ted Williams, etc. enjoying a smoke. Also, Wheaties (the Breakfast of Champions) and Royal Desserts had baseball players on cards as advertisers. This was in addition to the older kids in the neighborhood using baseball trading cards and a clothespin to create a 'motorcycle' sound on their bikes by attaching them to their bike frame causing the cards to hit the spokes.

With the popularization of television, there was constant vying for what was on. At this time there always seemed to be a baseball game on. On channel 9 the Brooklyn Dodgers were on and on channel 11 the Giants and Yankees were on depending who was at home. (Only home games were televised in these days). My main TV interest at seven years old were the puppet shows like Howdy Doody, Kukla Fran and Ollie & Rudy Kazootie, and action adventure westerns with cowboys like Hoot Gibson, Roy Rogers,

Gene Autry (future Angels owner), and Hopalong Cassidy, my favorite.

It was probably the beginning of the summer of 1953 that my relationship with baseball really began. My family consisted of Dad, Mom and my sister Carole – four people in a three bedroom colonial, but somehow it always seemed that from time to time other people were living with us, like uncles and their families. (I don't remember using the bathroom until I was twelve years old). Both my parents were avid sports fans and so were all of the other people in our house, so there was always, it seemed, a game on the TV or the radio.

It was also at this time that I got interested in collecting baseball trading cards. In 1953 there were two companies that produced cards – The Topps Company and Bowman Company. The Topps cards were like a painting from a picture while the Bowman were an actual picture with nothing on the front, thus, to find out who the player was, you had to turn the card over, which initiated my "baseball education". (Some card collectors of today consider the '53 Bowman cards, the best looking set ever). As an eight-year old, I did not yet have a favorite team. Because of the fine colored pictures, I collected Bowman cards rather than the Topps cards. As I recall, I didn't know they were Bowman cards, their wrapper had Joe DiMaggio written on them thus whenever I went to the candy store I used to ask for the "Joe DiMaggio" cards.

Collecting these "Joe DiMaggio" cards was a main factor in me choosing the St. Louis Cardinals as my favorite team. As an eight-year old, I was most impressed by their uniforms (the bright two cardinals perched on a bat and their colorful hat which had a blue cap, red bill and red interlocking S T L). My favorite cards were their three future Hall of Famers, Stan the Man Musial, Red Schoendienst, and Enos "Country" Slaughter.

During this time I became more involved in learning about baseball. An early memory was when my mom and I were in the "books for kids" section of a toy store. There were books of Bugs Bunny and Donald Duck, but what caught my attention were books about the baseball stars of the early '50's. I recall seeing books on the Pirates' home run hitter, Ralph Kiner (he led the NL in homers in his first seven seasons 1946-52), the Yankees' All-Star catcher, Yogi Berra, the Dodgers' dynamic leader, Jackie Robinson and Cardinal great, Stan Musial. These books were about twenty something pages – were probably for an 8 – 10 year old and had plenty of photos. I sweet-talked my mom into buying me the Stan the Man book. One of the photos was of Stan the Man with his son. At this point in my life I wished I was Stan the Man's son. A strange ironic twist is that I think my dad had the same wish (that I was Stan Musial's son).

Turning into a St. Louis Cardinal fan, I followed the National League a lot more than the American League. Since I was a new baseball fan I became more aware that the Yankees were "evil". The people in my house would continually comment on how lucky they were. (It was probably around this period that the saying "Rooting for the Yankees was like rooting for United States Steel" was started). Because of being a follower of the National League and the people in my house being anti-Yankee, I became a Yankee Hater. Also, whenever I got Yankee cards in a pack of cards, I would use them on my bike to make the motorcycle noise. (With the value of these cards now - the Mantle card itself is worth around $1,500.00- I must have used a couple of hundred thousand dollars to make a motorcycle sound...ahh, hindsight).

Also, during the summer of '53 I went to my first baseball game. It was at the Polo Grounds – a doubleheader, the Giants and Cardinals on June 14. As a fledgling Cardinal fan my interest in rooting for them was reinforced by their sweep of the doubleheader. Also, my favorites Stan the Man and Red Schoendienst had a bunch of hits. I think that Wilmer "Vinegar Bend" Mizell and Harvey "the Kitten" Haddix, St.Louis' 20-game winner, were the winning pitchers in the twin-bill. Mizell's nickname was for his hometown, Vinegar Bend, Alabama and Haddix' was because of his fielding style that was similar to that of his former Cardinal teammate, Harry "the Cat" Brecheen, regarded as the NL's best fielding pitcher in the '40's.

Let me give some background on why my parents were not Yankee fans. My father was born in 1914 and was five years old when Babe Ruth was traded to the Yankees. Living in the NJ suburb of Verona, which was about ten miles from New York City, he became a Yankee fan rooting for Babe Ruth, Lou Gehrig and the rest of them. For 14 or so years he was a Yankee fan. That was soon to end. In the mid-1930's, in the middle of the depression, my father helped make ends meet during this period by being a caddie at the Montclair Country Club. One of the golfers he caddied for was

George Weiss who was an executive with the Newark Bears, the main Yankee minor league team. Weiss, who later became the Yankees' General Manager, would tip his caddie like he would later pay his Yankee players of the 1950's – very cheaply (he even tried to cut Mickey Mantle's salary in 1957; the same year he was the American League Most Valuable Player). Caddies relied on the tips received from their golfers. Weiss' stinginess really aggravated my father and since the Newark Bears were the Yankees' farm team, my father changed his baseball loyalties from the Yankees to the New York Giants and became a Carl Hubbell and Mel Ott fan (the Giants' future Hall of Famers).

My mother also grew up a Yankee fan. She did not marry my father until she was 28 years old - in 1941 - an unheard of age for that time. Up until getting married, my mom would be considered a real maverick woman. During the depression, she had a job, had a '34 Ford, and was a basketball star in a women's industrial league. She was known as Stella All-Star, and I can remember her winning prizes at Palisades Amusement Park shooting baskets (swish-swish). Being an athletic person, she enjoyed baseball and was a Yankee fan for two reasons. The first reason was she rooted for the Newark Bears, the Yanks' top minor league club. In the late 1930's she would go to many Newark Bears games. She had an old autograph book and I can remember seeing signatures of George "Twinkletoes" Selkirk and Joe "Flash" Gordon that she got when they were on the Bears.

The second reason was that she grew up in Bloomfield, NJ. In the same neighborhood lived Hank Borowy who became a Yankee star pitcher in the early 1940's. He was the starter for the AL in the '44 All-Star Game and was 56-30 (.651 %) as a Yankee. He was sold to the Chicago Cubs in the middle of the '45 season, even though he was 10-5 and was one of the best in the AL. The price was just under a $100 thousand, a mighty sum in 1945 (a war year). I think the Yankee fans must have thought that their owner was Harry Frazee (the Red Sox owner who traded the Babe) as this was probably the reason the Yanks missed out on the '45 pennant. Borowy led the Cubs to the World Series (their last) by going 11-2 and leading the NL with a 2.13 ERA (for the year he was 21-7, and would be the only pitcher in this century to post 10 victories in each league in one season – it did not occur again until 2002 when Bartolo Colon won 10 games for the Montreal Expos and 10 for the

Cleveland Indians going 20-8 for the year). You could see how important he was to the Cubs pennant run as they beat out the Cardinals by only three games. The Sporting News, the weekly newspaper, known as "The Bible of Baseball" selected him as the NL Pitcher of the Year even though he only pitched a half of the year in the league. He is the last Chicago Cub pitcher to win a World Series game. My mom stopped being a Yankee fan after they traded away her former neighbor, Borowy. She then became a National League fan probably rooting for Stan Musial because of his Polish ancestry. She always referred to Musial as "Stash".

In 1953 the Korean War was finally over. In the country there were plenty of anti-Communism feelings throughout the land. Senator Joe McCarthy of Wisconsin spearheaded an Anti-Communism Committee of sorts, claiming seemingly everybody as being a "Pinko" (a Commie lover). Anyway, Senator McCarthy was on television quite a bit, and since the whole country had an air of anti-Communism, naturally my house, with whoever was living there at the time, was pro-American and hated the Commies (also known as Reds). The anger against these "Reds" was the same fervor expressed by the people in my house when the Yankees were on TV. This is one reason I felt the Yankees were something "evil" and should to be treated like Commies or 'Reds' – but in baseball the real Reds were in Cincinnati. (During this time the Cincinnati team modified their name from Reds to Redlegs).

The 1953 season was quite a year to begin following baseball. It was the first time in 50 years that a franchise moved. The Boston Braves moved to Milwaukee where they captivated the nation's fans by finishing runner-up to the Brooklyn Dodgers after finishing next to last in 1952. They were led by their second-year slugger Eddie Mathews who hit about 30 homers in the first half of the season chasing the famous Babe Ruth record of 60. He cooled off and hit another 17 to finish with 47. Although, not really caring about the American League, I was aware of the great year Al Rosen, the Cleveland third baseman, had - he led the league with 43 homers and 145 RBIs and batted .336 missing the batting crown by one point to Mickey Vernon's .337. Despite his near Triple Crown year and the usual fine pitching Cleveland had, they again were runner-up to the evil Yankees. In the '53 World Series, once again the Yankees played their Brooklyn neighbors, the Dodgers, for the fourth time since 1947. As in the previous three meetings ('47, '49 and '52) the Dodgers lost.

Take note that at this time baseball was comprised of an American and National League of eight teams each. The winner of each league was the pennant winner and would face each other in the World Series. New franchises started over the next decade, but it wasn't until 1969 when baseball expanded to 24 teams that each league split into an East and West division, thus necessitating the creation of a league playoff to determine the pennant winner.

1953
The Yankee Glove

It was in 1953 when I got my first glove, and believe it or not, it was a Yankee glove. Here's how I happened to select a glove from a member of my most hated team. Our house had a sun porch adjacent to our dining room. It had a couch in it but basically it was a storage area for my sister's and my toys, as well as an assortment of "old stuff". It was the spring of '53 when I found among the "old stuff" a baseball glove. It was not like the current 1950 gloves – the fingers of the mitt were unattached (no rawhide string connecting them). I remember the glove was either a Pie Traynor or Paul Waner model (memory lapse). I did not know who either player was but my father told me the player was a Pittsburgh Pirate star of the 1920's and '30's.

My dad laughed when he saw me with this old glove. He said that when we go on vacation he will get me a modern glove. Our vacation was usually at the Jersey shore town of Manasquan. One of my mom's basketball teammates had a sporting goods store in Manasquan and above the store were rooms where we stayed for our vacation.

We went on vacation in July and while there I was to choose a glove. There were two gloves I was interested in; one was a Yankee-Phil Rizzuto model and the other a Sam Mele model. Mele was an average outfielder with the Washington Senators (led the AL in doubles with 36 in 1951), and was later more famously remembered for being the manager of the 1965 pennant winning Minnesota Twins. The choice was difficult for me – the Rizzuto glove was better but not by a lot and he was a member of the hated Yankees. Anyway, my dad convinced me to forget the name on the glove and pick the one I liked (the price was about the same for each). Against my better judgment I picked the Rizzuto glove. I used the glove through 1953 and into 1954.

11

In 1954 and 1955 my favorite player, Stan "the Man" Musial, started to play first base. I wanted to follow his lead and become a first baseman. Also another factor was that I no longer wanted to use the Rizzuto glove. Rizzuto hit under .200 in 1954 (.195) and I did not want to be identified as someone who had a glove of a player who could not even hit .200. In these times the other kids always wanted to know whose model glove you used. My eldest son, Mike, later followed in my footsteps by choosing a Fred Lynn (of the hated Red Sox) model for his first glove. My son's reason was that Lynn was in the opening montage of "This Week in Baseball" making one of his patented over the fence catches.

For Christmas in 1954 I asked for and got a first baseman's glove. I don't remember whose model glove it was but I made sure it was not a Yankee player. (I think it was a Ferris Fain model – he led the American League in batting in '51 & '52).

In the spring of 1955 I did not sign up to play Little League, but I did play for my fourth grade class. Since I was the only kid with a first baseman's glove I became the first baseman. I soon found out having a first baseman mitt was not a good idea. This type of mitt restricts you from playing other positions. You do not see the other infielders, outfielders, and pitchers using a first baseman's mitt.

In 1956 I figured I'd be playing Little League ball. I did not want to be thought of as only a first baseman, but I did not want to go back to using the Rizzuto glove. Anyway, it was February of '56 and I was in a toy store that had a sporting goods section, when I saw this great looking glove. It was a Major League Ted Williams model made by the Wilson Company. Most of the new gloves of this period were very stiff and required a lot of oiling to make it loose and flexible. This glove was already loose and flexible. This glove was huge for my 10-year old hand but being flexible I had no problem with it. The price of this glove was $25.00 - quite a price for a glove in 1956. My birthday was the next month (March) and I told my mom this would be fantastic gift. She agreed that it would but that dad would have to give an OK. I had my doubts, I did not know if he would want to spend so much for a glove. In order to try to convince him, I showed him my baseball cards and that this glove was better than the ones the players on the cards had. He said we'll see since I had a relatively new mitt. It became the best birthday gift ever. Sometimes I think he allowed me to get this glove because it was a Ted Williams model. My dad being anti-Yankee was a big Ted Williams fan.

At last the Rizzuto glove would never be used again. I think it might still be in the pile of "old stuff" in the sun porch.

1954

Say Hey! New York Wins The World Series. Why Am I Happy?

The year 1954 began pretty well for Yankee fans. Their retired superstar Joe DiMaggio made what many thought was his greatest catch when he married Marilyn Monroe, arguably the most glamorous woman of the time. However, unlike a baseball, this catch was flubbed as they split before the end of the year.

This baseball season began with a major change. The St. Louis Browns, hoping to attain the attendance success of the Milwaukee Braves in '53 after their move from Boston, moved to Baltimore and became the Baltimore Orioles. (In 1901-02 the American League had a team in Baltimore, named the Orioles, that moved to New York in 1903 becoming the NY Highlanders; and later changed their name to the Yankees).

As 1954 began I was a certified Yankee Hater and a St. Louis Cardinal fan. Being a Cardinal and Stan "the Man" Musial fan, I mostly followed the National League. Going into the season the Brooklyn Dodgers were expected to three-peat (they won the NL flag in '52 & '53). I was hoping my Cardinals would give a good account of themselves. They started the year with some major changes. They bought Yankee ace Vic "The Springfield Rifle" Raschi, who won 21 games three years in a row (1949-51) and was 13-6 last year. The Yank management was irked by Raschi not signing his '54 contract, so in order to show the rest of the team not to squabble over their contract they sold him to the Cardinals. Actually, the Yanks considered Raschi to be aging - he was 35, plus they had a replacement in the wings - their top minor league pitcher, Bob Grim. The second move was the Cardinals traded their veteran All-Star Country Slaughter to the hated Yankees for some minor leaguers (one was Bill Virdon, who would later come back to haunt

14

the Yanks). The Cardinals could afford to trade Slaughter because it opened an outfield spot for Wally Moon, who became the NL Rookie of the Year by hitting .304 and scoring 109 runs. Another Cardinal rookie showing great promise was pitcher Brooks Lawrence who put up a 15-6 slate. Despite these changes the Cardinals finished sixth. Raschi proved the Yanks were right in letting him go as he became "The Springfield Pistol", finishing up with an 8-9 record.

My favorite player Stan the Man had his usual stellar year hitting .330 with 126 RBIs. He also hit 35 homers including a day in May when in a doubleheader against the eventual pennant winning Giants he set a Major League record for homers in a day with five.

The National League race was in New York between the Giants and Dodgers. The Brooklyn team had a great effort from their star center fielder, future Famer, "The Duke of Flatbush" Snider (40 homers) and their perennial NL All-Star first baseman Gil Hodges (42 homers) as they each had 130 RBIs. However, their All-Star MVP catcher of '53, Roy Campanella, had an injury plagued year missing over 40 games only hitting .207. Plus, their former ace, Don Newcombe, returned from his two years of military time but did not yet regain his skill only going 9-8. They just couldn't catch their National League neighbors. The Giants won by 5 games over Brooklyn.

The Giants were led by their returning serviceman Willie Mays. After missing two years, Willie, known as the Say Hey Kid, took the New York city by storm. He proved he was a true five tool player - hit for average and power, run like a gazelle, throw like a howitzer with accuracy and catching anything hit this side of Manhattan. (In my over 50 years of following the game he is the best player I've ever seen). The Say Hey Kid was the National League MVP - he led the NL in hitting .345, belted 41 homers and drove home 110 runs. Outfielder Don "Mandrake the Magician" Mueller, who possessed great bat control, was second in hitting in the league with a .342 average, and future Famer Monte Irvin, the other outfielder had 19 homers. The left side of the infield, third baseman Hank Thompson (26 homes, 86 RBIs) and shortstop Alvin Dark (.293, 20 homers, 93 runs scored) provided more pop to the offense. The Giants had a somewhat secret weapon in their arsenal, pinch-hitter deluxe Dusty Rhodes. For the year, in only 164 at bats, he hit 15 homers and drove in 50 runs, mostly in clutch situations. At this time, the Giants played in the Polo Grounds - it was an oval shaped stadium thus center field was almost 490 feet while the right field pole was about 260 feet and the left field pole about 280. These seats could have been the best seats for souvenirs seekers. Rhodes, a lefty, had a knack for hitting 265 foot homers into the right field stands.

The Yankees hoped to extend their World Series Championship run to six straight. Yankee Manager Casey Stengel won five consecutive pennants but never won more than 100 games. They figured if they can win a 100 they would be a shoo-in pennant winner. Their main competition would come from the Cleveland Indians, who were bridesmaids three years running. The Yanks got rid of Raschi, one of their three aces over the past five championships. They still had Allie Reynolds and Eddie Lopat and budding star Whitey Ford. To replace Raschi they had rookie Bob Grim who won 16 games in the minors in '53. He did not disappoint - winning Rookie of the Year with a 20-6 record. The Yanks also had some new players for their offense; third baseman Andy Carey hit .302, Irv Noren .319, and Bill "Moose" Skowron .340. The Yanks' two meal ticket stars, Yogi Berra (AL MVP, .307, 22 homers, 125 RBIs) and Mickey Mantle (.300, 27 homers, 102 RBIs), both had stellar seasons. Yankees' pitchers Ford, Reynolds, Lopat, Grim and Tom Morgan were a combined 72-27. Johnny Sain, in relief, won 8 and saved 22. It seemed like another cakewalk for the Yanks as they just won and won. They won 103 games, more than in any of their previous five pennant winning years.

However, the Cleveland Indians, no doubt tired of their runner-up status, had other ideas. They had a strong offense. Future Famer Larry Doby led the league in homers (32) and RBIs (126). Second baseman Bobby Avila led the league in hitting (.341) while last year's MVP third baseman Al Rosen had another All-Star year hitting .300 with 24 homers and 102 RBIs. Doby probably deserved to be the AL MVP but he and teammates Avila and pitcher Bob Lemon equally divided 15 first place votes as Yogi snuck in with 7 first place votes to win the award.

Bringing to life that famous baseball axiom, good pitching beats good hitting, it was their hurlers that were the major factor of them winning and winning, even more than the Yankees. Their future Hall of Famers, Bob Lemon and Early Wynn each won 23 games to lead the league, "The Big Bear" Mike Garcia won 19 and Art Houtteman won 15. An aging superstar, at 35, future Famer Bob

"Rapid Robert" Feller chipped in with a 13-3 record. Also, another future Famer, "Prince" Hal Newhouser, was talked out of retiring and registered 7 wins and 7 saves. In addition two rookie relievers, lefty Don Mossi and righty Ray Narleski combined for 11 wins and 20 saves.

Despite their winning ways the Yanks just could not catch the Indians. Their only faint hope would come in September when they would have to sweep the Indians in a doubleheader. Instead the reverse happened; Cleveland swept them in the twin-bill behind Lemon 4-1 and Wynn 3-2 to seal the pennant.

The Yanks, despite 103 wins, lost the pennant by 8 games to Cleveland, who set an American League record with 111 wins. The Major League record is held by the 1906 Cubs who won 116 games - in 154 games - which was tied by the 2001 Seattle Mariners (of course that was done in a 162 game schedule).

The Indians were a heavy favorite to win the World Series. The Giants' offense was on a par with Cleveland but their pitching staff was rated nowhere near that of the Indians. The Giants' staff was led by newcomer Johnny Antonelli. The southpaw was obtained in a trade with the Braves for 1951 Giant hero Bobby Thomson, who hit the famous "Shot Heard Round the World" to win the pennant. This trade infuriated many of the Giants' fans as Thomson was the Giants' best hitter in '53. However, they soon forgot about it when Antonelli became the league's best pitcher with a 21-7 record and 2.30 ERA. The other starters were righties Ruben Gomez (17-9), the veteran Sal "the Barber" Maglie (14-6) and Jim Hearn (8-8) while Don Liddle (9-4) threw from the portside. Maglie was known as "the Barber" because his inside pitches gave batters close shaves. However, the Giants' pitching staff's strength was their bullpen as future Famer Hoyt Wilhelm (the owner of baseball's nastiest knuckleball) and veteran Marv Grissom combined for 22 victories and 26 saves. Still the Cleveland staff was rated far superior with four future Hall of Famers.

Game 1 was at the Polo Grounds in New York. The contest was tied at 2 going into the eighth inning as "the Barber" and Lemon were locked in a pitching duel. In the eighth the Indians had two on with lefty hitter Vic Wertz coming up. Giant skipper Leo Durocher brought in Don Liddle for a lefty/lefty match-up. Well Wertz got all of it - it seemed the ball would wind up in the Harlem River. The Say Hey Kid in center turned and with his gazelle-like speed ran the ball down and with his back to the plate made his famous over the shoulder catch in front of the center field bleachers. Only in the Polo Grounds would the ball be caught because of its unusual shape. Liddle was taken out after Wertz's blast and supposedly said to his replacement Marv Grissom "OK, I got my man." Grissom stayed in for the rest of the game and for 2 1/3 innings kept the Tribe scoreless to get the victory because of the heroics of a bench player. In the bottom of the tenth inning the Giants put two on with one out. Pinch-hitter deluxe Dusty Rhodes was sent up to bat for Irvin. Lemon was still in there for the Indians. Possibly thinking Rhodes would take a pitch, Lemon maybe made it too good as Rhodes hit a 265 foot fly to right. Unfortunately, due to the Polo Grounds oval shape, the ball landed into the right field stands for a game-winning 3-run homer. Ironically, Rhodes' fly homer was almost 200 feet shorter than Wertz's eighth inning blast of 450. It was a sign of things to come.

The Indians figured game 1 was a fluke and it probably looked that way as game 2 started with Antonelli falling behind 1-0 as he gave up a dinger to the Tribe lead-off man Al Smith. Wynn, the Tribes' other ace, kept the Giants off the board for four innings when Rhodes ruined things again. With two on in the fifth Dusty again was sent up to pinch-hit for Irvin. He singled to center to drive in the tying run and set up the go ahead run. Rhodes stayed in the game and in the seventh showed he can also hit them far as he blasted a long homer to give the Giants an insurance run. It wasn't needed as Antonelli threw shutout ball after Smith's first inning homer. The Giants won 3 - 1.

The Indians couldn't believe what was happening. All because of Dusty Rhodes - in game 1 it was Rhodes 3, Cleveland 2 and in game 2 it was Rhodes 2, Cleveland 1.

In game 3 the Tribe started their 19-game winner, the Big Bear, Mike Garcia. He was opposed by 17-game winner Ruben Gomez. Cleveland being home figured things would be better. Not so, the Giants scored in the first and had a rally going in the third when again Rhodes was sent up to pinch-hit for Irvin. Again he came through with a 2-run single that also set up the third run of the inning. Gomez went 7 1/3 innings for the 6-2 victory. Cleveland did get a moral victory in that they got Rhodes out twice (he stayed in the game after his pinch-hit).

Lemon started game 4 hoping to keep the Tribe from being swept. Not to be. The Giants did not need Dusty as they got off to a 7-0 lead routing Lemon. The Indians came back to make it 7-4 in the seventh but Wilhelm and Antonelli came in to put down the Indian uprising.

The Giants swept the Series. Giant stats were put up by Alvin Dark (.412, 7 for 17) and "the Magician" Mueller (.389, 7 for 18) while Hank Thompson hit .364 scoring 6 runs, but it was Dusty Rhodes who was the hero. He was 4 for 6 with 2 homers and 7 RBIs in only 3 games. Also, the supposedly inferior Giant pitching staff had a 1.46 ERA while the heralded Tribe staff was 4.84. Antonelli posted a win and a save with a 0.84 ERA in 10 2/3 innings of work.

The only star for Cleveland was Wertz. Despite the Say Hey catch he was 8 for 16 with 2 doubles, a triple, a homer, and a .938 slugging %.

The New York streak continues. Every World Series game since 1949 was won by a New York team as '49, '51, '52 and '53 were all Subway Series. In '50, the Phils were swept like this year's Indians.

A New York team won the World Series but I was happy since it was the Giants (not the hated Yankees) and I was a National League fan.

1954
A Yankee Christmas Tree

It was December 1954. As far as sports went I was happy because (being a National League fan) the Giants won the World Series, but being a typical nine-year old, I really wasn't thinking of baseball. Thanksgiving was just over and all the men folk watched the annual Detroit Lion/Green Bay Packer game. Being a novice football fan, I cheered for the team that won - so the Lions who won the previous two NFL championships became my team (you might say in 1954 I was a front runner; but nowadays I root for the Jets and Giants). They had future Hall of Famers Bobby Layne, Doak Walker, Yale Lary and other stars of that era. Also, I was a fan of Elroy "Crazy Legs" Hirsch, the Los Angeles Rams' Hall of Fame receiver. I was probably a fan of his because I saw a movie of his life – and he played himself.

So like I said I wasn't really thinking about baseball. It was the second week of December and time for our traditional Christmas tree hunt. This was usually a big fun event for our family. Plenty of places sold the trees in our town of Belleville, but we would go into the neighboring town, Bloomfield, to get ours.

Well it was the second week of December and my Dad announced that it's Tree Day. After dinner we would go for the tree. We drove the few miles into Bloomfield and stopped at the lot that had rows of trees. Mom and Dad went one direction and me and my sister Carole, another. Naturally, brother and sister couldn't agree on what tree to get. I wanted this one and she wanted that one. Well my parents saw us arguing and came over. In order to break up our bickering, my mom pointed over to a man who was talking to other customers. She said "See him, he's Hank Borowy and he was a Yankee star pitcher of the early '40's." I think he had a real estate office and used the lot to sell Christmas trees during December. Well my mom thought she was doing something good by telling me

20

this information. The reverse happened. My stomach turned into knots. I just could not have a Yankee Christmas Tree in my house. This crisis and the typical 9-year old's anxiety about making it onto Santa's nice list, would not make this an enjoyable Christmas.

I said to my parents that all the trees here don't look good - we should go to another lot, in Belleville.

They were perplexed because before my mom told me about Hank Borowy, I had a tree picked out. My sister ratted me out - she told them the trees are OK he doesn't want one from a Yankee pitcher. I think my parents probably thought this kid needs help… (which is still up for debate today).

My mom called me over and told me the Borowy story – that the Yanks traded him in 1945 and he helped the Cubs get into the World Series and even won 2 games for them. She stated that was why she hasn't rooted for the Yanks since they traded him. She said we'll get the tree from a Cub pitcher.

At an early age I learned how to rationalize. After all what would Christmas gifts be without a tree to be under? So in 1954 we had a Cub Christmas Tree (and I some how squeaked onto Santa's nice list - whew!).

1955
The CATCH

The Yanks won over 100 games and could not win the pennant in 1954 while in the five previous years they had 90 plus victories and won all five Series. I thought the Yanks would be done in '55. The "Chief" Allie Reynolds retired, Lopat and Sain would be gone. So where was the pitching going to come from? Well, the General Manager, George Weiss, traded with the relocated Baltimore Orioles. From them they got Bob Turley who won 14 games for a team that lost 100 games and Don Larsen who had potential even though he lost 21 games. Also, lefty Tommy Byrne came back from the minors. The new Chairman of the Board, Whitey Ford, led the staff with 18 wins and even led the AL with 18 complete games (a feat he was generally not known for). Turley chalked up 17 wins while Byrne chipped in with 16. Larsen had a 9-2 season and relievers Tom Morgan and former National League MVP for the pennant winning Phils of 1950, Jim Konstanty, combined for 14 wins and 20 saves.

Yogi Berra repeated as the American League MVP, his third, hitting 27 homers and coming in third in the RBI race with 108. Mickey Mantle continued to improve leading the league with 37 homers while batting .306 and driving in 99 runs. Hank Bauer had 20 homers and scored 97 runs.

Cleveland was expected to repeat as American League Champs, but possibly the impact of being swept was too much to overcome. Their stars of '54 all had lackluster years. Al Rosen hit 50 points lower than in '54, batting champ Bobby Avila dropped 69 points and Larry Doby had 51 less RBIs. Even their pitching staff faltered. Early Wynn, Bob Lemon and Mike Garcia had a combined 19 less wins than in '54. However, Rookie of the Year Herb Score (16-10) kept the Indians in the race. In fact the Yankees did not take over first place until the middle of September. The Indians resumed their customary place as runner-up. The Yanks were 96-58 and beat them out by 3 games.

Being a Cardinal fan, I concentrated on following the Senior Circuit, the NL. However, the race was over very quickly as the Dodgers started the season with 10 straight wins and 22 out of their first 24. They beat out the Milwaukee Braves by 13 1/2 games. The defending champs, the Giants, finished third, miles behind the Dodgers despite The Say Hey Kid improving his power numbers from last year (51 homers, 127 RBIs while batting .319). The three best center fielders in baseball all played for the teams in the Big Apple – it was Willie, Mickey and the Duke (although the Phillies had a fair one in future Famer Richie Ashburn, but he was a singles hitter).

The Brooklyn offense was revitalized by a healthy return of their future Famer, catcher Roy Campanella. He kept pace with his backstop rival Yogi Berra by also winning his third MVP award by hitting .318 with 32 homers and 107 RBIs. The Dodgers' old reliables, Pee Wee Reese (.282, 99 runs), Duke Snider (.309, 42 homers 136 RBIs and The Sporting News Major League Player of the Year), Gil Hodges (.289, 27 homers 102 RBIs), Junior Gilliam (110 runs) and Carl Furillo (.314, 26 homers 95 RBIs) helped the Dodgers make it easy for their pitchers. Rookie Don Zimmer contributed 15 homers and 50 RBIs in half a season. Having a bad year in '54 after returning from military service, Don Newcombe regained his skills by going 20 - 5 and was equally effective with the lumber batting .359 with 7 homers and 23 RBIs.

With the Dodgers running away with the pennant, I concentrated on my Cardinals. They again did poorly finishing seventh. Last year's rookie ace Brooks Lawrence was a disappointment finishing at 3-8. He was traded to Cincinnati after the season and had two good seasons with the Redlegs winning 19 in '56 and 16 in '57. My favorite Stan the Man had a great year for most, but not by his standards, he hit .319, which was third in the league, with 33 homers and 105 RBIs. His finest moment came in the All-Star Game. With the score tied at 5 apiece in the twelfth inning, he blasted a Frank Sullivan pitch deep into the right field stands for a National League game-winning home run.

The Cardinals again had the Rookie of the Year, center fielder, Bill Virdon, who they got from the Yankees in the Country Slaughter trade, but it was another rookie that captured my interest.

In December of '54 I was kind of upset that the Cardinals traded their third baseman Ray Jablonski. In each of his first two years, he drove in over 100 runs and was an All-Star in '54. I hoped they had a good replacement - they did, it was Ken Boyer, brother of Major Leaguers, pitcher Cloyd and infielder Clete. Being able to see the Cardinals 15 or so times a year on TV, I instantly became a Ken Boyer fan. He hit .264 with 18 homers and was third in stolen bases with 22. However, it was not his bat that I admired, but his glove. Not only was Boyer quick but he had excellent range even playing about 20 games at shortstop. He also had a strong, accurate throw to first. His fielding was recognized as he won five Gold Gloves throughout his career. Boyer would prove out to be a five tool player. After 1955 I wanted to be a third baseman.

The '55 Series was again between old rivals. Since 1947 this would be the fifth meeting between the Dodgers and Yankees, with Brooklyn still hoping to win their first. At least the streak of a New York team winning every World Series game will continue.

There were some varying views on who would win. Would the Dodgers be able to compete against a good adversary since their run to the pennant was so easy, or would the Yankees be exhausted from going through a tight pennant race?

Another factor in most of the past Dodgers/Yankees World Series was that the Dodgers always seemed to have better regular season batting statistics. The main reason for this was that Ebbets Field in Brooklyn is a band box while Yankee Stadium is only friendly down the lines, especially in right field. Dodger homers at Ebbets Field became long outs at Yankee Stadium, especially in left field. (All of the Dodgers top hitters batted from the right side except the Duke).

The Yanks would have the advantage getting four home games if the Series went seven games.

The Series started with the team's aces facing each other. It appeared to be better to have won tough, meaningful games to win the pennant than coasting into the Series. The Brooklyn ace, Don Newcombe, "got nuked" giving up three homers - two to Joe Collins the Yankees' first baseman and one to the Yankees' first black player Elston Howard. Despite being the Dodgers' ace, manager Walter Alston did not use Big Newk the rest of the Series (either because of injury or ineffectiveness). The Yankees' ace Whitey Ford started for them and got the victory even though he gave up homers to the Duke and Furillo. The Dodgers made it close on the famous steal of home by Jackie Robinson. The ball beat Jackie but Yogi had the glove in the middle of the plate so when Jackie slid he hit the plate before he hit the glove. Yogi vehemently argued the safe call in one of the games classic catcher/umpire confrontations, but it was to no avail. This run put Brooklyn down by one but they could not get another and lost a tough one, 6-5.

In game 2 the Yanks started another lefty, Tommy Byrne, against the Dodgers. With their right-handed hitting line-up, except for the Duke, the Dodgers expected to even the Series. But it wasn't to be as they were "byrned" by a 4-2 score to be down 2 games to none. To rub salt in the wound, Byrne, a good hitting pitcher (.238 lifetime), drove in 2 runs in their 4 run fourth that was the margin of victory. No team has come back from a 2-0 deficit to win a seven game Series, so the Dodgers had their work cut out for them.

The Series moved across the river to Brooklyn and nowhere did that saying "Home Sweet Home" prove to be more true. The Brooklyn manager, Walter Alston decided to give his young pitcher Johnny Podres a unique birthday gift as it was his 23rd birthday. It was a World Series start. He came through with a complete game as the Dodgers won 8-3. His battery mate Campanella gave him the best birthday gift - a single, double, homer and 3 RBIs.

Morale was up in Flatbush as the Dodgers tried to even up things in game 4. The Dodgers fell behind 3-1 early in the game but scored 3 in the fourth and 3 more in the fifth to go on to an 8-5 win. The Dodgers' three big guns the Duke, Hodges and Campy all blasted round-trippers. Campy for the second day in a row had a homer, double and single.

The Series was tied at two. The Dodgers, still not using Newcombe for whatever reason, went with rookie Roger Craig to try to put them up 3 games to 2. Craig went 6 innings and was relieved by Clem Labine in the seventh with a 4-2 lead. Labine gave up a run in the eighth as the Dodgers won 5-3. The Duke paced the offense with two more homers (which gave him 4 for the Series making him the only player to accomplish this feat twice in the Fall Classic – he also did it in '52); but the key was a 2-run homer in the second inning by utility outfielder, Sandy Amoros, that gave the Dodgers a 2-0 lead. Amoros was in the line-up to give the team another left-handed bat to face the Yankee righties. Also, being very fast, he was often used as a defensive replacement late in the games to protect leads.

The Yanks couldn't wait to get out of Brooklyn; they probably thought that most of the Dodger homers would have been outs in the big Yankee Stadium ballpark.

The Dodgers in game 6 at the Stadium would not or could not use big Newk. They had good fortune in winning with rookie Roger Craig in game 5 so Alston started another rookie, Karl Spooner. It didn't work this time as the Yanks scored 5 in the first with Moose Skowron's 3-run homer being the big hit. Dodger pitchers kept the Yanks shut out for the rest of the game, but it was too late.

Yankee ace Whitey Ford was masterful tossing a four-hit complete game. The Yanks won 5-1. The Series was deadlocked at three. For the past two games Yankee star center fielder Mickey Mantle did not play due to an injured leg. In the seventh game he would only be available to pinch-hit. Both teams had other starters with injuries. Snider and Bauer despite leg injuries played in the deciding game 7, but Don Hoak replaced Jackie Robinson, who also had a leg injury, at third base for Brooklyn.

Alston chose Johnny Podres to start the deciding game - after all he was now a year older from last week. Stengel chose Byrne hoping he could duplicate his game 2 victory. For three innings the hurlers matched goose eggs, though the Yanks had a third inning threat end in a most unusual way - with two out Phil Rizzuto walked and Billy Martin singled, then Gil McDougald hit a chopper to third that Hoak would have had to eat loading the bases except that the batted ball hit Rizzuto as he was sliding into third causing him to be called out ending the rally. Then in the top of the fourth Campy doubled and scored on a single by Hodges. The Yankees tried to tie it in the bottom of the inning on a lead off two-bagger by Yogi that the Duke and left fielder Gilliam let fall between them but Podres buckled down and kept him from scoring. In the sixth Reese singled, was eventually bunted to third and scored on a sac-fly by Hodges... it was 2-0 Dodgers.

In the bottom of the sixth the Series came to a climax. The Dodgers made some defensive moves. Second baseman Zimmer was pinch-hit for, so the left fielder Gilliam moved to second and the speedy Sandy Amoros went to left field. Billy Martin, the Brooklyn nemesis, led off and worked his way on with a walk. Gil McDougal then bunted for a hit. Two on and no outs - Brooklynites thoughts went to "Wait 'til next year" once again. Yogi was the next batter. Yogi was a left-handed pull-hitter and the defense played him accordingly. Yogi surprised everyone when he sliced a drive headed for the left field corner. At the least it seemed to be a ground-rule double and the Yanks would be down 2-1 with runners on second and third with no outs - if it stayed in play the score would be tied. Sandy Amoros was playing in left-center for the pull hitting Berra. He got a real good jump on the ball as he and the ball were seemingly in a race headed toward the left field wall. Fortunately, being left-handed his glove was on his right hand and as the ball was hit to his right he was able to snare the drive (I was real happy Sandy won the race). If Amoros was right-handed he probably would not have been able to make the catch. Anyway, not only did he make the catch but he was able to stop, whirl, and fire a strike to shortstop Reese who fired to Hodges at first to double up McDougald who was running on the seemingly sure double. The Yanks instead of the score being tied or at least 2-1 with runners on second and third and no outs, now only had a runner on second with 2 outs - Podres retired Bauer for the third out.

Some people nowadays think that was it for the Bronx Bombers, but they again mounted a threat in the eighth as Rizzuto led off with a hit and after Martin made an out McDougald bounced a hard shot off of the third baseman Hoak. The tying runs were on base with the clutch hitting Berra and Bauer coming to the plate. Podres was up for the challenge and got Yogi on a fly out and whiffed Bauer to put Brooklyn one inning away from their first World Series title. In the ninth Podres retired the side in order with Howard's ground out - Pee Wee to Hodges ending it as Brooklyn FINALLY got its crown as Baseball's Best Team.

Brooklyn wins 2-0 to take the Series. Podres for Mayor!!!

No more "Wait 'til next year" for Brooklyn.

The Yanks were stunned. Two years in a row – no World Series Championship. All because of the CATCH!!

1955
Want A Yankee Autograph? Why?

It was during this summer that reinforced my reasons for hating the Yankees. My dad worked most weekends, so it was my mom who would take me and my sister to see a game. Naturally she took us to a Cardinal (the team I was for)/Giant games at the Polo Grounds. My sister Carole was "daddy's little girl", so she rooted for my dad's team, the Giants, and was a Say Hey Kid, Willie Mays, fanatic. My mom also took us to Yankee Stadium to my disapproval.

One of the games I remember was against the Chicago White Sox. I really didn't care to go but I guess someone gave us the tickets. My mom got me to go by telling me they were managed by Marty Marion who was a former St. Louis Cardinal All-Star shortstop who won the MVP in 1944. At this time I was becoming knowledgeable about the history of baseball, especially the Cardinals and knew about Marion so I did not feel that bad about going.

I do not remember that much about the game except that the White Sox won. I think it was Billy Pierce who won and Nellie Fox and George Kell had some key hits.

After the game we waited outside the Stadium for autographs, but we would only want them from the White Sox. I would not even consider getting an autograph from a Yankee. I recall getting the program signed by outfielder Jim Busby and first baseman Walt Dropo. Then White Sox manager Marion came out of the visitor clubhouse exit. He stated he doesn't sign for Yankee fans. I was ten years old then. I had on a St. Louis Cardinal cap and blurted out "I can't stand the Yankees and I'm a Cardinal fan". Looking at me with a St. Louis cap on my head, he grinned and said "I guess you are" and signed my program.

Most of the autograph seekers waited at the Yankee clubhouse exit. I remember a car pulling up and police setting up an aisle as Mickey Mantle went into the car and it took off. I saw the Yankee manger Casey Stengel being driven away in a limousine.

But the thing that really made an impact on me with was that there was this notable Yankee star (don't want to mention his name) that was driving a red convertible. I guess it was his wife in the front seat. Anyway, a bunch of autograph seekers would run up to his car and as they reached the car, he would drive away about 100 feet. The seekers would chase the car and again the car would drive another 100 feet. This went on another couple of times before the car sped off. The player did not sign any autographs.

I thought "What a way to treat your fans". I thought the player was a real jerk and the Yankee fans that kept chasing the car only to get nothing were "pretty stupid".

Just another reason to give me a lasting impression to hate the Yankees!

1956
Little League --Yanks Grin and BEAR It

In 1956 I was 11 years old and decided that I would play Little League ball. Little League is from 8 years old until 12. I always thought that was a big age gap, so I never signed up to play. My ball playing was usually playing for my school class or just pick-up games with sometimes less than nine on a team. Well when I was 11, I figured I had only one age above me to compete against.

In February our town paper had a notice to those wanting to play Little League that they would have to sign up by the beginning of March. I had my dad sign me up. Also, this year my dad got me the Major League Ted Williams glove for my birthday in March.

Once you signed up for Little League, tryouts were held and all the players were evaluated. In early April at the tryouts I felt I gave a good account of myself. I had this huge glove and snagged all the fungos hit to me.

I've always heard that infielders should have small gloves so it's easier to find the ball in order to make a quicker throw to first, or any base that you are throwing to. When it was my turn to take grounders in the infield, I felt invincible with my new glove. Nothing got by me, even a few bad hoppers were snared. As for throwing, I guess my arm was average but I would get rid of the ball quickly and was pretty accurate, and I had no problem finding the ball in my big glove.

Once the tryouts were complete, your manager would call informing you of what team you were on. In our town we had teams that were the names of some of the Major League teams. Naturally there were the three New York teams, the Yankees, Dodgers and Giants and I remember the Cardinals, Pirates and Cubs. There were no Senators, A's or Red Sox. There were other team names that were not named for Major League teams. These included the Aces, Clippers, Bombers, Demons and Bears. Is it coincidental that

30

Clippers, Bombers, and Bears are Yankee-related (Columbus Clippers, Bronx Bombers, and Newark Bears? Could be since our town is located so close to New York).

Well about two weeks after the tryouts, I received a call from my manager. He told me his name was Mario and gave me his phone number and told me when our first practice would be. While he was giving me this information, I was sweating out what the name of the team was.

There is no way I wanted to be on the Yankees. After manager Mario gave me the practice information I asked him the name of the team. He said, "We're the Bears". At first I was relieved that the team name was not the Yankees, but soon realized that the Bears are the name of the legendary minor league team of the hated Yankees - the team my mom used to see play back in the '30's.

After I hung up, I gave my dad the information that manager Mario gave me. My dad saw I did not appear happy and asked me what the problem was. I told him I'm glad I'm not a Yankee but that I don't want to be a Bear, because of the Yankee affiliation.

Sometimes I think now, that my dad was thinking "Where is this kid coming from". Anyway he explained to me that he hates the Yankees, too and is glad that my Little League team is not the Yankees. As for being the Bears, that's like being from Chicago (the football Bears). He told me "Look the Bears used to be the Yankee minor league team, but it is not in existence anymore". There wasn't really anything I could do about it so I just accepted the fact that I was a Bear.

We had a few practices, like five or six, before the season began. Manager Mario basically had no coaches so my dad said whenever possible he would help out, hitting fungos and grounders, throw some batting practice, etc.

Our team was decent, three quality pitchers and some OK hitters. At the first practice I planted myself at third base (wanted to be like Ken Boyer). With my big Ted Williams glove nothing got by me so I was to be the third baseman. There was twelve teams in our league and we did well coming in third.

There are two games I remember. It was the middle of the season and we were playing the Pirates. It was the one before the game against the Yankees.

In our league there was usually only one umpire (they were for the most part high school kids). The umpire could either be behind home plate or behind the pitcher at the back of the mound. This was our first game with the umpire behind the mound. In the second inning a Pirate hit the ball to me. With my big vacuum cleaner type glove, I naturally caught the ball, but when I raised up to throw to first the umpire who was calling pitches from behind the mound was standing in my way. If I threw to first my normal way the ball would have struck him in the head. In the 1940's there was an All-Star pitcher named Rip Sewell, who twice won 21 games. He was known for the "eephus" pitch. It was like a pop up - he'd throw to the catcher and it usually crossed home plate for a strike, most players couldn't hit it except for Ted Williams who hit it for a home run in the '46 All-Star Game.

I threw an eephus-like pitch to first base so I would not hit the umpire in the head. I did not have Rip Sewell's accuracy. I not only threw it over the umpire's head, I also cleared the first baseman's head as well. Boy was I mad. In the fourth inning, a hard one hopper was hit to me − I had all the time in the world but this umpire is looking straight at me waiting for me to throw. He was right in the line of the throw so again my eephus throw cleared the field. Manager Mario and my dad agreed this was a problem and said I'd have to move front or back to get the umpire out of the line of the throw. I am sure Ken Boyer didn't have this problem. The Pirates had poor pitching so we won the game easily, so my throwing miscues didn't cost us the game.

The next game was against the Yankees. We were tied for third place at the time. One of the Yankee players was a classmate. He was a good hitter. From playing softball in gym class I knew he was a lefty who had an inside-out swing that sent laser shots down the third base line.

Before the game I was really concerned about the umpire being behind the mound to call pitches. I was hoping he was one who liked to be behind the plate - no dice - he was behind the mound. I was really up for this game. I felt playing the Yankee team elevated my performance as I had the adrenalin flowing.

Before the game, Manager Mario gave us our pre-game pep talk. While he was doing this my dad went out and was talking to the umpire.

In the first inning the clean-up batter, my lefty hitting classmate, was up with a runner on second. I moved closer to the line despite Manager Mario telling me to play him like a lefty and move closer to the shortstop. Before he could call time and come out on the field to instruct me to move over a pitch was thrown. As usual, a hard shot down the third base line looked like it was headed into the left field corner - but wait I had on my basket sized Ted Williams glove. I snared it in the webbing. As I turned to throw to first wondering how to compensate for the umpire obstacle there was none. The umpire was lying prone on the ground watching the play. With no obstacle and the ball hit so hard I easily threw out my classmate to end the inning. Manager Mario thanked me for not listening to him.

My dad took me aside and told me about his little conversation with the umpire. It went something like this, "Look if the ball is hit to third, the kid has a rocket arm to first about head high, so anything hit that way it would be a good idea if you ducked".

In the third my classmate hit me another smash - which with the big glove was no problem to handle, the umpire went prone and I easily threw him out again. Looking into the dugout my dad gave me the thumbs up sign.

In the sixth my classmate forgot his inside-out swing and pulled a homer over the right fielder's head. No matter, I had a few hits and RBIs and we won by three. We were now in third by ourselves and finished up there.

Although not winning first place, the Bears finished ahead of the Yankees!

1956
Yankee Juice

It was the summer of my first Little League season playing for the Bears. Usually after a game some of us Bears would stop at the local drug and candy store and slurp up a beverage. Each of us had our preferences - Coca Cola, 7-Up, Pepsi and mine was Yoo-Hoo. I was a chocolate addict, so naturally a chocolate drink was my favorite.

At home my dad always bought a six-pack of Coca Cola and 7-Up. I told him that I liked Yoo-Hoo and at the next supermarket visit can he get me Yoo-Hoo instead of Coca Cola.

It was on one of these summer days I was watching a game on TV and drinking a Yoo-Hoo. My uncle Walter, my mom's brother, came over; he was a Yankee fan and knew I hated them. He saw me drinking a Yoo-Hoo and asked how I liked drinking Yankee juice. "What?" I said. He told me that Yogi Berra was a Vice President for Yoo-Hoo, thus it's Yankee Juice.

Although I did not go cold turkey, I reduced my consumption of Yoo-Hoo considerably.

1956

Past Yankee Failures

(1926 Alexander the Great and 1942 The MAN Arrives)

In 1956 the Yankees reverted to their old form and won the American League (again over the usual runner-up, the Indians). They also won the World Series so I won't mention any more about it.

As far as my beloved St. Louis Cardinals, they came in fourth two games under .500. Stan the Man had his lowest batting average ever (.310, which was fourth in the league) but did lead the league with 109 RBIs. My other favorite Ken Boyer had a super sophomore year. His .306 average was fifth in the league as was his 98 RBIs - he also clubbed 26 homers. (Take Note: During this era when a player batted around .290, hit more than 20 homers, and drove in about 90 runs he was considered a star).

The highlight of the season for me was the All-Star Game. Stan the Man hit a homer (increasing his All-Star home run record to five) and Ken Boyer started at third base. At this time there was no All-Star game MVP selection but if there was, Boyer would have won it. He made three scintillating plays in the field and was the batting star getting three hits. The National League won 7-3 as Say Hey also homered while for the AL Ted Williams and Mantle went deep.

In 1956 I completed sixth grade. My favorite subject was ancient history. I was really enthused about learning about the early civilizations (Egyptian, Greek, Roman, etc). All through my school years I aced history. This carried over to my leisure time as I was constantly reading about the history of baseball, especially anything about the St. Louis Cardinals. Whenever we were assigned a book report, mine would be one about the Cardinals.

Also, on TV there was this program, I think it was called *This Year in Sports*. Whenever the year was a Cardinal World Series

35

Championship year, I would make every effort to watch it. Naturally, I enjoyed the Pepper Martin led champs of '31, the '34 Gashouse Gang winners with the Dean Brothers and Joe "Ducky" Medwick, the '44 Series with the cross-town Browns, and of course the '46 mad dash for home by Country Slaughter which was the deciding run.

But the two years that I enjoyed the most were the years 1926 and 1942. The Cardinals both times defeated the hated Yankees. I must have read several accounts of both Series.

Up until I started following baseball closely (1954 was my first full year of doing so) the Yankees had won 16 World Series and lost only 4, and half of them were to the Cardinals. The Cardinals up to 1954 had the best National League World Series record winning 6 and losing 3.

Anyway, in 1926 the Cardinals won their first pennant. They were the last team in the National League to capture the pennant. Just winning the pennant was quite an achievement-playing in the World Series was just gravy.

The Cardinals had seven of their eight position players hit over .290 (in this era, the '20's & '30's hitting prevailed). Hall of Famer first baseman Jim Bottomley led them with a league leading 120 RBIs, and his 19 homers were second in the league. Third baseman Les Bell had a career year batting .325 and finished fourth in the NL with 17 homers and third in RBIs with 100.

Rogers Hornsby was the player manager for the Red Birds. The managing aspects of the job appeared to take its toll on his batting performance. He hit just .317 with 11 homers and 93 RBIs, a good year for most, but not for "the Rajah". Unbelievably, the five previous years his batting average was over .400. In any event he did manage them to their first pennant.

They did not have a great pitching staff. Flint Rhem, a flake of sorts, had a career year (20-7). Willie Sherdel won 16. Future Famer Jesse "Pop" Haines was 13-4. However, the surprise of the staff was Grover Cleveland Alexander, known as "Old Pete". The Cardinals got Pete on waivers from the Chicago Cubs in June. Pete was supposedly a problem. He was 39 years old - was an alleged alcoholic and had epilepsy. Besides how many more wins could he have left in him - at the time he became a Cardinal he already had amassed 315 victories.

Arriving in St Louis revitalized him. He was in 23 games for the year and had a 9-7 record. He led the team with a 2.91 ERA. Most people probably thought that was it for Pete, but the best was yet to come.

The Yankees won the pennant by three games over Cleveland. The famous Murderers' Row was in its infancy. Naturally the Bambino (Ruth) led them - hitting .372 while leading the league in homers (47) and RBIs (145). Two of their future Famers were in their second full season - first baseman Lou Gehrig hit .313 with 16 homers and 20 triples and was second in runs scored (135), and center fielder Earle Combs hit .299 and scored 113 runs. Another future Famer, rookie second baseman Tony Lazzeri hit .309 was third in homers (18) and second in RBIs (114). Also, Bob Meusel, the left fielder missed almost a third of the season but still hit .315 with 12 homers and 81 RBIs.

The pitching staff was led by future Famers Herb Pennock (23-11) and Waite Hoyt (16-12). Their other ace was Urban Shocker (19-12). Shocker was one of the game's tragic stories - less than two years later in 1928 he died from heart problems. In 1927 he went 18-6 for the fabled Murderers' Row supposedly knowing he did not have long to live. The four-time 20-game winner finished with a 187-117 (.615 winning %) slate for his shortened career.

The Series looked like a no-brainer - the Yanks would win, the question is in how many games?

The Series started and in game 1 the Cardinals scored in the first. The Yanks came back with one in the bottom of the first. The rest of the game was a pitching duel between Sherdel and Pennock. The Yanks scored the tie-breaker in the sixth for a 2-1 victory. In order to go back to St. Louis with the Series evened up, Old Pete had to come through.

The Yankees and everyone thought it was over as the Yanks quickly took a 2-0 lead at the end of two, but that was it as St. Louis pulled a "shocker". After giving up a lead-off single in the third, Pete retired 21 consecutive batters. The Cards' batters evened the score in the third and put the game away with 3 in the seventh off of Urban Shocker. Cardinal right fielder Billy Southworth, an acquisition from the Giants in mid-season, had 3 hits, including a homer and 3 RBIs. Southworth would later torment the Yanks as Cardinal skipper in 1942.

The Cards returned home and had Pop Haines ready to do the job on the mound and at the plate. The knuckleballer threw a four-hit shutout making it 16 consecutive innings Murderers' Row did not score. The Cards won 4-0 with half the runs coming on a 2-run homer by the pitcher Haines. The Cardinals probably surprised even themselves as they were up 2 games to 1.

It was all the Bambino in game 4. The Cards started their flakey 20-game winner, Flint Rhem. In two at bats Ruth hit 2 off of Rhem into the Mississippi River. Rhem left the game in the fourth losing 3-1. The Cards showed life though and rallied to take a 4-3 lead. But their relievers continued to get bombed including another homer by Ruth giving him 3 for the game. Although the Cards tied the Yanks with 14 hits, they were outscored 10-5. Series was now tied at two apiece.

Game 5 was almost a repeat of game 1. Sherdel against Pennock locked in another duel. The Cards were winning 2-1 in the ninth when the Yanks tied it on a pinch-hit. The Yanks won it in the tenth on a sacrifice fly by Lazzeri. Sherdel was again a tough-luck loser. In the Series, he pitched 17 innings with a fine 2.12 ERA but was 0-2.

The Cards were going back to the Stadium in bad shape. They would have to win both games to take the Series. The Cards went with Old Pete again. The offense gave him a quick lead scoring 3 in the first. It was all he needed as the Cards put the game away with 5 in the seventh. Southworth had a double and triple and tallied 3 times, while Les Bell had 3 hits, including a dinger and 4 RBIs. But the story was Old Pete, another complete game victory. The Yankee batters must have been thinking, well at least we won't have to face that old man Alexander, any more.

Game 7 featured Waite Hoyt winner of the 10-5 victory and Pop Haines who won the game 3 shutout. The Bambino hit three for Hoyt in game 4 so in game 7 he put the Yanks on the board with a third inning blast. The Cards took the lead with three runs in the fourth on Yankee miscues in the field.

In the seventh the Yankee threat came about. Combs led off with a single. Haines was able to get two outs, but walked Ruth and Gehrig loading the bases. With two out, super rookie Lazzeri was up. What happened next has been written about many different ways. The Yanks could not believe their eyes. Haines developed an open blister and could no longer throw his knuckler, so Old Pete was summoned to the mound. Some stories say he was sleeping off a hangover in the clubhouse. Another story had manager Hornsby telling Pete, after his complete game victory in game six, not to celebrate as he may be needed tomorrow.

In any event, Old Pete was in there against the young slugger. Hornsby was telling Pete how to pitch to Lazzeri. Pete possibly was thinking "I got 324 wins and some of them with mediocre teams, and twice in this Series I put the Yanks down, and this guy is telling me how to pitch - yeah he can tell me how to hit, but pitch - no way". Pete came inside hard with a pitch that can only be fouled off. Well Lazzeri smashed it but it went foul, as Pete knew it would. It did not miss being a Grand Slam by much, but Pete put it where he had to. The outside corner now belonged to Pete. The confrontation ended on an outside breaking ball that sent Lazzeri down swinging.

This was still only the seventh inning - two more to go. Well, the 39-year oldster breezed through, until the Bambino came up. Being a wise old man he walked him. It was on a full count and was written that it was probably strike three, but the Babe's stature possibly influenced the umpire to call it a ball. Bob Meusel was up next. The previous year (1925) he led the American League with 33 homers. Anyway, Ruth broke for second base hoping to surprise the Cardinals and get into scoring position. It didn't work out as a throw from catcher Bob O'Farrell, the NL MVP, to player-manager Hornsby nailed the Babe by plenty. The Cards won their first Series in a huge upset. One reason for Ruth's steal attempt was that the Yanks thought there was probably no way they would be able to get two consecutive hits off of Pete. Maybe one hit but no way would they get two.

Old Pete was too much for the Yanks - 20 1/3 innings with a 1.33 ERA, 17 Ks and two victories and one huge save.

Please note that almost everything I've read indicates this was Pete's last hurrah. What a bunch of baloney. In '27 at 40 years old, he was 21-10 and was second in the NL with a 2.15 ERA. In '28 at 41 years old he was 16-9 helping the Cards to their second pennant. At age 42, in 1929, he won 9 games for the Cards.

In 1952 a movie was made about Old Pete. Pete was played by former President Ronald Reagan and his wife by Doris Day. I'm not sure but I think the film people of Hollywood made the Lazzeri strike out end the game in the movie. The name of the movie was "The Winning Team."

In 1942 it was eight years since the Cardinals were in the World Series - not since the 1934 Gashouse Gang defeated the Detroit Tigers. During this eight year period they had good teams finishing runner-up four times. The Cardinals' chance of winning was greatly diminished when they got rid of their All-Star first baseman Johnny Mize. He was traded to the New York Giants. For six years Johnny Mize was the National League's best hitter winning two home run titles, a batting championship, always hitting well over .300, and driving in more than a 100 runs winning one RBI title. His offensive absence would hopefully be picked up by a rookie named Stan Musial.

In 1941, Musial was called up by the Cards as they chased the Dodgers down to the wire. The Cards could not overtake Brooklyn, but it was not due to Musial not producing - playing in the last 12 games he hit .426. When he came up his teammates referred to him as 'Musical', but that quickly ended because of the "tunes" he played with his bat.

Most people know the Musial story. A promising pitcher in the minors, he played the outfield when not pitching because he hit so well. While he was playing in the outfield, he hurt his shoulder diving for a ball. Thinking he was going to be a pitcher he thought his baseball career was over. His minor league manager was Dickie Kerr, who won two games for the White/Black Sox in the 1919 World Series. Kerr, being a good Major League pitcher knew a good hitter when he saw one - even if he had a strange corkscrew batting stance. Kerr would convince Musial he could play in the Majors and the rest is history.

In '42 Musial joined Country Slaughter and Terry Moore, one of the best fielding center fielders ever, to create one of baseball's best defensive outfields. They could all cover a lot of ground. At shortstop the Cards had Marty Marion who because of his height 6'2" and long arms that gobbled up everything was known as the "Octopus". The staff was led by Mort Cooper who was the league's best pitcher and MVP (22-7, 1.78 ERA and 10 shutouts), and rookie standout Johnny Beazley (21-6, 2.13 ERA). Mort's brother, Walker, was an All-Star catcher.

Slaughter led the offense leading the NL in hits (188), triples (17) and total bases (292) and was second in NL batting (.318), third in RBIs (98), and slugging % (.494). Musial, in his rookie year was third in the league in hitting (.315) with 10 homers and 72 RBIs.

Marion led the league with 38 doubles. The Cardinals were more than 10 games out of first place trailing the Dodgers. Then they caught fire. They won 43 of their remaining 51 games (43-8). They won the most games in the National League (106) since the 1909 Pirates. You might think winning the pennant would be a snap - but no, the Dodgers pushed them to the end winning 104.

The Cardinals' opponent was ho-hum, who else but the New York Yankees. The Yankees had won five of the last six World Series. From 1936-41, only the 1940 Cincinnati Reds, who beat the Detroit Tigers, were able to break up the Yankee monopoly.

The Yanks won 103 games. Their batting attack was led by superstar Joe DiMaggio (.305, 21 homers, 114 RBIs which was second in the league), Charlie "King Kong" Keller (26 homers, 108 RBIs - both third in the league), and MVP second baseman Joe "Flash" Gordon (fourth in the league in batting .322 and RBIs 103).

But it was their four starters that gave them the pennant by 10 games over the Boston Red Sox. Ernie Bonham was 21-5 with a 2.27 ERA and Spud Chandler was 16-5 and 2.38 ERA. My mom's neighbor from Bloomfield, NJ, Hank Borowy, was 15-4, good for second in the AL with a .789 winning % and he had a 2.52 ERA. All three of them were in the top five in the league in ERA. If that wasn't enough, their veteran star, future Famer, Red Ruffing had a 14-7 slate.

No way could the young inexperienced Cardinal team derail the Yankees' locomotive. But do not forget the Cardinal skipper was Billy Southworth who tormented the Yankees in the 1926 World Series won by the Red Birds.

As the Series began, it looked like the prediction was right. St.Louis looked like anything but a team that won 106 games. For seven innings Mort Cooper only gave the Yanks two runs, but in the eighth they scored three more. The Cards made four miscues which did not help.

Anyway, the Cards could not do anything against Ruffing. He had a no-hitter with two outs in the eighth inning when Terry Moore singled to spoil the effort. The Yanks scored twice in the ninth to make it a 7-0 lead. Ruffing needed one out in the bottom of the ninth when all of a sudden the Cardinal bats erupted. He gave up four hits and the Yanks sent for Chandler. He was not effective giving up two hits. The Cards made the score 7-4 had the bags loaded with rookie star Musial at the plate. Chandler got him to ground out to give the Yanks the win.

Even though the Cards lost, it seemed like they won. Their wild comeback in the ninth inning inspired them giving them confidence that the Yankee invincibility was just a myth.

Game 2 was between the team's 21-game winners, Ernie Bonham and the Cards rookie Johnny Beazley. Beazley had a 3-0 lead going into the eighth but the Yanks scored three times to knot the score. In the bottom of the eighth, Musial did come through with a single to score Slaughter to make it 4-3 Cards. The Yanks weren't dead. In the ninth, Slaughter, who just scored the go ahead run, secured the victory by nailing a Yankee runner attempting to advance to third on a hit to right for the second out. Cards won 4-3.

With the Series even at one apiece, the Series shifted to Yankee Stadium. The starters were Chandler and Ernie White, the Cardinals' sore armed pitcher for most of the year (he was 7-5). The sore arm was fine as he threw a six-hit shutout. Playing in the Stadium with its expansive outfield was advantageous for the Cards' fleet footed outfielders, as all three - Musial, Slaughter and Moore - made crucial plays robbing Yankee batters of extra base hits (two of them might have been homers) to thwart any Yankee rallies. Chandler pitched well for the Yanks only giving up 3 hits. The Cards scored a run in the first and one in the ninth for its 2 runs. With White pitching and super defense, it was all that was needed. Cards went up 2 games to 1 with a 2-0 victory.

The Cards were down 1-0 in the fourth inning of game 4. With my mom's neighbor Borowy on the mound, the Cards blasted him and his reliever for six runs. With NL MVP Mort Cooper pitching well, it appeared with a 6-1 lead, this game was history. Not so. The Yanks came back with 5 in the seventh to tie the score. It looked like the Yankee momentum would carry them to victory. Not so. Cards' reliever Max Lanier, who was 13-8 for the year came in and put down the Yanks for three innings while his mates tallied 3 more times. Cards won 9-6 and needed only one more to take the Series.

In game 5 it was Beazley, the rookie, against the veteran Ruffing. Going into the ninth the score was tied at 2. Two Famers went yard earlier in the game, Rizzuto for the Yanks and Slaughter for the Cards. In the top of the ninth, Cards' rookie Whitey Kurowski hit a 2-run homer to give the Cards a 4-2 lead going into to bottom of the ninth. The Yanks' final hopes were over in a flash when their MVP Flash Gordon was picked off second base by catcher Walker Cooper. It ended a horrible Series for Flash, as he was 2 for 21 at the plate.

Cards won the game 4-2 and took the Series 4 games to 1, winning 4 straight. This year, the Yanks were not INVINCIBLE – but rather INVISIBLE.

Editor's Note: To my father's dismay, the Bronx Bombers won the 1956 Series in seven as Don Larsen threw his historic perfect game in game five, winning 2-0, and Johnny Kucks blanked Brooklyn 9-0 as Yogi nuked Don Newcombe for a pair of 2-run bombs in the finale. My dad says that the last pitch of Larsen's gem that was a called strike three to pinch-hitter Dale Mitchell was so high that it must have been on drugs. He thought that the umpire Babe Pinelli, who was retiring after the Series, just wanted to be part of baseball history as there never has been a no-hitter in the World Series. Thus was born my dad's Pinstripe Intimidation theory.

1957
Little League -- No Cigar for the Yanks

In the spring of 1957, I decided again to play Little League ball. I was 12 and it would be the last year I would be eligible. Our local town paper had an announcement notice that sign-ups were taking place and had to be in by the beginning of March. I had my dad sign me up. I soon received notification that evaluation tryouts would be the first week of April.

As the tryout date approached, I got out my glove that was oiled up, a ball placed in its pocket and tied with cord since the '56 World Series ended.

Anyway, I rode my bike to the tryouts. We were split into groups, some of us fielding/ throwing and some of us hitting.

I was with the first group that was evaluated on fielding. With my big glove I felt I did pretty well - handled all the grounders flawlessly and ran down a few long fungo shots. Like I've said, all I had to do was throw up my arm with the big glove and the ball would land in it.

Next came the batting part of the tryouts. While I was waiting my turn I observed two things: 1. The adult that was pitching was wearing a cap with the hated interlocking NY of the Yankees. 2. He was throwing meatballs (easy to hit pitches) to the batters. I figured that I would be able to really blast some shots off of this guy with the hated Yankee cap.

As I was waiting my turn to bat, I was busy trying to find a good bat to hit with (the league provides bats). I could not find a decent bat. They were all so light, they felt like toothpicks. I think they were 29-ounce bats. Well my turn to bat came and I still could not locate a 31-ounce bat.

Each batter was given ten swings, really not much to be evaluated on but with so many kids, that's what it was. So there I am standing at the plate against this adult pitcher with a Yankee cap on, throwing meatballs, and I have this toothpick in my hands. My timing was so off as it was the first time this year that I swung a bat that after eight swings I showed little ability. I fouled off a couple, even whiffed two of them, and hit a couple off the end of the bat. The eighth pitch was embarrassing as I broke the bat. Instead of using one of the 29-ounce bats provided for the tryouts, I saw one of my teammates from last year who had his own bat, so I asked him, "Hey, I got two swings left, can I try your bat?" He said "Sure".

Anyway, I took his bat and quickly grimaced - it was a Mickey Mantle model. But it was a 31-ounce bat and it felt good in my hands.

It worked out pretty well, as I finally hit a couple of good ones off the Yankee-capped pitcher. The first swing with the Mantle bat produced a hard grounder through the box into center and my last swing was a gapper into right center. I was sorry my ten swings were over.

As I walked over to the batting evaluator I was thinking "No wonder Mantle is such a good hitter, it's his bat". The evaluator made mention to me of how good my last two swings were. Instead of mentioning my difficulty with the light bat, I just said that I was a little rusty; you know first time batting this year.

When I got home my dad asked how the tryouts went. I told him with the glove I was like Say Hey in the outfield and Ken Boyer in the infield. I said if the league is using 29-ounce bats, I'm going to have to get my own bat.

The next day my dad and I went to the sporting goods store to get a bat. (Bats at this time were only made of wood - aluminum bats were a thing of the future). Since we lived within ten miles of New York City the model bats they had were of the three New York City teams. The Carl Furillo bat felt OK, but the one that felt the best was a Hank Bauer model. Hank Bauer was the Yankee right fielder who was a solid player (he made a few All-Star teams in his career and holds the record for hitting safely in 17 consecutive World Series games). I really didn't want a Yankee player model bat.

My dad convinced me to get the one that felt the best, and told me that even though he also could not stand the Yankees, he respected the clutch hitting that Bauer provided for the Yankee offense. When I agreed to the get the Bauer bat, my dad said better get two just in case one breaks.

Driving home I thought of a solution to the dilemma of having a Yankee-Bauer model bat. When I got home I took my bats to the garage and got some sandpaper. On one bat I sanded off Hank Bauer's name and then took a pen and wrote in Stan the Man. With the other bat I sanded off Hank and only the A and U of Bauer and replaced it with an O and Y and wrote in Ken in order to have a Ken Boyer bat.

The next week I got a call from my manager. I was not home when the call came so all my mom told me was when the first team meeting and practice would be, but she wasn't given the name of the team.

When I went to the first practice I saw that our manager was the guy with the Yankee cap who pitched during the batting evaluations of the tryouts. I mentally cursed that "Oh no, I'm on the Yankees". Wasn't to be, he was just wearing the cap. Anyway, the name of the team was the Demons. My sister Carole, who was two years older than me, thought this was an appropriate name for a team that I would be put on, as I was a typical pain in the neck younger brother.

I guess for traveling purposes the league tried to keep the kids from the same part of town on one team, thus the other three 12-year olds (Mike, Bob and Nick) on my block were on my team. With the four of us as the nucleus we did OK - coming in third place and all of us made the All-Star team.

The game I remembered most was against, guess who? The Yankees; and I recall them being pretty good and the game was in the middle of the season.

In 1957, in our town anyway, kids would try smoking at about 12 years old. In those times everyone smoked (movie stars, athletes, politicians, etc.). When you were 12 there was peer pressure to smoke so you'd be cool. I'm only speaking for the boys. Try as I did, I could not get the hang of it. I hated the hot smoke, inhaling made me dizzy, I would be coughing plus I would become teary-eyed from the smoke - did I look cool? To this day, my wife gets angry with me because we do not utilize our fireplace because I can't stay in the room with smoke. Instead she improvises and uses candles in the fireplace.

Our Little League field was part of a large sports complex – football stadium, track and high school baseball field. The complex was surrounded by woods. This is where most of the pre-teens would go to smoke.

The day of the game against the Yankees, Mike, who was one of the guys on my block on the team and lived right across the street from me, said, "Let's go to the woods before the game". We usually didn't do this when we had a game.

We went to the woods and when we got there Mike whose idea it was said, "Look what I got". It was a big cigar that he took from his dad's cigar box. Mike lit it, had some puffs and passed it around. I took one puff and sort of gagged. I didn't look cool. After 20 minutes or so we had to go to the field, so Mike took the cigar, doused off the lit part, wrapped it in his handkerchief and put it in his pocket.

After our pre-game fielding practice the game started. The Yankees were up first and we got them out without them scoring. In the bottom of the first we had one on and one out and Mike, our cigar guy, was getting ready to bat. Here's what happened.

In 1957 the batting helmets were made of layers of cardboard and went around your head and ears. The ear sections had holes in it so when you ran you heard a loud, annoying whoosh in your ears. Mike was going to minimize the noise by taking out his handkerchief and use it to plug the ear holes. He forgot all about the cigar.

I was the clean-up hitter and was standing in the on-deck area, when all of a sudden Mike pulled out the handkerchief and out fell the cigar. It was like the E F Hutton commercial, when everyone stops and listens when E F Hutton talks. All of us guys must have had the same thought, the coaches were going to rat us out. After the seemingly long silence, the coaches started laughing. The Yankee team did not see this and wondered what was going on.

With our coaches laughing our team loosened up and rallied – Mike got a hit and I followed with another with my Stan the Man Bauer bat and we went on to defeat the Yankees.

The only thing I figured on why the coaches did not rat us out to our parents was that they did similar things in their youth.

1957
The Yanks Are LEW-SERS

The 1957 season was marked by events that took place in 1951 and in 1954.

The Yankees throughout the years have been known for acquiring quality veteran players who still had something left to help them in their pennant drives to the World Series.

In 1951 the Yanks thought they needed some pitching help, so again, out came their wallet to acquire the Boston Brave pitcher Johnny Sain. He was a 20-game winner four times since 1946. In '51 he was not having a good year. The Yanks offered $50,000 (a tidy amount in those days) and threw in minor leaguer Lew Burdette in order to entice the Braves to make the trade.

The trade worked out for both teams. In the short term, Sain helped the Yanks to three championships. In the long term, the Braves won out. Burdette became a top National League pitcher. In 8 out of 9 years, he won over 15 games. The year he didn't he was a fine 13-8. He became a 200-game winner in his near Hall of Fame career; his 203-144 record is similar to a few in the Hall, such as Hal Newhouser (209 -150).

Burdette was a legendary pitcher of his time because of his unique pitch. It was a sinker ball that was allegedly made to sink because of the foreign substance on it — normally referred to as a spitball. It was never proven that he threw the spitball, but the movement on his sinker was a major concern for all the batters he faced.

His effectiveness with this pitch was never more pronounced than in the '57 World Series, when he was seemingly taken over by the spirit of the famed Christy Mathewson, (who hurled three shutouts in the 1905 World Series against the Philadelphia Athletics).

In 1954, the New York Giants decided they needed more pitching to make a run for the pennant. They were interested in Boston Brave lefty Johnny Antonelli, who was a .500 pitcher in 1953 (12-12). In order to get him, they had to give up their 1951 "Shot Heard Round the World" hero Bobby Thomson. The Giant fans were up in arms about giving up their hero for a .500 pitcher. Thomson had 26 homers and 106 RBIs in '53.

The Giants really made out in this trade. In 1954, Antonelli was the league's best pitcher (21-7) leading them to the World Championship. He continued to be a winner for the Giants, winning 20 in 1956 and 19 in 1959.

This trade appeared to be a bad break, literally, for the Braves. In 1954 Thomson broke his leg during spring training. Waiting in the wings for a chance to show his talents was what was to be the last Negro League player to make the Majors, Henry (Hank) Aaron, who became known as the Hammer. Ironically, with his name starting with two 'A's, he's listed as the first position player in the baseball register, which is appropriate since he's first in homers and RBIs.

Taking advantage of his shot at playing regularly, Aaron displayed his talents. After a solid rookie year in '54, he became a full fledged National League All-Star outfielder putting up stats comparable to the Duke (Snider), the Man (Musial) and the Say Hey Kid (Mays). He won the batting title in '56 and the home run and RBI crown in '57, and beat out Stan the Man for the '57 National League MVP award.

Once again, in 1957, the Yanks were heavily favored to win the pennant and Series. Their main opposition figured to be from the perennial bridesmaids, except for '54, the Cleveland Indians. The Tribe had three 20-game winners in 1956, Early Wynn and Bob Lemon and the second year phenom Herb Score, who was showing the talent to be a left-handed Bob Feller. In his first two years, the fireballing southpaw led the league in strikeouts as he won 16 in 1955 and 20 in 1956.

In 1955, the Philadelphia A's were sold to Arnold Johnson. At the time, the Yankee Triple A minor league team was located in Kansas City. Johnson, who was a millionaire, was friends with the Yankee owner, millionaire Dan Topping, and their General Manager, George Weiss. They made an arrangement that the Yanks would move their farm team to Denver and open up Kansas City to be a Major League city. In Philadelphia, the A's had to compete against the National League Phillies, who seemed to be the city's favorite, having been in the 1950 Series and showcased All-Stars Richie Ashburn, the center fielder, and perennial 20-game winner Robin Roberts. The joke in Philadelphia was that there were no Athletic supporters.

With the A's owner and the Yankee owner being friends, there were constant trades between the two franchises. The Yankees always had plenty of players to trade, so when they needed a specific piece to complete their team and the A's had that player, a trade would be made between the two. These trades kept the Yankees winning up until the mid-60's. During this period, the Yankees acquired key players such as Ralph Terry, Bobby Shantz, Clete Boyer, Bob Cerv, Country Slaughter, Ryne Duren, and Roger Maris.

This year, the Yanks led the American League with an ERA of 3.06. The second place Chicago White Sox were second with a 3.35 ERA. But, the White Sox offense was nowhere near the Yankee offensive might. The White Sox leaders in homers were Larry Doby and Jungle Jim Rivera with 14, while for the Yanks, Mantle had 34, Yogi 24, Bauer 18, and Moose Skowron 17.

The Yankee run to the pennant was made easier by their trade with Kansas City. A couple of things about the Yankee/Kansas City trades. One American League General Manger said something to the effect that it is a lot easier to win when you have your farm team in the league. The other was that the abbreviated letters KC actually stood for "Kissin' Cousins" not Kansas City. Anyway, the Yanks needed some more pitching – so their Kissin' Cousins supplied them with the little lefty (5'6") Bobby Shantz and Art Ditmar. Shantz was the American League MVP in 1952 (24-7) for the Philadelphia A's, but was later plagued by a sore arm. The Yanks always had the money so they could afford to gamble on Shantz. Together, Ditmar and Shantz were 19-8, and Shantz led the league with a 2.45 ERA.

The Yanks also had the "Sturdi"est staff in the league. Tom Sturdivant led them with a 16-6 record and was second behind Shantz in ERA (2.54). The Chairman of the Board, Whitey Ford, missed a couple of months due to injury, but was effective when healthy (11-5, 2.56 ERA). Their two 1954 acquisitions from the Baltimore Orioles were also very good, "Bullet" Bob Turley (13-6) and Don "Perfect Game" Larsen (10-4).

Their offense was led by Mickey Mantle, who repeated as AL MVP. He was the fore-runner to the Barry Bonds walk-a-thon. After his Triple Crown performance of last year, AL pitchers decided to walk him 146 times and, although his power numbers dropped, he did lead the league in runs (121). The Mick had 94 RBIs, was third in homers with 34, and his .365 batting average was the highest of any American Leaguer since 1940, except for Ted Williams who accomplished it three times. Unfortunately for Mick, this was one of those years, when Teddy Ball Game became the oldest player (at 38) to take a batting crown with a .388 average (too bad Ted's legs were so old or he may have hit over .400 again). Williams was selected as The Sporting News Major League Player of the Year for a record setting fifth time. Interestingly, this was the year that GM George Weiss tried to cut MicKs salary because he didn't win another Triple Crown - hey what'd you expect from someone who was a lousy tipper for my dad who caddied for him back in the '30's. Other contributors to the Yankee attack were Moose Skowron (.304, 17 homers, 88 RBIs) and Yogi (24 homers, 82 RBIs).

The '57 Yanks outscored and out pitched all the other teams, so it was no surprise that they won the American League pennant by 8 games over the Chicago White Sox. The Yanks' main rival in the '50's, the Cleveland Indians fell apart in May when Yankee Gil McDougald hit a line drive that hit Indian Herb Score in the eye. He was done for the year (and this basically ended Score's career). At this time, his career record was 38-20 and the Red Sox tried to buy his contract for a million dollars (an unheard of sum at the time) before this incident. Score came back and lasted four years but was never the same – he was 17-26. The other two Indian 20-game winners in '56, Wynn (14-17) and Lemon (6-11), had bad years.

The Yanks of '57 did not have its major battle on the field. Their battles on the field were nothing compared to what happened in May.

It was Billy Martin's 29th birthday. His best friends, Whitey Ford and the Mick decided to have a party for him. The Yanks that came were the old-timers - naturally Ford and Mantle, also Bauer and Yogi came with their wives. Johnny Kucks, the only newcomer, and his wife also went.

After dinner the Yankee group decided to go the Copacabana to see entertainer Sammy Davis, Jr. While watching the show, another group was making racial insults to Davis. The Yanks, who since

1955 had Elston Howard on their team, were in no mood for hearing these racist comments directed at the talented Davis.

The Yankee group told that idiot group to shut up. The drunken idiot group was looking for trouble and challenges escalated between the groups. The Copa's security men came and things seemed to cool off. But, in the men's room, one of the idiot drunks was laid out on the floor, knocked out cold. The Copa's people got the Yankee group out of there through the back doors. Anyway, the New York dailies got the story and plastered it all over their newspapers.

GM George Weiss probably came close to a coronary when he saw his morning papers. The players were fined and some were benched, but not so that they would jeopardize losing a game. It was undecided who laid out the idiot drunk in the men's room (there was speculation that the former marine Bauer landed the blow). The Yanks said it was one of the Copa's men.

George Weiss never liked Billy Martin. This Copa brawl is the straw that broke the camel's back. Weiss blamed Martin for leading Mantle and Ford astray and overall was a bad influence on the team. Martin never could figure out how he could be such a bad influence. In 1950 he roomed with Rizzuto, in '55 with Yogi and '56 with Mantle-and all three were voted American League MVPs. Maybe Weiss didn't like having MVPs, as he would have to give them a bigger contract.

Martin's 29th birthday was probably his worst. About a month after the Copa incident, Weiss made a trade with his Kissin' Cousins. It was a belated birthday gift for Billy from Weiss – a trade to the A's. Weiss justified the trade. He got Harry "Suitcase" Simpson. The year before "Suitcase" was the A's All-Star, driving in over 100 runs and hitting 21 homers. And Weiss would not have to put up with the Martin, Ford and Mantle hi-jinx. For Weiss, winning the pennant was a lot easier then handling the Copa incident.

Being a Cardinal fan my attention again was generally focused on the National League. I was able to go to a couple of Giant/Cardinal games and Dodger/Cardinal games. At this time I did not realize this would be the last time I would be able to see a National League game in New York until 1962. I had no idea that Brooklyn and the Giants would move to the West Coast. Really you can't blame them, especially with seeing the attendance the Braves were drawing, California would be an untapped market. Also, the Polo Grounds and Ebbets Field were ancient, and New York would not build them a new stadium.

The Brooklyn Dodgers were the favorite to three-peat in the National League. Last year the Braves only missed the pennant by one game and were expected to give the Dodgers a run of their own. The Dodgers seemed to be getting old. Jackie Robinson, their symbolic leader, was 37 and retired instead of reporting to the Giants, who he was traded to. What an INSULT!! Jackie was NOT particularly fond of his Manhattan neighbors. The Duke hit 40 homers and drove in 92 runs. Hodges hit .299 with 27 homers Furillo hit .306 and Gino Cimoli batted .293 but that was it for their offense. Pee Wee hit .224 and Campy .242. Newcombe, who won 27 games in 1956, was below .500 at 11-12. Podres was only 12-9 despite leading the NL with 6 shutouts and in ERA (2.66). The Dodger bright spot was an ornery, hard throwing right-handed 20-year old Don Drysdale, who was 17-9. In their last year in Brooklyn the Dodgers came in third, 11 games out of first.

My favorite team, the Cardinals, gave me an exciting year. For most of the year they battled the Braves for the pennant. The Cards' staff was no match for the Braves' staff. Larry Jackson and Lindy McDaniel were both 15-9 for the Red Birds and Sad Sam "Toothpick" Jones (he always had one in his mouth while pitching) was 12-9. This could not compare to the Braves' mounds men, Warren Spahn with his patented high leg kick was 21-11 (one of the staggering 13 times he was a 20-game winner) and won the Cy Young Award, Bob Buhl was 18-8, and Lew Burdette was 17-9.

The Cardinal offense is what kept them in the chase. Stan the Man led the league in hitting (.351) and was second in slugging % at .612. He banged out 29 homers and had 102 RBIs, and was runner-up for the MVP award behind the Hammer, Aaron. (However Sports Illustrated magazine still selected Musial as their Sportsman of the Year). Their outfielders complemented Musial in the power department. Wally Moon and Del Ennis hit 24 homers each and Ken Boyer chipped in with 18. Yes, Boyer was in the outfield for over 100 games. Why the Cards would move him from third base is beyond me. The Cards picked up Eddie Kasko to play third. Boyer proved to be a star defensive center fielder, but after this year went back to third base where he would win his five Gold Gloves. I don't know if moving to the outfield had an adverse effect on his average

(.265), but after moving back to third he became a perennial .290-.300 hitter. The Cardinals came in second place, 8 games out.

The Braves had a lot of injuries in '57, but their replacements seemed to come through. However, their main guys, Aaron and future Famer Eddie Mathews, did not get hurt. The Hammer led the league with 44 homers and 132 RBIs, while Mathews hit 32 with 94 RBIs. Aaron and Mathews hitting 3 & 4 in the line-up were maybe the most potent 3 & 4 hitters since Ruth and Gehrig. The Braves solidified winning the National League flag with a trade in June with the New York Giants. The Giants got back their 1951 hero Bobby Thomson and second baseman Dan O'Connell for Giants' second baseman Red Schoendienst. The former Cardinal great hit .310 and, with both the Giants and Braves, led the league with 200 hits. He was always a superlative fielder and combined with shortstop Johnny Logan to give the defense a superb double play combo. Aaron was the only outfielder who played the whole season. As an outfielder, he won three Gold Gloves. The fleet-footed Billy Bruton was in center until he got injured. Left field was a patch work of veteran "Handy" Andy Pafko, Bob "Hurricane" Hazel, who hit over .400 in 134 at bats, and Wes Covington, who hit 21 homers in less than 100 games. An injured Bruton didn't play in the Series. Aaron showing his versatility took Bruton's place in center.

The Series was ready to begin. For New York City, no big deal, it was just another Series. For Milwaukee, the whole city was ecstatic and the suds were flowing in the nation's beer capital.

The Series opened in Yankee Stadium. The match-up was Ford against the Cy Young Award winner Warren Spahn. For 4 innings they matched goose eggs. The Yanks broke through in the fifth for 2 runs and added one in the sixth. The Braves couldn't do anything against Ford, except in the seventh when a Covington double and Schoendienst's single gave the Braves their only run. Yanks and Ford beat Spahn 3-1.

For the past 9 World Series, a New York team has won 47 consecutive games (from 1949 thru the first game of 1957). Game 2 had former Yankee farmhand Lew Burdette, he of the famed sinker "spitball" going against the American League ERA leader, little (in stature) Bobby Shantz.

The Braves opened the scoring in the second when Aaron tripled and Joe Adcock singled him in. The Yanks countered when Jerry Coleman's single drove in Country Slaughter. The next batter was the pitcher Shantz. He pulled a shot down the left field line. Covington was the left fielder. He was not regarded as a good defensive outfielder. The Yankees would disagree. Covington raced toward the fence, threw up his glove to backhand the long drive to end the inning. Yankee fans were thinking "Shades of Sandy Amoros". With two on and two out, if Covington did not pull off this spectacular catch, the Yanks would have had scored two runs with a runner on second. But, instead the inning ended 1-1. In the third, Logan and Bauer matched homers, so after three it was 2-2. In the fourth, the Braves strung together hits by Joe Adcock, Andy Pafko and Covington to score 2 runs to make the score 4-2 Braves. Burdette must have been thinking "That's it, no more runs – no not just this game, I mean for the Series, from me anyway". Braves won 4-2. For the first time in 48 World Series games a New York team did not win.

The Series moved to Milwaukee. The Braves' fans festive time was ended quickly. Tony Kubek was the AL Rookie of the Year, playing over 35 games at three different positions - third, short and outfield. He hit .297 but only hit 3 homers. After 18-game winner Bob Buhl retired the lead-off man Bauer, Kubek came up. It must have been a strange feeling for Kubek, as Milwaukee was his hometown. He promptly angered his neighbors by hitting a homer. The Yanks went on to score 3 in the first, but for them and Mickey Mantle something bad occurred. Mantle was on second when Buhl tried to pick him off. The throw was off line, and with Mantle diving back and Schoendienst trying to catch the errant throw they became entangled. Mantle, attempting to get free from Schoendienst to go to third, injured his shoulder. This injury bothered him on and off for years.

The Yanks continued to bomb Brave pitchers and won 12-3. In fact, Milwaukee's now hated son, Kubek, hit another homer almost reaching his regular season total of 3. The only positive thing for the Braves was Aaron hammering a 2-run homer in the fifth. The Yanks were up 2 games to 1.

Game 4 had Spahn against the Yanks top pitcher in '57, Tom Sturdivant. The Yanks took a quick 1-0 lead in the first. In the fourth, Mathews doubled to put runners on second and third with Aaron up. With first base open the Yanks opted not to walk him. Aaron showed them his carpentry skills by hammering his second Series homer over the left field fence. Frank Torre, Joe's older

brother, also hit a homer in the inning to make the score 4-1. With
Spahn on the mound throwing like an All-Century Team pitcher, the
game seemed to be an easy Brave victory. But in the ninth the great
lefty faltered - with two outs, Yogi and McDougald hit safely. The
next batter, Ellie Howard with a full count on him blasted a 3-run
game tying homer. In the tenth Spahn was still in there, but with two
outs, an infield hit and a triple by Bauer gave the Yanks a 5-4 lead
and a probable 3-1 lead in the Series. All that was needed was to get
the Braves out in the bottom of the tenth.

Pitching for the Yanks was Tommy Byrne who relieved in the
eighth. Byrne always had a tendency to be a bit wild. The Braves
sent up Nippy Jones to pinch-hit for Spahn. Nippy did not play
much – he had 21 hits and hit .266. Since he did not play much, he
probably had plenty of time to keep his cleats polished. Byrne
uncorked a low breaking pitch that hit Nippy in the shoe and rolled
to the back stop. The umpire did not see the ball hit his shoe and
called the pitch a ball. The Brave third base coach beat Yogi to the
ball so he couldn't rub the polish off. The coach showed the umpire
the polish on the ball and Nippy Jones was awarded first base. Felix
Mantilla went into to run for him. Nippy could than re-polish his
shoe. Still it was only a runner on first. Then Schoendienst
sacrificed him to second. Stengel then took out lefty Byrne and
brought in Bob Grim, his top reliever who had 12 wins and 19
saves. Grim was a righty and was facing righty, Johnny Logan. The
righty/righty switch move blew up when Logan belted a double
down the left field line to tie it up at 5. With lefty slugger Mathews
up and first base open, the Yanks could have had righty Grim face
righty Aaron. The Yanks chose their poison. Since the Logan
righty/righty match-up didn't work – Stengel let it go with the lefty
(Mathews) - righty (Grim) match-up. Good choice! Mathews blasted
a 2-run run game-winning homer. You could say it was a 'Grim'
day for the Yanks, as they were Nipped by the Braves 7-5 to tie the
Series at two games apiece.

I was in seventh grade in 1957. During the Series, us that
collected baseball cards would flip them against the wall. Some of
us flipped Brave cards and others Yankee cards. Naturally I flipped
Brave cards. The card closest to the wall won. The most coveted
cards were the Mantle and Aaron cards, especially the Aaron card
because when the Topps Company made his card they reversed the

photo negative, thus the 1957 baseball card of Aaron has him batting left-handed.

Game 5 was on a Monday, the match-up was Whitey against Lew. The reason I remember this game more than any other is that we watched the game in school. Our gym class was on Monday in the afternoon. Our gym teacher was Ed Berlinski, who was another of my mom's neighbors from Bloomfield NJ and a former college football star at North Carolina State and was also our high school baseball and football coach. During the fall his classes would be teaching us football and then having a two-hand touch game. But on this Monday he took us to the auditorium. There was a TV on the stage. He said that today we're going to watch the World Series. The guys in my class were split – many were Giant and Dodger fans who also hated the Yanks.

The game was a masterful pitching performance by both hurlers. Ford only gave up six hits, but three of them were in the sixth inning, and with two outs, successive hits by Mathews, Aaron and Adcock gave the Braves the only run of the game. Lew made good that he would keep the Yankees scoreless as he threw a seven hit shutout. The Yanks thought they had a run in the fourth when McDougald clubbed a long fly to left. Again the reputed poor fielding Covington was on his horse and as he reached the wire fence, leapt high and caught the ball as it was headed over the wall. After bouncing off the wire fence he fell to the ground ball in glove. Braves won 1-0 and were up 3-2 in the Series. It was my best gym class ever.

In game 6 Buhl was hoping to win the Series for the Braves. He gave up a 2-run homer to Yogi in the third. Reliever Ernie Johnson then went in. Frank Torre closed the gap by homering in the fifth. Aaron hammered a homer, his third of the Series, to tie it at two. But then that Yankee magic appeared in the bottom of the seventh, when Bauer's long fly to left hit the foul pole for a homer and a 3-2 lead that held up. The Series was knotted at three games apiece.

Spahn would have been the Braves' starter in the deciding game, but he had a terrible flu so again it was in Lew's hands...or his saliva? The Yanks would have rather faced a healthy Spahn then Burdette. Larsen started for the Yanks. He did not do badly, but the Braves scored four runs in the third – aided by the Yanks messing up a chance for a double play. It didn't matter as the Yanks couldn't do anything with Lew. He threw a seven-hit shutout. It was 23 consecutive scoreless innings he threw against the mighty Yanks. He was the first pitcher to win three complete Series games since the Indians' Hall of Famer Stan Coveleski did it in 1920 (ironically, Coveleski's bread and butter pitch was the spitball, but it was legal back then). The Cardinals' Harry "the Cat" Brecheen won three games in the 1946 Series, but one was in relief. His performance was the best since Christy Mathewson's three shutouts in 1905. Of course, he must have thanked Wes Covington for his two great catches in games 2 and 5.

Aaron had a great Series hitting .393 with a triple, 3 homers, and 8 RBIs. But mainly it was Burdette, the Yankees' former minor leaguer who made the Yankees out to be "LEW-SERS'.

1958
California Here I Come

In 1958 the Yankees took all the marbles so I won't mention too much about the year. The big event of the year was the National League's two New York teams moving to California - the Brooklyn Dodgers to Los Angeles and the New York Giants to San Francisco.

At this time I did not realize the impact it would have on me. I would not be able to see my Cardinals play this year. Also, I was used to seeing them on TV fifteen or so times a year, now even that was out. Most of my following the National League was from one of the NY radio stations that used a ticker to recreate the Giant games. Also, I was able to pick up, with some static, the Cardinal station from St. Louis. Since they were one hour behind us, their games started at 9:00 p.m. Eastern Standard time so I could only listen to half of the game before going to bed (during the school year).

As 1958, started I was optimistic about St. Louis' chances to win the pennant since they made a run for it the year before.

The Cardinal owner, August Busch was also the owner of Budweiser Beer, and his suds created a lot of money. When contract time came, he made Stan the Man the first $100,000 player in the National League. After all, he led the league in batting and was runner-up for MVP in '57.

In '58, the Man was 37 and his power numbers dropped to 17 homers and 62 RBIs in 135 games. However, he did make a run for the batting championship hitting .337 to finish third. The Phils' Richie Ashburn hit .350 to win it and the Say Hey Kid was runner-up at .347.

The highlight of the season for the Cardinals was in May. Stan the Man had 2,999 hits. The Cardinals had a game in Wrigley Field in Chicago before returning home to St. Louis. Fred Hutchinson, the Cardinal Manager, did not start Musial so he could get his 3,000 hit in front of his hometown fans.

Anyway, the way the things were going for the Cardinals, it did
not work out that way. The Cards were losing in the sixth inning.
The Cardinals had a chance to score so Hutchinson sent up Musial
to pinch-hit. Against the Cub pitcher, Moe Drabowsky he lined a
double into left for his 3,000 hit. Stan the Man became the first
Major Leaguer to reach 3,000 hits since Paul "Big Poison" Waner
did it in the early 1940's.

My other favorite, Ken Boyer, had a good year. He was moved
back to third base and won his first Gold Glove award. At the plate
he stopped trying to pull everything and learned how to take the
outside pitch to the opposite field. He hit .307 with 23 homers and
90 RBIs. But, outside of Boyer and The Man, their offense was
weak.

The Cardinal pitching was also down. Lindy McDaniel and
Larry Jackson, who were both 15-9 in '57, were a combined 18-20
in '58. Sad Sam "Toothpick" Jones pitched well, finishing second
in ERA (2.88), but with little run support, was only 14-13 (no
wonder he was sad). The Cardinals finished up in sixth place.

The Braves again took the National League pennant. Warren
Spahn and Lew Burdette each won 20 games. On the offensive side
Hank Aaron and Eddie Mathews each hit over 30 homers.

Getting back to the big event of the year (the two New York
teams move to the West Coast), the Dodgers and Giants both did
well at the gate. The Dodgers played in the Los Angeles Coliseum.
It was sort of like the old Polo Grounds (shaped like an egg). Left
field was only 251 feet, but with a 40-foot screen, while right field
was like five miles. These dimensions were right up the Dodger
catcher Roy Campanella's power alley. But it would never happen
as during the winter on an icy road, Campy got in a car accident that
left him paralyzed for life.

The other former Brooklynites were aging and their power
skills were fading. The question in southern California was could
the Duke of Flatbush (Snider) become the Duke of Los Angeles; the
answer is no, Los Angeles already had a Duke (John Wayne).
Snider, gave it a good effort batting .312 with 15 homers; but he
only played in 106 games due to injury. The other "Boys of
Summer" slugger Gil Hodges hit 22 homers, but only drove home
64 runs. The Dodgers came in next to last, but the owners had to be
happy with the money they made with an attendance of 1,800,000
(in this era, attendance of over a million was a franchise goal).

The Giants, the Dodgers' northern neighbor in San Francisco, came in third place. They showed off their new star Rookie of the Year, Orlando Cepeda, who hit .312 with 25 homers and 96 RBIs. The Giant owner was also happy as they drew 1,200,000 fans to a stadium that only had a capacity of 25,000. This was almost double what the Giants drew in their last year in New York. The Giants played in Seals Stadium while waiting for Candlestick Park to be built.

Editor's Note: Most people remember negative events from their childhood. Well my dad's bad memories tended to revolve around the Yankees winning and this year was no exception. The Milwaukee Braves, who were trying to repeat as champs, were up 3 games to 1 against the Yanks. Only once before (in 1925 when the Pittsburgh Pirates came back from that kind of deficit to defeat the Walter Johnson led Washington Senators) had a team come back to win three in a row to take the Series. The Yankees won the next three contests, winning game 6 in extra innings and game 7 by scoring 4 runs in the eighth, breaking a 2-2 tie.

1959
White Sox WYNN the Pennant

As the 1959 season was to about to start, the Yankees were again the American League favorite. After all, since 1949, they won every pennant except for 1954. The manager of the only team to break their streak, the '54 Cleveland Indians, was Al Lopez who was now managing the Chicago White Sox.

In '58, the Chicago White Sox and Cleveland Indians made a trade. The White Sox irritated their fans by trading All-Star outfielder, Minnie Minoso to Cleveland for veteran pitcher Early Wynn and outfielder Al Smith. Minoso hit over .300 in '57 with over 100 RBIs. Wynn was 14-17 and at 39 years of age did not appear to be winding up his career on a positive note. He came up in 1939 with the Washington Senators, was traded to Cleveland and was a 20-game winner four times. He was an ornery pitcher and there is a story that goes something like this. He was once asked "Would you knock your mother down if she was at the plate?" Wynn said something like "You're damn right - did you ever see her hit?"

Well, in '58 the trade was still in Cleveland's favor. Minoso hit over .300 again to go with 24 homers. Wynn was 14-16 for the second place Chisox.

In '59 Minnie had another All-Star year again batting over .300 with 21 homers. But the White Sox got even with the trade as Wynn had his last hurrah. He was 22-10 with a 3.16 ERA and won the Major League Cy Young Award (it wasn't until 1967 that each league gave an award).

Here is some perspective on Minnie Minoso belonging in the Hall of Fame. Possibly due to baseball's slow acceptance of integration, Minnie didn't make the Majors until 1951 at the age of 28 (after starring for the New York Cubans in the Negro Leagues). In his first year he finished second in the AL in batting (.326) and runs (112), and was fourth in the MVP voting. Despite these numbers he wasn't selected Rookie of the Year - it went to the Yanks' Gil McDougald (.306, 72 runs) who came in ninth in the MVP voting. During his twelve full seasons, the seven-time All-Star was always in the top ten in most offensive categories – he led the league in triples and stolen bases three times, batted over .300 eight times, had 100 RBIs four times (as many as Mantle), scored more than 90 runs ten times (a major feat in the 1950's). In his late starting career, he finished with 1963 hits, a .298 average (the same as the MicKs and a point above Al Kaline's) with 1023 RBIs and 1136 runs scored. The Gold Glove Awards did not start until the latter stages of Minnie's career (1957). Minnie showed that he could still flash the leather as his defensive skills won him three Gold Gloves - in '57, '59 and '60 (and he wasn't a kid then). Growing up during this time, when I think back to the AL All-Star outfield of the 1950's I see the Mick, Teddy Ballgame and Minnie (some might say Al Kaline, but he was only there for half of that decade becoming a star in '55). Minnie has the qualifications making him worthy enough to have a plaque in Cooperstown.

Pitching was the Chisox strong point. The league's second best hurler was Bob Shaw 18-6 and 2.69 ERA and even 3 saves. In addition, their usual ace Billy Pierce had 14 victories. To complement the starters, the White Sox had two of the best relievers in the league in Turk Lown and former Cardinal Gerry Staley. They combined for 17 wins and 29 saves - almost half of the White Sox's 94 wins.

This team was known as the Go-Go Sox because of their speed and "Punch and Judy" offense. They only had two players with over 10 homers – catcher Sherman Lollar with 22 and Al Smith (who they also acquired in the Wynn deal) with 17.

Their offense consisted of the Hall of Fame double play combination, second baseman Nellie Fox and shortstop Luis Aparicio. The typical White Sox rally would start with Aparicio getting on (he led the AL in steals his first 9 seasons), stealing second, and Fox would either sacrifice him to third or drive him in with one of his 191 hits (second in the AL). Fox, who will always be remembered for having a huge wad of chewing tobacco in his cheek when he played, was second on the team with 70 RBIs despite hitting only 2 homers. His .306 batting average was fourth in the league. He was also selected American League MVP.

The Chisox defense was another integral part of their winning ways. Their defense was especially strong up the middle – Lollar catching, the Hall of Fame double play combo, and Jim Landis in center, who caught everything east of the Mississippi.

Surprisingly, it wasn't the hated Yankees that the White Sox had to hold off. It was the Cleveland Indians who were once again bridesmaids. Their stars were Minoso and new American League power hitter, Rocky Colavito, who tied Washington Senator Harmon "Killer" Killebrew for the AL home run crown with 42 round-trippers including a record-tying four in one game in June against the Orioles. Colavito was also renowned for his howitzer-like throws from the outfield (best in the AL). The saying in the American League was "Don't knock The Rock". (Take Note: Cleveland appeared primed for another pennant run in 1960 being led by The Rock, but just before the '60 season opened, Colavito, the AL home run co-champ was dealt to Detroit for the AL batting champ, Harvey Kuenn who hit .353, but with little power. The Tribe fans were livid toward Cleveland GM, Frank "Trader" Lane swapping their favorite player for a singles hitter. During the '50's Cleveland came in second place five times and took the pennant in '54. After this trade the Indians would become a virtual fixture in the lower end of the AL standings for the next 35 years until 1995 when they won the AL pennant. "The Curse of The Rock" was set in stone even though Colavito returned to the Tribe in '65).

Pitchers Cal McLish at 19-8 and Gary Bell at 16-11 were the mainstays of the Tribes' staff. Another Indian star was Tito Francona with a .363 batting average, 20 homers, and 79 RBIs, but didn't qualify for the batting title crown with only 399 at bats. His other major baseball accomplishment was having a son, Terry who was a role player for the Expos in the '80's and went on to be manager of the Boston Red Sox in 2004 leading them to the World Series Championship (to do so they had to defeat the hated Yankees in the ALCS in historic fashion; more on that later).

The Yankees had a great year, in my eyes anyway. They came in third (79 -75), 15 games out of first place. Since I could only watch the Yankees on TV, I had a pretty good year watching them lose. (Not to be negative, I had a pretty good year watching their opponents win).

The Yankees got off to a horrible start. It became a season that was filled with injuries. The Yanks usually overcame this type of injury situation in the past to win, but could not do it in '59.

I really enjoyed it when the Yanks landed in last place on May 20. The Yanks haven't lived in the cellar since 1940. The Yanks finally called their Kissin' Cousins (the A's) and were able to get Hector Lopez. He helped revitalize the offense and the Yanks climbed to within two games of first place by the end of June when they ran into the Go-Go Sox. The Sox won 3 out of 4 and the Yanks never recovered, as they became the Going-Going-Gone Yanks.

The Yankees demise was basically the only positive thing for me in '59. My team, the Cardinals finished seventh, 16 games out of first. My favorite, Stan the Man, had a horrible season, showing that his age of 38 was catching up to him. He hit only .255 with 14 homers. My other favorite, Ken Boyer put together another All-Star year, hitting .309 with 28 homers (three of them were inside the parkers, all in a three week period – from May 30 to June 14) and 94 RBIs. Boyer also had a 29-game hitting streak – the longest in the Majors since Musial's 30 in 1950. Despite the Cardinals' dismal record, they did have six players on the NL All-Star team. Besides the Man (a sentimental pick) and Kenny, pitcher Vinegar Bend Mizell (13-10), catcher Hal Smith (.270), first basemen/outfielder Bill White (.302 - he was traded by the Giants for Sad Sam Jones) and Joe Cunningham (.345) were also on the team. Cunningham, a lifetime .291 hitter with a career .403 on base % (ranked 51st all-time), gave the Hammer a run for the batting crown, but settled for the runner-up spot as Aaron won it with a .355 mark.

The Windy City was having a good year as the fifth place Cubs' Ernie "Lets Play Two" Banks (.304, 45 homers, 143 RBIs) was selected the NL MVP for the second year in a row.

The major individual performance of the season was turned in by the Pirates' Harvey "the Kitten" Haddix who was purring for 12 "purr"fect innings against the heavy hitting Braves only to lose the game in the thirteenth inning. Often forgotten about in this historic contest is that the Braves' hurler Lew Burdette, the '57 Series Yankee Killer, tossed a 13-inning shutout for the victory.

The Giants appeared to have won the National League pennant going into the last two weeks of the season, but they lost seven of their last eight allowing the Dodgers and Braves to pass them as they tied for first. There would be a Braves/Dodgers playoff for the

NL flag. Although losing the pennant, the Giants' toothpick chomping Sad Sam Jones, who they got in the Bill White trade, had to be happy with his performance leading the NL in ERA (2.83) and tied for most wins with 21 – The Sporting News selected him as Major League Pitcher of the Year.

In the two out of three playoff series, the Dodgers won two straight to take the flag. The Braves, after losing the opener 3-2 on catcher Johnny Roseboro's sixth inning homer and Larry Sherry's 7 2/3 innings of shut out ball, appeared to have the playoff tied leading 5-2 in the ninth inning behind their alleged master of the spitball, Lew Burdette. But then in the ninth maybe Lew's mouth was getting dry as Wally Moon and Duke Snider singled and Gil Hodges drew a walk as Lew was taken out – Norm Larker followed with a 2-run single and Carl Furillo tied it up at five with a sac-fly. The Dodger skipper Walter Alston sent in Stan Williams in the tenth and he responded with three scoreless innings. In the bottom of the twelfth with two outs Hodges walked and Joe Pignatano singled followed by Furillo hitting a hopper up the middle – Felix Mantilla the back-up shortstop for the injured regular Johnny Logan fielded the ball but made an awkward throw to first on a bounce that got by Frank Torre, the first baseman, as Hodges sped home with the pennant winning run. The Dodgers jumped from seventh place from the year before to become the National League Champs.

The Dodgers were led by a last hurrah from a couple of veteran Brooklynites. Hodges hit 25 homers with 80 RBIs in only 125 games, and the Duke (in 126 games) hit .308 with 23 homers and 88 RBIs. Gold Glove second baseman Charlie Neal was on the All-Star team and cranked out 19 homers batting .287 and scoring 103 runs. A key acquisition they made was the left-handed hitting Wally Moon, who hit .302 and had an inside-out swing that launched fly balls over the Coliseum's short left field screen for home runs – most of his 19 homers were of this type and were known as "Moon shots".

The Dodger starters could not match the Brave starters. Warren Spahn and Lew Burdette were both 21-15 and Bob Buhl was 15-9, but that was pretty much it for their mounds corp. Don Drysdale had 17 victories to lead the Dodger staff and Johnny Podres won 14. But they had the depth to tie the Braves for the regular season and beat them in the playoffs.

The '59 Series match-up was set - the Dodgers and White Sox. I was a National League fan but if the White Sox won it would not bother me that much. After all, the last time the White Sox were in the World Series it was the one to forget – the 1919 Black Sox Series that they supposedly threw (actually, all the conspirators were actually acquitted – how?). This was a Series I could enjoy watching no matter who won.

The Sox won the first game in a rout. Wynn looked like Cy Young, throwing eight scoreless innings. The Go-Go Sox had a power display in the 11-0 thrashing led by National League veteran, Ted Kluszewski. He was at the end of his career hitting only 4 homers for the season. But in this Series Big Klu must have felt like he did when he was bashing 40 a year for the Reds in the mid '50's – he use to have his sleeves cut out at the shoulders so his massive arms would be free to swing the bat without ripping apart his shirt. In game 1, Big Klu hit 2 homers and a single to drive in 5 of the 11 runs.

The Sox looked good in game 2 leading 2-1 in the seventh. The Dodgers sent up Chuck Essegian to pinch-hit, hoping for him to get on. It was unlikely he would homer as he only hit one for the year. Well, "Boom", he tied it with a homer and after a walk, Charlie Neal hit a homer (his second of the game). It gave the Dodgers the lead for good. Larry Sherry, in relief, got the win to even the Series at one.

The Series moved to Los Angeles and since it was held in the Coliseum, new attendance records were set with each game having crowds surpassing 90,000. Don Drysdale and Dick Donovan in game 3 were pitted in a scoreless duel. In the seventh, the Dodgers scored twice when Brooklynite veteran Carl Furillo knocked a pinch-hit single with the bases loaded. Don Drysdale ran into trouble in the eighth, but again Sherry came in and got the Sox out. The Dodgers won 3-1.

In game 4, the Dodgers got to Wynn in the fourth for 4 runs. Roger Craig was on his way to victory when the Sox tied it in the seventh with Lollar's 3-run homer being the big hit. The old vet Hodges hit a homer in the eighth to give the Dodgers the lead. Sherry was brought in again and kept the Sox from scoring and was the wining pitcher as LA won 5-4.

The Chisox started Bob Shaw in game 5 against a young lefty named Sandy Koufax. They had an old fashioned pitching duel with Shaw winning 1-0 to keep alive the White Sox chances.

In game 6, Wynn again started. In the third, the Duke hit a 2-run homer and that was followed by a 6 run rally in the fourth. The Dodgers had an 8-0 lead but when old Klu hit a 3-run homer in the bottom of the fourth in came that guy again, Larry Sherry. He blanked the White Sox for the rest of the game.

The Dodger victories had the old Brooklynites as heroes with the Duke, Hodges (9 for 23, .391) and Furillo all getting big hits. Neal was LA's big stick batting .370 leading them in hits (10 for 27), runs (4) and RBIs (6). But it was Larry Sherry who was the hero. He had 2 wins, 2 saves and gave up only one run in 12+ innings of relief. He was Series MVP as they celebrated in southern California with 'Sherry' instead of champagne.

Old Klu was the star for the White Sox getting a double and three homers among his 9 hits and a record 10 RBIs for a 6 game Series. Aparicio, the Sox go-go guy, batted .308 but was only was 1 for 2 on steal attempts and only scored once.

Meanwhile, the Yanks were paying no attention to the '59 Series. They were busy formulating plans to pry home run hitter Roger Maris from their Kissin' Cousins.

1960
an aMAZing series

The Yankees were always in the market for left-handed pull hitters that can take advantage of Yankee Stadium's short right field porch. They must have been overjoyed in 1958 when Roger Maris was traded by Cleveland to the Yankee "farm team", their Kissin' Cousin A's. Maris was a lefty pull hitter tailor made for Yankee Stadium. In '58 he hit 29 and in '59 was leading the league in hitting before an operation sidelined him. After their disastrous '59 season, the Yankee brass decided that Maris was just what they needed.

The Yankees gave up an aging Hank Bauer and Norm Siebern and pitcher Don Larsen, considered washed up at the time, to get Maris. Siebern was a lefty-hitting outfielder but his power was to right-center, not down the friendly 301 foot fence in right field.

Maris was just what the doctor ordered. He hit 39 homers, one behind league leader Mantle, and led the league in RBIs (112) and slugging % (.581). He was the AL MVP. The Mick, in addition to his 40 homers, drove in 94 runs.

The Yanks also received a pop in their offense from their solid defensive infield. Moose Skowron, the first baseman, showed what he could do when playing a whole season (.309, 26 homers, 91 RBIs). Kubek and Clete Boyer (Ken's little brother) combined for 28 homers on the left side. Clete was as good a fielder at third as Ken (some say better), but he could never dethrone Brooks Robinson for the AL Gold Glove; however he did win one in the NL for the Braves in 1969. Catchers, Yogi and Ellie Howard combined for 26 homers. The Yankees led the league with 193 homers.

The Baltimore Orioles put together a young team (were known as the Baby Birds) and were on the Yankees' back going into September. Their young infielders, first baseman Jim Gentile, shortstop Ron Hansen, and third baseman Brooks Robinson all had more than 85 RBIs. Their young wings on the mound were Chuck Estrada (18 wins) and Milt Pappas (15 wins).

The White Sox tried to defend their '59 title by adding much needed offense. They did so in getting Washington Senator slugger Roy Sievers (28 homers and 93 RBIs) and reacquired their former All-Star Minnie Minoso (20 homers, 105 RBIs and a .311 batting average). It was their pitching that failed them. In 1959, Early Wynn and Bob Shaw, together, were 24 games over .500; in 1960 they were only one game over .500. Still they chased the Yanks and still had a shot at the pennant at the end of August.

Going into September any of the three teams could take the flag with any kind of a hot streak. The Yanks must have thought they were in Hell, as they got so hot they won their last 15 games of the season to beat out the Baby Birds by eight games and the defending White Sox by ten.

The Yanks had no real pitching stars in '60. Art Ditmar, a former Kissin' Cousin Athletic, led them with a 15-9 record and was fourth in the league with a 3.06 ERA. Jim Coates was 13-3 and their usual ace Whitey Ford was 12-9 with a 3.08 ERA (fifth in the league), but ended strong, winning his last three games.

In 1960 my focus was still in following the National League, even though the only way was by radio from the static-riddled St. Louis radio station. My mom saw that I really missed seeing the Cardinals play - so it was probably in late June when she said the Cardinals are playing in Philadelphia and they are having a Sunday doubleheader. We would take the train from Penn Station in Newark to Philadelphia (the Phils' ball park was close to the train station). In the first game, the Cardinals had Ernie Broglio on the mound in relief. I don't recall if St. Louis was ahead or the score was tied when Tony Gonzalez hit a game-winning homer in the bottom of the ninth. I was not in a good mood; after all, this was a horrible Phillie team.

It looked like this was going to be a perfectly lousy day for me. The Cards were down in the second game, 3-1 in the ninth, when their catcher Hal Smith, (not to be confused with the Pirate catcher Hal Smith) banged out a 3-run homer to give the Cards a 4-3 lead. Broglio was already in the game in relief and was left in for the Phillies ninth. Again he had to face Gonzalez. This time he got him out. Cards won 4-3, so at least my day had a win and a loss, as did Broglio's. I think it made his record 5-4 at that point.

The Cardinals then decided to use Broglio as a starter because at the end of May, they traded Vinegar Bend Mizell to the Pirates for Julian Javier. Broglio surprised everyone by becoming the best pitcher in the league as he won 16 out of 19 to be 21-7, but lost his last two starts to finish at 21-9. Had he won those last two games he probably would have won the Cy Young Award. The pennant winning Pirates' Vernon Law was 20-9 and took the award. Broglio led the league in wins (21), winning % (.700) and was second in ERA (2.75).

The Cardinal staff really turned things around and I was hoping, like the Dodgers of '59, that St. Louis could make the leap from seventh place to first. Larry Jackson came back to win 18 games and Lindy McDaniel became the leagues best reliever winning 12 and saving 26 games. Also, getting his feet wet, was a fireball throwing rookie named Bob Gibson.

My guy, Ken Boyer led the offense. He was third in the NL in slugging % (.562), fourth in total bases (310) and homers (32), and fifth in batting average (.304) and RBIs (97).

Musial, at age 39, came back with a respectable season increasing his average by 20 points from last year to .275. Playing in about two-thirds of the games, he was second on the team with 17 homers.

The Cards made a run at the Pirates but, in a late season five-game series against them they did not fare so well so it was farewell to their pennant dreams (actually Broglio won the first game and Gibson the second as St. Louis cut the Pirate lead to three games, but then this deck of Cards came tumbling down as they dropped the last three to be six games out of first). They finished third – 9 games out. Even the Braves beat them out for the runner-up spot. What's amazing is that the Braves didn't win it all. Spahn won 21, Burdette 19 and Buhl 16. The Hammer (40 homers and 126 RBIs), Eddie Mathews (39 homers and 124 RBIs), Joe Adcock (25 homers, 91 RBIs), and Del Crandall (his .294 led the team, 19 homers, 77 RBIs) provided plenty of offense. The Braves, mysteriously (to me anyway), finished 7 games out.

The Pirates were a surprise winner to some, but really it shouldn't have been that much of a surprise as they basically had the same nucleus of the team that came in second in '58. But in 1960, they had two more years to mature to become pennant winners.

The Pirates were solid in all phases of the game. They had a good pitching staff. Law won the Cy Young Award and Bob Friend was 18-12. The staff got a big boost when they got Vinegar Bend Mizell from the Cardinals and he went 13-5 for them. (I sometimes think that if the Cards kept him they would have won the pennant, forgetting that trading Vinegar Bend created the opening for Broglio to be a starter). Another former Cardinal, Harvey "the Kitten" Haddix, won 11 games. (Remember, Mizell and Haddix were the winning pitchers in the first baseball games I ever went to - a doubleheader sweep in '53 at the Polo Grounds). The final piece to the staff was ace reliever El Roy Face. Although not as good as his record setting 1959 performance of 18-1 in relief, he was still very effective as he won 10 and saved 24 games.

The defense was exceptional. In the outfield they had Roberto Clemente, possibly the best right fielder ever, and in center was Bill Virdon, a former Yankee farmhand given up in the 1954 Slaughter trade with the Cardinals. Virdon was one of the best in the league and can really run down the long drives that were hit in spacious Forbes Field. In left, Bob Skinner, was an NL All-Star.

Playing the infield in Pittsburgh was not easy. It seemed like a cement mixer poured the infield. It was known for its cement like hardness - and after a few innings it would get chopped up and look like it came under a mortar attack. To handle the grounders, they had ex-marine Don Hoak at third (no ball would ever try and eat him up), at short they had Dick Groat (and possibly his All-American hoop days at Duke and a short stay in the NBA gave him his sure handedness). At second they had a young Bill Mazeroski, probably the best middle infielder prior to Ozzie Smith.

First base was a different story. Starting was Dick Stuart who only played because of his bat (he once hit over 60 homers in the minors). His fielding prowess, or lack thereof, eventually earned him the name "Dr. Strangeglove". Rocky Nelson platooned with him. Together they hit 30 homers and drove in 118 runs. Catching was shared by Smokey Burgess and Hal Smith (not the Cards' Hal Smith), who both hit over .290 and combined for 18 homers.

The offense was led by National League MVP Dick Groat, who led the league with a .325 average. Clemente had his first great year hitting .314 and leading the team with 94 RBIs. (I think Roberto should have been the NL MVP, but actually the fiery Hoak with 17 homers and 79 RBIs was runner-up).

The season highlight for me was going to the All-Star Game. It was at Yankee Stadium. My mom got tickets and for me it could not have been better. The National League won 6-0, and the Cardinals in the game excelled. The Man, at 39 years old, hit a pinch-hit homer extending his All-Star Game home run record to six. My other guy Ken Boyer capped the scoring with a 2-run homer in the ninth. Cardinal pitchers Larry Jackson and Lindy McDaniel each threw a scoreless inning. The Say Hey Kid, though, was the National League's star of the game hitting a homer and two singles.

But the best moment for me came with the Pirates' Bob Skinner batting and he fouled one back. Our seats were pretty far back in the mezzanine so it was improbable a foul ball could reach our seats, but the ball took a weird bounce off a railing and was headed our way. I was sitting between my friend and my mom. The ball was headed toward my mom's right. She and other fans reached for it. The ball went off of about five hands (in front and behind us), including hers. The fan two seats away from her wound up with the ball!

Well let's get to the Series. The Yanks as usual were heavy favorites. It was thought at the time that it would be like the last Yankee/Pirate World Series in 1927 when Ruth, Gehrig and the rest of the Murderers' Row demolished the Pirates in four straight.

In game 1, the Yanks ran into the long arm of the 'Law' - Vernon Law that is. The Cy Young Award winner went seven innings only giving up two runs. In the first inning, it looked like the 1960 version of Murderers' Row would do in the Pirates when Maris hit a homer to put the Yanks up 1-0. The Yanks started Art Ditmar, their top winner for the year. With hindsight it is thought they should have started Whitey Ford, who was only 12-9, but won his last three starts. Ford wouldn't even start game 2, as he would be saved to start game 3 at Yankee Stadium where he was so dominant. If Ford opened the Series he could have been available if there would be a seventh game, but who thought the Pirates would make it a seven game Series? (Not too many people outside of Pittsburgh). Well, Ditmar couldn't hold the first inning lead and did not last the inning. A walk, a couple of muffed plays by the Yanks on Pirate steal attempts, and a walk and hits by Groat, Skinner and Clemente gave the Pirates a 3-1 lead after one inning.

The Yanks almost broke the Law in the fourth. With two runners on, Yogi blasted a long drive to right center − two runs would score and the score would be knotted at 3. But no, the Yankee threat was thwarted by the long arm of Bill Virdon, their former farmhand, as he darted to the wall, jumped, and snagged the drive. This disheartened the Yanks so much that in the bottom of the inning, (showing a sign of things to come), Bill Mazeroski slammed a 2-run homer and, in the fifth, that guy Virdon drove in the Pirates' sixth run. Law was taken out after 7 innings, as he was pitching with a sore ankle that he injured just before the season ended. (I believe it was during the pennant clinching celebration). To finish off the Yanks, the Pirates brought in Roy Face. At 5'8" and 150 lbs., he hardly looked intimidating on the mound, but hitters generally could not handle his famed forkball that dropped right out of the strike zone. He did give up a 2-run pinch-hit homer to Elston Howard in the ninth. Pirates won 6-4…Don't mess with the Law.

Going into game 2, "Beat-em Bucs" signs were all over the place. The Pittsburgh fans were hoping the game 1 victory would give them momentum. Didn't happen! The '60's Murderers' Row woke up. The Yanks rapped out 19 hits in the 16-3 rout that looked more like the score of a Giant/Steeler football game. Mantle led the barrage with 2 homers and 5 RBIs. The Yankees' friend in Pittsburgh for game 2 seemed to be mostly on the Pirate pitching staff, as six of them contributed to their defeat. The Buc starter was really a friend - Bob Friend, their 18-game winner. Bullet Bob Turley scattered 13 Pirate hits in going 8 innings.

With a day off the Pirates had time to rest, lick their wounds, and be ready for game 3 at the big park in the Bronx. They were ready all right. The Bucs started the future North Carolina Congressman, Vinegar Bend Mizell. The former Cardinal got shell-shocked in the first inning, as the day of rest did not cool off the Murderers' Row bats. The Yanks put up 6 runs before most of the fans were even in their seats. Singles hitter, second baseman Bobby Richardson, who had only one homer for the season, capped the first inning scoring with a Grand Slam. Mantle continued his hot hitting with 4 hits including a double and homer. Yanks won 10-0. The Yanks only needed one run anyway as Ford tossed a four-hit shutout. Yanks were up 2 games to 1, and the cakewalk was on.

In game 4 the Pirates would need some 'Law' and order to pull even at two games apiece. Vernon supplied the pitching and offense to carry the Bucs. Law gave up a homer to Skowron, and was down 1-0 going into the top of the fifth. The Bucs got two on with Law coming up. As a hitter he was not an automatic out, as he had a respectable lifetime batting average over .200. Law doubled driving in one to tie the game. Virdon, that guy again, quickly untied it with a 2-run bloop single. In the seventh the Yanks rallied. Law probably didn't help his bad ankle by running around the bases in the fifth. He gave up a run and the Yanks had two on. The Bucs' skipper Danny Murtaugh figured it was time to have the Yanks "Face" the forkball. The Yankees left fielder Bob Cerv was the batter. He was a power hitter who hit 38 homers for the A's in 1958. Face threw a pitch that didn't fork. Cerv blasted one to right center. Virdon sprinted toward the Yankee bull pen, leapt, and the leather of Virdon again ruined the Yanks' chances of scoring. It was clearing the fence when he caught it. Face than stuck a fork in the Yanks for the remaining two innings.

The Series was tied at two apiece. In the Yankees two wins they outscored the Pirates 26-3. In the games the Pirates won they barely outscored the Yanks, 9-6.

With the Series tied the Yankees again started their top winner Ditmar, while the Bucs went with the Kitten Haddix. The Yanks didn't know what Haddix they would see – the 1959 Haddix who threw 12 perfect innings the year before against the heavy hitting Braves, only to lose in the thirteenth inning, or the 1960 pitcher who was 11-10 with an ERA around four.

Ditmar, who didn't last one inning in the opener, was better in this outing – he at least lasted until the second inning. In the second, the Pirates had hits by Dick Stuart and Smokey Burgess and a 2-run double by Mazeroski to take a 3-0 lead. It would be enough as the '60's Murderers' Row could only muster 2 runs, one on a homer by Maris.

Haddix was somewhere between his perfect game and his 11-10 season record giving up only two runs and five hits in 6 1/3 innings. When he tired in the sixth, the Yanks again would have to Face the forkball. Roy kept the Yankees hitless over the rest of the game, giving up only one base on balls in the final 2 2/3 innings. The Pirates won 5-2 and went up 3 games to 2, needing only one more to have the Yanks 'Walk the Plank'.

In game 6 the Yanks, again found a friend in the Bucs' starter Bob Friend. The Yanks' Murderers' Row pounded him for 5 runs by the third inning, and they continued to find more friends on the Pirate staff as the final score was 12-0. Yogi and Maris each had 3 hits, catcher John Blanchard had 3 doubles, but it was again their singles hitter Richardson who did the most damage with a pair of triples and 3 RBIs.

The Yanks only needed one run as the Pirates once again could do nothing with Ford. Whitey threw his second shutout giving up seven hits and one walk.

The next day I told my mom I was too ill to go to school (it would have made me sick to miss this game). The finale was set. It was to become one of the most memorable games in baseball history. It seemed that it was a game that nobody wanted to win. Law and order would not prevail in this contest, although in the game's first five innings it appeared that it would.

Vernon Law was hoping to join Lew Burdette as the only other pitcher to win three games in a World Series against the Yankees. Law was given a quick 4-0 lead after two innings courtesy of first baseman Rocky Nelson's 2-run homer in the first and Virdon's 2-run base hit in the second. Yanks' pitchers, starter Bob Turley and Bill Stafford, gave up the 4 runs. The Yankees then brought in the diminutive Bobby Shantz, who for four innings cooled off the Pirate bats.

Law seemed to be tiring in the sixth as his ankle injury may have been acting up. He gave up a Skowron homer in the fifth, but when he put two on in the sixth, the Buc skipper Murtaugh figured it was time to make the Yanks Face the fork ball one last time. Well, not this time. Roy didn't have it. Mantle singled in a run and Yogi banged out a 3-run homer. Yanks were up 5-4 – so much for Law's third victory. I thought I should have gone to school (at the time of Yogi's homer I would have been in English class).

The Yanks increased my level of anguish when in the eighth they tacked on two more runs to make the score 7-4 with only six outs remaining. Yankee fans were probably rationalizing it is only right that the Yanks win, as in all three of their victories they demolished the Pirates, while the three Pirate wins were squeakers.

The Yankees still had reliever Shantz in to start the eighth – it would be his fifth inning of work, his longest stint of the year. Oh well, he could rest all year probably thought Stengel, the Yankee skipper. It looked like leaving Shantz in was a good move. After Gino Cimoli led off with a pinch-hit single, Virdon was then up and he hit a hard bouncer to Tony Kubek at shortstop. Yankee fans were probably so happy to see Virdon hit this sure double play bouncer, as the former Yank farmhand was such a nemesis with his glove and clutch hits. The Yankees and their fans happiness did a quick 180 degree turnaround for what happened next.

Kubek was perfectly positioned to field the ball and start an easy 6-4-3 double play. As he was ready for the last hop, the hard hit ball took a weird bounce off the beat up rock hard infield and struck Kubek in the throat. Kubek went down like a ton of bricks. With Kubek laying there fighting to breathe, Cimoli was safe at second and Virdon at first. The plot thickened as instead of having two outs and nobody on, the Bucs had no outs and the tying run at the plate. Naturally Kubek had to be taken out. Play resumed and the Yanks kept Shantz on the mound.

The next batter was Groat who, showing the Yanks why he was the NL batting champ, singled to left to cut the Bucs' deficit to two. Stengel then took out Shantz and brought in Jim Coates. Playing National League ball, the runners were sacrificed to second and third. Coates then got Nelson to fly out to short right – so now he only needed one more out to get out of the inning. It looked like the strategy worked when Roberto Clemente bounced a grounder. The Yankee first baseman Skowron had to move toward second to field the ball. With his momentum going toward second he thought he would not be able to stop and beat the speedy Clemente to first. He did have time, though to throw to the pitcher Coates, who should have been covering first. For some reason Coates didn't get over there in time. Clemente was safe as Virdon scored and it was now just a one run game.

The next batter was catcher Hal Smith. Smith was in the game because Smokey Burgess was taken out earlier for a pinch-runner. Hal was not an easy out, as in only 253 at bats he hit .295 with 11 homers – so he had some clout in him.

Coates was maybe still angry over the previous play (possibly he thought Skowron should have made the play unassisted). Smith, who ironically was also a former Yank farmhand, had a full count when Coates, not wanting to walk him, made the pitch too fat and it was clobbered over the left field wall for a 3-run homer. Bucs were up 9-7 and Forbes Field was rocking.

My anguish of a half-hour ago was dissipated and I thought of how glad I was being home from school. The heck with English class! Only three more outs and the Bucs would be champs and the Yanks would be losers. But I am not stupid, (although some may disagree), and I know the Yankees with their talented players would not make these three outs be easy.

The Yankee spirits must have been really lifted when they saw their ol' friend take the mound in the top of the ninth. Bob Friend, who had an ERA of about a thousand (actually it was around ten) did not disappoint. He gave up two quick singles to Richardson and pinch-hitter Dale Long and was yanked out and Haddix, the game five winner, came in. He got Maris out, but the Mick singled in a run to make the score 9-8. With one out and runners on first and third Yogi came up and resulted in arguably one of the headiest plays in Series history.

He hit a hard bouncer down the first base line. Rocky Nelson speared the ball. (Had "Dr. Strangeglove" Stuart been playing first, the ball might have been a double into the right field corner). Anyway, since Nelson was close to the bag he stepped on first. Mantle seeing him touch first knew the force was taken off, so he surprised Nelson when he decided to get back to first. Mick dove back evading the tag try by Nelson. During this play McDougald scored the tying run. It's all nines - ninth inning and the score tied at 9-9, does anybody want to win? It seemed years ago that Law and Turley started this game. Ralph Terry, who came in to get the third out after Hal Smith's homer, stayed in the game for the Yanks. He would be facing Mazeroski leading off the ninth for the Pirates. The Pittsburgh fans were hoping he would start a Series ending rally. In game 1 he hurt the Yanks with a 2-run homer that the Bucs won by two, but he definitely was not considered a home run threat (he hit 11 during the season). What happened next stunned the nation's fans.

Terry's first pitch was high, so with a 1-0 count on Maz he brought the next pitch in lower – but not low enough. It was a pitch he could handle – and be belted it. My first impression was that it would go over left fielder Yogi's head for at least a lead-off double – but the ball just kept going and going until it whizzed over the left field wall. As the ball cleared the wall I jumped off my sofa so high that I thought I would leave a head print on the ceiling. The game that would not end – did. Pirates won 10-9 to take the Series 4 games to 3. It was a good day to miss school.

This was the first time the Series ended on a walk-off home run. Maz's shot today is still considered the second most famous event in baseball history – behind the Thomson homer in '51.

Looking at the stats no one would believe the Yankees lost. They out hit the Pirates .338 to .256, scored twice as many runs 55 to 27, and had an ERA that was half of what the Pirates was (7.11 to 3.54). The Yanks had four regulars hit over .330, four had 10 hits or more, and three had more than 8 RBIs, while the Bucs didn't have one batter with any of those totals. Richardson (.367, 11 hits) won the Series MVP via his record 12 RBIs.

I thought Maz should have been Series MVP – he hit .320 and his hits were instrumental in three of the Pirate victories – plus he performed his usual flawless defense. But Maz's performance was recognized as he was later selected as the Player of the Year by The Sporting News.

The Yankees not only lost this aMAZing Series, they also lost their manager Casey Stengel and General Manager George Weiss. The Yanks sugar coated their departure saying they agreed to leave as both were over 65 years old. Typical Yankee loyalty is rewarded?????

1961
M & M's Leave a Bad Taste in My Mouth

The year was 1961 and it became one of baseball's most memorable ones, but not for me. The Yankees for the first time since 1949 did not have Casey Stengel managing them. They got rid of him after the Yankees were defeated by the Pirates in the '60 Series. Their new manager was Ralph Houk, who was a Yankee back-up catcher for Yogi from 1947-54. Naturally with Yogi as back-stopper, Houk only saw limited action in his eight years (.272, 43 for 158). He was known as the Major due to his rank in the military during WWII. The Yanks won the pennant and the Series as Ralph Houk was made out to be some sort of genius. What a bunch of bull – with the talent the Yankees had they would have won the Worlds Series even if Daffy Duck was the manager (well, maybe not Daffy).

The most notable event of the year was the chase to break the Bambino's home run record of 60 by Mickey Mantle and Roger Maris. The Bambino's record was arguably the nation's most cherished sports record of all time. The chase to break this record captivated the country. The top spot for the home run lead see-sawed between Mantle and Maris all through the summer as they replaced those little round candies as the nation's most famous M & M's.

The race for the home run record went into September with both of the M & M's having a shot at it. Then Mantle bailed out of the race when he developed an infection of sorts from a shot he received for a cold. The Mick wound up with 54 round-trippers, the most ever by a runner-up. It was up to Maris alone to challenge the Babe. He did it, or didn't he? Let me explain. Maris broke the record with his 61st homer in the season's last game. The problem was that it was in the 162nd game - the Babe hit his 60 in a 154 game season. Prior to the season reaching the 154 game mark the baseball commissioner Ford Frick (a former Babe Ruth crony) decreed that in order to break the Babe's record of 60 it would have to be done during the first 154 games like Ruth did. If the record was broken after the 154th game it would be marked with an asterisk showing it was broken in a 162 game season.

The 1961 year was the first season the Major Leagues had a 162 game schedule. The reason for the extra eight games was due to baseball expansion. One of the reasons for the expansion was to thwart the formation of the Continental League that was to become a rival of the present Major League. Former Cardinal and Dodger executive Branch Rickey was to spearhead this new Continental League.

The American League expanded first. They put a team in Los Angeles (the Angels) and replaced a team in Washington, DC (the Senators), as the original Senators left the nation's capital for the untapped market of Minneapolis/St. Paul becoming the Minnesota Twins. In 1961 the American League would have ten teams with a 162 game schedule.

The National League stood pat in '61 and had a 154 game schedule. In 1962 they would put a team in New York and in Houston. I was really elated over the news that next year I would be able to see the Cardinals play in New York.

With the chase to break the Bambino's record by the M&M's, I attended several Yankee games this year for a couple of reasons. One was that until 1962, they were the only team in town and the other was that, being a history buff, I wanted to see history made in person, even though it was being done by the M & M Yankees.

During the summer I would go to my relatives who lived in the Greenpoint section of Brooklyn. From there it was a half-hour subway ride to Yankee Stadium. I would go to the games with my cousin Ron and my Godfather uncle Eddie, both Yankee fans. In fact, my cousin and I went to all three games in the beginning of September when the Detroit Tigers came to town ready to overtake the Yanks for first place.

The Tigers had their own version of M & M – it was C & C (Cash and Colavito). "Stormin' Norman" Cash led the league in hitting (.361) and had 41 homers and 132 RBIs. (Take Note: Cash continued to be a power hitter for several more years but never again batted over .283 – after his playing days he admitted he was using a corked bat in '61). Rocky Colavito "rocked" 45 homers to go with

140 RBIs. Plus their future Famer, Al Kaline, was second in hitting at .324, scoring 119 times. Most people would not believe this fact, but the '61 Tigers actually outscored the M & M-led Yankees 841 to 827.

To get back to these three games, they were probably the worst three games in a row I ever attended. Detroit lost the first game 1-0 when the Yanks scored in the ninth. In the middle game Maris hit 2 homers to lead the Yanks to victory. The third game the Tigers had a one run lead going into the ninth. The Mick hit his second homer of the game to tie the score and the Yanks went on to win and sweep the series. Had Detroit not blown the last game they could have stayed in the race 2 1/2 out instead of 4 1/2 out. What was really disappointing to me was that the Yanks even beat my favorite AL pitcher Frank Lary (a.k.a. "The Yankee Killer", 27-13 lifetime against them) – this year he was 23-9 (I wished he was 24-8). Anyway, this weekend the M & M's left a bad taste in my mouth as they coasted the rest of the way to the pennant.

As for my Cardinals, I had hopes that them chasing Pittsburgh for the pennant last year was a sign of good things to come.

If I told you that my guy Ken Boyer has his career high batting average (.329, third in the NL), was fourth in hits (194) and runs scored (109), hit 24 homers and had 95 RBIs – that Stan the Man at 40 years of age hit .288 with 15 homers and 70 RBIs in two-thirds of a season – that St. Louis had the second best team batting average (.271) - that the pitching staff had the league's lowest ERA (3.74) – that they finished five games ahead of the defending champion Pittsburgh Pirates, that maybe they won the pennant. Nope – they came in fifth place – six games over .500 and 13 games behind the pennant winning Cincinnati Reds. Even though they led the league in lowest ERA their aces from last year did not come through. Ernie Broglio, the Cy Young Award contender in '60 went from 21-9 to 9-12 and relief ace Lindy McDaniel's combined wins/saves were cut in half from 38 to 19.

The Cincinnati Reds, who finished sixth last year (67-87), improved by 26 games this year (93-61) to capture their first pennant since 1940. Future Famer Frank Robinson was their big gun - the five tool player was the league MVP (.323 average, 37 homers and 124 RBIs). Robinson was the most aggressive player of his time. He would crowd the plate daring the likes of Drysdale and Gibson to knock him down which they did (he led the league in being hit by a pitch seven times in his career). His answer to the brush-backs would be to send a line shot someplace. He was also the best at taking out (and I don't mean for dinner) the shortstop or second baseman in breaking up a potential double play. Oh, how I wished he was on the Cardinals.

The Reds' second banana with the lumber was Vada Pinson who was second in the league with a .343 average, hit 16 homers and led the league in hits (208). Their offensive attack was complemented by their corner infielders, first baseman Gordy Coleman and third baseman Gene Freese. Ironically they had identical stats in doubles (27), homers (26), and RBIs (87).

The Reds had some good arms on the mound. The first Little Leaguer to make the Major Leagues, Joey Jay, tied for the most wins (21-10). Jim O'Toole was second in wins (19-9) and was second in ERA (3.10). Bob Purkey chipped in with 16 wins. But much of the staff's success can be due to their excellent relievers. Jim Brosnan, who was the author of the baseball book "The Long Season", won 10 in relief and was tied for second in saves with 16 by teammate Bill Henry.

Cincy had to hold off the Los Angeles Dodgers. The Reds had the edge in hitting but the Dodgers matched up with them on the mound. Johnny Podres, the Brooklyn hero of 1955 was 18-5 and Sandy Koufax, their pitcher full of potential, learned how to pitch instead of just throw and also won 18. Their young hard-throwing intimidator, Don Drysdale, chalked up 13 victories. The Dodgers were a couple of years away from taking it all.

It was during the September series between the Yankees and Tigers when I was over my relatives in Greenpoint Brooklyn. I was saying since the Yankees always seem to be in the World Series it would be a cool idea to go to a World Series game, even though I still had hopes that Detroit would take the AL flag. Well the Yanks won the pennant so I planned to put my cool idea into happening In order to go to a World Series game in New York it would be a weekday game. The weekend games were scheduled in Cincinnati. I would have to convince my parents that I would have to take a day off from school in order to go to a Series game. My parents said OK after I convinced them I would not have any adverse results from missing school. After all, last year I stayed home to see the Mazeroski homer (of course I was ill that day).

I called my uncle Eddie; he was not working on Thursday, the second game of the Series. We did not have tickets. What we would have to do is to arrive there early to get in line for a bleacher seat.

The Series opened on a Wednesday. The Cincy pitcher Jim O'Toole pitched a superb game. In seven innings he gave up six hits, but two of them were home runs, one by Elston Howard and the other by Moose Skowron. The problem for the Reds was that the Yankee pitcher Whitey Ford was even better. Whitey only gave up two hits in blanking the Reds for his third consecutive shutout in World Series play.

That night I went to my relatives in Greenpoint so my uncle Eddie and I could get an early start to get to the Stadium to ensure getting a good spot in line for tickets. That morning my uncle and I got to the Stadium by 7:00 a.m. I was pretty much surprised by the amount of fans waiting in line for the ticket booth to open. It was very chilly in the morning but there was plenty of interesting baseball chit-chat so at least the time did not seem to drag.

Eventually the ticket booth opened. We got our tickets and entered into the bleachers. These were unreserved bleacher seats – the other side had reserved bleacher seats. Once you entered the seats were first come first serve. Actually these are not seats. Bleachers are just long pieces of board with numbers on them designating the seating space. Someone with a big butt may need two seats (as is my case today?).

Waiting four to five hours for the game to start you would think I'd be bored to no end. But no, I kind of enjoyed the whole adventure. Just soaking up the atmosphere of being at a Series was exciting. I spent the time getting a bite to eat, digesting the World Series program from cover to cover, and talking sports with my uncle and the other fans. What really surprised me was that there were many National League fans at the game. I really could not imagine American League Yankee fans at the Cincy ball park, Crosley Field.

The Reds had their big winner Joey Jay going against Ralph Terry. Terry rebounded well after giving up the Mazeroski homer to end the '60 Series. He went 16-3, was second in winning % (.842), and had a better ERA (3.15) than the Cy Young Award winner, his teammate Ford (3.21).

The game was scoreless for three innings. In the fourth Gordy Coleman blasted one. It was coming toward us in the right field bleachers. The ball curved away from us but still went into the stands for a 2-run homer. Cincy was up 2-0 and was I happy. Not for long. I guess Jay couldn't stand prosperity. In the bottom of the fourth he walked Maris, then gave up a 2-run homer to Yogi (close to the same spot Coleman had just hit his) to tie the score at 2-2.

In the fifth the Reds broke the tie on some aggressive base running. Utility infielder Elio Chacon was on third with two outs. A pitch from Terry got away from the catcher Howard, but it did not go far. Chacon broke for home and beat the tag by Howard to put Cincy up 3-2. The Reds put the game away with hits by a most unlikely hero. Twice, the Reds had third baseman Gene Freese up with a runner in scoring position. Johnny Edwards, a rookie catcher who hit .186 in less than 150 at bats, followed Freese in the line-up. The Yanks elected to walk Freese both times to face Edwards, but the strategy failed, as twice Edwards came through with RBI hits. Edwards showed it was not a fluke as he did go on to make three NL All-Star teams.

These cushion runs weren't needed as Jay shut out the Yanks the rest of the way. Reds won 6-2 and I was happy. But that was it. The Yanks won the last three to take the Series 4 games to 1. At least I was at the one game they lost.

In game four Ford started and pitched five more scoreless innings before coming out of the game with a foot injury. Combined with the three previous shutouts he tossed in Series play, he now had 32 consecutive scoreless innings. This broke the record of 29 2/3 scoreless innings held by that famous Boston Red Sox lefty Babe Ruth (in the 1916 & 18 Series).

It was not a good year for the Babe. First, his home run record of 60 was broken - even if there was an asterisk by the new record (since removed). Now his World Series pitching record of 29 2/3 scoreless innings went by the boards.

At least the Babe still has the career home run record of 714. It is unthinkable that any hitter would ever be able to "hammer" out more than 715 homers.

1962
There's a New Kid in Town

In 1962 it was just another year for the Yanks. They won a third consecutive pennant and won the World Series in 7 games, when Bobby Richardson snagged Willie McCovey's line drive with runners on second and third and two outs in the ninth inning to give the Yanks a 1-0 Series ending victory.

The American League was so devoid of talent that Mickey Mantle won the MVP award playing in only 123 games and having 377 at bats. However, to his credit, he made the most of them hitting .321 with 30 homers and 89 RBIs. Personally, I thought Richardson should have been MVP. Besides his excellent fielding (like the last out of the World Series), he was the catalyst of the offense, leading the league in hits, 209 while hitting .302 (sixth in the league). The new asterisked-single season home run record holder, Roger Maris, had good power stats hitting 33 homers with 100 RBIs, but since it did not measure up to last year's numbers, he was the recipient of many Bronx Cheers in Yankee Stadium whenever he did not come through.

Two new strangers made the American League pennant chase a little interesting until the Yankees pulled away. The Minnesota Twins, one year removed from the nation's capitol gave the Yanks a run but faded in the stretch to come in second, five games out. They were managed by Sam Mele, whose glove I opted not to get in 1953, when I chose the Rizzuto glove instead. The Twins had a solid hitting line-up as all the regulars reached double figures in homers. They were led by future Famer Harmon "Killer" Killebrew, who led the league with 48 homers and 126 RBIs, and Bob Allison (29 homers, 102 RBIs). Killebrew's nickname (naturally derived from his last name) was very appropriate as that's what he did to American League pitches winning six home run titles. The Killer smashed some of the longest round-trippers (573 for his career) from the late '50's into the early '70's. I used to visualize AL hurlers trembling on the mound staring at the 5'10", 213 lb. slugger as sawdust dropped from the handle as he tightly gripped the bat awaiting the pitch.

The Twins had two top starters. For years, Camilo Pascual always pitched well for the Washington Senators, but with usually negligible run support. Now with some runs to work with, Pascual became a 20-game winner and led the league in Ks (206), shutouts (5) and complete games (18). Southpaw Jim "Kitty" Kaat had 18 victories. Jim's nick & last name were very appropriate as he fielded his position like Harry "the Cat" Brecheen and Harvey "the Kitten" Haddix. Kaat's cat-like reflexes on the mound earned him 16 Gold Gloves. Along with this collection of hardware and his 283 wins Kaat should have enough credentials to get a call from the Hall.

The other surprise team in 1962 was the Los Angeles Angels. In only their second year of existence they finished in third place, 10 games out. Their top stars were Leon "Daddy Wags" Wagner who supplied the power (37 homers and 107 RBIs) and tiny (5ft 5in) Albie Pearson whose 115 runs scored led the league. Rookie Dean Chance was their ace at 14-10, but it was another newcomer, Bo Belinsky, who got most of the ink in the LA headlines via his no-hitter in May against the Orioles and his off the field playboy exploits with some of Hollywood's top foxes (for a short time he was engaged to Mamie Van Doren, but I guess he struck out).

The American League, since 1949, had become so boring with the Yanks winning all but twice ('54 and '59), even their fans stopped coming to the ball park. In '62 the Yankees attendance dropped a quarter of a million – from 1,747,725 in '61 to 1,493,574 in '62. This drop was also attributed to the New Kid in town at the Polo Grounds.

In '62 I had no intentions of going to any Yankee games. I would go to the Polo Grounds when my team, the St. Louis Cardinals, would come to town. There was only one exception to this plan.

I was 17 at the time and was going to be a senior in high school. It was a Saturday in July when our doorbell rang. I answered the door and saw one of our neighbors from three houses down on the other side of the street. He was somewhere in his 50's, as was his wife. I haven't really had any dealings with these neighbors as they kept to themselves except for when I was a kid (about 11 or 12 years old). All of us kids on the block would play softball and stickball in the street. This neighbor's front lawn was in deep right field. He did not appreciate it when the ball would land on his lawn or in his wife's garden. He would holler at us and sometimes keep the ball. Anyway, that was probably four or five years ago. What was he doing at my front door? Returning the balls that he confiscated?

I looked at him quizzically when he stated that he knew my father and I were sports fans and that he had two tickets for Sunday's game against the Angels. He worked for a company owned by Bill "Moose" Skowron. I think he might have been an accountant or something for Skowron's company. These tickets were for Skowron's company's box seats. He wasn't a sports fan and he didn't want the tickets to go to waste, so he thought that my dad and I could use them.

I took the tickets and went into the kitchen and told my dad what took place. Both of us were bonafide Yankee Haters, but thought these have to be pretty good seats, so we decided to go.

As we drove up the Garden State Parkway to the George Washington Bridge, my dad and I were planning our strategy. Since we were going to be sitting in the box seats of a company owned by a Yankee, it probably would not be proper to root against the Yankees. We didn't want our neighbor to look foolish if people from the company knew he had given the tickets to Yankee Haters.

We got there with time to spare, parked the car and went into the Stadium. As expected these were great seats, a few rows behind the dugout. The game started and the Angels got off to an early lead. I don't remember the actual score but the Angels won rather easily. A couple of times I slipped and started to clap when the Angels did something positive. My dad had the same problem. A couple of times the other fans looked at us – like who are we rooting for? But as the game moved along we got better with our acting. As the Angels were winning easily, we would say to each other so the fans close by could hear us, "We'll get them next inning," or we would holler at the umpire if a close call went against the Yankees. On the ride home my father and I laughed all the way about being Yankee "fans".

However, the real story in New York this year was the Mets. The fledgling organization really aggravated the Yankee brass by having former Yankee brain trust George Weiss as General Manager and Casey Stengel as manager.

All the teams in the league had to make players available to stock the new expansion teams (the Mets and the Houston Colt 45's). The Mets went mostly for name players that were in the twilight of their career or had past ties with, the New York teams. These included former Yankee Gene Woodling and former Brooklynites Gil Hodges, Don Zimmer, Roger Craig and Charlie Neal.

The Mets would complete the worst record in Major League history (40-120) that still stands today (although the 2003 Detroit Tigers made a run at it with 119 losses). Their All-Star was Richie Ashburn. For the year the future Famer hit .306 and, at 35, probably had a few years left; but no that would not happen. Playing for such an inept team seemed to take too much out of him, as he retired and became an announcer for the Phillies.

Frank Thomas provided some offense with 34 homers and 94 RBIs. Their first baseman was "Marvelous" Marv Throneberry who became loveable because of his ineptness. His fielding made Dick "Dr. Strangeglove" Stuart look like a Gold Glover. Not to be out done by his fielding, his base running was also something to marvel at. I believe there was a time when Throneberry was standing on third with an apparent triple. The opponent appealed that Throneberry didn't touch second base. The umpire agreed and Throneberry was called out. When the skipper, Casey came out to argue, the umpire told him to forget about it, he also missed first base.

The spark of the team was utility player "Hot Rod" Kanehl who played all the positions except pitcher and catcher. Their pitching staff was hindered by a poor defense. Roger Craig lost 24 games, Al Jackson 20, Jay Hook 19, and Craig Anderson 17.

The Mets did lead the league in pitchers named Bob Miller. They had a righty Bob Miller (1-12) and a lefty Bob Miller (2-2).

All of this ineptness, and yet close to a million fans came to see these loveable losers. Part of the attraction was to see the former New York players, but most of it was National League fans able to see baseball again. I know - I was one of them. When St. Louis came to town I would make every effort to see the games.

The 51-year old Polo Grounds seemed to be on its last legs. The Mets had Shea Stadium being built and would be ready for the 1964 season. I loved watching the games at the Polo Grounds. All the seats past the foul poles were for general admission. General admission was only $1.30 and with the foul poles only 260 -280 ft., you can get a good seat if you got there early.

When the Cardinals came to town on the weekend, I would go to my cousin's house in Brooklyn. We would take the half-hour subway ride to the Polo Grounds and get there for batting practice. We always had seats next to the wall so we could shoot the breeze with the players shagging flies during batting practice.

At one of the Cardinal visits, my cousin and I witnessed Stan the Man's four consecutive home runs - it was over two games. He smacked a pinch-hit homer in one game then smashed three in a row in the next game. The Man was 41 years old, but you would not know it the way he hit this year. He came in third in hitting (.330), had 19 homers and 82 RBIs. Not bad for an old Man!

My guy Ken Boyer's batting fell under .300 for the first time in four years, but he still had a good year hitting .291 with 95 RBIs and 24 homers. He had a career high 109 runs scored. First baseman Bill White, future National League Commissioner, led the Cards with 102 RBIs and was fourth in hitting behind the Man at .324.

On the mound Bob "Hoot" Gibson was 15-13 and second in the NL in Ks (206) and fifth in ERA (2.85). I was a big Hoot fan, as he is one of my all-time favorite players. The nickname is from the cowboy of the same name who starred in so many of them B-movie westerns that I enjoyed watching in the early '50's. Ironically, with Hoot being one of the league's hardest throwers, his fastball looked like it was fired out of a six-shooter. His 'deMEANor' on the mound was such that it rivaled the Dodgers' Don Drysdale's reputation as the NL's most ornery and intimidating pitcher. The Cards again finished in the second division in sixth place – six games over .500.

Again the NL baseball fans in the country enjoyed another exciting photo finish, unlike the Yankee (American) League. It was like the old Dodger/Giant pennant race in New York in '51 - except now it took place in California. The defending NL champs, the Cincinnati Reds, did their best winning 98 games as Bob Purkey at 23-5 tried to hurl them to repeat as pennant winners but it just wasn't enough as they finished up in third place behind the two California teams. The Reds' NL MVP of last year, Frank Robinson, even improved on his '61 stats batting .342 with 39 homers and 136 RBIs.

Both teams had an explosive offense. For the Giants, the Say Hey Kid was still at the top of his game leading the league with 49 homers and was second with 141 RBIs. Orlando Cepeda had 35 homers and 114 RBIs and Felipe Alou had 25 homers and 98 RBIs. Their catchers Ed Bailey and Tom Haller combined for 35 homers and 110 RBIs.

The Dodgers countered with Tommy Davis who led the league in batting (.346) and RBIs (153). Frank "Hondo" Howard blasted 31 homers and had 119 RBIs, and Willie Davis smacked 21 homers with 85 RBIs. But their power was not their most important offensive weapon. It was the NL MVP Maury Wills, who set a Major League record with 104 stolen bases, (Ty Cobb had the previous record of 96) had 208 hits and scored 130 runs.

On the mound San Francisco had Jack Sanford (24-7), future Famer "The Dominican Dandy" Juan Marichal (18-11), Billy O'Dell (19-14), and former White Sox ace Billy Pierce (16-6).

Don Drysdale led the Dodger staff, winning the Cy Young Award (25-9). Johnny Podres won 15 and Stan Williams 14. Sandy Koufax won 14 games and lost 7 – but that was up until the middle of July. He had problems with his fingers and was gone until the end of September (in his few autumn starts he was ineffective). With a healthy Koufax, the Dodgers would have most likely won the pennant in a cakewalk.

In the fall of '62, I started my senior year in high school. One of the guys (Bill) who I rapped with was a die-hard Dodger fan. From the time school began after Labor Day, he would constantly ridicule me about my Cardinals. This went on until the last week of the season. Low and behold, the Dodgers had a three game series with St. Louis. The Dodgers needed to win only one of the three to take the National League flag.

Didn't happen! The Cards swept the Dodgers, and with the Dodgers' usual weapon – pitching. The Cards only scored a total of six runs in the three-game sweep. The scores were 3-2, 2-1 and 1-0. Gibson won the 1-0 game on a homer by Gene Oliver. The Cardinal sweep allowed the Giants, who won their final game 2-1 on Willie Mays' eighth inning homer against the Houston Colt 45's, to tie the Dodgers, necessitating a playoff.

When I saw my friend in school after the Dodgers got swept, I made no mention of baseball, I just said "Hey Bill, what's new". His response was a quick mean glare.

As for the best of 3 playoff, the Giants won the opener rather easily 8-0 behind Piece's three-hit shutout and a pair of homers by

Mays (LA made a futile attempt using Sandy to start the opener but he could not find his pre-injury stuff) - and they seemingly had the second game well in hand when the Dodgers rallied and went on to an 8-7 victory to force a winner take all finale. Like in 1951, the Dodgers had a lead (this time 4-2) going into the ninth. The Dodger reliever, Ed Roebuck, was cruising having thrown three scoreless frames. In the ninth the Giants scored four runs on only two hits – Matty Alou led off with a pinch-hit single followed by an out, two walks and a line drive infield single off of RoebucKs hand by the Say Hey Kid scored one run – Stan Williams, LA's 1959 playoff hero, replaced Roebuck on the mound to restore order – it did not work – a Cepeda sac-fly tied it at 2. Two more walks and an error plated two more Giant runners making it 6-4. Pierce then went in and retired LA easily in the ninth. Ironically the Giant manager was Alvin Dark who was their shortstop back in '51 when Bobby Thomson hit his famous pennant winning blast. My friend Bill was not too happy as it was "Shades of '51" for Dodger fans.

After the Series in November, the Yankees and Dodgers made a trade.

Since Stan Williams blew the playoffs for the Dodgers, their front office probably thought it would be best to trade him. The Yankees were looking for pitching and must have figured Williams would do well in Yankee Stadium with its big dimensions. After all he won 14 plus for three straight years with the Dodgers.

Who would the Yanks give up? Well, they had a young Joe Pepitone up in 1962 to get his feet wet. He was being groomed to take Bill Skowron's first baseman's job. Skowron had a good year in '62. He hit .270 with 23 homers and 80 RBIs in only 140 games. It did not matter, he would be history.

Like I said, Moose was traded for some needed pitching and he was expendable as Pepitone was waiting in the wings. (Or was it possibly because of a game in July, his company's box seats had a couple of Yankee Haters in them – and it got back to the Yankee front office).

1963
Dodgers Return to New York with Brooms

In 1963 the Yankees had another stroll to the pennant. They won by a boring 10 1/2 games ahead of the Chicago White Sox. The Chisox led the league in ERA and had the league leaders in Gary Peters (19-8, 2.33 ERA) and Juan Pizarro (16-8, 2.39 ERA). In '63, I was completing my senior year in high school. My strongest subject was history – the only question I got wrong on the history final was regarding the Spanish conquistador "Who was Pizarro?" I answered it correctly; he was a lefty pitcher for the White Sox. The teacher had no sense of humor – I knew the answer was "conquered the Incas of Peru". The Chisox had little offense. Their leader was Pete Ward, the third baseman, who was fifth in hitting .295 and had 22 homers. Dave Nicholson also hit 22 homers, but in 443 plate appearances he struck out 175 times.

I was hoping the Minnesota Twins would continue to improve from their runner-up spot last year. Their potent offense returned as they led the league with 225 homers. Harmon Killebrew led the league with 45, Bob Allison was third (35) and Jimmie Hall fourth (33). Camilo Pascual again having some runs to work with won 20 games (21-9 with a 2.37 ERA, third in the league). But he was their only effective pitcher.

The talent pool was so low in the American League that the Yanks won easily despite having no significant contributions from the M & M's. The Mick missed about 100 games and had only 172 at bats, but had 15 homers and a .314 average. Maris missed almost half the season, but had 23 homers and 53 RBIs. Picking up the offense was Elston Howard who had his third superb season in a row, but this was even better than the 1961 season when he hit .348. He hit .287 with 28 homers and 85 RBIs and was the league's MVP. Joe Pepitone took over at first for Skowron and made the All-Star team. He led the Yanks with 89 RBIs and socked 27 homers. Tom

93

Tresh also supplied some pop to the offense belting out 25 homers in his sophomore year. Being a switch-hitter, the Yanks were hoping maybe another Mick is on the way.

The Yankee defense and pitching was what put them over the top. Their infield of Clete Boyer and Joe Pepitone at the corners was best in the league and Bobby Richardson and Tony Kubek were a double play combo since their Denver minor league days.

The Yanks' staff was just plain great. The Chairman of the Board, Whitey Ford, led the league in wins (24-7), winning % (.774) and had a 2.74 ERA. The '62 Series hero Ralph Terry, after a slow start, won 17 games and tied for the lead in complete games (18). But it was two newcomers that came on the scene that brought the most excitement. Jim Bouton, known as "Bulldog", was a hard throwing right-hander who was sort of a cross between the 1949–53 aces Vic Raschi and Allie Reynolds. The Bulldog put so much effort in his delivery that his hat would usually fly off his head. He followed his 7-7 '62 rookie year by finishing behind Ford in wins (21) and winning % (.750). At the time no one knew that Bouton would become Major League Baseball's Public Enemy Number One, when in 1969 he wrote "Ball Four", the controversial book about clubhouse stories that were never to be written or talked about.

The other newcomer was a lefty, Al Downing, who was called up in July. He started off fast and throwing low-hit games, the Yanks were hoping they had the next Sandy Koufax. Downing was not as tall as Sandy, but a little bit taller than Whitey Ford. At the time I thought he was a cross between Koufax and Ford, and his rookie stats showed he had the potential to be as good. He went 13-5, completed 10 of his 22 starts and had 4 shutouts. He led the league in Ks per 9 innings and fewest hits per 9 innings. The Yankee relief corp was headed by lefty, and former NBA Laker, Steve Hamilton and righty Hal Reniff, who combined for 9 wins and 23 saves.

The National League again was different from the American League. They had a pennant race. Up until the middle of September, only one game separated the Los Angeles Dodgers and "my" St. Louis Cardinals.

The defending champion San Francisco Giants had productive years from their future Hall of Famers – Say Hey hit .314 with 28 homers and 97 RBIs and Willie McCovey tied Aaron for the home run crown with 44. Juan Marichal had a Cy Young type season (25-8 and 2.41 ERA), but as good as he was, he was no Koufax. The major drop in production was from the Giants other starters. Jack Sanford, Billy O'Dell, and Billy Pierce had 59 victories in 1962, this year they had only 33, a difference of 26 wins. One of Marichal's wins was a major highlight of the season. On July 2, the 22-year old was in a 16-inning pitching duel with the 42-year old Warren Spahn, who was 23-7 for the year. After 9 innings Alvin Dark the Giants' skipper tried to take out Marichal a couple of times but he would not come out as long as that oldster Spahn was in there. The Say Hey Kid mercifully crushed a homer in the sixteenth off of Spahn to give the youngster the 1-0 victory.

The Dodgers' winning year can be credited to their pitching. The runner-up Cardinals out hit the Dodgers by 20 points (.271 to .251) and outscored them by over 100 runs. Sandy Koufax had one of the best years ever for a pitcher. He was 25-5 with a 1.88 ERA. He threw 11 shutouts and led the league with 306 Ks against only 58 walks. The mystifying question of the year was – how did he lose 5 games? Don Drysdale won 19 and Johnny Podres won 14. The other star on the mound was Ron Perranoski, the ace lefty reliever. He won 16 in relief and saved another 21.

The Dodger offense was woeful. All of their players had severe reductions in their stats from last year. (It should be noted that a major reason for this was that the baseball increased the upper part of the strike zone to its pre-1951 height - the top of the shoulders - in an attempt to create a more even balance between batters and pitchers). The catalyst Maury Wills did hit over .300 (.302) but had more than 60 fewer stolen bases and scored 47 less runs. Tommy Davis again led the league in batting (.326) but his RBI total dropped from 153 to 88 and his homers went from 27 to 16. He and Frank "Hondo" Howard were the only Dodgers to hit more than 15 homers. Hondo hit 28 homers (fifth in the league) but his RBIs dropped by 55. Howard was known as Hondo, after the movies western character played by John Wayne. Howard, not to be confused with the AL MVP Elston, was the Majors' biggest and possibly strongest player. He was listed at 6'7" and was a college basketball star at Ohio State. At one time he held a rebounding record at Madison Square Garden with 32. Interestingly at this time, there was another basketball star from Ohio State starting for the NBA Boston Celtics. He was John Havlicek and his nickname was also Hondo. Another ironic twist was that the baseball Hondo was taller than the basketball Hondo. Strange that those two guys from Ohio State were nicknamed after a guy, John Wayne, who played football for Southern Cal (USC).

Even catcher Johnny Roseboro and center fielder Willie Davis' stats were lower than last year's. Despite just about the whole line-up suffering through a bad season, the Dodgers still won the pennant. Doing more with less had to be one of the Dodger mottos for 1963. Of course having Koufax Incorporated on the mound makes it easier to do more with less.

St. Louis made a good run at the Dodgers. In late August the Cards were six games out. They then put together a tremendous run that I have never seen before. They went out and won 19 out of 20 games. However, the Dodgers were no shrinking violets – they put on a good run of their own winning 14 out of 20. So, during this 20 game stretch, St. Louis only gained five games. They were only one game out and had a three game series with the Dodgers. With Koufax scheduled for the middle game (couldn't get too optimistic about winning that one) the Cards would have to win the other two to deadlock the race. In the first game I picked up the static-y St. Louis station. Podres started for the Dodgers and the crafty lefty won 3-1. The Cards only run came on a homer by Stan the Man, who announced that this was his last season. He was trying his best to get into another World Series (his last was in 1946). The Dodger gimme game was a ho-hum 4-0 whitewashing by Koufax. The Cards were now three games out. If they can salvage the finale they would still be in the race only two games out. Remember the fall of the Dodgers in '62 (of course they did not have Koufax).

In game 3 the Cardinals chances could not have looked better. They were winning 5-1 going into the eighth inning with their emerging star, Hoot Gibson, six-shooting them down. The Dodgers, even with their ineffective offense, scored three in the eight to make the score 5-4. Then in the ninth the Dodgers sent up a rookie, Dick Nen, who promptly hit a game-tying homer. I just about broke my radio, knocking it off my night table. Who was Dick Nen? It was probably his only meaningful hit in his career. He played parts of six years with 185 hits and 20 other homers. His greatest feat, other than this Cardinal crushing homer, was having a son. Not being a proficient hitter, I guess he told his son Robb to become a pitcher. Robb Nen was one of the better relievers from 1992-2002. Anyway, the Cards lost this game in extra innings and that was it as they just played out the rest of the season.

The Cardinal run at the pennant was attributed to a few changes that eventually will bring about success in 1964. The Cards traded for the 1960 MVP Dick Groat. The former Duke Basketball All-American solidified the Cardinal infield. In fact, the St. Louis infield started the All-Star game for the National League. Bill White at first, Groat at short and Ken Boyer at third all were voted in and Julian Javier was picked when an injured Mazeroski had to be replaced. Groat was third in the league in hitting (.319) and led the league in doubles (43). He also was the MVP runner-up behind Koufax. The other change the Cards had was handing the catching reins over to 21-year old Tim McCarver. In his first full season he hit .289 and was very good defensively.

The Cardinal infield corners Boyer and White provided the power numbers. Boyer hit 24 homers and was second in the league with 111 RBIs. White hit over .300 again, led the team with 27 homers and was third in RBIs, just behind Boyer with 109.

What St. Louis needed was more offensive output from its outfield. Center field was held down by Curt Flood, arguably the best defensive center fielder this side of Say Hey. Flood was an asset to the offense. Not having a lot of power, he was a table setter – he'd get around 200 hits and could really motor around the bases. The other outfield spots did not produce much offense. (Generally, a team's top hitters are usually the right and left fielders, either hitting for average or putting up power numbers – some of the ideal ones were Aaron, Al Kaline, and Frank Robinson).

I was hoping that Stan the Man would come close to his '62 stats, but at 42, that was a pipe dream. Although he did provide some clutch hits, his average fell from .330 to .255. He knew it was over (he retired with a slew of National League batting records). The Cards tried a lot of players, including Charlie James, who was tagged Musial's caddie, who had 10 homers and 45 RBIs in two-thirds of the year.

The Red Birds' pitching staff would normally be good enough to be considered best in the league, but not this year against the Dodgers' Koufax-led staff. Former ace Ernie Broglio regained his 1960 form and led the team with an 18-8 record. Hoot Gibson continued his improvement and matched Broglio's 18 wins. Veteran

Curt Simmons was 15-9 and was fifth in ERA (2.47). Twenty-two year old Ray Sadecki was also showing promise winning 10 games.

Once again, for me it was, "Wait 'til next year" for St. Louis. At least after this run there was some genuine hope.

In New York the Yankees' battle to win the pennant was matched by their quest to win the attention of New Yorkers and their media. Their counterparts, the Mets, improved over 25% as they increased their win total from 40 wins in '62 to 51 in '63. The Mets' ineptness continued as Ol' Casey Stengel captivated the media with stories and reasons why they lost. Fans, including me, continued to flock to the rundown Polo Grounds to see these lovable losers. A new reason to come for Brooklyn fans was that the Mets got Brooklyn's former star, Duke Snider. Duke getting close to the end of his storied career did hit 14 homers. Roger Craig pitched well but still lost 22 games despite a 3.78 ERA.

This year, the Mets had over a million fans come to see their lack of play. Meanwhile the Yankee attendance dropped almost 200,000 from '62, and they won the pennant. With the World's Fair and the Mets having a state of the art new stadium opening in Queens in 1964, the Yankees' front office was starting to sweat about losing the attendance battle of New York.

A few games I remember were the Mets versus Cardinals. My cousin Ron and I would go to about six of these games. Once Stan the Man said he was hanging up his cleats, I made sure I would attend his last games in New York. So naturally on the Cards' last trip to New York my cousin and I went. Unfortunately, for me and the Man, the Mets won the last two games of the series. Another game I recall is, (even though it may be hard to believe), the Mets were pounding St. Louis' pitching. In the old Polo Grounds, the bullpens were on the playing field in the power alley areas. The bullpen had some type of awning over the bench. Anyway, I went out there and leaned over the wall saying "let's get somebody throwing" (like I'm the manager or something). One of the Cardinals in the 'pen, Bobby Shantz, looked up and said "Get the hell out of here before I kick you in the butt". As a concerned Cardinal fan I walked away mad telling my cousin, I didn't like Shantz as a Yankee and I don't like him as a Cardinal. I put the horns on him hoping the Cards trade him.

In the spring of '63 I graduated high school. My only real goal was to be a history teacher. I thought I would get a job for a year or two to make some funds for college. During the spring of '63 my uncle Walter, (the one that told me drinking Yoo-Hoo was drinking Yankee juice), informed me that the US Post Office was giving an exam in June. Not knowing what I would be doing, I set out to take the exam in June of my senior year. In September the Post Office called me and informed me that I passed the exam and would start employment in October. I quickly asked the date hoping it would be the end of October so I would be free to see the Series. The Post Office personnel department told me they still had paperwork to process for all the new hires, so I would start October 26. Yay, I'd be able to see the World Series!

The World Series was about to start. Just like last year when the Giants/Yankees World Series went from being borough to borough to coast to coast, this year's Dodgers/Yankees Series would go from a former borough to borough Series to being coast to coast.

In game 1 it was a match-up of the games best pitchers, Koufax (25-5) versus Whitey Ford (24-7). Whitey was the American League's best, but no one was as good as Sandy. Game 1 turned out to be a very bright day for Sandy and the Dodgers. With the lefty Ford going, the Dodgers decided to bench the left-handed hitting Ron Fairly and played the right-handed hitting Moose Skowron at first. This was sort of a surprise because Moose had a terrible year. He seemed to have been traumatized by no longer being in Yankee pinstripes. Playing in only about half of the games, he hit only .203 with just 4 homers and 19 RBIs. The Moose played more like a Mouse (maybe because he was in Disneyland, USA). Anyway, playing against the Pinstripes probably made Moose realize he was no longer a Yankee, as he had a super Series.

The Dodgers broke the game open in the second. Hondo Howard drove a cannon shot off of Whitey that crashed into the 408 ft mark on the center field wall. The ball got there so fast and hard, that the wall was probably now 410 ft. The ball bounced halfway back to the infield. Even the Yankee fans that were used to Mantle's powerful blasts were even stunned by this Howard shot. Moose then came up, and squashing his Yankee emotions, singled in Hondo with the Series' first run. Dick Tracewski, the platoon second baseman, then singled setting the big at bat of the game. Yankee Stadium was known for its deep power alley dimensions, but also for its short right field foul line (296 ft). All through baseball history the Yanks had lefty home run hitters from Ruth to Maris. In fact, Yogi had a patent on hitting balls around that short foul pole for homers. Well this time the Dodger catcher Johnny Roseboro, who only had 9 homers for the year, put one up in the air that hung fair for a 3-run homer. Dodgers were up 4-0 with Koufax going. The Dodgers put up another run in the third on three hits by Junior Gilliam, Tommy Davis, and Moose with the RBI hit. The Dodgers now had a 5-0 lead with the best pitcher in the world on the mound. It was a no-brainer to say the game was unofficially over.

Sandy started the game with five straight Ks and continued to pile them up throughout the game. Koufax had a shutout going into the eighth. The Yanks had a runner on via an infield hit. Maybe this upset Sandy as Tom Tresh hit a two out 2-run homer. It didn't matter; the score was now 5-2. In the eighth, Sandy tied the World Series strike out record of 14 that was held by his former Brooklyn teammate Carl Erskine. Sandy had two outs in the ninth and the Yankees sent up pinch-hitter Harry Bright. Poor Bright – here he is in his home park batting in the World Series and almost all of his supposed Yankee fans were rooting for him to strike out. The 'Bright' day concluded for Sandy and the Dodgers as Harry obliged by fanning to end the game and give Sandy the new Series record of 15 strikeouts.

For game 2 my Godfather, Uncle Eddie from Greenpoint Brooklyn called me and he had two reserved bleacher seats for the game. My cousin Ron didn't want to miss school so I was the next option to go. After the Dodger/Koufax victory, I took the bus to New York Port Authority and took the subway to my uncle Eddie's where I would spend the night. Since we had reserved seats we did not have to get there early, like we did in '61 when we had to wait in line to get unreserved bleacher seats. The match-up was rookie Al Downing against old Yankee nemesis Johnny Podres. Both managers Ralph Houk and Walter Alston opted to use their lefties in Yankee Stadium since it was harder for right-handed hitters to hit homers than it was for lefties. Another reason that the Yankees chose Downing to start instead of Ralph Terry was that a lefty could better keep the Dodgers' road runners (Gilliam, the Davises, and especially Wills) from stealing bases or getting a good lead off of first.

The Dodgers again drew first blood putting up a deuce in the first to have a two run lead even before the Yankees batted. The Dodgers' motto for this game was "Where there's a Wills there's a way". Maury singled off Downing in the first. One of the reasons

Downing started, besides being good, was his ability to keep runners close to first or pick them off. The strategy appeared to work as Downing picked off Wills. Right away I thought, 'what the? – don't they know about his pick-off move!' I guess Pepitone, the first baseman didn't know of it either – he was coming in for a sacrifice bunt. Downing threw to the stunned Pepitone whose throw to second failed to nail Wills who raced to second on the pick-off throw. Gilliam singled Wills to third. Willie Davis than hit a fly to right that Maris possibly should have caught (I think he slipped). He didn't catch it and Willie Davis had a two-run double. You really put yourself in a hole when you give the crafty Podres a two run lead before he threw a pitch. In the fourth inning the Yanks suffered another embarrassment. The Moose came up and banged out a homer into the right field stands. I was surprised at the fans cheering 'Mooooose' after this homer – well maybe it was 'Boooos'. The Davises put together a run in the seventh, as Willie doubled and Tommy tripled (Tommy's was his second triple of the game tying Richardson's feat in the '60 Series). The score was now 4-0 and Podres was cruising. Podres knew how to keep the ball in the park. Mantle was 0 for 4 but all of his at bats were long fly outs to the deep power alleys that the speedy Davis guys could easily catch.

The Yanks escaped complete humiliation when in the ninth Hector Lopez doubled. You don't mess around when you have a Perranoski to extinguish fires. He came in and gave up a run-scoring single to the Yankee Howard (Ellie) – but that was it. Brooklyn, oops, Los Angeles won 4-1 and went up 2 games to zip and heading back to LA for some home cooking.

There was the customary day of travel (this time though, it was all the way across the nation). The Yankee problems were further compounded by an injury sustained by Maris when he ran into the fence in game 2. He injured his arm taking him out of the rest of the Series. This is just what they needed, to lose Maris. But possibly the other Yanks envied Maris in the aspect that he wouldn't have to face the Dodger pitching – it wasn't something to look forward to, and they didn't even face Drysdale yet.

Game 3 starters were the right-hander match-up of Bulldog Bouton and the intimidator, Drysdale. Again, as in game 2, the Dodgers scored on some strange doings in the first inning. Gilliam walked and was on first with two out when Bulldog threw a wild pitch that allowed Gilliam to get into scoring position. Tommy

Davis then hit a hard shot that caromed off the mound and then glanced off of second baseman Richardson's leg into right field allowing Gilliam to score. Bouton then shut down the Dodgers for seven innings only giving up three hits. The Yanks' reliever Reniff also pitched a hitless/scoreless inning. You might think with this excellent pitching the Yanks maybe won the game. Nope – Drysdale, used to getting little run support, made the flukey one run stand up. In this game he mimicked Koufax from the right side. He only gave up three hits and a walk while fanning nine. Dodgers won 1-0 and were up 3 games to zip. Los Angeles hardware stores were having a run on brooms (especially with Koufax going for the clincher the next day).

The Yanks put their hopes on Ford to keep them alive. The Yanks had a Ford, but the Dodgers had a Mercedes (Koufax) – who would win? Again it was Hondo, who Ford must have had nightmares about all winter. He blasted a Ford pitch in the fifth - well over 400 feet into the left field stands where few balls have ever been hit (I think Bob Uecker caught it). The Mick finally came through with only his second hit of the Series in the seventh, but what a hit – he showed Hondo someone else can blast them in a Ruthian way. The score was tied at one but only for the half inning. In the bottom of the inning Gilliam hit a grounder to third base - Boyer made a fine play on it and threw to Pepitone. The throw would have easily beaten Gilliam except that it was lost by Pepitone trying to locate it out of all the white shirts of the fans in the seats behind third base. The throw bounced off the fence and went into right field allowing Gilliam to get all the way to third base. Willie Davis then put the Dodgers up 2-1 with a sac- fly. The Yanks threatened in the ninth. Richardson singled, but then Sandy struck out Tresh and the Mick. The game appeared to be over when Elston Howard grounded to Wills who tossed to Tracewski. As the umpire was calling Richardson out at second the ball fell out of Tracewski's glove. Wait - game and Series is not over – the Yanks have the tying run in scoring position. With Sandy on the mound, he got Hector Lopez on another grounder to Wills to give the Dodgers the four game sweep. Bring out them brooms!!!!

In Brooklyn it took the Dodgers until 1955 to win their only World Series. They have been in Los Angeles only six years and already have won it twice.

One more thing about Moose Skowron. Naturally Koufax was the Series MVP, but the most valuable position player would be Moose. Tommy Davis hit .400 (6 for 15) and Hondo had the two big blasts that traumatized Ford, but Moose was 5 for 13 (.385) with 3 RBIs. Also Moose had to be satisfied with the performance of Pepitone, the replacement for him. Pepitone had only two singles in 13 at bats (.154) and contributed in the field to two of the losses – (the botched pick-off in game 2 and missing Boyer's throw in game 4). I don't know if Moose's Series performance revitalized him or if he realized he didn't have to be a Yankee to be productive. After the Series he was sent back to the American League and had two productive years hitting .282 with 17 homers in 1964 and hitting .274 with 18 homers in 1965.

About three weeks after the Series I started work. I was a clerk in the Newark Post Office. I was an 18-year old kid and was amazed of the amount of people working there (about a 1,000 or so). Most of the work force at this time was still men. I did a lot of different jobs with the mail and encountered many other workers. Since they were men, the chatter was usually about sports, especially baseball. Football wasn't that big yet and the NBA was boring (even worse than the Yankee dominance was the Celtic dynasty – beginning in 1957 the Celtics won 11 out of 13 NBA titles). A lot of these guys were former athletes back in the '40's and '50's. One guy played with Larry Doby in Paterson in the '40's, another guy pitched against my mom's neighbor Hank Borowy in the late '30's – I remember him saying the score was 1-0 but I don't recall if he won or not. Another guy I worked with told me he graduated high school in Donora, PA with Stan the Man.

These guys I worked with furthered my baseball knowledge. One of the guys I worked with everyday was Frank Molinaro. He would tell me about his son Bobby's baseball ability, who was 13 at the time. Bobby went on to play parts of eight seasons in the American League in the '70's and '80's (.264 lifetime average, .291 in 1980 for the Chisox). Sometimes I couldn't wait to go to work to hear these stories. Through them I understood how good Bob Feller, Ted Williams, Johnny Mize, and Stan the Man were back in the '40's and '50's.

1964
It's All in the CARDS

(Editor's Note: Be prepared – this is a long chapter)

In all my years of following baseball, the year 1964 continues to be my greatest ever for obvious reasons. After rooting for St. Louis for the past eleven years they finally won the World Series.

It was a most unusual season, as up until the last three weeks of the season you couldn't get a nickel for St. Louis' chances to win the pennant. But they put on such an unbelievable streak, and due to other circumstances they won the National League flag, only to have to face the heavily favored and hated Yankees in the Series.

Well, when it comes to fate, and it's "All in the Cards", you just can't lose.

When the season began in April, I was a working man for about half a year. I worked the 6:00 p.m. - 2:30 a.m. shift. Like previously stated, I worked with a lot of guys and the usual banter was about baseball (in 1964, football and basketball were not nearly as popular). Another thing I found out at work is that outside of former Giant and Dodger fans, the most popular National League team was the Cardinals. There was a bunch of them at work, and I would usually chew the fat with them. (The Mets really didn't have a fan base until '69).

During spring training, I would talk to these co-workers about the Cardinals' chances in '64 and we generally agreed that this could be their year. After all, they just about scared the blue out of the Dodgers last year when they went on a 19 out of 20 winning streak that just fell short as they finished as runner-ups.

Going into the year they had three solid starters in Ernie Broglio, Hoot Gibson and Curt Simmons who combined for 51 victories in 1963. Ray Sadecki, hopefully could develop into another

104

top starter, (at 22, he won 10 games last year). With Bill White, Julian Javier, Dick Groat, and the captain, Ken Boyer, they had the 1963 National League All-Star infield. Also improvement from their young catcher Tim McCarver (at 21, he hit .289) could be expected. The outfield was a question mark. Curt Flood, the lead-off man, was solid, and it was hoped that Charlie James, who was known as Musial's caddie, could take over for the Man as he retired in '63. The other outfield position was really an unknown. Possibly Mike Shannon would be ready - in '63 he had a cup of coffee (8 for 26, .308). He, like Tim McCarver, turned down a football scholarship (quarterback at Missouri U.) to play baseball. Like in 1958 and 1961, I was anxious for the season to begin, anticipating a fun year.

The '64 Yankees had a big change. Ralph Houk, the manager from 1961 to 1963, became General Manager. Who would manage this team that was so talent laden that only Daffy Duck could mess up their run for the pennant? Their choice to take over the managerial reins was probably a surprise to some, as they selected Yogi Berra. Yogi was known as a clutch player who was noted for his 'Yogi-isms' - like "It ain't over 'til it's over." Most of his sayings had a lot merit when analyzed. Yogi would prove to them that he was no Daffy Duck. (I don't know why I keep picking on poor Daffy).

Another possible reason for selecting Yogi was the battle for the NY sports pages. Hopefully Yogi's comments would be able to compete against Casey Stengel who was managing the cross-town Mets. The New York media seemed to favor these hapless, inept losers rather than the boring, always winning Yanks. Another factor was the battle for fans, as it was showing up as the Mets' attendance increased, while attendance at the Stadium decreased. Adding to this concern for the Yanks was that the Mets were opening their new state of the art stadium in Queens (Shea Stadium). Also in 1964, New York hosted the World's Fair right in Queens - next to the new stadium. The Mets would eventually win the attendance battle - even though they were the National League's cellar dwellers, they outdrew the American League penthouse residents (the Yanks) 1,732,597 to 1,305,638.

During the first half of the year I had little to cheer about. The Cards were playing .500 ball. At least I was able to see them play at the new Shea Stadium. It was a nice stadium but I preferred the old Polo Grounds where for a $1.30 you could get a general admission seat and be right on top of the action. At Shea, like Yankee Stadium, you were more removed from the field.

All through June and July I watched, read, and listened to St. Louis play .500 ball. At work I would usually go to lunch at 11:00 p.m. and go to my car and pick up the end of the Cardinal game from their KMOX station that I could pick up in Newark, NJ. I would usually return from lunch being frustrated because of what I considered was dumb moves and decisions by the Cardinal manager Johnny Keane. Rooting for the Cardinals, I was not a Keane fan. During my half hour lunches, he'd make a move - I'd second guess him, and I'd be right. I never thought the Cards had a chance with him as the skipper.

The highlight of the first half of the season was the All-Star Game. It was being played at Shea Stadium, since it was brand new and the World's Fair was across the street (so to speak). My cousin Ron and I decided to get tickets for the game. I took a vacation during the week of the All-Star Game and spent time at the World's Fair with my cousin except for the game.

The 1964 All-Star Game turned out to be great for a Cardinal (and National League) fan. If the National League won it would knot the mid-summer classic at 17 apiece. At this time in baseball the All-Star Game was a big deal. The Leagues did not like each other. For the most part you were a National League fan or an American League fan. The players at this time generally played their whole career in one league. The only exceptions were veteran stars changing leagues when their big years were over - like Greenberg, Mize, Slaughter, and Sain. This year though, the Phils traded for Detroit Tiger star pitcher Jim Bunning, who had on off year in 1963.

St. Louis had good representation for the All-Star Game. They had 3/4 of their '63 All-Star infield return. Ken Boyer started at third, Dick Groat at short and Bill White was a reserve at first. Curt Flood was a reserve outfielder.

In the fourth inning, Billy Williams, the Chicago Cubs future Famer, homered to tie the score at one, and later that inning, my guy Boyer hit one to put the Nationals up 2-1. He also singled in the second. I must be good luck – I go to two All-Star Games and Boyer hits a homer in each one. In the next inning a Cardinal strikes again, as Groat doubles home a run for a 3-1 lead. The Americans came back with two in the sixth and one in the seventh to take a 4-3 lead.

Entering the bottom of the ninth the Americans had the game seemingly well in hand. They had "the Monster", Dick Radatz, the Red Sox reliever, on the mound. Radatz would have looked more appropriate being on the gridiron – he had defensive end size (for this era) at 6'6" and 230 pounds. In '63 and '64 he put together two of the finest relief pitching seasons ever. In '63 he won 15 and saved 15 and bettered that in '64 with 16 wins and 16 saves with an ERA under 2.29. To the Nationals, he truly looked like the Monster. In the seventh and eighth he got four of the six outs on Ks with his blazing fastball. But in the ninth, Radatz made the mistake of giving up a lead-off walk to the Say Hey Kid. Mays promptly stole second and scored on a single by his Giant teammate Orlando Cepeda to knot the score at four. Flood went into run for Cepeda, who had taken second on the throw home. Radatz gave up an intentional walk, got two outs, and was now facing Johnny Callison. All year long Callison was getting clutch hits that kept the surprising Phillies in first place. Well Radatz threw his best fastball, but Callison hit a "monster" shot for a 3-run All-Star Game-winning homer. The National League finally tied the American League with 17 wins apiece in the mid-summer classic.

It was only appropriate that a Phillie would win the All-Star Game (their ace Jim Bunning even put on a show fanning four, in his two inning scoreless stint), as it appeared to be their year. With the All-Star game being the season mid-point they were in first place by 1 1/2 games over the San Francisco Giants. Both teams see-sawed between first and second place all through the first half of the season. The Phillies only real blemish in the first half of the season was being the victim of LA's Sandy Koufax no-hitter on June 4.

Another reason that it looked like a Phillie year was that the season highlight was a pitching performance by their ace Jim Bunning. Bunning already had tossed a no-hitter for Detroit in 1958. Having started his National League career in fine form, he was slated to pitch on Father's Day against the Mets. It was only fitting for the future Famer and Congressman from Kentucky to pitch on this day, since he was the father of an "almost baseball team" (he had seven kids at the time). Anyway, for this day, Bunning was the "Perfect" Dad, throwing a Perfect Game – take that Sandy!

The Phillies really only had two stars as position players. Callison, the All-Star MVP, was steady all year. He was tied for third in the league with 31 homers and was fifth in RBIs (104) and in total bases (322). It seemed whenever a hit was needed he got it. Had the Phils taken the flag he would be the shoe-in MVP (as it was, he was runner-up). Coming on the scene to help Callison was a rookie third baseman named Dick Allen who was far from being a Ken Boyer in the field but could he pound the horsehide. Despite leading the league in strikeouts, he made enough contact to hit .318 (fourth in the league) and led the league in three categories - runs scored (125), triples (13), and total bases (352). He also found time to club 29 homers and drive in 91 runs. Although Allen often whiffed (he was in the top three in strikeouts seven times), when he did made contact the ball would just seem to just explode off his bat (his lifetime average was .292 with power - 351 homers). He ran away with the Rookie of the Year award. The rest of the team was comprised of basically complementary players, like Cookie Rojas who hit .291 and playing just about all the positions (for whoever was hurt or needed a rest).

The downfall of the Phils was their pitching even though they had a lefty/righty combo that challenged the Dodgers' Koufax/Drysdale duo. Bunning continued pitching well after his Perfect Game and finished 19-8 with a 2.63 ERA (fifth in the league). His lefty counterpart was Chris Short, who after becoming a starter in May, went 17-9 with a 2.20 ERA (third in the league) - but that was all the Phils had. Art Mahaffey and Dennis Bennet each won 12, but were generally hurt or ineffective when the Phils had the greatest collapse in baseball history. They had a 6 1/2 game lead with only twelve games to play. It looked like the Phillies' fans could get their Series tickets – but the Phillies' skipper Gene Mauch started to manage by pushing the panic button. He began to pitch Bunning and Short with only two days rest during the stretch drive. It did not work. You might say that the Phillies' pennant run came up a little bit "Short".

The Cards were six games out with twelve to go. While the Phils were collapsing with their ten game losing streak, the Cards won eight in a row, and the Reds won nine in a row. All St. Louis had to do was beat the lowly Mets to take the flag. On a September Friday night, Al Jackson looked like Koufax and beat Gibson 1-0. On Saturday the Mets looked like Murderers' Row by bombing Sadecki and others to the tune of 15-5. Luckily the Phils rebounded to knock off the Reds. Going into the season's last game, St. Louis and Cincy were tied for first with Philly one game out. A Phillies win and St. Louis loss would make it a three-way tie. There would be no need for a playoff, as the Phils' Bunning whitewashed the Reds 10-0 and the Mets resorted to being themselves as the Cards, after trailing 3-2 after four innings, trampled them 11-5 to win the pennant.

Actually, St. Louis began their pennant quest at the end of July when they were one game under .500. They just lost to the Phils' Chris Short and still had a game Saturday and a doubleheader on Sunday against the league's pace setter. On this Saturday I was over relatives in Lakewood, NJ. Lakewood picked up the Philly TV stations so we were watching the game. The Cards had led throughout the game with Boyer having hit a homer. The next time he came up I told my mom – "hey $5.00 if he hits another homer" – after all, what's a player's chance to have a multi-homer game. Boom, there goes my $5.00 as he sent another into the stands. The Cards were winning 10-2 in the ninth when the Phils put up a big rally scoring seven times to only be down by one. I recall the last out being a long fly that was caught at the fence. This game sparked them as the Red Birds took 46 of their last 67 games, including sweeping the doubleheader the next day.

It was the addition of four new players, three of whom were acquired during the year that was instrumental in St. Louis taking the flag. The first was Roger Craig. Poor Roger lost 46 games in the Mets' first two years, and must have felt like he was in heaven, (even though he wasn't traded to the Angels), when the Cardinals got him. He was only 7-9 but had a fine 3.25 ERA and had a big clutch win during their win streak at the end of the year.

The second acquisition was probably one of baseball's most famous trades. It was done just before the trading deadline. The Cards were desperate for outfield help. Only Curt Flood was having a productive year. He led the league with 211 hits and batted .311. Charlie James failed to take the Man's spot. Ernie Broglio, the Cards' 18-game winner from last year got off to a slow start at 3-5. The Cards traded him for the young Cub outfielder Lou Brock – Lou who? He was a speedy inconsistent hitter (.258 in 1963) whose main claim to fame was hitting a homer into the Polo Grounds bleachers (only the second to do it). Maybe that was his problem as a Cub; he thought he was a home run hitter instead of the line drive hitter he became. Most Cardinal fans, including myself, were rather livid about this trade for this Brock guy. After all, Broglio won 18 in 1963 and 21 in 1960, when he also had a slow start. Most people thought Bing Devine, the St. Louis General Manager, needed a lobotomy. Nowadays, after Brock put together a Hall of Fame career, people forgot what they thought of at the time of the trade and thought how could the Cubs have been so stupid? Broglio did nothing for the Cubs (4-7). A consolation for me was that the Cards also shipped them the only Cardinal I didn't like, Bobby Shantz, who I put the jinx on the year before.

All Brock did when he came to St. Louis was hit .348, socked 12 homers and scored 81 runs in only 103 games. (Lou would go on to be one of my all-time favorite players). He fit in perfectly in the two spot behind lead-off man Flood. Just think if he stayed with the Cubs and became this good – what a line-up they would have had - Brock, Ernie Banks, Billy Williams and Ron Santo. With Brock in left, the Cards now only needed a right fielder. The first week of July they called up their best minor league outfielder Mike Shannon. Nicknamed "Moon Man" for his flakiness, he filled the bill. He had a rifle arm and was a good fielder. He also provided enough pop with the bat - hitting nine homers with 43 RBIs in half a season.

The Cardinals' last piece to the puzzle was to get a decent reliever. Their Triple A farm team in Jacksonville had the answer. He was a 38-year old journeyman, Barney Schultz, whose main pitch was the knuckleball. He had it really fluttering this year, as he was 8-5 with a miniscule 1.05 ERA in 86 innings when he was called up. The Cards' General Manager Bing Devine called him up the beginning of August. All old Barney did was win one and save 14 with a 1.65 ERA in 30 games. The old knuckler was really dancing down the stretch as he showed up in seven of the last nine games and did not allow a run.

The acquisition of these four players was done by the GM, Bing Devine. But he was not around to see what the fruits of his labor accomplished. The Cardinal owner August Busch, the owner of Budweiser Beer, fired him in the middle of August when St. Louis was in fifth place. Even though he was fired, The Sporting News selected Devine as Baseball's Executive of the Year. Bing may have been thinking, "Hey, Mr. Busch, have a beer on me."

Another factor to the Red Birds' rise to the top in the second half of the season was that Groat, after a slow start, wound up at .292 and, despite only one homer, drove in 70 runs. Also, like Groat,

Bill White, was on the All-Star team despite a terrible start. He was going for his third straight .300 average/100 RBI season (a noteworthy achievement in the '60's) - by mid-season it didn't look promising. But he went on a tear averaging nearly an RBI a game for the second half of the year. He finished up batting .303 with 102 RBIs and 21 homers. White came in third in the league MVP voting behind Boyer and Callison. Besides Flood, the other Cardinals to hit consistently the whole season were sophomore catcher, Tim McCarver (.288) and Boyer who was selected the NL MVP and The Sporting News Major League Player of the Year. Kenny batted .295 with 24 homers and drove in a league leading 119 runs.

The Cardinal staff was only so-so during the first half of the year. Ray Sadecki surprisingly was the team's most consistent, winning four games every month since May to become a 20-game winner (20-11). Curt Simmons was a decent 12-9 by August then became unbeatable winning his last six to finish at 18-9. Hoot Gibson was mediocre, up until mid-August (10-10). It was a disappointing season up onto that point – after all a lot was expected from him after his 18 victories last year. Anyway, he came on real strong firing his blazing fastball to win nine of his last eleven to have an outstanding 19-12 record.

Not only did St. Louis have to overtake the Phils, they had to keep pace with the Reds who had the same idea as the Cards – to overtake the stumbling Phils and capture the flag. Cincy took twelve of thirteen to move into first place, only to lose four out of their last five to finish second. It was a sad year for Cincy for another reason. Their manager Fred Hutchinson had been diagnosed with cancer. For the most part Dick Sisler ran the team. A good portion of the country pulled for the Reds to win it for Hutch. (Hutch did not make it to 1965 as he passed on in November).

The defending champion Dodgers had an awful year. In 1963 they won it all despite a weak offense. Hoping their offense would regain the effectiveness of '62, the reverse occurred. The player's stats declined even more in '64. Only Koufax could rise above it. He was heading for another 25 victories, but in August he hurt his arm sliding into a base. He pitched two more games to go to 19-5. In the middle of August his season had ended. His ERA of 1.74 led the league. His righty counterpart Drysdale was second at 2.19 but was only 18-16 due to losing four games 1-0. The Dodgers came in sixth 13 games out.

In 1964 I was more aware of how the Yankees and the American League were doing because at work there were plenty of Yankee fans. As stated before, in '64 the Yanks went from Major Houk (he was a Major in WWII) to Major Berra (he was a 'major' contributor to ten World Series titles.). The guys at work would argue if Yogi was a good manager or not. The Yanks, the Chisox, and the Orioles were competing for the top spot. At the end of July and beginning of August the Yanks held on to first and had a slate of fifteen games in a row against the Orioles and White Sox. It was during these games that the Yanks called up their top minor league pitcher, Mel Stottlemyre who was 13-3 at the time. The Yanks did not fare well as they lost 10 of the 15. This 5-10 record against their main contenders resulted in the infamous Harmonica Incident.

After losing four in a row to the White Sox, the Yankees were in their bus leaving Comiskey Park for the airport. Phil Linz, the Yankees' utility infielder, was the free spirit type that was now showing up in American sports. Yogi and his coaches were sitting in the front of the bus, being silent, as is expected after four losses in a row. The bus became stuck in traffic. Linz was sitting in the back of the bus. In order to idle away the time Linz took out a harmonica (he was learning to play it). He started to play "Mary Had a Little Lamb." When Yogi heard the music he said something to the effect to stop it. Supposedly Linz did not hear what Yogi said and asked the players sitting near him if any of them heard what Yogi said. The Mick, (a known prankster), said that Yogi said to play it again. So he did. Yogi came to the back of the bus and told Linz what to do with the harmonica. Linz tossed the harmonica to Yogi who swatted it so hard it hit Pepitone in the leg causing a cut. Yogi and Linz started jawing with each other. Finally Yogi went back to the front saying this will be settled later. The Mick picked up the harmonica, and he and Ford started to make jokes about the harmonica to break the tension. Linz was fined $200 but sheepishly made out like a bandit when a harmonica company gave him a reportedly $20,000 endorsement contract, a $19,800 profit. (Actually I was at a baseball affair in November 2004 and Linz was there. So I briefly had a discussion with him about this incident and he told me that he really received $10,000, still a nice bit of change in 1964).

Most people credit this incident as being the spark the Yanks needed. But after the incident they lost two more to be six games out. Stottlemyre ended the six game losing streak and the Yanks took off. They didn't have to play the contenders anymore and feasted on the weaker teams to the tune of 22 out of 28 and took the pennant by one game over the Chisox and Baltimore. The White Sox put on a rush winning their last nine but it wasn't enough.

Mantle came on strong and was second in MVP voting with 35 homers, 111 RBIs and a .303 average. (The Orioles' Brooks Robinson was the AL MVP batting .317 with a league leading 118 RBIs). The other 'M', Maris, chipped in with 26 homers and 71 RBIs and Pepitone put up 28 homers and 100 RBIs. But I thought Elston Howard was their main man. I thought he was better than his MVP year of 1963. He was third in the league in hitting at .313 and had 84 RBIs.

Whitey Ford was again Chairman of the Board being second in the league in winning % (.739, 17-6), shutouts (8) and ERA (2.13). Bulldog Bouton was 18-13 and lefty Al Downing was 13-8 leading the league in Ks (217). But it was two late additions that put them over the top. August call up Mel Stottlemyre was 9-3 with a 2.06 ERA. September addition Pedro Ramos was an actual life saver. In his one month with the team he won a game in relief and saved seven others. In 13 games and 22 innings he had a microscopic 1.25 ERA. Only winning the pennant by one game you could see how important it was to pick up Ramos. However, to the delight of the National League pennant winner, Ramos would be unavailable to participate in the World Series since his acquisition was after the September cut-off for eligibility.

In 1964 the Yankees had another obstacle to overcome, but it was not on the playing field. It came out in August, in the heat of the chase for the flag that the Columbia Broadcasting System (CBS) would purchase the Yankees for $14 million. This brought up a huge outcry from many. I really hated (and still hate) following any of the legal entanglements that baseball gets into. I just enjoy the game on the field. Anyhow, the deal and sale was approved, and CBS owned the Yanks. They assumed they got the golden goose, as the Yankees, including 1964, had been in 14 of the past 16 World Series. They naturally did not know it at the time but all they got was a paper tiger. (All during the CBS tenure as owners, the Yanks were a bad team. During this time 1965-1973 the Yankees proved to be the best TV sitcom that CBS produced. I guess CBS got tired of the laugh track and looked to cancel this sitcom. In 1973 they would take a $4 million loss and sold them to some little known shipbuilder from Cleveland named George Steinbrenner).

The Yankee players didn't let this change of ownership distract them as they took their fifth consecutive American League flag – and with their third different manager (Casey in '60, the Major in '61 –'63, and Yogi in '64).

That was the difference between the leagues. The Cardinals were the fifth different team since 1960 to represent the National League (Pittsburgh in '60, Cincy in '61, San Fran in '62, LA in '63, and now St. Louis.) At least the Yankee players were able to see a lot of the country.

The Series was set – the Cards and Yanks in their fifth Series as opponents. The Cards won in '26 and '42 – the Yanks won in '28 and '43.

This year the weekend games would be in New York. Once St. Louis won on the last day of the season I called my cousin Ron in Brooklyn and told him it would be good to get reserved bleacher seats. You had to buy a strip for three games (for the three games it would be $9.00 a person). My other cousin Don also wanted to go to the weekend games. Don's father was my uncle Walter who told me about Yoo-Hoo being Yankee juice back in 1956. Don, who was 11 at the time, was a Yankee fan like his dad.

In the 1960's there were no World Series night games, and since I worked the 6:00 p.m. - 2:30 a.m. shift I would be able to watch the games from St. Louis on television. I was off on the weekend and Monday was Columbus Day, so I was off for the holiday.

Both teams had a starter injured and would not be available for the Series. The Yanks lost shortstop Tony Kubek (Linz would take his place), and Cards lost second baseman Julian Javier (Dal Maxvill would play second). It appeared that neither team benefited by these circumstances, or so it seemed.

The Series opened on a Wednesday. The Yanks were heavy favorites, with one of the factors being experience, having been in the past four Fall Classics. St. Louis only had three players with any World Series time – Dick Groat at short and Bob Skinner, a reserve outfielder, with the 1960 Pirates and Roger Craig with the Dodgers of '55, '56 and '59.

The nervousness the Cards had was minimized by the antics of the back-up catcher, Bob Uecker, before he became an actor and TV sitcom star in "Mr. Belvidere" and the movie "Major League." Uecker only had 21 hits and batted under .200 for the season, but his comedy routine kept the team loose. During batting practice of the first game, he picked up a tuba left by one of the bands for the pre-game activities. He started to shag the flies with the tuba. He cracked up his teammates (and maybe the tuba) relieving any tension they might have had.

In the first game the Yanks started Whitey Ford. Whitey was the Series all-time top winner (10), but he did lose his last three Series decisions giving him the most Series losses (7) as well. The Cards started their 20-game winner Ray Sadecki. They would have probably preferred to start their best pitcher Gibson. However Gibson pitched the previous Friday losing the 1-0 game to the Mets Al Jackson, and also pitched four innings on Sunday in the pennant clincher. He'd go on Thursday.

The Cards opened the scoring in the first on hits by Brock and Groat and a sac-fly by Ken Boyer. The Yanks came back in the second on a 2-run homer by Tresh and hits by Clete Boyer, (who stole second) and Whitey (which scored Boyer). Linz walked putting Whitey on second. Richardson singled and Whitey tried to score but Brock gunned him down at the plate. Had he been safe the score would have been 4-1. Instead Ford had to go back to the mound and maybe was tired from running around the bases. The Cards reached him for a run on hits by Shannon and Sadecki. Both hurlers had RBI hits in the second.

The Yanks put another run on the board in the fifth and it stayed 4-2 going into the bottom of the sixth. Ken Boyer led off with a single. After an out, Moon Man Shannon came up. Well, he launched a 'moon shot' - it hit the big Budweiser sign in back of the stands, possibly a 500 foot homer. Score was tied at four. Ford, maybe having flashbacks of Hondo Howard blasts in '63, promptly yielded a double to McCarver. Downing came in to pitch and gave up a pinch-hit to Carl Warwick to break the tie. The Cards scored another on a triple by Flood to make it 6-4. The Yanks came back with one in the eighth to make it a one run game. However, Barney Schultz knuckled down to business and got Mantle to ground out with two on to finish their threat. The Cards put it away with three in the bottom of the inning, with BrocKs two-run double doing the most damage - Cards won 9-5. At least the Yanks had a moral victory – their five runs were one more than they scored in the entire 1963 Series.

Unknowing to everyone, Ford was done for the Series. He would need an operation on his arm. It was Whitey's last Series and he wound up with a 10-8 Series record.

Hoot Gibson hopefully was rested enough as the Cards hoped he could shoot down the Yanks to go up 2 - zip. The Yanks countered with their rookie ace, Mel Stottlemyre. Mel was 13-3 in Triple A and 9-3 with the Yanks (22-6 for the year). Unlike the fireballing Gibson, Stottlemyre had a great sinkerball and would usually get more than half his outs on ground balls to the infield.

At the start of the game it must have looked to the Yanks that they were facing a right-handed Koufax. Hoot started the game like Sandy did in game one of '63 – five consecutive Ks. Singles by Shannon and Maxvill gave the Cards a 1-0 lead in the third, but the Yanks tied it in the fourth on doubles by Howard and Pepitone.

In the sixth the Yanks broke the tie in what I refer to as Pinstripe intimidation. Mantle walked and then Pepitone was supposedly hit by a pitch. The only person in the world who saw it that way was the plate umpire. Most people would think I'm biased for my Pinstripe intimidation theory. Ever since 1953 when I started to follow baseball I think that umpires, even if it is subconsciously, give the close calls to the Pinstriped Yanks.

This umpire's call probably took away from Hoot's focus as he surrendered an RBI single to Tresh that gave the Yanks the lead. They scored twice in the seventh and four in the ninth and won 8-3. Stottlemyre went the route for the victory.

I was full of anticipation for game 3 at Yankee Stadium. I would be at the game in the reserved right field bleacher section with my Yankee-fan cousins Ron and Don. The match-up was Bulldog Bouton and southpaw Curt Simmons in a battle of 18-game winners. This would be Simmons first Series. He was a Phillie Whiz Kid in 1950 and his 17 wins helped put them in the Series. But just before the Series, Simmons got drafted and the Yanks didn't have to face him. (The draft board was probably comprised of Yankee fans).

Both pitchers were on their game. The score was tied at one going into the ninth inning. The Yanks scored first on an RBI double by Clete Boyer. The Cardinal run was driven in by Simmons (another RBI hit by a pitcher).

Simmons was still throwing fine after eight innings – but in the ninth St. Louis had two on with Simmons due to bat. Simmons was a decent hitter as evidenced by his RBI hit in the fifth, and in 1962 he hit .303 with 20 hits. Anyway, Keane took him out for pinch-hitter Bob Skinner. Bouton came in making the pitch too fat. Skinner blasted it toward us in the right field bleachers. As the ball was headed our way I was thinking the Daily News headlines would be "Yanks get Skinned", my cousin Ron was muttering something angrily and my 11-year old cousin Don's eyes had tears starting to form. Hitting a blast to right center in Yankee Stadium isn't always the best thing to do - it can be compared to hitting a blast in the Grand Canyon. Maris, who was playing center, ran it down – my cousins were happy, while I was muttering angrily, 'that in any other park it's a 3-run homer'.

Barney Schultz took the mound in the ninth. The Mick was leading off. In game one Schultz got him out in a big spot. Naturally I was hoping the old knuckler would be dancing. No dice, no fluttering – the pitch came in like a meatball with extra sauce. A Mantlesque shot wound up in the third tier in the right field stands. My 11-year old cousin Don was uncontrollably jumping up and down hollering joyfully "I knew it, I said a Hail Mary and an Act of Contrition." (No doubt to the delight of his Sunday school teachers). I was stunned. To this day it remains my worst single moment of following baseball. I did not watch the TV news or read the paper the next day. The news was all about the Mantle homer that not only won the game, but gave Mantle the World Series home run record with a total of 16, passing the Babe. Another one of Ruth's records falls in the Fall Classic.

All the way back to my cousin's in Brooklyn, I was thinking I'm a jinx and I am not going to the game tomorrow. I'll give my ticket to my uncle Eddie - he'll go to the game with his son and nephew. I'll watch it on TV.

On Sunday my cousins went to the early church services at St. Stanislaus which was around the corner. Since I was not going to the game I went to the late Mass. I also figured that if I go to church after my cousins, that God would respond to the more recent prayers. I hoped that my prayers would at least negate my cousins' earlier ones. I came back from church and waited for the game to start. Meanwhile my mom and Aunt Mary were in the kitchen talking and preparing dinner.

The pitchers were lefties, Al Downing and Ray Sadecki. The Cards went out in the first. The Yanks came up as I was anticipating a good performance from Sadecki, as his opening game stuff was hit pretty hard. It wasn't to be.

The Harmonica Kid, Linz, led off with a double to right. Like I said before, Linz is a free spirit type and tried to steal third. It's generally considered a Cardinal sin to attempt to steal third with none out. Well it turned out to be a sin for the Cardinals, when they had Linz in a run-down but botched it up with Linz winding up on third. Maybe this shook up Sadecki as he gave up a double to Richardson, and a single to Maris. Mantle came up and hit a single to right. However, he must have been thinking he was back in the '50's when he could really fly. He tried to stretch it into a double testing Moon Man Shannon, who had the best arm in the league this side of Clemente. Shannon threw a rocket to second to easily nail the Mick. That was it for Sadecki – four batters and four hits and two runs in only 1/3 of an inning – and that was thanks to Moon Man's throw to second.

Roger Craig was brought in to restore order. Since Craig was a starter 19 times during the season, relieving in the first would almost be like starting the game. After having lousy seasons in New York with the Mets in '62 and '63, Roger was due for some success in The Big Apple. However, the first batter, Elston Howard gave him a unfriendly welcome by singling in Maris with the third run of the inning. However after that, Roger made it lights out for the Yanks in his 4 2/3 innings of work. The Yanks did threaten in the third, but again the Mick came to the Cards' aid. After two outs Mantle and Howard walked. While Mick was on second, Dick Groat showed off his smarts as a Duke graduate by cleverly telling Mantle about his game-winning homer yesterday. The Mick may have been gloating as Groat snuck in behind him. Craig knew what was going on and spun around picking off Mantle - his second goof on the bases and it was only the third inning.

As the sixth inning began, Al Downing still looked like Koufax; in five innings he had five Ks and only gave up a weak hit and one walk. The Yanks should have known that the sixth was going to be a problem. Carl Warwick, (emulating Dusty Rhodes), was already on base in three consecutive games as a pinch-hitter (2 hits and a BB). He made it four with a lead-off single. He hit for Craig, so at least the Yanks wouldn't have to face him for the rest of

the game – his reliever could not be as effective as he was. Flood
followed with a hit. After an out, Groat hit a seemingly perfect
double play ball to second and Richardson seemed to have had
plenty of time to get the speedy Flood at second. However for some
reason Richardson had a problem getting the ball out his glove,
(maybe he was waiting to see if Linz was playing "Mary Had a
Little Lamb"). He made a bad toss to Linz and with Flood sliding
hard, Linz couldn't hold the ball. Maybe the Yanks were hurting
without Kubek playing as he and Richardson were a double play
tandem since their minor league days – and Richardson just wasn't
as comfortable with Linz at short. What a turn of events – instead of
the inning being over, the bags were loaded with the league's MVP
coming up, Ken Boyer.

My emotions were running wild. I was hollering "yeah, yeah",
after the Yanks messed up on the double play. My mom came out of
the kitchen wanting to know what was going on. I told her, "bases
loaded one out and guess who's up". She said "It's got to be
Kenny". I blurted out – "$10.00 for you if he hits one out".
Naturally of course she said "Sure" – after all what were the chances
since only one time did a National League player ever hit a Grand
Slam in World Series play (Chuck Hiller of the 1962 SF Giants).

Downing's first pitch was off the plate for a 1-0 count. His next
pitch is what people today say was a mistake. Most people say that
since Downing had one of the league's best fastballs and led the
league in Ks that's what he should have thrown. Possibly Downing
knowing Ken Boyer was a good fastball hitter wanted to cross him
up. Also, Boyer only had one hit for the Series, although yesterday
he hit a couple of fly-outs into the canyon. Anyway Downing threw
the change-up, and it changed the score – from down 3-0 to up 4-3.

I jumped off the chair, probably higher than when Mazeroski
homered in '60 – (but my mom jumped higher, she got $10.00). I
didn't care. I would have spent that much if I went to the game. But
the game wasn't over. The Yanks had almost half the game to play
and Craig was done.

The Cards brought in Ron Taylor, who had 8 wins and 7 saves,
but an ERA over 4.00. At this point the Yanks figured on getting
some runs. They say imitation is the sincerest form of flattery – so
Craig must have been flattered by Taylor's outing. It was probably
even better than Craig's. In Taylor's four innings, he only had
allowed one base runner, a walk to the Mick (he probably thought

it's easier to get him out running the bases). It was a good thing too, since the Cards didn't score after Ken Boyer's slam.

My uncle and cousins arrived back in Brooklyn and were not too happy, so all I said was "Good game". To this day, this is my best day ever following baseball. Funny-my worst and best day in my over 50 years of following baseball were 24 hours apart.

One thing that stood out for me regarding game 4 is that God does respond to the most recent prayer!

For game 5 my cousins had school – they weren't off for the Columbus Day holiday. They gave me their tickets and I asked a co-worker and his brother to go – they were Yankee fans, which was appropriate since my cousins were Yankee fans.

Game 5 was a rematch of the game 2 starters Stottlemyre and Hoot. This game turned out to be a pitcher's duel reminiscent of the '63 Series. It was scoreless until the fifth when the Cards scored twice – bringing to life the saying 'that baseball is a game of inches'. With one out Gibson hit a blooper to left that Tresh probably should have caught, but missed it by inches. Flood then hit a grounder to second but like yesterday Richardson muffed a double play ball that would have ended the inning. Brock then singled in Gibson and sent Flood to third. Still with one out, Bill White grounded another double play ball to Richardson. Richardson threw to Linz who had to hurry his throw to Pepitone because the jet-like Brock was bearing down on him. (Again it appears that the Yanks missed having Kubek at short). Pepitone caught it but my umpire intimidation theory didn't work - White was safe by inches as Flood scored the second run.

The two run lead held into the ninth as Hoot was shooting down Yanks with his fastball. The Mick led off and got on by a boot by Groat. After one out, Pepitone came and hit a shot at Gibson hitting him in the hip which caromed toward the third base line. (Gibson was also a very good basketball player at Creighton University and I read he played with the Harlem Globetrotters and this play resembled one of their acts). This one play personified Gibson's athletic ability, as in one motion, going away from first base, he grabbed the ball, and with his body falling toward third, threw his best fastball of the game – a submarine-type that beat Pepitone by an inch. (Hoot was quite a fielder and went on to win nine consecutive Gold Gloves – from 1965 -'73). The Yanks must have thought that the first base umpire had "Cardinal intimidation". I don't know if

Hoot got hurt on the play or lost his focus, but the next batter, Tresh crushed a regular fastball that was kind of fat. Score is tied 2-2 and I felt sick (ghosts of Ruth and Gehrig were acting up). Yankee fans say if the umpire didn't blow the call on Pepitone the Yankees would have won 3-2. I say no. If Pepitone was safe, Hoot would have pitched differently with two on base.

The Yanks still had Pete Mikkelson in there to start the tenth; he got the Yanks out of a jam in the eight and tossed a good ninth. He walked White to start the inning. Ken Boyer was up next. Another Cardinal rule in baseball is that the clean-up hitter does not sacrifice (one reason is that most of them don't know how). I knew Ken Boyer could bunt (after all, his rookie 1955 Topps baseball card depicts him bunting). Boyer laid down a beauty, caught the Yanks by surprise, and he had a bunt single. Groat followed with a missed sacrifice attempt, which trapped White in a run down. When the Yanks tried to get him going back to second, Bill alertly turned and beat the throw to third. After Groat forced Boyer, the Red Birds' top Series hitter, Tim McCarver, came up with runners on the corners and one out. The Yanks had a lefty Steve Hamilton ready in the 'pen. The ex-NBAer was almost an automatic out for left-handed hitters. Yogi opted to leave in Mikkelsen. After just missing a 3-run homer that made the count full, Mikkelsen came in too fat. McCarver blasted one into the Canyon. It was headed our way – my co-worker and his brother were not happy. At first I thought it was at least a sac-fly, then double or triple, and then it landed in the right field stands. Cards were up 5-2 with Hoot out there.

In the Yankee tenth Richardson got a hit. With two outs Maris hit a foul pop into the third base box seats. Ken Boyer made a tremendous lunge into the stands (and since this was not Wrigley Field), the fans got out of the way, and Boyer caught the ball to end the game. There is nothing better than going home up 3 games to 2.

A while back I saw an article about the most famous home runs in baseball history (i.e. Thomson's shot in '51, Maz in '60, the Hammer's #715). Mantle's, Ken Boyer's and McCarver's in games 3, 4 and 5 all were listed in the top 25.

Naturally, in game 6, I was watching and anticipating a victory for a St. Louis World Series Championship. The pitchers were the game 3 starters Bulldog Bouton and the crafty Simmons. After the Yanks went out in the first, the Cards started off like Bulldog was a "whipped puppy", as Flood and Brock led off with hits putting runners on first and third. Bouton induced White to ground into a double play. A run scored but the rally was over as Bouton went back to being a Bulldog.

Simmons kept the Yankee hitters off stride and held onto the 1-0 lead until he committed the Cardinal sin of giving up a two-out RBI hit to his adversary Bouton (seems like a lot of RBI hits by the pitchers). With the scored tied at one in the sixth, the M & M's were anything but sweet to Simmons as they banged out back to back homers to give the Yanks a 3-1 lead. After Simmons left the game, the Yanks put up five more runs to win 8-3 forcing a seventh game.

Poor Simmons he wound up with a fine 2.51 ERA but St. Louis lost both games he started. Sadecki had an 8.35 ERA but the Cards won both of his starts. So much for stats!

For game 7 both teams had their game 4 starter available (Sadecki and Downing). However, they both chose to go with their game 5 starters (Gibson and Stottlemyre) with only two days of rest. The Cards broke the scoreless tie in the fourth on some aggressive base running and shoddy Yankee fielding. Ken Boyer ignited the rally with a single, Groat walked and then McCarver grounded to Pepitone, who forced Groat at second. However, the shortstop Linz, possibly aware that McCarver had good speed for a catcher, rushed his throw which got by Stottlemyre who was covering first, allowing Ken Boyer to score. Moon Man then singled to put McCarver on third. With Maxvill up Shannon broke for second. As Howard threw to second, McCarver broke for home and scored. Maxvill then drove in Moon Man. Cards were up 3-0.

The Yanks sent up a pinch-hitter for Stottlemyre in the fifth, so Downing came in to pitch. He showed why it was probably not a good idea to start him. His first batter was Lou Brock, who hit a blast, like another Lou (Gehrig), onto the right field roof. Bill White singled and Ken Boyer doubled. White scored on a Groat ground out and Boyer, who had good speed, scored on a sac-fly to short right by McCarver beating Mantle's throw (he didn't have a Moon Man arm). The Cards were now up 6-0 and I was pretty happy – but not for long. The Yanks cut the lead in half in the sixth, two hits and the Mick coming up. He rocked one to the opposite field, into the left field bleachers. It was now 6-3.

In the seventh with two outs Ken Boyer, not to be outshone by Mantle, also slammed a home run into the left field bleachers (which left him a triple short of a cycle). It was now 7-3.

Hoot had a four run lead going into the ninth. He was running on fumes. He was alternating Ks and homers. He K'd Tresh and Ken's brother Clete homered, then he K'd Blanchard, but Linz homered. Richardson broke the alternating. He already set a Series record of 13 hits and had M & M following him. Richardson ended the suspense and popped out to Maxvill to give the Cardinals the World Series Championship.

The Yanks may have won five consecutive pennants, but out of the five only two World Series Championships.

The Cards had a bunch of heroes. Naturally Hoot was the Series MVP with his two complete game victories and a Series record 31 Ks. McCarver hit .478 and won game 5. Brock hit .300, Warwick tied a pinch-hitting record and there were Craig's and Taylor's relief performances in game 4. And then there was my favorite, Ken Boyer. His heroics are not given their due. He only hit .222 but his hits were all instrumental in the St. Louis victories. (In the games, the Yanks won, Boyer was 0 for 12). Boyer's lead-off hit in game 1 started the winning rally. In Game 4 his 'Slam was the winner. In game 5 he had a bunt single that set up McCarver's game-winning homer, and in the finale he had one of the best game 7 for a batter in Series history as his single, double and homer were responsible for four runs.

You would think everything would be great in St. Louis. August Busch, the Cardinal and Budweiser owner was all set to give the manager Johnny Keane a new contract. During the year when the Cards were seemingly going nowhere it was a forgone conclusion Keane would be fired at the end of the year (supposedly the former 1934 Cardinal Gas House Gang shortstop Leo "The Lip" Durocher was all set to take over). Before Busch could offer the contract, Keane resigned.

Half-way across the country Yogi was expecting to be re-hired with a raise or maybe a multi-year contract. Everybody was surprised when Yogi was fired. "Why?" was the big question. He got his team to win the pennant over the Orioles and Chisox, who were both maybe better than the Yanks. Plus he took the Cardinals to seven games without Ford being of much use. What a turn of events for Yogi (and George Steinbrenner wasn't even around yet). Probably it was Major Houk, the ex-military man, wanted more of a General Patton-type manager and Yogi did not fit that bill. One reason that Keane submitted his resignation to the Cardinals was that it was already a done deal that he would become the Yankee manager in '65.

CBS's new team lost the World Series but at least they had the manager of the World Series Champions.

1965
The Yankees Get a KEANE Manager

For the first time in my life I felt elated since I went through the off-season having my team being the World Series Champions. I was now anticipating a repeat championship. Their starting line-up was intact and their three top starters were back. They did trade their fourth starter Roger Craig for Cincy's Bob Purkey. They also traded for Tracy Stallard, famous for giving up the famous Maris 61st homer, from the Mets. Even though he had 20 losses in 1964, the Cards were optimistic that Stallard would have a successful season, like Roger Craig did in '64.

The big change was the manager. Johnny Keane, more or less, told the owner, Gussie Busch, what to do with his contract renewal. Personally I was not a Keane fan. I was glad when Red Schoendienst (and not the rumored Durocher) replaced him. Red was the Cardinal All-Star second baseman when I began following baseball, and he was one of my favorite players, even when he played for the Giants and Braves, going on to a Hall of Fame career.

I couldn't wait for the season to begin. At work I would rap with other Cardinal fans about another championship, probably against the Yankees again – after all they won nine of the past ten American League pennants. However, I cautioned my Cardinal fan co-workers that don't count the Yankees in because they have a" Keane" manager.

The Cardinals did not keep up their part to have a repeat Yankees/Cardinals Series. They had a horrible year. During this era, most players began to fade in their mid-30s. This year Ken Boyer and Dick Groat were 34 and Curt Simmons was 36. All three had huge drop-offs from '64. Out of their All-Star infield only White put up decent numbers (24 homers, .289 average but his 73 RBIs were 29 less than in 1964). Boyer, coming off of his MVP year, hit 35 points lower, 11 fewer homers, and 34 RBIs fewer than in 1964.

Groat only hit .254, and Julian Javier missed more than half the year.

In the outfield Curt Flood had another fine year hitting .310. Lou BrocKs year was decent (.288 average, 63 SBs, 107 runs) but it was also a drop from his .348 of '64. Moon Man Shannon missed a third of the season, but when he played it was like he was out in space. Tim McCarver did OK at .276 and 11 homers, but missed a lot of games.

The pitching is where the Cards really were off the mark. Last year Simmons and Ray Sadecki were 38-20 – this year they would be 15-30. Hoot was the mainstay of the staff with his first 20-win season (20-12). The staff was so bad that the only other double digit winners were the new additions Purkey (10) and Stallard (11).

With this type of performance the Cards finished a dismal seventh – one game under .500.

The Dodgers scored less runs than all the teams except the expansion Houston Colt 45's, oops, wait I mean the Houston Astros, their new moniker as they were now playing in the Astrodome, and Mets. Sweet Lou Johnson and Jim Lefebvre led LA in homers with 12 while Willie Davis with 10 was the only other Dodger to reach double digits in home runs. As a team they only hit 78 homers with Drysdale blasting 7. In fact Drysdale was their best hitter - in addition to his homers he batted .300 (39 for 130) with 19 RBIs. However, they also yielded the lowest amount of runs, courtesy of the dynamic duo of Koufax (26-8, 2.04 ERA, and Major League record 382 strikeouts) and Drysdale (23-12, 2.77 ERA), plus reliever Ron Perranoski (6 wins & 17 saves) coming out of the 'pen. Their anemic offense was just enough to get their two aces a couple of runs to post their 49 victories. In fact in September Sandy threw his fourth career no-hitter defeating the Cubs 1-0 as their pitcher Bob Hendley was a hard-luck loser as he tossed a one-hitter.

The Giants came in second finishing two games out despite MVP Say Hey with his 52 homers and McCovey with 39 homers. Marichal was 22-13. But the Koufax/Drysdale tandem was just too much to overcome.

My only solace in 1965 was the performance of the Yanks. When Keane signed with the Yanks, he probably thought he was walking into a dynasty. Nowadays, reading about the '65 Yanks, it says that CBS got a paper tiger, but people at that time thought the Yankees were still a juggernaut. The team of '65 was a young team and had World Series experience. Only Ford and Howard were in their mid-30s fading skills age. Their infield was young – Pepitone was 24, Richardson 29, Kubek and C. Boyer 28. The Mick was the old man in the outfield at 34. Maris was 31 and Tresh 27.

Their pitchers, outside of Ford, were all young and already proved to be good. Bouton was 26, Downing 24, and Stottlemyre 23. Their relievers also appeared to have several years ahead of them – Ramos was 30, Hamilton 31, and Mikkelsen and Reniff 26.

This was a team I thought that even Johnny Keane couldn't screw up. The Yanks proved me wrong. I don't know if the Yankees resented the National League manager, but they didn't produce and were beset with injuries. Their only infielder to hit over .250 was Clete Boyer (and that by one point at .251). Tresh was the only asset in the outfield, hitting 26 homers with a .279 average. Maris only had 155 at bats. The Mick was hurt most of the year missing a third of it – he hit .255 with 19 homers. The catcher, Howard, was hurt, also missing a third of the season and posting poor stats (.233, 9 homers, 45 RBIs). The Yanks had a team batting average of only .235.

On the mound the Yanks didn't do much better. Stottlemyre was one of the league's best at 20-9, and old man Ford was 16-13. Bulldog Bouton was in the doghouse all year (4-15). Downing was 12-14 and had a decent 3.40 ERA, but suffered from the weak Yankee offense. Ramos was effective out of the 'pen with 5 wins and 19 saves. (Poor Pedro, for years he was on lousy teams. He finally gets to the dynasty Yankees and literally gets them into the 1964 Series only to be ineligible. Now the '65 season begins and Pedro is full of hope which is quickly squashed as the Yanks turned into the Washington Senators of his past). An interesting Yankee pitching note: When I was in seventh grade my high school (Belleville, NJ) had an All-State pitcher named Jack Cullen. Well in '65 Cullen made it to the Yanks and was 3-4 with a 3.05 ERA.

The Yankees finished in sixth place with a record of 77-85 and 25 games out. For Yankee Haters, The Glory Years Part 1 began.

The Minnesota Twins won the pennant even with slugger Harmon Killebrew missing 50 games (he still hit 25 homers). Batting champ Tony Oliva (.321) and shortstop MVP Zoilo Versalles who led the league with 126 runs, 12 triples (tied with Bert Campaneris) and 45 doubles (tied with Carl Yastrzemski) were the top Twin batsmen.

"Mudcat" Grant, who was the AL's top pitcher leading the league with 21 wins, 6 shutouts and a .750 winning %, and Jim Kaat (18 wins) were the "Twin" aces. Al Worthington showed his worth in the 'pen with 10 victories and 21 saves. Camilo Pascual was hurt most of the year, but he did go 9-3. Pascual and Pedro Ramos, both from Cuba, were teammates on those lousy Senator teams of the 1950's. The Senators are now the Twins (American League Champs). Pedro probably wishes he never left them lousy Senators.

One other American League note was that the Los Angeles Angels changed their name to the California Angels.

The Series was going to begin on a Jewish holiday. The Dodgers' Sandy Koufax observed the holiday, so Drysdale had to open the Series. Poor Dodgers, they only had a 23-game winner starting instead of a 26-game winner.

The Twins took advantage of not having to face Sandy. Similar to the way General Grant took Richmond, Mudcat took Los Angeles in the opener, 8-2. In game 2 the Ks met - Koufax and Kaat. After five scoreless innings, the Twins scored 2 in the sixth. The Dodgers only got one run off Kaat and lost 5-1.

The Dodgers were down 2 games and had their unheralded lefty Claude Osteen to get them back in the Series. Osteen was 15-15 but had a fine 2.79 ERA. He met the challenge tossing a five-hit shutout to put the Dodgers back in it. Drysdale got even with Grant beating him 7-2 to even the Series and Koufax got even with Kaat throwing a four-hit shutout. Dodgers were up 3 games to 2 and had Osteen ready to wrap it up. Mudcat would face him on two days rest and beat him 5-1 (he also belted a 3-run homer), deadlocking the Series at 3 games apiece. The Dodgers had Drysdale with three days rest ready to go, or Koufax with two days. They wisely chose Sandy with Drysdale ready in relief. Not necessary, Koufax threw another shutout – a three-hitter. Sandy threw 18 scoreless innings and gave up only seven hits within three days. Naturally he was the Series MVP – his second in three years. The Dodger batters had a "fairly" decent average of .274 especially when you consider they only hit .245 for the year. For LA Ron Fairly led their offense (.379, 11 for 29, 3 doubles, 2 homers, 6 RBIs, 7 runs scored). Again this must have aggravated Brooklynites as it was the Los Angeles Dodgers' third World Series title in eight years – while in Brooklyn they only had one in over fifty years.

In the New York battle for fans, the Mets outdrew the Yankees by over half a million. One reason for that may have been that the Mets picked up Yogi as a player/coach. The Mets even though they came in last place again, had the funniest quips going. Yogi and Casey were back together. However, that was short lived as Casey injured his hip and at 75 had to retire after about 100 games. Coach Wes Westrum took over for him.

Another factor that would keep the Yankee Hater Glory Years going was that Major League Baseball enacted a draft, whereas all high school and college players would be selected by teams in inverse order of their place in the standings. No longer could the Yankee $$$$ sign the cream of the crop - at least not for ten years when free agency would emerge.

1965
I Become a Yankee (Sort of)

I was being drafted, no, not by a Major League team, but by the U.S. Army. I guess I sort of would be like a Yankee. At this time the Vietnam War was escalating. I was notified to report to the induction center in Newark on October 20, so I took off two weeks from work prior to that. I was able to watch the whole 1965 Series.

On October 20 I went down to the induction center. The people there were from my town and North Newark, which borders my town. There were about 10 guys I knew from my town. After going through paperwork and some physical checks, we boarded a bus to Ft. Dix in central New Jersey. I was sitting next to this guy Domenick. We talked on the way to Ft. Dix. I found out he came over from Italy when he was ten, and he was a soccer and track star at Barringer (the North Newark High School). Eventually we were put in the same battalion and while on leave seven months later I went over to his house and saw his sister. To make a long story short, I married her three years later. So I was sitting next to my future brother-in-law.

We arrived at Ft. Dix in the afternoon and were hustled around – being assigned a barrack, getting uniforms, inoculations, etc. Another traumatic event was getting your hair cut (all of it, buzzzzzz!). At this time short hair was out and the Beatles look was in. My hair was never too long but since I was going into the Army I let it grow longer than usual.

Well there I am, in the chair with the clippers going buzzzzzz. My hair is falling all over the floor. The army barber shop had a radio on. What they announced on the sports round-up floored me. Here I am losing my hair and the announcer saying –"the Cardinals and Mets just completed a deal, Ken Boyer to the Mets for Al Jackson, their best pitcher, and third baseman Charlie Smith". I thought, "What is it with the Cardinals always getting Met pitchers," (they had Craig and Stallard and now Jackson).

October 20, 1965 was a bad day for me and Ken Boyer. I was drafted into the U.S. Army, so I was sort of a Yankee and Boyer was traded to the lowly Mets. I didn't know who was worse off, me or Boyer. He would have probably changed places with me if he could.

1965
The Babe at Fenway

From Ft. Dix we were sent to Ft. Devens in western Massachusetts for basic training. In November the Vietnam War was heating up. The Ia Drang Valley battle just took place (that was the backdrop of the 2002 Mel Gibson movie "We Were Soldiers" that was based on the 1992 book by Harold G. Moore and Joseph L. Galloway). At Ft. Devens most of us who were at the induction center in Newark on October 20 were assigned to the newly formed 196th Light Infantry Brigade. The Army was trying something new – we would stay together as a unit for our two year period. I didn't feel that good about being in a light brigade. The last light brigade I recall was the Lord Alfred Tennyson famous poem "The Charge of the Light Brigade" – and they did not fare too well.

Anyway, it was in the middle of our eight weeks of basic training when our platoon leaders wanted to know who wanted to go the Boston Patriots (they weren't called New England yet) game. In 1965, the AFL and NFL were enemies. In order to put people in the seats the Patriots gave tickets to the Army. In case you don't know, basic training is not a pleasant experience so I figured going to a pro football game (even if it was the AFL) would be a great diversion. Besides I'd get to see Fenway Park.

We had about five or six Army buses ready to roll to Boston. To get there we had to go through Cambridge where Harvard University is located. As our olive drab colored caravan went through Cambridge the student peaceniks were hollering at us and throwing things at the buses. We were all draftees and didn't want to be in the Army but what could we do. We opened our windows and shouted back, giving them finger and arm gestures, and throwing whatever we could at them. It would not surprise me if some of these peaceniks are now in Congress.

We finally got to the game. I was awed by being in Fenway, but a gridiron instead of a diamond takes away some of the effect of being there. I thought it was ironic that I was where Babe Ruth started his career, and the Patriot quarterback was Vito "Babe" Parilli. I'm not kidding when I say I saw the Babe play at Fenway.

The weather was damp and cold. I and a lot of the other soldiers spent the second half in the walkway. I don't even know who won the game. However, I have to give credit to New England football fans who stare Old Man Winter in the face to cheer for their teams.

Our bus caravan back to Ft. Devens took a different route. It didn't go through Cambridge.

1966
From the Penthouse to the Basement in Two Years

As the year began I just finished up basic training. In January our unit, the 196th Light Infantry Brigade, would begin Advanced Infantry Training (AIT). When in the army you are with guys from all over the country. I soon discovered the Yankees were hated by the rest of the country. In our little amount of leisure time I would spend time talking a lot of sports stuff and playing touch football. While in AIT I was sent to D Company. My future brother-in-law, Domenick, and most of the others from my home area stayed in C Company, so I had to make some new buddies.

To build company camaraderie, a basketball league was started with each company having a team. Although not having played for the high school team, I thought I was a decent player having played a lot of pick-up on the playgrounds. I was a good shooter and being 5'10" and 190 pounds could set a good pick. However, when they had the tryouts I could see I was out of my league. These guys were All-Stars in high school and were much faster and taller than me except our star, flashy Ed Courton who was only 5'8". He was quick and scored about 20 a game in college (he got about 30 ppg for us). One of our forwards was the dependable, sweet-shooting Charlie Houston, who told us about his cousin, Wade Houston who was playing at the University of Louisville. (Wade eventually coached his son Allan at the University of Tennessee, who was an NBA star with the NY Knicks). Also, there was our instant spark guy, Bob Marsh, and the do-everything rugged Bill Garman, who were main ingredients in our team's success. But one of the guys I hung around with was a real workhorse for the team with his rebounding and scoring. He was Bruce Bergey, who was 6'5", fast, strong, and could get off the ground. He would tell me about his brother Bill, a linebacker at Arkansas State, (before he went on to NFL stardom with the Philadelphia Eagles making All-Pro four times). Bruce played a year for the Kansas City Chiefs as a tight end and then played in the Canadian Football League (CFL). I was surprised I made the team, even though I was a scrub. I averaged 2 points, 1 rebound and 1 foul per game in my five minutes or so. We went undefeated and won all our games by over 20 points. This was a great diversion from everyday Army life.

As spring was approaching our unit was sent to Camp Drum by Watertown, New York for military maneuvers. It was pretty cold there, (it snowed in May), and I didn't think it was a good place to train if we were going to a humid, hot place like Viet Nam. Word was out that our unit was to be deployed in the Dominican Republic, replacing the 82nd Airborne in June so we had a month or so of riot control training which is what you do there. However, the Dominican Republic had a political change of some kind and the US troops were pulled out so our destination would be Viet Nam.

One of my traits is I have a problem with authority or superiors, especially if I don't agree with them. It's not that I don't do what they want but I sometimes question it and make smart aleck remarks about it. As a kid my dad made me stand in the corner a lot, in school I got detention, at work my bosses sometimes hollered at me, referees or umpires threatened to toss me out of the park when I coached and my wife is often mad at me all because of my mouth. So in the Army I became an expert on KP (Kitchen Police detail) because I'd question and smart aleck my sergeants. As a soldier I was probably more of a Beetle Bailey type than a GI Joe. In fact, if you asked me who my favorite Beatle was, it wouldn't be John, Paul, George, or Ringo, it would be Beetle Bailey. (Actually my preferred music is Motown such as the Temptations, the Supremes, etc.).

As the '66 baseball season was approaching, being in the army made it difficult to keep abreast of what was going on. There was another franchise changing their location. The Milwaukee Braves moved their teepees to Atlanta becoming the Major Leagues' first team in Dixie. Naturally I was hoping St. Louis would rebound from sixth place and I was also interested in the Mets, outside of the Cards. I was always pulling for them to improve and now that Ken Boyer was with them my interest increased.

The Cardinals again came in sixth. The Cards traded Groat and White to the Phils at the end of 1965 for pitcher Art Mahaffey (1-4) and Alex Johnson (.186 in 25 games), who both were ineffective. After 20 games, Ray Sadecki was traded for Orlando Cepeda, and he led the Cards offense (.303, 17 homers). Moon Man returned to respectability (.288, 16 homers). McCarver and Brock again had decent years, but Flood's batting fell to.267.

For St. Louis their star remained Hoot Gibson, who again was one of the leagues' best (21-12, 2.44 ERA). Al Jackson, who they got for Boyer, pitched well (2.51 ERA), but must have felt like he was with the Mets, as his record was only 13-15. Getting some time on the mound were Nellie Briles (4-15) and a 21-year old, Steve (Lefty) Carlton.

The Mets, with Ken Boyer in the line-up, improved by 16 games; and it was the first year they didn't lose 100 games. Boyer's year was similar to the year before, as he was second on the team in homers (14) and hit .266. The Mets also escaped the cellar and played over .400 ball. They were 7 1/2 games ahead of the last place Cubs. (Funny, that in only three years these two cellar dwellers would fight it out for the 1969 NL East pennant).

The no-offense Dodgers won the National League flag again, by one and a half games over their rival Giants. Koufax and Drysdale shocked the baseball world by becoming a holdout tandem. The Dodgers backed down and paid Sandy $125,000 and Don $110,000. Sandy justified his raise by going 27-9 with a 1.73 ERA and 317 Ks. Drysdale didn't live up to his salary (13-16, 3.42 ERA). However, some of his possible wins were picked up by "the Vulture", Phil Regan. Nicknamed so because of his scavenger-type ability to pick up wins, he was the leagues' top reliever (14-1, 21 saves with an ERA better than Sandy's at 1.65). Somehow, the Dodgers held off their rival Giants despite the seasons of their Famers (Say Hey hit 33 homers, McCovey 36 and Gaylord Perry was 21-8, 2.99 ERA). Poor Marichal could never get a Cy Young award with Sandy around – he was 25-6 with a 2.23 ERA.

In May, our unit found out we were going to Viet Nam, since the Dominican Republic deployment went by the boards. Sometime in August we'd be on our way to 'Nam. Sometime in May I was home on a weekend pass as was my buddy Domenick from C Company. Since we lived only a few miles apart we decided to go out and party. When I went to pick him up, he wasn't ready so I went into his house. As I entered I saw a young attractive girl around 18 or so. I knew Dom had a big family but was unaware he had a younger sister. We talked a little, and then Dom and I went out. After the weekend, on the way back to Massachusetts, I asked him about his sister. He didn't think she was going with anyone. So the next week I was off I asked her out. I guess she didn't have her glasses on because she said yes.

This year the CBS writers couldn't come up with a better horror show than what the Yankees scripted. They were hoping that 1965 was an aberration. The Yanks eliminated the suspense early by losing 16 of their first 20. Johnny Keane was not feeling too keen at this time as the Yanks fired him. Unfortunately he passed away within a year of his firing.

With the Yanks in last place, GM Major Houk came out of the front office to try to lead his troops to victory like he did in the Battle of the Bulge in WWII. However, on a comparable level if the troops he led in WWII were as effective as these Yanks, the United States would be part of the Third Reich.

The Yankee pitching finished up in the middle of the pack as far as ERA went, but their won-loss record did not reflect this. Stottlemyre, who won 20 in 1965, lost 20 this year despite a 3.80 ERA. Ford was hurt most of the year but was 2-5 with a low 2.47 ERA and Bouton was 3-8 with a low 2.70 ERA. Their best pitcher was Fritz Peterson at 12-11.

The Yankee offense was in bad shape. The Mick missed a third of the season but bounced back from a miserable '65 to hit .288 with 23 homers. Pepitone hit 31 homers and Tresh hit 27 but only hit .233 as did Maris but with only 9 homers. The Yanks matched their '65 batting average of .235. In addition, by the end of the year their former World Series double play combo would be gone as Kubek retired at the young age of 28 in 1965 and Richardson would retire at only 30 after the '66 season. All of this combined to have the Yanks (70-89) finish in last place for the first time since 1912. With the Mets not coming in last, it seemed New York would avoid having a cellar dweller, but the Yankees would not let that occur for the city. (Maybe CBS thought that being like the Mets would help attendance, as the Mets' fans kept coming despite the team's inept play. The Mets again clobbered the Yanks in the attendance war).

Let's get back to the real war. I don't remember which one it was, but one of President Johnson's daughters got married in August of '66 when I went to 'Nam. Our unit, the 196th Light Infantry Brigade, raised the number of military personnel in 'Nam to 300,000. We were near the Cambodian border close to a big hill known as Black Virgin Mountain. Being the first troops in this area we had to build a base camp. Everybody had a detail specialty - mine was becoming a bunker engineer, which consisted of mostly filling sandbags. One of my sergeants, who was known as Sgt. "Jelly Belly", tried to motivate me by calling me the Stan the Man of sandbags since he knew I was a Cardinal fan. Sgt. Jelly Belly was quite a character – he won $3.00 on a dare to swan dive off of a dike into a rice paddy, but really he should have only taken $2.00 since his dive was more like a belly flop.

After we got the base camp in decent shape, and had some free time, we dug out some of our recreation equipment - some bats, mitts, and softballs. We found some open area and laid out a softball field. I was with the mortar platoon of D Company. We had four squads of five or six. Anyway, we had a game –squads 1 & 2 vs. 3 & 4. I was pitching for 1 & 2 and Sgt Jelly Belly for 3 & 4. I was a good hitter with no speed so I was noted for running home runs into doubles. But I did get the winning hit off of Sgt Jelly Belly. I could tell he wasn't happy.

A few days later, our D Company recon platoon said they wanted to play us. Our mortar platoon team (consisting of all four squads) was put together by Sgt. Jelly Belly. I guess he was still mad at me because he didn't pick me. Some of the guys he did pick asked me what position I'd be playing since Sgt. Jelly Belly would be pitching. They were surprised he didn't pick me as I was a better softball player than a basketball player. Anyway I watched the game and saw Sgt. Jelly Belly get lit up as we got crushed. Some of the guys said we lost because I didn't play. I said nah! We lost by too much for me to matter – but maybe if I pitched it could have been different.

In 'Nam it was hard to follow baseball. But we did get the army paper "The Stars and Stripes" and our communication bunker had a radio. Having breakfast on Oct. 6, I heard some of the guys saying they had the World Series on in the big communication bunker (it was always manned). The game was on 2:30 a.m. or something like that in Viet Nam time. The Orioles won the game 5-2 with Moe Drabowsky (who's previous claim to fame was giving up Stan the Man's 3000th hit) setting some kind of Series strikeout record, with six in a row and eleven in relief. Frank and Brooks Robinson both went yard for the Birds.

My tent was close to this bunker so I found out who was manning it on the a.m. shift and asked him to wake me when the World Series began. So at 2:30 a.m. he woke me up and I went to listen to the game. Koufax was going against some young guy Palmer, who I knew little about, but he was the Orioles top pitcher at 15-10.

The Orioles won the pennant fairly easy thanks to one of baseball's most lopsided trades. The Reds traded Frank Robinson (who Cincy felt was an old 30) for Milt Pappas, a solid Oriole pitcher. Pappas had a very good career winning almost 100 games in each league (110 in AL, 99 in NL) but was nowhere close to Frank Robinson's career, who in my opinion should have been on the All-Century Team. Rumor was that Cincy really traded him because he would question authority and be curt with the quips (he was sort of like me, except for a little more baseball talent). All he did for the O's was win the Triple Crown (.316, 49 homers, 122 RBIs) and was the AL MVP becoming the first player to win it in both leagues. Combining with his namesake, Brooks, and Boog Powell, they all had over 100 RBIs. The O's also had Luis Aparicio (.276, 97 runs scored) at short. A batter would have needed one of our 106 recoilless rifles to drive a ball through the left side of the infield with Brooks at third and Aparicio at short.

Joining Palmer on the hill were starters Dave McNally (13-6), Steve Barber (10-6) and Wally Bunker (10-5) while relievers Stu Miller and Eddie Fisher (not the singer) totaled 14 wins and 26 saves. Miller was known for having the slowest change-up in the Majors and is often remembered for being charged with a balk in the 1961 All-Star Game when the notorious wind at Candlestick Park in San Francisco (ironically his home field as he was a Giant then) blew him and his 165 lbs. off of the mound in the ninth inning causing the AL to tie the game – despite that he wound up getting credit for the win in the NL's 5-4 ten inning victory.

My old Yankee nemesis, the old Marine from the Copa Incident in '57, Hank Bauer, managed this team. I wonder if the Orioles used any "Stan the Man Bauer" bats like I did back in 1957.

The game went on for four innings until Dodger center fielder Willie Davis became Palmer's best friend. In the fourth inning Davis, lost two balls in the sun and threw one into the stands (this was uncharacteristic of Davis who would eventually win three Gold Gloves). Dodgers were down 3-0 and this Palmer guy was not going to let the anemic Dodger offense do anything. When the O's got 2 in the eighth, I went back to my tent for a few more zzz's. Palmer won 6-0 on a four-hitter beating the famous Koufax (of course on this day he had Paul Blair in center, not Willie Davis).

Unknown to everyone, it was Sandy's last game, as his arthritic elbow put an end to baseball's greatest pitcher ever. He was medically forced to retire after a 27-win season. This guy Palmer, who beat him, went on to become sort of a right-handed version of Sandy, winning three Cy Young Awards and having a stretch of being a 20-game winner in eight out of nine seasons during the '70's.

The Dodgers lost the next two games by the score of 1-0 (on solo homers by Blair in game 3 and Frank Robinson in game 4). Wally Bunker (an appropriate name considering where I was) threw a six-hit shutout in game 3 and Dave McNally did even better in game 4 tossing a four-hit whitewashing. The Dodgers would wind up being shutout the last three games of the Series scoring only 2 total runs (even worse than the 1963 Yanks). Frank Robinson was Series MVP via his triple, 2 homers and 3 RBIs (which was one more than the whole Dodger team had).

Prior to going to 'Nam, my mother had surgery for breast cancer (it was the end of May). In the middle of October, about a week or so after the Series, our unit was to partake in Operation Attleboro, up to that point the largest operation of the war. Our mortar squad's job was to be ready to protect our 105 howitzers if we were attacked. We were there about a week when one of our sergeants came up to me and informed me that he had bad news. He told me my mother had passed away. A Viet Cong mortar round would not have shocked me more than this news did.

The Army got me home as soon as possible. Since my dad lost his wife and his brother a few months apart, the Army did not send me back to 'Nam. I was reassigned to Ft. Dix, NJ.

1967

The Yanks Couldn't Give a HOOT about this World Series

As the year began I was back at Ft. Dix, where I began my army career. When I arrived there for my new unit, I informed them that I had two years of experience working in the Newark, NJ Post Office. They assigned me to be the mail clerk for the 1st Advance Infantry Training (AIT) Brigade. (The Brigade consisted of six companies). Within a month I streamlined the whole working process of the mail so that when five more companies were added, me and the other clerks could handle it and still have some free time. I shed my Beetle Bailey image and became the GI Joe of the mail room which resulted in a promotion.

There were three of us Brigade Mail Clerks. If we worked hard, two of us could process the morning mail and later we would catch up with the paper work. There was this Friday night that I had to get home. I still lived in Belleville which was 70 miles from Ft. Dix. The other clerks told me to head out on Thursday night and they'd cover for me on Friday. Well, early Friday morning one of my buddies called and said the other guy went on sick call. I told him to hang tight and that I would be there in an hour or so. I quickly washed up, threw on my Army fatigues, jumped in my car, and headed down the Jersey Turnpike. I was about halfway there, going about 75 mph, (the speed limit was 60 mph). However, even at 75 mph vehicles were still passing me. I'm driving along when I see in my rearview mirror the red and blue lights of a NJ State Trooper. He pulled me over, but I wasn't that concerned as I was in my Army uniform. I figured on getting a warning (I don't know, I thought there would be a common respect thing between the military and State Troopers – like I'm heading back to my base to serve my country). Obviously he could have cared less and gave me the ticket.

After he left I was seething, I surmised that he must be a Commie – after all who else would give a serviceman a ticket during a war? Where was Senator Joe McCarthy of Wisconsin when you needed him? (I forgot that the Senator passed away in 1957).

I had to go to court in Monroe, NJ. I never heard of Monroe and was surprised that there was a town named for Joe DiMaggio's ex. I went to court properly prepared – a fresh haircut, a starched uniform complete with my Vietnam ribbons and Combat Infantryman's Badge, and spit-polished shoes that would have made Nippy Jones of the 1957 Braves proud. While waiting with my fellow traffic violators there was a consensus that GI Joe (me) was a lock to beat the rap. The judge looked like he was from the WW II era and hopefully he'd be patriotic and give me a warning. Wrong again. The judge suspended my license for 30 days and fined me $25. Once again I thought, "Senator McCarthy, where are you?" I could not understand central NJ. To me it seemed to be populated by Commies. I would never want to live there. ("Never" ended three years later when I bought a house smack dab in the middle of central Jersey in South Brunswick - the town next to Monroe).

Being the Brigade mail clerk gave me ample time to follow baseball. Every morning I would get the Philadelphia newspaper on the way to pick up the mail. If a game from Philly was on in the afternoon I'd listen to it on the mail room radio.

As the season began, the Red Sox, who finished only a half game ahead of the cellar dweller Yanks in '66, were given little or no chance to win the pennant. The Cardinals were expected to do a little better than Boston in the American League, but they too were given little hope to take the National League flag.

The Cardinals winning the pennant was even more of a surprise considering that their ace, Hoot Gibson, was out for almost two months after getting smacked in the leg by a line drive on July 15 by Roberto Clemente. Gibson, after getting up from the line drive, showed the type of competitor he was by facing another batter unaware that his leg was broken. He was headed for another 20-win season, but this incident ended that. St. Louis was in first at the time and the other teams thought they would fold like a deck of cards. St. Louis brought Nellie Briles out of the 'pen – and all he did was win nine straight and finished 14-5 for the year. A young Lefty Carlton won 14 games and Ray Washburn chipped in with 10 more. But the surprise was Dick Hughes (16-6, 2.66 ERA), who was runner-up for

NL Rookie of the Year and should have probably won it. He only had this one good year as a sore arm the next year ended his career. Hoot came back in the beginning of September and won three in a row to finish at 13-7.

The offense was led by NL MVP Orlando "Cha Cha" Cepeda (25 homers, .325 average, and league leading 111 RBIs), Lou Brock (.299, 206 hits and a league leading 113 runs) and Curt Flood (.335, fourth in the league). Tim McCarver, who was the MVP runner-up, chipped in at .295. But the surprise was the former Yankee, Roger Maris. With "Cha Cha" leading them the Cardinals were known as "El Birdos".

After two years with the CBS comedy team, the Yankees, Maris was calling it quits until the Yanks told him to wait, and they traded him to St. Louis for Charlie Smith. Who is this Smith guy? He got traded to St. Louis for a star (Ken Boyer) and then dealt to the Yanks for another star (Maris). Roger Maris hated the big city and agreed not to retire when traded to St. Louis. Roger never regained his home run swing from a wrist injury sustained with the Yanks. Maris didn't provide a lot of stats (.261, 9 homers), but his presence and leadership fit the Cards like a glove.

One of the company mail clerks in my Brigade was from St. Louis. I told him when they come to Philly we'll go to a game (about an hour away). We went to the game and sat in the stands by third base. Dick Allen was the Phillie third baseman and was known for his glove of stone. Throughout the game I kept hollering for the St. Louis batters to hit it to Allen. Allen kept on glaring toward us. Anyway, late in the game with the score tied a hard one was hit to him and he botched it up and the Cards went on to win.

The Cards won the flag rather easily by 10 1/2 games over San Francisco. The Giants' star was the Cy Young winner, Mike McCormick (22-10). This was his teammate Juan Marichal's year for the award - with Koufax retired and Hoot injured he was the favorite, but no, he picked the wrong time to have an off-year. Despite a low 2.76 ERA his won-loss slate was only 14-10.

The Mets fell back into the cellar, again losing over 100 games. However, the future showed promise. The Mets had the NL Rookie of the Year in pitcher Tom Seaver who had a terrific season. He was 16-13 with a 2.76 ERA.

The Yanks improved from last year to 72-90 as they won two more games than in 1966 and climbed out of the basement to finish ninth. Their offense was horrible. As a team they hit .225. Mantle led them with 22 homers, but hit only .255. The offense was so bad that their RBI leader was Pepitone with 64.

Stottlemyre again pitched well with a 2.96 ERA, but due to a lack of offense, finished with a 15-15 record. Downing was 14-10 with a 2.63 ERA. Ford was in only seven games and had a low 1.64 ERA, but was 2-4 due to little run support. It was Whitey's last year.

During the summer I went to a Yankee/Red Sox game that was pretty funny. I was home on leave and I was getting serious with my army buddy DomenicKs sister. Every weekend I'd be over her house and we would go out. Her name was Josephine. Her family was Italian and she was the 13th child of 14. Needless to say with in-laws and cousins the family was so big they should have had their own zip code. I was the first non-Italian to become a member of this family. There are several now, but I was the pioneer. (You know that movie "My Big Fat Greek Wedding" – well I was like John Corbett, who played the groom in the movie). While I was on leave some of my future in-laws decided we would go see the Red Sox play the Yanks. The year before, the Red Sox finished only a half game ahead of the basement Yanks but this year they were in the hunt for the pennant. Josephine hated sports and did not want to go, but we were just short of kidnapping her and took her with us.

Our seats were next to the left field foul pole. Josephine knew some of the basics of baseball like 3 outs, 3 strikes, 9 innings etc., but she was full of questions that had the surrounding fans in stitches. Her first question was when the ground crew went out to get the infield ready for play after fielding practice. Since we were at field level she said, "Hey, they can't start the game until they remove that pile of dirt in the middle of the infield." I had to explain the pitcher's mound to her. When the Red Sox took the field in the bottom of the first the fans around us were hollering "Hey Yaz, Hey Yaz", Josephine was perplexed "What's a Yaz?" she asked. I had to explain that Yaz is easier to say than Yastrzemski and that he is one of the greats in the league. In the third inning the fans were cheering when a Yank stole second base. Josephine asked what's the clapping for - I told her the Yanks just stole second base – she said "What are you talking about it is still there?" Later in the game a ball was called foul that was probably fair because it kicked up some chalk from the foul line. Naturally the manager argued it was fair. Anyway, I then explained to Josephine the foul line and foul pole that we were sitting close to. She asked what happens if the ball hits the foul pole? I said it's a home run – she stated that is stupid it should be called a fair pole if it's going to be a homer. I told her that's a "fair" point. I then pointed to Yaz who was right in front of us and said "See Yaz, that's what the Yanks consider a foul Pole." Josephine, being only five feet tall, had this comment go over her head. She hasn't been to a professional game since.

In the American League, it was the year of Yaz. He carried the Red Sox from ninth place in '66 to the penthouse this year. Yaz with his unique batting stance of the bat held excessively high over his head hit .326, had 44 homers, and 121 RBIs to win the Triple Crown (Killebrew also had 44 homers). Yaz also led the league in hits (189) and runs (112); and not to neglect the defensive side of the game also won his third Gold Glove (he won a total of seven in his career). Yaz even had to do more after their other star Tony Conigliaro was hit in the head by a pitch about two-thirds into the season and missed the rest of it. George "Boomer" Scott provided some line-up protection for Yaz batting .303 (fourth in the AL) while booming out 19 homers.

The pennant race went down to the wire. The Red Sox had to win both games against the Twins, while the Tigers had to lose. Yaz came down the stretch with a smoldering bat (in the previous 10 games he batted .444, 16 for 36 with 4 homers and 11 RBIs) and the Twins couldn't extinguish it. In the final two games Yaz went 7 for 8 with 5 RBIs – his 3-run homer led the Bosox to a 6-4 win in the first contest. The Twins took a chance in the final game starting their 20-game winner Dean Chance for the third time in eight days but Jim Lonborg, the Cy Young Award winner with a 22-9 record, ruined the Twins chances with a 5-3 victory (Yaz's hit drove in the go-ahead run). The Tigers were playing after the Red Sox game and a victory would tie them forcing a playoff – no need, the Angels beat the Tigers. The Red Sox ended a 21-year pennant drought..

It was a repeat of the '46 Series – the Cards and Red Sox. (The Cards won it 4 games to 3 on Country Slaughter's mad dash for home in game 7). The Cardinals had a rested Hoot to start the Series, but the Bosox star, Lonborg had to pitch on Sunday so he couldn't open the Series. The Bosox started Jose Santiago. If I told you that he only gave up two runs and even hit a homer off of Hoot, you would think that maybe the Red Sox won. But that was the only run they got as Gibson went all the way for a 2-1 victory. Brock had four hits and on two of them ran around the bases and scored on RBIs by the former Pinstriper, Maris.

In game 2, Lonborg had a no-hitter until two out in the eighth when Julian Javier doubled. He tossed a one-hitter, and Yaz supplied the runs with two homers in the 5-0 victory. In game 3, Brock had a triple and a bunt and scored twice. Shannon hit a two-run moon shot and Nellie Briles, Gibson's replacement during the year, emulated Hoot as the Cards won 5-2.

Game 4 was just about over before it began. After the Bosox went out in the first, the Cards scored four times on six hits driving out Santiago. With Hoot going it was all over as he threw a five-hit shutout. Lonborg came back in game 5 to keep the Bosox alive. He won 3-1 as he only allowed a homer by Maris in the ninth. Lefty Carlton took a tough loss only giving up an unearned run in six innings. In game 6, the Red Sox pounded eight Cardinal pitchers in an 8-4 win to force a seventh game. Yaz had three hits including a homer and shortstop Rico Petrocelli hit 2 homers.

The deciding game match-up was Hoot and Lonborg. They both had already won two games giving up only one run. The only problem was Hoot had three days of rest while Lonborg only had two days. The Cards won 7-2 and Hoot even hit a homer.

This year in Boston it was known as the "Impossible Dream" (from the popular song by Jack Jones in 1966) - but eventually the Red Sox Nation had to wake up. Naturally Hoot was the Series MVP. Brock hit .414 with 12 hits scoring 8 runs. Maris batted .385 with 10 hits and drove in 7 runs and Javier hit .360 with 3 doubles and a homer. Yaz's storybook year ended with him hitting .400 in the Series, 10 for 25, 2 doubles and 3 homers, but he missed out on getting the ring.

After the Series, I finished my two-year stint in the Army and returned to work at the Newark Post Office. My Cardinal fan co-workers and I rapped about the World Series and thought maybe St. Louis was on its way to becoming a dynasty. Another thing I noticed at work – the Yankee fans were in hiding – like in a spider hole or something. Seems like in general they just couldn't give a Hoot about baseball.

1967
The Ring: No, not the World Series Ring

As summer began, Josephine and I decided to get engaged for her birthday in early September. I had to get her an engagement ring. It was going to be tough to get a nice one on an Army salary. My family told me about a Post Office truck driver that was also a part-time jeweler. Since I was a fellow postal employee and a soldier he'd give me a good deal. I met him and picked out the ring. I didn't know how I was going to pay for it.

In July, my answer of paying for the ring came to be. In the Army, the company clerk hands out your pay at the beginning of the month. (You always want to stay in the good graces of the company clerk for various reasons). On this day, my mail clerk buddy and I were in line for our money. The camp was also running a raffle for $1.00 per chance (first prize was a '67 Camaro) conveniently at the pay table (no one would refuse the company clerk). My buddy was in front of me and was overpaid by $20. Since he had found money, he bought 21 tickets. I bought my ticket and told my buddy if I won the car I'd give him mine. About a week later, the raffle officer called me informing me that I won—second prize, a Honda Super 90 motorcycle. My buddy was mad he didn't buy another ticket, or at least why couldn't have I won first prize because then he would have wound up with my car – but hey, the Camaro wasn't my color anyway.

Part of the winning package included free riding lessons. I had a blast learning to ride, but wasn't really interested in becoming a biker. My family asked me what I was going to do with my motorcycle because they had someone who was interested in buying it. The amount was just about what would cover the cost of the engagement ring. I decided to sell my motorcycle, since this was my found money. When my buddies heard that I sold my motorcycle for an engagement ring they concluded that I was either crazy, in love, or had post 'rice paddy' stress syndrome - or all three.

I couldn't have written a better script to the end of the year. In no particular order, the Cardinals won the World Series, my tour of duty was over, and I got engaged (?).

1968

Forget Pinstripes, This Year it's Tiger Stripes

As 1968 began Josephine and I were engaged. Our engagement was for about a year, which was sort of normal at this time (nowadays some marriages don't last that long). Our wedding was to be on a Sunday at the end of August.

Even though planning the wedding, getting a place to live, buying furniture etc. cut into my following baseball, I still found time to do so. Also, before the season began, I got a position on the day shift as a Post Office window clerk. One of the clerks at the office where I trained and worked at was Aldo Cerone. He told me his son, Rick, was the All-State quarterback at Essex Catholic High in Newark, NJ and was also quite a catcher (he had a decent Major League career mostly with the Yankees).

In baseball this was the year of the pitcher. The American League hit .230 (the A's led the AL at .240) – Yaz won the batting title again but was the only one to hit over .300 (at .301). Only Ken "Hawk" Harrelson (109) and Hondo Howard (106) cracked the century mark for RBIs. The National League did not fare much better hitting .243 (only the Reds batted over .252) and only Willie McCovey (105) had more than 100 RBIs.

In September in a Giant/Cardinal series, Giant Gaylord Perry and Cardinal Ray Washburn pitched back to back no-hitters. The Dodgers' "Big D", Don Drysdale broke a pitching record tossing six consecutive shutouts while throwing 58 2/3 straight scoreless innings (despite this feat he was only 14-12 for the year).

The Cardinals resembled the Dodgers' championship team of the early 1960's (little hitting, superb pitching). Flood, was one of five National Leaguers to hit over .300 (.301), and Brock, (who led the league with 46 doubles, 14 triples, and 62 stolen bases), were the catalysts of the offense. Only Cepeda (16) and Moon Man Shannon (15) had double digit homers.

The pitching was outstanding. Gibson took over NL domination where Koufax left off. He set a lively ball ERA record of 1.12 and finished 22-9 (how did he ever lose? – 5 of his 9 losses were by a 1-0 score). He had a 15-game winning streak (ten of them shutouts) in route to the MVP and Cy Young Award. He was joined on the mound by Nellie Briles (19-11), Ray Washburn (14-8), and Lefty Carlton (13-11).

St. Louis easily beat out San Francisco by nine games. Poor Marichal, known for his "leg"endary high leg kick during his wind-up, was 26-9 with a 2.43 ERA but was runner-up again for the Cy Young Award to Hoot. Marichal needed to have those stats last year.

The National League surprise team was the Mets. With new manager Gil Hodges at the helm, they improved by 12 games to finish ninth but their young players showed promise. Tom Seaver avoided that sophomore jinx and had a fine 16-12 slate but he was surpassed by Jerry Koosman at 19-12. Outfielder Cleon Jones just missed hitting .300 and finished at .297.

In the American League the Detroit Tigers coasted to the pennant with both pitching and hitting (eight players reached double figures in homers). The other noteworthy news was that last year's cellar dwellers, the Athletics, snuck out of Kansas City and relocated in Oakland, California. With a change of scenery the A's improved their record by 20 games (82-80) finishing in sixth place one game behind the Yankees.

The CBS comedy act in New York was becoming less funny. The Yanks improved to finish fifth, four games over .500 (83-79). Mel Stottlemyre was the star again reaching the 20-win mark (21-12, 2.45 ERA). Mel would have probably been a Hall of Fame pitcher if the Yanks had an offense like their 1949-1964 teams. Stan Bahnsen was Rookie of the Year (17-12, 2.06 ERA) and Fritz Peterson was 12-11 with a 2.63 ERA.

The Yankee offense was the worst in the league. They hit only a ridiculously dismal .214. The Mick led the Yanks with 18 homers but hit only .237 causing his career average to fall below .300 - Mick would call 1968 his last year as he would finish with a .298 lifetime average. Only Roy White at .287 and 17 homers was productive. Now the Yanks know how the other teams in the '50's and early '60's felt when it was "Wait 'til next year".

The Tigers only hit .235 (third baseman Don Wert batted a meager .200 and the regular shortstop Roy Oyler was worse at .135 in 111 games) but banged out 185 homers to lead the league. Willie Horton led the offense (.285, 36 homers, 85 RBIs), while runner-up MVP catcher Bill Freehan hit 25 homers and drove in 84 runs. Jim Northrup had 21 homers and 90 RBIs and veteran Stormin' Norman Cash hit 25 homers (without cork?). Dick McAuliffe led the AL with 95 runs scored. The Tigers won despite their veteran All-Star Al Kaline missing a third of the season – still he had 10 homers, 53 RBIs and a .287 average.

Detroit won because of two pitchers that marched to the beat of a different drummer. Denny McLain became baseball's first 30-game winner since Dizzy Dean did it for the Gashouse Gang Cardinals of 1934. McLain was 31-6 with a 1.96 ERA and 280 Ks. He, like Gibson, was MVP and Cy Young Award winner. Denny McLain was more like Dizzy Dean than just being a 30-game winner. He was always doing crazy antics. He was known for consuming a six pack or two of Pepsi a day and flew to Vegas to play an organ at one of the clubs there.

The other off-beat pitcher was Mickey Lolich. He was easily overshadowed by McLain's year but he complemented him with a fine 17-9 record. Lolich looked like a pitcher you could bunt against because of his rotund-ness, but he was really a decent fielder. He was also referred to as baseball's worst hitter (but don't say that to Nellie Briles). Lolich would drive to the stadium on his motorcycle… (no, it wasn't mine).

McLain's antics were exemplified when he won his 31st game. The Tigers had a large lead with Mantle coming up. At the time Mantle was tied with Jimmy Foxx on the all-time home run list at 534. McLain was a Mick fan and told his catcher Freehan he was coming in with a fat one. Mick thought it was a trick so he didn't swing. Freehan told him he's going to make it fat again. Mick still didn't believe it – he let two fat ones go by. Freehan again told Mick "C'mon Mick". The third one Mick parked to pass Foxx. The funny part was that the next batter, Pepitone, motioned to McLain to do the same for him – naturally Denny made him eat dirt.

McLain was one of baseball's tragic figures. He was like Dizzy in that he only had five great consecutive years going 105-52. He also shared the Cy Young Award with Mike Cuellar in 1969. Like I said his playing days were similar to Dizzy's, but his post-playing days were more like Pete Rose's as he was involved with some criminal element and spent some time incarcerated.

It was the beginning of the summer and I was anticipating being married by the end of it. Not so. My dad had a sense that most people like a Saturday wedding, so since he was paying for half of the wedding he asked Josephine if we could possibly change to a Saturday even if it meant delaying the wedding. Without even consulting me (like I'm only the groom) my dad and Josephine changed the date to October. When I heard October, I was hoping it would be the latter part of the month (at this time the Series was in the beginning of October) so it would not interfere with the Series. Nope, the wedding would be October 5th. When my co-workers saw me aggravated over this they said, "You should be glad your wedding is postponed you have two more months of freedom". I told them, "No. I'm aggravated over my wedding being in the middle of the Series".

The Detroit manager, Mayo Smith, made one of the more daring moves in Series history. The Tiger shortstop position (Roy Oyler, Dick Tracewski and Tom Matchick) didn't even hit .200, so he took his centerfielder Mickey Stanley and put him at shortstop, and moved right fielder Jim Northrup to center to make room for Kaline in right who was coming back from an injury. The move paid off handsomely as Stanley played an excellent shortstop.

The Series opened in St. Louis and it was supposed to be the best match-up ever, Hoot vs. McLain. Hoot was almost untouchable as he scattered five hits and set a new Series K record with 17. McLain was his own worst enemy when he walked two in the fourth that combined with hits by Moon Man and Javier to give the Cards a 3-0 lead and with Hoot's smoking six-shooter that's all that would be needed.

In game 2, Lolich evened the Series at one going the route in an 8-1 victory. Lolich was a top quality pitcher, so his performance on the hill was not a surprise – but his third inning homer was, since he had a reputation as baseball's worst hitter. Briles really didn't have it as evidenced by Lolich's homer. Horton and Cash also banged out homers.

The third game was my wedding day. I didn't have those getting married jitters as I was hoping the Cardinals' pitcher, Ray Washburn wouldn't have any either. While I was getting wedding ready, Kaline homered to put the Tigers up 2-0. In the fourth the

Cards were rallying. The ushers (three of them were Josephine's brothers, Domenick, Benny and Lou – the other was my cousin Ron) and I were in my house watching this; meanwhile the car was waiting to take us to Sacred Heart Cathedral in Newark, NJ for my wedding. My dad ordered us out of the house... NOW! It was a half-hour ride. On the way there, Tim McCarver hit a 3-run homer. Cards were up 4-2. We arrived at the Cathedral and waited for the priest in the back room. From previous meetings, the priest knew I was a Cardinal fan. As soon as he arrived he told me Cepeda just hit a 3-run homer. Priests (I think for obvious reasons) should always root for the Cardinals. Washburn went six and was the winning pitcher. During the ceremony there was a slight lull. The priest just about shocked me when he looked at Josephine, then me, and said very quietly, "Must be the seventh inning stretch about now." Josephine and I both said "I Do"!

At the reception, before going on his break the band leader asked us what our wedding song was. We didn't have one so he said, "Have one when I get back". We couldn't agree on anything – I asked her how about "Going to the Chapel" she said "No". Well the band leader came back and asked us for our song. I shook my head at him and kidding around said "How about "Take Me Out To the Ball Game"." Josephine rolled back her eyes. She has no sense of humor except for marrying me. She then told the band leader "OK you want our wedding song, it's "What Kind Of Fool Am I" by Sammy Davis Jr. And that is our wedding song.

On Sunday in game 4, Gibson again beat McLain 10-1. Denny only went 2 2/3 innings and gave up four runs. Hoot even hit a homer, (so there, Lolich). After the game Josephine and I started our drive to Miami for our honeymoon.

On Tuesday, the Cards were hoping to wrap it up and it looked that way as in the first inning they got a 3-run homer from Cepeda. The Tigers scored two in the fourth to make the score 3-2. We were listening to the game on the radio while driving through North Carolina. The station was full of static and irritating to Josephine. She wanted to turn it off, but I said "Hey it's the Series." She said I hope the Cardinals lose and put a jinx on them. Her jinx worked. In the fifth Brock doubled and tried to score on a single by Javier. Horton made a great throw to Freehan. Brock, with his speed, was sure he would score so he didn't slide. Freehan made a swipe tag and Brock was called out. He was probably safe but it's what the umpire calls that's final. Actually, if Brock slid he would have had to gone through Freehan, who was built like The Great Wall of China, and had the plate blocked and outweighed Brock by over 30 pounds. With the Tigers losing 3-2 in the seventh manager, Smith let Lolich bat. Amazingly he came through with a hit that started a 3-run rally, with Kaline's bases loaded single being the big hit. I thought Smith was crazy to let Lolich bat - maybe he figured Lolich was going to be the next Bambino after homering in game 2.

Well the Cards were still up 3 games to 2. The Tigers started McLain with two days of rest so I figured, if the Cards hit him with three days of rest last time, they'll do OK today. We were at poolside at the motel in Miami when the game started. I told her I was going to the room to get some towels. When I put the TV on in our room it was the third inning with the Tigers up 2-0. Well, I was shocked to see the Tigers tie the Series record for runs scored in an inning with ten. The big blow was a Grand Slam by Northrup. Josephine still doesn't know why it took me over an hour to find some towels. McLain and the Tigers won going away, 13-1.

So what, the Cards had Hoot going and all he's done was win seven Series games in a row with an ERA around 1.00. The Tigers had their motorcyclist Lolich ready.

The next day I watched the game at the outdoor bar that was adjacent to the pool. For six innings the game was scoreless. In the sixth Lolich picked off Brock and Flood. That's the kind of game it was for St. Louis. In the seventh, Hoot gave up two out hits to Cash and Horton. Northrup then hit a long fly to center – no problem with Flood out there. Wait, Flood took a step in, and as he then went back, the ground gave way costing him time to get back. It was a 2-run triple. Freehan then doubled in Northrup. The Cards weren't doing anything against Lolich except for a last-try homer by Moon Man. Tigers win 4-1 and win their first Series since 1945, when they beat my mom's neighbor Borowy and the Cubs.

Lolich was the Series MVP 3-0, 1.57 ERA. Hoot again sets a new Series K record (35) beating his own record of 31 in 1964. He was 2-1 with a 1.57 ERA. Brock tied the Series record with 13 hits including 3 doubles, a triple, and 2 homers while hitting .464. Kaline hit .379 with 11 hits including 2 doubles and 2 homers with 8 RBIs, while Cash had 10 hits batting .385.

As 1968 was in the book, something had to be done about the pitching dominance of the game. In 1969, the strike zone was reduced to its pre-1963 dimensions and the height of the mound would be lowered.

1969
What a METamorphosis

In 1969 New York City was again becoming the nation's sports capital. In football, Broadway Joe Namath delivered on his New York Jets guaranteed Super Bowl victory over the Baltimore Colts (a sign of things to come for these two cities). In basketball the Knicks were putting together one of the best teams ever with former Chicago White Sox pitcher Dave DeBusschere being a main ingredient in its success. In baseball you have the Mets – Who?? Supposedly when someone asked if the Mets had a chance to win it all, it was answered "There will be a man on the moon before the Mets win a World Series."

In '69 the mound was lowered and the strike zone reduced, but that wasn't the major change. Baseball celebrated its century anniversary by adding four teams, the Montreal Expos and San Diego Padres in the National League and Seattle Pilots and Kansas City Royals in the American League. Each league was split into East and West divisions. The division winners would meet in a playoff to determine the pennant winner.

In the National East St. Louis was expected to repeat. They traded Cepeda for Joe Torre and he did well hitting (18 homers 101 RBIs) and Brock hit .298. On the mound Hoot won 20, Carlton 17 and Briles 15. Despite this they came in fourth.

All year it looked like the Cubs would finally end their 50+ year drought. They had the pitching with future Famer Fergie Jenkins (21 wins), Bill Hands (20 wins), Ken Holtzman (17 wins) and Phil Regan, the Vulture reliever (12 wins with 17 saves). At the plate their stars were pounding the ball - Ernie Banks (23 homers, 106 RBIs), Ron Santo (29 homers, 123 RBIs) and Billy Williams (21 homers, 93 RBIs). Also, Jim Hickman (21 homers) and catcher Randy Hundley (18 homers) chipped in offensively. The Cubs had it all – except fate.

They led the third place Mets by ten games in the middle of August. And they still led the Mets by two in the first week of September. But the Mets swept them and it was all over. The Met locomotive couldn't be stopped – it just rolled on and on. They went 39-11 down the stretch to coast to the National East title winning 100 games - then in the postseason they won 7 of 8. They won 45 of their last 57 games.

There were two theories on why the Cubs were overtaken by the runaway Mets (they finished 8 games behind them). In one of their celebrated series at Shea, a black cat ran across the Cub dugout – bad luck for the Cubs. The other theory was that on July 20th, Neil Armstrong and Buzz Aldrin took a little stroll on the moon. The Mets were a sure thing now. (At this time I was unaware about the Cubs having a Billy Goat hex put on them in the 1945 World Series).

The Mets were an unbalanced team - this had nothing to do with their mental state. Their sticks could not compare with the Cubs. They really only had three quality hitters – Cleon Jones hit .340 (third in the league), Tommie Agee (had 26 homers and led the team with 76 RBIs) and Donn Clendenon, who they traded for in July, had 12 homers in half of a season. Art Shamsky, although only playing in 100 games, also helped out at the plate batting .300 and smacking 14 homers. One reason it seemed the Mets attack appeared not to be as good as other teams was that their manager Gil Hodges played all of his players, platooning them like Old Casey used to do when his Yanks beat Hodges' Brooklyn teams. (At least Hodges learned something in those losses). Another reason the Mets won was their excellent defense, especially up the middle – Jerry Grote with the mask, Bud Harrelson, Ken Boswell and Al Weis at second and short, and ball hawk Agee in center.

However the strength was their pitching. The Cy Young winner, Tom "Terrific" Seaver went 25-7 with a 2.21 ERA and Jerry Koosman went 17-9 with a 2.28 ERA. Gary Gentry won 13 and a young Nolan Ryan went 6-3. This strength extended into the bullpen. The Mets were clutch and adept at winning games in the late or extra innings. Their ace relievers, Tug McGraw and Ron Taylor, combined for 18 wins and 25 saves.

You could tell what kind of magical season the Mets were having when on September 12 they swept a doubleheader from the Pirates winning both games by a 1-0 score with their pitchers

Koosman and Don Cardwell driving in the runs - and on September 15 when Lefty Carlton set a new Major League record striking out 19 Met batters but lost the game 4-3 as Ron Swoboda belted a pair of 2-run homers (he only had 7 other homers for the year).

One thing about Seaver - at this time he was New YorKs top media personality. He was on TV, in the newspapers, and magazines. I was 24 years old then and I was about 5' 10" and 200 lbs. I was a post office window clerk in downtown Newark, and would have a hundred or so customers a day. I was built and had my hair styled sort of like Seaver's. Several customers commented on how I resembled him (yeah, my fastball isn't as fast as his change-up). My sister only lived a mile from me so I was over there two or three times a week and I mentioned to her what the customers said about me resembling Seaver. Well you know how siblings are – she laughed and said "Yeah you look like Seaver". Well a couple of days later her neighbor comes over and says to my sister "You know Carole, your brother reminds me of Tom Seaver."

The Mets' runaway in August and September captivated the New York area. I even think a bunch of Yankee fans joined the Mets bandwagon. Even I was pulling for the Mets, (and not because some customers said I look like Seaver). Just like other people in the beginning (in 1962), people who rooted for other teams also pulled for the Mets as a second team –but then they were the loveable losers. I also developed a liking for the Mets when Ken Boyer was traded to them. Mets-mania was running rampant. They outdrew the CBS sitcom in New York by a million. The Mets had over 2 million for the first time and led the league in attendance.

The Yanks, under the former genius Major Houk finished a game under .500 (80-81, 28 1/2 games out). Stottlemyre again was the ace with a 20-14 record. Fritz Peterson had 17 wins, but Stan Bahnsen hit that sophomore jinx going 6-16. The Pinstripers at the plate were more like hospital candy stripers. Pepitone hit 27 homers and Bobby Murcer returned from the service to hit 26. Murcer, like Mantle, was an Oklahoman and there was a build-up that he'd take his place as the next Yankee star.

In the American East you would think the Tigers would repeat as every regular had double-digit homers and Lolich and McLain (co-Cy Young Award winner with Cuellar) combined for 43 wins, but no, they were runner-up, 19 games behind the Baltimore Orioles.

The Orioles' pitching and hitting were outstanding and they also had the league's best defense. Mark Belanger (winner of 8 Gold Gloves) was as good a shortstop as Brooks Robinson was a third baseman so getting a ground ball hit to left seemed to occur as often as Halley's Comet. And at second base they had the Gold Glove winner Davey Johnson who was on the All-Star team. They missed tying the league record for wins by two games (they finished with 109). Their top three aces were co-Cy Young Award winner Mike Cuellar (23-11), Dave McNally (20-7) and Jim Palmer (16-4). They were managed by Earl Weaver, whose main strategy was the 3-run homer. They had four big bangers – Boog Powell (37 homers 121 RBIs), Frank Robinson (32 homers 100 RBIs) Brooks Robinson (23 homers 84 RBIs) and Paul Blair (26 homers 76 RBIs). Even the light-hitting Belanger aided the offense with a surprising .287 batting average, and his double play partner Johnson (.280) showed he could also swing the bat.

In the American West, Minnesota won behind the batting of MVP Harmon Killebrew (49 homers and 140 RBIs led the AL) and Tony Oliva (.309, 24 homers, 101 RBIs). The Twin 20-game winners were Jim Perry (20-6) and Dave Boswell (20-12). They held off the Oakland A's who were led by former Arizona State All-Americans Reggie Jackson (47 homers, 118 RBIs) and Sal Bando (31 homers, 113 RBIs).

Baltimore swept the playoffs winning two of them by one run. The second game was a classic. McNally pitched an 11 inning shutout to win 1-0. McNally wouldn't let Killebrew beat him (he walked him five times).

The National West was won by Atlanta. Geographically they should have been in the East, but the league didn't want to break up certain rivalries. The Braves outclassed the Mets in the hitting phase. Aaron hammered 44 homers, drove in 97 runs and hit .304. Cepeda had 22 homers and 88 RBIs while Rico Carty hit .342 with 16 homers. On the mound the future Famer knuckleballer Phil Niekro was 23-13 and former NBA player (two years with the Detroit Pistons) Ron Reed was 18-10.

The National League playoff match-up was Mets pitching vs. Atlanta hitting. However, the Met pitching was poor with an ERA of 5.00 and the Hammer homered in all three games. But at the plate the Mets did a reversal – they scored 27 runs and had 37 hits in a three game sweep. Cleon Jones hit .457 with a homer and 4 RBIs,

Agee had 2 homers hitting .357 and Ken Boswell, who only hit 3 homers all year, hit two in the series. This offset Aaron's .357, 3 homers, 8 RBIs performance.

As for the Mets pitching, only a young Nolan Ryan was effective, going into the third game in the third inning, keeping the Braves at bay while the Mets rallied for the win. Despite the lack of good pitching, the Mets still pulled off the sweep.

The Mets and Orioles match-up had the Baltimore juggernaut a heavy favorite, despite that man on the moon theory. (This match-up eerily paralleled the Baltimore Colts/NY Jets meeting for this year's Super Bowl). Ten months earlier the Broadway Joe Namath-led Jets silenced the heavily favored Colts in Super Bowl III).

It looked like the odds-makers were right when in the Series opener Seaver was not so terrific and gave up a lead-off homer to Don Buford. The Mets' batters couldn't do anything against the Cuban change-up that was Cuellar's calling card as the O's won 4-1.

In game 2 Koosman was looking like another pitcher whose name began with a K (Koufax). He threw six hitless innings before Paul Blair singled. Brooks Robinson singled him home to tie the score at one. Clendenon homered in the fourth for the Met run. In the Mets' ninth with two outs they put together three consecutive hits by Ed "the Glider" Charles, Grote and Weis to take the lead 2-1. With two outs in the bottom of the ninth, Koosman walked Frank Robinson and Boog. Ron Taylor came in to extinguish the fire getting Brooks Robinson to ground out.

The Series moved to Shea for game 3 and it was all Tommie Agee. In the first he greeted Palmer with a homer to give the Mets the lead 1-0. Because of his glove, that was all that was needed. The Mets' Gary Gentry was pitching when the O's had two on when Elrod Hendricks smashed one to the 396 ft. sign for a sure two-run double or triple. But Agee raced back (he was one of the best) and snow coned it saving two runs. The Mets scored two in the second and one in the sixth for a 4-0 lead going into the seventh. Gentry walked the bases loaded, which brought in Nolan Ryan. Blair hit a laser shot into right-center. It could even have been an inside-the-parker – but no, Agee made a diving catch to keep at least three runs from scoring. The Mets went on to win 5-0 with Agee saving Met hurlers 5 runs with his leather. These catches rank with those of Say Hey in 1954 and Amoros in 1955, (and I would include Covington's 2 catches in 1957 as well).

In game 4 it was again the Cy Young Award winners going at it. Seaver had a 1-0 lead in the ninth, courtesy of another clutch homer by Clendenon off of Cuellar. In the ninth Frank Robinson and Boog singled. Brooks Robinson was up next. (He must have thought of not to hit it to center with the vacuum cleaner Agee patrolling there). So he sent a bee-bee shot into right. It would tie the score and maybe Powell could score also. But wait, Ron Swoboda was out there and imitated Agee by making an all-time great diving catch. Frank Robinson tagged up after the catch to tie it and forced extra innings. (Three of the best catches in Series history are in back to back games). Anyway, in the tenth the Mets had runners on first and second when J.C. Martin bunted. The Oriole pitcher Pete Richert fielded it and threw to first except that the throw hit Martin's wrist and bounced away allowing the runner, Rod Gaspar, to score from second to win the game. The hero of the game for the Mets was the umpire who should have called Martin out for interference because he appeared to be out of the base path while running to first.

The Mets were hoping not to leave New York and win game 5 and the Series. The Orioles scored three in the third when the pitcher McNally made like Lolich in last year's Series and hit a two-run homer (the third year in a row a pitcher hit a Series homer). This was followed by a Frank Robinson solo shot.

In the sixth the Mets made it a one run deficit on a replay from 1957. Cleon Jones was up – McNally threw a pitch that was called a ball. Cleon said it hit his shoe. In 1957 his namesake Nippy Jones had the same thing happen to him so they showed the umpire the polish on the ball. Remembering this, the Mets showed the umpire the ball with the polish on it so Cleon was awarded first. Clendenon hit another clutch homer to make the score 3-2. Al Weis, who hit 3 homers all year, tied it with a homer in the seventh. The Mets won it on doubles by Cleon and Swoboda in the eighth.

The Mets had many heroes. The pitching staff's ERA was 1.80. Koosman was their ace at 2-0 with a 2.04 ERA. And then there was Agee and Swoboda with their spectacular catches. Light-hitting utility player Al Weis swung a heavy bat (.455, 5 for 14, a homer and 3 RBIs). Donn Clendenon, with his 3 clutch homers, was MVP.

Gil Hodges pulled off one of the greatest managerial feats in baseball history. Combined with his outstanding playing career, he now looked like a lock to be on his way to Cooperstown. Here it is

2006 and he's not in. Why? I don't know. (Since he became election eligible there are 22 players that are now in the Hall that he received more votes than – i.e. Snider, Mathews, Killebrew). But I do know that as a kid in the 1950's watching Brooklyn play St. Louis I feared Hodges lurking in the on-deck circle more than I did their three Famers - Campy, the Duke and Jackie - whenever the Dodgers were rallying against my Red Birds. Gil was an eight-time All-Star, had over 100 RBIs in seven consecutive seasons (quite a feat for this era), and when he retired in the beginning of 1963 he had the most career home runs (370) for a right-handed hitter in NL history - only Jimmie Foxx (534) in the AL, at this time, had more than him. His performance on the diamond helped the Dodgers win seven pennants and two World Series. Despite being right-handed, he was considered to be the best defensive first baseman of his time, as evidenced by his three Gold Gloves (1957-59). The Gold Glove awards began in 1957. His enshrinement in the Hall is long overdue.

Men Walk on the Moon and the Mets Win a World Series. What a <u>METamorphosis</u>!!!!!

1970
Yankees Improve, but Orioles Fly Away with It All

This year was pretty busy for me so a lot of my attention was diverted from my passion of following baseball. In February my son was born. Naming him was a small problem. My in-laws have a tradition that you name your first son after the father's father and the second son after the mother's father (we have four nephews named Frank). My dad's name is August and it's not that I don't like the name (after all the Cardinals' owner's name is August Busch). However, I did not want to name my son after any relative, including me, but being named for a baseball player is something else which is why I tried to convince Josephine to agree on Ken or Stan for obvious reasons. She didn't care for either name. We wound up agreeing on Michael as I always liked the song "Michael Row the Boat Ashore", but we compromised and chose August as his middle name.

Once we became a family we needed a home, so house hunting took up a lot of time. We bought a house in South Brunswick in central Jersey (about 40 miles from Newark), but I wasn't too happy about it being next to Monroe - that town I had to go to traffic court in when I was in the Army.

The Yankees improved dramatically in 1970 – by 13 games. They were 93-69 but still finished 15 games behind the high flying Orioles in the AL East. Had they been in the NL East they would have been the champs since Pittsburgh won it with only 89 wins. Fritz Peterson (20-11), Stottlemyre 15 wins and Stan Bahnsen 14 wins led the pitching staff. Relief was provided by Jack Aker and Lindy McDaniel who combined for 13 wins and 45 saves. Only Bobby Murcer (23) and Roy White (22) reached double figures in homers. Danny Cater hit .301 and Rookie of the Year Thurman Munson, a young rugged catcher, hit .302.

The Orioles again made a run at the league record for victories but fell three short. They had three 20-game winners - Mike Cuellar and Dave McNally (both had 24) and Jim Palmer (20). It was a little easier to pitch when you got the run support the Orioles' offense gave them. Nine players reached double figures in homers. Boog Powell, the AL MVP, led the team (35 homers, 114 RBIs) while the Robinsons, Frank (.306, 25 homers, 78 RBIs) and Brooks (15 homers, 94 RBIs) also belted the horsehide.

In the AL West there was a game of musical cities as the Seattle Pilots after only one year of being there left the Pacific Northwest and turned up in the recently vacated city of Milwaukee becoming the Brewers. The Twins, again easily won the West with Harmon Killebrew (41 homers, 114 RBIs) and Tony Oliva (.325, 23 homers, 107 RBIs) leading the offense. Jim Perry (24-12) won the Cy Young Award while Jim Kaat was 14-10. But it was their Twin relievers that carried them to the AL West title. Former Dodger Ron Perranoski, the lefty Twin won 7 and saved a league high 34, and Stan Williams, the righty Twin won 10 and saved 15.

In the AL playoffs the Orioles again beat the Twins in a three game sweep. Palmer won the clincher 6-1 tossing a six-hitter. Their bats rang up 27 runs and a .330 average. Brooks Robinson hit .583 and Boog .429 to lead the offense.

Pittsburgh won the NL East by 5 games over the Cubs. The Bucs' lumber propelled them to the top – Roberto Clemente (.352), Manny Sanguillen (.325), Bob Robertson (27 homers, 82 RBIs) and future Famer Willie "Pops" Stargell (31 homers, 85 RBIs). Stargell was one of the NL's most feared sluggers and it was interesting to see beads of sweat forming on the foreheads of pitchers as the imposing Buc would ferociously whirl his lumber like a windmill at the plate waiting for their reluctant pitch. The Mets, who I was becoming more of a fan of, came in third. Seaver won 18 and led the league in ERA (2.81) and Ks (283). The Cards came in fourth. Hoot was the NL Cy Young Award winner leading the NL in wins (23-7) and winning % (.767).

In the NL West, rookie manager Sparky Anderson began forming the Big Red Machine in Cincinnati. They coasted to the division title by 14 1/2 games. Johnny Bench, the NL MVP, (.293, 45 homers, 148 RBIs) had the best power stats ever for a catcher, and is still regarded as the best defensive catcher ever. He and Tony Perez (.317, 40 homers, 129 RBIs) were the most important cogs in the 'Machine. The other cogs were Pete Rose (.316, 15 homers, 120 runs), Bobby Tolan (.316, 16 homers, 112 runs,), Lee May (34 homers, 94 RBIs) and Bernie Carbo (.310, 21 homers). On the mound Jim Merritt won 20, Gary Nolan 18 and Wayne Simpson and Jim McGlothlin 14.

In the NL playoffs the Pirate hurlers kept the 'Machine bats in check, only giving up nine runs in the three games – but the Cincy staff was better only allowing three runs to sweep the three games. The opener was a classic as the Reds' Gary Nolan and Dock Ellis dueled each other for nine scoreless innings - Cincy rallied for 3 runs in the tenth for a 3-0 victory.

There's an old baseball adage - good pitching beats good hitting. The Oriole staff lived up to this by throwing a wrench into the gears of the Big Red Machine holding them to a .213 average while they hit .292 to win the Series in five games. Brooks Robinson continued his torrid hitting .429 with 2 homers. Frank Robinson and Boog each had 2 homers and Paul Blair hit .474.

But the big reason the O's dismantled the 'Machine 4 games to 1, was the Reds' insistence to hit the ball to third base. The Reds, especially Lee May, hit liners, lasers, swinging bunts toward third, you name it, it didn't matter. They were all sucked up by the human vacuum cleaner Brooks Robinson. He leapt, dove, threw off balance - it was the greatest display of fielding in the Series. Baseball people knew how outstanding Brooks Robinson was, but being on the national stage, the Series, let everyone know it – don't hit it to third when you play the Orioles. Brooks would go on to be selected to The All-Century Team in 2000.

1971
The Yanks' Pennant Hopes are for the Birds

After being second in the AL East last year, the Pinstripers had envisioned winning the division and pennant, but these hopes and dreams were really for the "Birds". The Orioles for the third year in a row took the division and playoffs, even though they won "only" 101 games, seven less than last year.

Most teams are satisfied with a 20-game winner, two of them is really good – but four of them! Yes, Dave McNally had 21 and Pat Dobson, Jim Palmer and Mike Cuellar all had 20. They were the first team to have four 20-game winners since the White/Black Sox of 1920, the year after they allegedly threw the Series. They came in second behind Cleveland in 1920 despite this feat.

Again the Baltimore offense supplied them with enough run support. Boog Powell and the Robinsons, (Brooks and Frank) all had over 90 RBIs, Merv Rettenmund hit .318 and Don Buford led the league with 99 runs.

The Yankees, even with good seasons, would have been hard pressed to beat the Baltimore Birds. The Yanks dropped 11 games from last year to finish fourth with an 82-80 record. Their offense did not provide enough runs as only two Yanks had over 11 homers. Roy White had 19 with a .292 average, and Bobby Murcer raised fan's hopes of him being another Mick by having an outstanding year hitting .331 (second in the AL) with 25 homers and 94 RBIs (fourth in the AL). Stottlemyre led the staff with a 16-12 slate; Fritz Peterson chalked up 15 wins and Stan Bahnsen 14.

Oakland won the AL West behind the Cy Young and MVP pitching of Vida Blue (24-8) and "Catfish" Hunter (21-11). Hitting were Sal Bando (24 homers) and Reggie Jackson (32 homers, second in the league).

Like the past two years, the O's swept the playoffs scoring five runs in each game while McNally, Cuellar and Palmer kept the A's bats in check as they all posted wins. Brooks Robinson kept up his torrid postseason average hitting .364 and Boog poked 2 dingers in the middle game.

In the NL East, the Pirates held off St. Louis to win the division. St. Louis' run at them was led by MVP Joe Torre (.363, 24 homers, 137 RBIs) and pitchers Lefty Carlton (20-9) and old Hoot (16-13). The Pittsburgh attack was led by Pops Stargell (.295, 48 homers, 125 RBIs), Manny Sanguillen (.319, 81 RBIs), Bob Robertson (26 homers) and Roberto Clemente (.341, 86 RBIs). Their mound leaders were Dock Ellis (19-9) and Steve Blass (15-8). Ellis was quite a character and it was rumored that in 1970 he was so high he didn't even realize that he tossed a no-hitter. Dave Giusti was a lifesaver in the 'pen with 5 wins and 30 saves.

The Pirates met the San Francisco Giants in the NL playoffs. The Giants were led by Bobby Bonds (33 homers, 102 RBIs) and pitchers Juan Marichal (18 wins) and Gaylord Perry (16 wins).

In the NL playoffs the Giants won the opener and then walked the plank in three straight to the Bucs. Clemente started to warm up at the plate hitting .333 with 4 RBIs, but it was Robertson who really did in the Giants - .438 (7 for 16), a double, 4 homers (3 in one game) and 6 RBIs. Dave Cash also swung a good bat (.421, 8 for 19, 5 runs scored). Rich Hebner (.294, 2 homers, 4 RBIs) supplied more pop and in game 3 his eighth inning homer off of Marichal was the margin of victory in the 2-1 win.

In the Series it looked liked the O's were going for a sweep as they took the first two games. The Bucs then shocked the baseball world by taking the next three. The O's bounced back with an extra inning win to deadlock it at three apiece. In the finale, Clemente homered in the fourth and the Bucs got another in the eighth as Blass tossed a four-hitter in a 2-1 victory.

Steve Blass was the Bucs' ace on the mound (he was 2-0 with a 1.00 ERA) winning game 3 by a 5-1 score, in addition to his deciding game win.

Brooks Robinson continued his solid postseason by hitting .318, but Clemente was something else. He had a hit in all 7 games, batted .414 and had 2 doubles, a triple and two homers among his 12 hits. At this time, probably only the real in depth baseball fan knew that Clemente was a superstar with his four batting titles, 11 consecutive Gold Gloves and NL MVP in '66, but like Brooks Robinson last year, Roberto (who naturally was Series MVP) put on a show in the national spotlight letting everyone now realize how great he really was.

It must have been tiresome for CBS to keep having these re-run episodes of the Yanks not being in the Series.

1972
No Flag, CBS Cancels the Yankee Sitcom

This year I had another distraction (a good one, though) that kept me from following my passion (baseball, duh!) with my usual zest. I was going to be a dad again. With Josephine being pregnant and doing things with Mike, who was two, I was pretty busy. In July my second son was born. Once again the name situation came up. Like I said when Mike was born, I don't like to name my son after a relative, but a ballplayer, yes. Again, for obvious reasons, I suggested to Josephine – how about Stan or Ken. She still doesn't have a clue why I picked these names. She said no – we agreed on Christopher as I always wore a St. Christopher medal. Poor Josephine – she hates sports and now will soon have another sports fanatic running loose in the house.

Despite not being able to put forth my usual effort of following the game, I was aware that the season started seven days late due to a strike. The other news was the lowly Senators left the nation's capitol for the Lone Star State becoming the Texas Rangers; and switched AL divisions with the Milwaukee Brewers - the change in locale didn't matter as the Rangers continued their dismal play losing 100 games despite the shortened season.

Following the Mets, along with St. Louis, I was stunned just like the rest of the baseball world was when Gil Hodges died of a heart attack in spring training. Yogi Berra was named manager – probably much to the dismay of the CBSers. Just what the Mets needed, another media attraction in Yogi. This year the Mets would outdraw the Yanks by almost a million fans. The Mets with little offense finished 10 games over .500. Outside of Yogi, their only marquee person was Seaver, who had a terrific 21-12 record. With some run support (the Mets hit .235) he would have possibly hit the 25-win mark. But even at that he would have been overshadowed by Lefty Carlton who had 27 wins for the Phillies, who only won 59 games for the season. Lefty was traded to the Phils because of a contract dispute with St. Louis owner Augie Busch. Had he stayed in St. Louis they would have had Lefty and Hoot Gibson, who was 19-12. The shortened season cost Hoot a shot at 20 wins.

The Pirates coasted to the NL East title behind the hitting of Pops Stargell (.293, 33 homers, 112 RBIs), Al Oliver (.312, 89 RBIs), Rich Hebner (.300, 19 homers, 72 RBIs) and Clemente. Roberto at 37 had another good year (.312) and on the last day of the season got his 3000th hit. Always in condition, he could have gotten another four or five hundred hits – except for one of baseball's most tragic accidents. On New Year's Eve he was flying relief supplies to victims of an earthquake in Nicaragua. The plane never made it there. Parts of the wreckage and the pilot were found, but not Roberto.

Steve Blass carried his '71 Series success into the '72 season winning 19, and Dock Ellis won 15, but I wonder if he knew it. But the meat of the staff were relievers Dave Giusti and Ramon Hernandez who combined for 12 wins and 36 saves,

The Reds won the NL West as easily as the Bucs took the East - by 10 1/2 games. The Big Red Machine traded Lee May for speedster Joe Morgan who led the league with 58 stolen bases and 122 runs and also hit 16 homers. Pete Rose (.307, 107 runs scored) and Tony Perez (21 homers, 90 RBIs) also produced but it was Johnny Bench who was the big cog (40 homers, 125 RBIs) winning his second MVP. Gary Nolan was their best starter (15-5), but it was their relievers Tom Hall, Pedro Bourbon and Clay Carroll (who combined for 24 wins and 56 saves) that were the strength of the staff.

In a down to the last out playoff series, the Reds prevailed. They were losing by one in the last inning of game five when Bench cracked a homer to tie it. Two singles and a wild pitch followed to give the Reds the flag.

In the AL West, Oakland was expected to repeat with their maturing team. Their owner was flakey Charlie Finley. He had his team look like a team from the 1890's as he paid them to grow moustaches. You wouldn't think they'd repeat based on Vida Blue's performance. The MVP of '71 (24-8) was a hold-out and finished at 6-10. However, Catfish Hunter (21-7), Ken Holtzman (19-11) and Blue Moon Odom (15-6) picked up the slack. Hall of Famer Rollie Fingers, with the handlebar moustache, really played the villain's role to other teams with 11 wins and 21 saves. The bats of Reggie Jackson (25 homers, 75 RBIs), Sal Bando (15 homers, 77 RBIs), Mike Epstein (26 homers, 70 RBIs) and runner-up MVP Joe Rudi (.305, 19 homers, 75 RBIs) provided plenty of hitting.

In the AL East, CBS was hoping to win baseball's version of an Emmy (the AL flag). They just couldn't do it, but it wasn't because of the efforts of Bobby Murcer who was doing his best to live up to the hype as him being the next Mick. He led the league in runs (102), and was second in homers (33). He finished third in hits (171), doubles (30), RBIs (96) and slugging % (.537). But only Ron "Boomer" Blomberg (14 homers) joined him with more than 10 homers.

It was the Yankee pitching which kept them in the race until the middle of September when they finally lost steam. Mel Stottlemyre typified the strange Yankee year. He had a 3.22 ERA and had 7 shutouts among his 14 victories, but he led the league with 18 losses. Their other starters were Steve Kline (16-9, 2.40 ERA) and two others who possibly may have done better if they were more focused on the game – Fritz Peterson was 17-15 and Mike Kekich 10-13. But the main reason the Yanks stayed in the race was reliever Sparky Lyle who won 9 and saved 35. The Yanks may have won the flag had they not traded 14-game winner Stan Bahnsen for a group of unknowns. All he did in 1972 was win 21 for the Chisox. Major Houk for the past seven years still couldn't find the missing genius ability he had in '61 and '62. The Yanks finished 79-76, 6 1/2 games out. CBS was ready to cancel its hit sitcom - I really didn't know who would want a bunch of re-run episodes of losing.

The Tigers won the AL East behind the pitching of Mickey Lolich (22-14) and Joe Coleman (19-14). They only hit .235, but had seven players with double digit homers led by Norm Cash (22). Al Kaline hit .313 but missed a third of the season.

In the AL playoffs the A's won a thrilling series 3 games to 2. They won the final 2-1 as the Tigers were really feeling blue – Blue Moon Odom went five and Vida Blue completed the final four combining on a five-hitter. Blue Moon was 2-0 hurling 14 scoreless innings. However, in the playoffs Oakland star Reggie Jackson injured his leg and would miss the Series and had to put off being Mr. October until next year.

Despite not having Reggie, the A's took the Series in seven games. Six of the games were decided by one run. The A's took the first two 3-2 and 2-1, Cincy the next 1-0, then the A's scored twice in the bottom of the ninth to win the fourth game 3-2. The Reds bounced back in game 5 scoring a run in each of the last two innings to win 5-4 and stay alive, and then won game 6 in the only game not decided by one run, 6-1. In the deciding seventh game the A's posted a 3-2 victory. Gene Tenace, the A's first baseman, accounted for all of his team's runs in game 7 as he drove in the first run and then the go-ahead run with a double and his pinch-runner scored the third run.

The MVP and star of the Series was the most unlikely player. It was Gene Tenace, who hit only 5 homers in 227 at bats and was only 1 for 17 in the playoffs. All he did in his first two at bats was blast homers. For the Series he batted .348 (8 for 23), had 4 homers and 9 RBIs, which was two more than the rest of the team had. On the hill Catfish chalked up two victories and Rollie had one to go along with a save.

The Yanks could look to next year – but who will be their owner? - Maybe NBC?

1973
You Gotta Believe: Yogi has the Last Laugh

As the year began it was announced who the new Yankee owner would be. It was a group headed by George Steinbrenner. Who cared? Nobody really cares about owners and the general fan would have a problem naming any of them. All through the history of the game only Connie Mack would probably be the one most remembered. Yeah, I know of the Dodgers' Walter O'Malley, the Red Sox' Tom Yawkey and the Cards' August Busch, but generally the owners stayed in the background. This new guy was a shipbuilder and was hoping to get the Yankees afloat. However, he initially came across as an owner who would let his baseball men run the team. Right - at this time, I was not aware of his past coaching experience of college football. Everyone would soon realize that he just can't stay away from the action despite his lip service to the contrary.

It was March when I was at work and walked by a radio and heard the most unusual trade in baseball history. It was not between teams – but between players. Pitchers Fritz Peterson and Mike Kekich traded families - spouses, kids and pets. Naturally this was a big news story, with most of the country viewing it with disdain. I think it had an adverse effect on their baseball performance last year and carried into this year. The public's negative reaction to this strange trade could have been the reason Peterson had a poor 8-15 record. As for Kekich, he was traded in June.

This situation, combined with the new Boss meddling, could not have been a pleasant time for Major Houk, who was used to managing without interference - CBS allowed him to run the show. Houk kept the Yanks around first place until the end of July when a famous home plate collision between the leagues' two top catchers, rivals Carlton Fisk and Thurman Munson resulted in one of the games more celebrated bench clearing brawls. This incident activated the somewhat dormant Yankee/Red Sox rivalry. Usually this kind of action elevates a team to a higher degree of play – but not this time. The Yankees were mediocre the rest of the year, finishing fourth in the AL East at 80-82. Maybe Houk was too busy making sure the players had proper hair length and no facial hair, as per the new Boss' memo, instead of figuring out how to win games.

This was the year that the American League enacted the Designated Hitter Rule whereas the pitchers would not bat – one of the non-pitchers would take their place in the line-up making the term DH part of the baseball dictionary (in the AL anyway).

The Yanks had some good years from a few players. Bobby Murcer had a stellar year as his .304 average and 286 total bases were fourth in the league, his 96 RBIs were fifth, and 182 hits were second. Munson hit .301 with 20 homers and newcomer Graig Nettles matched Murcer's 22 homers. The Yankees had the first batter in baseball to bat as the DH. He was the "Boomer" (Blomberg) and he was the Yanks' primary DH. Only playing 100 games due to injury he batted .329 with 12 homers and 57 RBIs. This foursome seemed to be a solid nucleus for the Yankees' future. Stottlemyre's record was like his teams – .500 at 16-16. Rookie Doc Medich was the best starter at 14-9. However it was relievers Sparky Lyle and Lindy McDaniel who totaled 17 wins and 37 saves who kept the Yanks from being in the basement.

Major Houk resigned after the season, possibly envying Yogi Berra's success with the cross-town Mets. All Yogi did was lead the Mets to the NL pennant. They were the only team in the NL East to be over .500 (82-79). In fact three teams in the NL West had a better record than the Mets. The Mets again crushed the Yanks in the attendance race by about 700,000.

The Mets' offense was pretty poor – with only Felix Millan (.290 average) and Rusty Staub being quality hitters. It was another terrific year for Tom Seaver, the Cy Young Award winner. He was 19-10 and led the league in Ks (251) and ERA (2.08). The other main contributor to this Met miracle was their reliever Tug McGraw (5 wins 25 saves). When things were going bad it was always his "You Gotta Believe" saying that brought them back. The Mets had to go to the last weekend of the season to clinch the flag.

One of the season's major feats was the Atlanta Braves setting a record of having three players with 40 homers. Hank Aaron hammered out 40 (leaving him one short of the Babe's Major

League record of 714), Darrell Evans belted 41 and the third was a real surprise, second baseman Davey Johnson, who finished runner-up with 43 – his previous high was 18. No wonder the Atlanta ballpark was referred to as the launching pad. Despite this barrage of heavy hitting the Braves finished fifth in the NL West. Pops Stargell led the NL with 44 circuit blasts.

The other outstanding achievement of the year was turned in by Nolan Ryan of the sub-par California Angels (79-84). He was 21-16 with a 2.87 ERA and set a new Major League strikeout record besting Koufax's mark by one with 383 Ks (and it's a lot tougher task to do in the AL with a DH rather than the NL with the usually easy to K number nine pitcher spot in the line-up).

The Mets' reward for winning their division was to be the victim of the Big Red Machine. Cincy had the bats going again. Pete Rose was MVP, leading the league with 230 hits and a .338 batting average. Speedy Joe Morgan was second in the NL with 116 runs and 67 stolen bases while clubbing 26 homers. Johnny Bench swatted 25 homers with 104 RBIs, while Tony Perez belted 27 homers and drove home 101 runs. Their top pitcher Jack Billingham, matched Seaver's 19 wins and Don Gullett had 18. The 'Machine won 19 more games than the Mets and outscored them by 133 runs. What a mismatch!

The NL playoffs were anything but a mismatch. Seaver lost game 1 to Billingham, 2-1 on homers by Rose in the eighth and Bench in the ninth. The Mets took the second game 5-0, scoring 4 in the ninth, behind Jon Matlocks shutout. In game 3 Jerry Koosman won 9-2. The game was marred by a donnybrook, when Rose slid hard into the Mets shortstop Bud Harrelson. Outweighed by at least 30 lbs., Harrelson did not back down and came up swinging and the melee ensued. Rose got even in game 4 with a twelfth inning homer to win 2-1 and tie the series at two apiece. In the finale Seaver got some runs to work with and beat Billingham, 9-2. So much for the mismatch - the Mets out hit the 'Machine .220 to .186 and had a lower ERA- Mets 1.34, Cincy 4.59.

In the AL East, Baltimore, making like past Yankee teams, won the title for the fourth time in five years. Their stars were pitchers Jim Palmer (22 wins) and Mike Cuellar (18). Their big bat came from Earl Williams who had 22 homers and 83 RBIs. He was from East Orange, NJ and I worked with his cousin Carl in the Newark Post Office, so I was pulling for the O's to beat the Oakland A's in the AL playoffs. Other Orioles who did well with the wood were Tommy Davis (.306, 89 RBIs), Al Bumbry (.337) and Rich Coggins (.319). It would be tough as the A's were loaded. They had three 20-game winners, Catfish Hunter (21-5), Ken Holtzman (21-13) and Vida Blue (20-9). Rollie Fingers saved 22 and won 7. For offense, they had MVP Reggie Jackson, who batted .293 and led the league with 32 homers and 117 RBIs. Sal Bando had 29 homers and 98 RBIs. Gene Tenace, showing his power surge in last year's World Series wasn't a fluke, connected for 24 homers and drove in 84 runs. In the league's first year of the designated hitter, the A's DH Deron Johnson came through with 19 homers and 81 RBIs.

In the AL playoffs it was again a five game series. The teams split the first four. Game 3 was a gem as Cuellar and Holtzman were locked in a 1-1 battle for 10 innings until Bert Campaneris ended it with a lead-off homer off of Cuellar in the bottom of the eleventh. In the finale Catfish pitched a five-hit shutout to win 3-0 for his second win of the playoffs.

Again, the World Series looked like a mismatch. The Mets took care of the Big Red Machine, now they were ready to do it to the Big Green Machine (the A's uniforms were green).

It seemed a possibility when, in game 5, Jerry Koosman and Tug McGraw combined on a three-hit shutout to win 2-0 to put the Mets up 3 games to 2 – but they'd now have to beat the A's in Oakland.

In game 6 Seaver pitched well, except to Reggie who had a pair of RBI two-baggers and a single and scored in a 3-1 victory. Anyway, the Mets couldn't touch Catfish. In the deciding game Oakland won the Series in the third on 2- run homers by Bert Campaneris and Reggie, who was the Series MVP. Holtzman and Fingers stifled the Mets batters in the 5-2 finale.

David doesn't always beat Goliath. Well, at least Yogi still had a job even though he lost the Series; unlike in 1964 when the Yanks axed him after the same scenario.

Dick Williams tried to pull a 1964 Johnny Keane by resigning because of owner Charlie Finley interfering with on field activities. Steinbrenner quickly gobbled him up. I didn't understand how managing for Steinbrenner would be an improvement over Finley. However, the deal was squashed by the league as Williams was still under contract to the A's.

With hindsight I think the Boss was thinking, "Although I want Williams I'd rather have Catfish and Reggie – but how??"

1974
There Goes the Boss

The start of 1974 would include some major changes. With the resignation of Major Houk, who became manager of the Detroit Tigers, it looked like the Yankees might have Baseball's first black manager, Elston Howard, a Yankee coach, was waiting for the call that never came. Ellie was a winner, having been in ten World Series and wearing four rings. The Yanks hired Bill Virdon, who helped make the 1960 Series a miserable one for the Yanks, to be manager. Also, this year the Yanks were playing their first year in Shea Stadium because Yankee Stadium was under renovation.

The season opened with the anticipation of a new career home run record. Hank Aaron finished 1973 with 713 homers, one short of the Babe's 714. He tied the record off of Jack Billingham, and then on April 8, he hammered # 715 off of Al Downing to take over the top spot – Sorry Babe!

This year in the AL East no team was going to run away with the division.

If you were told of Boog Powell's stats (12 homers, 45 RBIs) and Brook Robinson's (7 homers, 59 RBIs) and that Jim Palmer was 7-12 you would surmise that the Orioles would be also-rans. But this year all the teams were devoid of stars. Bobby Grich led the O's with 19 homers and 82 RBIs. Their three starters Mike Cuellar (22-10), Ross Grimsley (18-13) and Dave McNally (16-10) were the backbone of the team, as they out raced the Yankees for the AL East title by two games. Both teams were hot down the stretch. The Yanks won 20 of 31. The back-breaker was an Orioles' three-game sweep in the middle of September. It was Baltimore's fifth East title in six years. The Orioles would end the season series against former Yank manager Houk and his Tigers. The O's won all three which infuriated the Boss as he claimed the Tigers and Houk didn't play their regulars so the O's world have a better chance to win and keep

178

the Yanks from winning the East flag. The Yanks were runner-up at 89-73 missing the AL East title by two games.

The new Boss' regime showed how the Yankee roster would be throughout the years – always changing. This year they had two new additions that led them in batting – Lou Piniella batted .305 and Elliott Maddox .303. Playing in Shea Stadium, Bobby Murcer missed the short right field stands of Yankee Stadium, and hit only 10 homers, but had 88 RBIs. His comparisons to being the next Mantle appeared to be fading.

The Yankee pitchers who kept them in the race were Doc Medich and Pat Dobson, who were both 19-15. Sparkly Lyle continued to be one of the league's best firemen winning 9 and saving 15.

Another distraction may have affected the Yankees, although I think it was a positive one that motivated the Yanks to their September drive that almost overtook the Orioles. The Boss was involved in some improper campaign contributions, something like that, as I don't really follow off the field stuff that closely. Baseball Commissioner Bowie Kuhn suspended Steinbrenner until 1976.

In the AL West, the Oakland A's continued their mini-dynasty, with a fourth AL West flag in a row. To replace an unhappy Dick Williams as manager Charley Finley chose Alvin Dark who won an NL pennant across the bay with San Francisco in '62. They held off Texas to win by five games. The A's were only one game better than the Yanks with 90 wins. They had Catfish, the Cy Young Award winner with a 25-12 slate, Ken Holtzman (19 wins) and Vida Blue (17 wins) with help from Rollie Fingers (9 wins 15 saves) to comprise the league's best staff. The offense had the usual cast of characters: Reggie (29 homers, 93 RBIs), Sal Bando (22 homers, 103 RBIs), Gene Tenace (26 homers), and runner-up MVP Joe Rudi (22 homers, 93 RBIs).

The A's beat the O's in another alphabet playoff series, 3 games to 1. After Cuellar won the opener 6-3 the A's took the next three – Holtzman threw a five-hit shutout in a 5-0 win, Blue tossed a four-hit shutout as he bested Palmer in a 1-0 squeaker on a homer by Bando in the fourth inning, and then won the final 2-1 behind Catfish, as an RBI double by Reggie was the A's only hit (Oakland did get 11 walks though, which helped their cause).

Boss Steinbrenner may have been thinking how nice it would be to have the Athletics back in Kansas City, when the Yanks could pick their Kissin' Cousins clean.

On a personal level I had major back surgery and was out of work for 14 weeks. I spent most of that time playing with my sons. Mike was 4 and Chris was 2. My wife thought she had three kids. It was during this period when I introduced my kids to baseball. Whenever Josephine wasn't home we would move the furniture, got the plastic bat and nerf ball and played ball. We used diapers as the bases. Some of my wife's favorite crystals were victims of our ball playing.

The Pirates won the NL East behind the lumber of Pops Stargell (.301, 25 homers, 96 RBIs), Al Oliver (.321, 85 RBIs) and Richie Zisk (.313, 17 homers, 100 RBIs). Jerry Reuss was their ace at 16-11. The Bucs beat the Cards out by 1 1/2 games. Lou Brock tried to run them to the title with a Major League record 118 stolen bases. Hoot Gibson was 39 years old and it was starting to take its toll as his record fell to 11-13. The Mets' defense of their title never materialized as they went a woeful 71-91. Seaver was not so terrific at 11-11 and for the first time had an ERA that was over three (3.20). However, sharing Shea with the Yanks, the Mets outdrew them by half a million.

NL MVP Steve Garvey (.312, 111 RBIs), Jim "The Toy Cannon" Wynn (32 homers, 108 RBIs – he was nicknamed for his 5'9" height), and Bill Buckner (.314) led the Dodgers to the NL West flag. Hurlers Andy Messersmith (20-9) and Don Sutton (19-9) were saved by some of fireman Mike Marshall's record 106 appearances (15 wins, 21 saves). Marshall broke new ground becoming the first reliever to win the Cy Young Award nosing out his teammate Messersmith.

The Dodgers took the Pirates in four games in the NL playoffs behind the batting of Garvey (.389, 7 for 18, 2 homers, 5 RBIs) and the pitching of Sutton (2-0, 0.53 ERA in 17 innings). Stargell was the only Buc to do anything with the lumber (.400, 2 homers, 4 RBIs).

It was a California World Series – LA Dodgers vs. Oakland A's. With the Series tied at one the A's beat the Dodgers in three straight to take the Championship in five games. Ironically four of the five games ended up 3-2, but the A's won three of them. Catfish and Holtzman posted wins and Blue Moon Odom was credited with the victory in the clincher as Rudi's seventh inning homer broke a 2-2 tie giving the A's the title as the Dodgers couldn't do anything against Fingers who came in to seal the deal. It was a three-peat for the A's. Rollie Fingers, with his handlebar mustache, saved two of them in addition to winning game one. In over 9 innings of relief his ERA was 1.93 and he was the Series MVP.

A couple of things occurred after the postseason. The first was that it became evident that Bobby Murcer would not become the next Mick. In October he was traded for Giant star Bobby Bonds, who like Murcer, had an off year. The second was that Charlie Finley messed up Catfish's contract and he was declared a free agent by arbitrator Peter Seitz. Ironically, a few years later I was at an arbitration hearing for the Post Office and the arbitrator was Seitz. I had one of my best lunch breaks as I was able to sit with Seitz and talk about baseball.

The last day of the year, the Yanks threw out hook, line and sinker and reeled in their big fish, I mean Catfish. For the past four years Catfish was a 20-game winner and showed he is a big time pitcher by virtue of his 7-2 postseason record. This definitely was not good news for the Yankee Hater.

1975
Yankee Title Chances Get LYNN-ched

The season began badly for a Yankee Hater as the Catfish deal was finalized the first week of the year, making the Yanks the AL favorites, along with Baltimore. Boston was not looked upon as a real threat to take the pennant.

However, the Bosox had two rookies that battered AL pitching. Jim Rice took over in left for Yaz, who was moved to first. All Rice did was hit .309 (fourth in the AL), had 102 RBIs (fifth in the league) and hit 22 homers, and he finished third in the MVP voting. His rookie teammate Fred Lynn took the MVP award. I was captivated by Lynn mainly because he looked like the second coming of Stan the Man. He was runner-up in batting (.331) to, naturally, Rod Carew's .359, led the AL in runs (103), doubles (47), slugging % (.566) and was third in RBIs (105). He also played center field with flair, always making spectacular catches. Although he surpassed his rookie MVP year in 1979 and had other quality years being a nine-time All-Star he was not the Man. The Crimson Hose also got productivity out of a future Famer, catcher, Carlton Fisk (.331, 10 homers in half of the season) and Cecil Cooper (.314, 14 homers in two-thirds of the season).

On the hill they were led by Rick Wise (19-12), making a case that being traded for Lefty Carlton a few years ago was not all that one sided, Luis Tiant (18-14), Spaceman Bill Lee (17-9) and Roger Moret (14-3). Tiant, a.k.a."El Tiante", was one of baseball's most entertaining characters gazing at center field during his unusual wind-up that resulted in 229 victories. He's another that I feel has the stats to be in the Hall.

The preseason AL East pick, the Orioles, finished second behind the return to the Cy Young Award form of Jim Palmer (23-11), and Mike Torrez (20-9). Lee May (30 homers, 99 RBIs), Ken

Singleton (.300, 15 homers) and Don Baylor (25 homers, 76 RBIs) led a balanced line-up. But they came in second, 4 1/2 out.

The other favorite, the Yanks were third (83-77) 12 1/2 games out. My fears concerning their new acquisition, the Catfish were realized as he tied for the AL lead in victories (23) with Palmer. However, Doc Medich (16-16) and Pat Dobson (11-14) failed to match last year's 19 wins apiece. Even Sparky Lyle had a down year (5-7, 6 saves) and wasn't their saves leader – it was rookie Tippy Martinez with 8 and a 2.68 ERA.

The Yankees' other newcomer, Bobby Bonds, also came through, hitting 32 homers and driving in 85 runs. He also became a 30/30 man with 30 stolen bases. Chris Chambliss hit .304 and Graig Nettles punched out 21 homers with 91 RBIs. But the big bat was provided by catcher Thurman Munson, who was battling Fisk for being the Majors' second best back-stopper behind Johnny Bench. Munson hit .318 with 102 RBIs.

The Yanks' year was going nowhere so in August the Yanks fired Virdon and brought in Billy Martin. He didn't do much better than Virdon. The firing probably came about in late July when the Yanks were still in the hunt. The Yanks faced Boston in a four game series at Shea. The Bronx Bombers took the opener - the Red Sox regrouped and "LYNN-ched" the Yanks by taking the next three.

I decided to take my son Mike to one of these games - it was his first baseball game. He was five years old and I thought it would be a good game to see. Although he was only five we played a lot of ball in the back yard. He had good eye/hand co-ordination and made some great catches, like Lynn. He didn't know why I hated the Yanks and he became a Lynn fan.

During this summer our niece Vita, who was 16 stayed with us. Unlike her Aunt Josephine, she was a big baseball fan. She had a crush on Yankee rookie Tippy Martinez. I asked her if she wanted to go to the game with me and Mike. I don't know why, but she opted not to go. Well, in order to get my son to soak up the complete experience we got to the game early to see batting practice. We got field level seats next to the fence. During the batting practice I saw Tippy Martinez in the outfield. I started hollering "Tippy, Tippy" and was waving for him to come over. He did and Mike, with eyes wide open, saw me tell Tippy about my niece having a crush on him. We shook hands. I was happy that Boston won and when I got home showed Vita the hand that shook Tippy's. She went bonkers. I think she wanted to 'Bobbit' (cut off) my hand. When we ate dinner, I had to make sure where Vita was in relation to the knives. In a couple days this passed, and since my hand was washed several times, she didn't want it any more.

Oakland won the AL West despite losing Catfish. Vida Blue (22 wins), Ken Holtzman (18) and Rollie Fingers (10 wins/24 saves) were able to hold off the Kansas City Royals who were led by the AL's budding new star George Brett, who batted .308 leading the league with 195 hits and 13 triples.

Reggie again led the A's attack with a league leading 36 homers and drove in 104 runs. Gene Tenace hit 29 homers, newcomer and former Cub star, Billy Williams belted 23 and Joe Rudi 21. It was the A's fifth West division title in a row.

In the AL playoffs it was a Red Sox sweep as Yaz (.455), Fisk (.417), and Lynn (.364) led a potent attack. El Tiante threw a masterful three-hitter winning the opener 7-1 while Wise went into the eighth inning in the 5-3 clincher. This dismayed the Yankee fans as for this playoff they were Athletic supporters.

Pittsburgh won the NL East over Philly behind their Lumber Company – Pops Stargell (.295, 22 homers, 90 RBIs), Dave "the Cobra" Parker (.308, 25 homers, 101 RBIs – nicknamed so because he attacks pitches like the cobra attacks its prey), Richie Zisk (.290, 20 homers, 75 RBIs), Al Oliver (18 homers, 84 RBIs) and Manny Sanguillen (.328 average).

The Mets improved by 11 games, primarily behind the arm of Tom Seaver, who like Palmer, returned to his terrific Cy Young form going 22-9 with a 2.38 ERA. The Mets came in third.

However, the Pirates' Lumber Company was no Big Red Machine. This year it was Joe Morgan's turn for the MVP. He used his trademark batting form which included his left arm flapping like a hummingbird to hit .327 with 17 homers and 94 RBIs. Johnny Bench (28 homers, 110 RBIs), Tony Perez (20 homers, 109 RBIs), Pete Rose (.317, 112 runs), George Foster (.300, 24 homers), and Ken Griffey. (.305, 95 runs) fueled the big 'Machine. On the hill starters Gary Nolan, Jack Billingham and Don Gullett all won 15 and Fred Norman was 12-4 while fireman Rawley Eastwick saved 22.

The 'Machine swept the Lumber Company, putting it in position to win their first World Series after losing in '70 and '72. Griffey (.333, 4 for 12, 4 RBIs) and Perez (.417, 5 for 12, 4 RBIs) together drove in more runs than the entire Lumber Company. Gullett and Norman won the first two games 8-3 and 6-1 respectively, and the Reds took the third game 5-3 in extra innings

Rice was injured at the end of the season. The question was "How crispy would the Red Sox attack be without Rice?" But without him they swept the A's. The next question was "Can they dismantle the 'Machine?"

Cincy was up 3 games to 2 (El Tiante won both of the Red Sox games) when game 6 was finally played after rain caused a three day delay. Because of the postponements El Tiante was able to start this historic game. I let my son stay up to watch, and he was happy as his favorite, Lynn, hit a 3-run homer to give Boston a 3-0 lead. The 'Machine came back to take a 6-3 lead but Bernie Carbo tied it with a 3-run pinch-hit homer. Mike went to bed and I watched the rest myself until 12:30 a.m. It was exciting especially Dewey Evans' fantastic catch robbing Morgan of a homer in the eleventh. Fisk led off the Boston twelfth with a long fly down the left field line. In a famous scene he seemingly willed it fair – it hit the foul pole for a game-winning homer. FisKs game-ending homer is rated as one of baseball's greatest moments

In the deciding game the Curse of the Bambino came out. The Sox took a 3-0 lead but Spaceman Lee gave Perez one of his noted change-ups that went into orbit to make the score 3-2. The Reds tied it in the seventh and won it on a single to center by Morgan in the ninth inning. Rose (.370, 10 for 27) was selected as the Series MVP. Rawly Eastwick was 2-0 in relief with a 2.25 ERA in 8 innings of work covering 5 games

When Christmas came I got my son a quality glove. It was a Fred Lynn model, his favorite player. Yes, there was another Yankee Hater in the family…but not for long.

1976
The Yanks Get BENCHED

The Boss came off of suspension as the season began. As usual, the cast of characters changed. It was the infancy of free agency. The Yanks ran away with the AL East. Their holdovers performed well – Thurman Munson (.302, 17 homers, 102 RBIs) was AL MVP, Graig Nettles led the AL with 32 homers, Chris Chambliss (.293, 17 homers, 93 RBIs) and Roy White (14 homers and league leading 104 runs) added additional pop. Additions Mickey Rivers, acquired in a trade for Bonds, hit .312 and scored 95 runs, and Willie Randolph played second like Bobby Richardson.

The new pitchers included Ed Figueroa (19-10), Dock Ellis (17-8), but I wonder if he knew he was a Yankee, and Ken Holtzman (9-7). Catfish had an off year at 17-15. Sparky Lyle bounced back with 7 wins and 23 saves.

Baltimore had 20-game winners in Jim Palmer (22-13), who won his third Cy Young Award, and Wayne Garland (20-7) and their offensive punch was provided by the trade acquisition of Reggie Jackson (27 homers, 91 RBIs) and Lee May (25 homers, league leading 109 RBIs). They came in second 10 1/2 games out. Boston was third as both Lynn and Rice did not match their rookie years.

Detroit wound up in fifth place but did provide the entertainment highlights for the year. It occurred whenever the AL Rookie of the Year, Mark "The Bird" Fidrych took the mound. He was nicknamed for his resemblance to Big Bird on Sesame Street. He was 19-9 and led the league with a 2.34 ERA and 24 complete games and was selected to start the All- Star Game for the AL. His rituals during the game included getting on his hands and knees to manicure the mound and also talking to the baseball. The conversation was one-sided with The Bird telling the ball what direction to go to as it entered the strike zone (I guess the ball listened based on the results). He captivated the country as TV ratings and crowd attendance soared every time he was scheduled to pitch. In September I immensely enjoyed watching The Bird on TV as he put up goose eggs as he blanked the Yankees 6-0 as the baseball apparently took his advice to avoid the fat part of the Pinstripers' bats. Sadly, this entertainment was only for this year as Fidrych had a bad knee and developed a sore "wing" that virtually ended his career.

The Yanks' easy run to the AL East title caused problems in my household. My sons and I would always have a game on TV – the Mets or the Yanks. Mike was 6 and Chris 4 at the time. Mike could not understand how I could root for the Mets and not the Yanks. He told me to root for both of them. I explained to him my reasons, but he said that was stupid and he was going to root for both teams. Another reason he started to be a Yankee fan was Rivers and Randolph. Mike really identified with them. Mike was thin, fast, and quick and can flash the leather like them. At least he still used the Lynn glove. Naturally Chris followed his older brother's lead and became a Met and Yankee fan. I wondered what I'd tell my dad, with me raising Yankee fans.

In the AL West, the Kansas City Royals broke the five year reign of Oakland. The Royals' George Brett was crowned batting champ (.333) just edging out teammate Hal McRae (.332). They beat out Oakland by 2 1/2 games. The A's owner Charlie Finley caused baseball plenty of turmoil as he sensed what free agency would do to the game so he made deals to get rid of his high priced players. Vida Blue was Yankee bound and Joe Rudi and Rollie Fingers were headed to Fenway; but Commissioner Bowie Kuhn voided the deals in the best interest of the game.

The Yanks were in the postseason for the first time since 1964. It must have been their return to the renovated Yankee Stadium that did it – Nettles and Chambliss were happy with the short right field stands. As a Yankee Hater all I'll say about the playoffs is that they won in five games. (Editor's Note: Chambliss' dramatic ninth inning homer gave the Yanks their first championship in over a decade).

In the NL East the Phillies rode the bats of Mike Schmidt (38 homers, 107 RBIs) and Greg Luzinski (.304, 21 homers, 95 RBIs) and the pitching of Lefty Carlton (20-7) and Jim Lonborg (18-10) to 101 victories and coasted to the title.

Sparky Anderson's Big Red Machine again steamrolled to an easy NL West title. Joe Morgan repeated as MVP (.320, 27 homers, 111 RBIs), Tony Perez (19 homers, 91 RBIs), George Foster (.306, 29 homers, 121 RBIs), Pete Rose (.323, 120 runs), Ken Griffey (.336, 111 runs) and Cesar Geronimo (.307) all were cogs in the big 'Machine. Surprisingly only their usual power man had a poor year – Johnny Bench (.234, 16 homers, 74 RBIs). Gary Nolan (15-9) and Pat Zachry (14-7) were two of seven Cincy hurlers to have double digit wins.

The 'Machine ran over the Phillies in three straight. Rose bloomed going 6 for 14 (.429) with two doubles and a triple. Griffey was 5 for 13 (.385) while Foster blasted two big homers. Bench showed signs of waking up (4 for 12 with a homer and double) and was hoping to show Munson who the game's best catcher was in the Series, as Thurman completely outshined him during the season. The Phillies' outfielder Jay Johnstone, who was known to be flakier than cereal, had one of the top "Post" season stats ever hitting .778 (7 for 9) with a 1.111 slugging %. Cincy and the Yanks met in the Series in 1939 and 1961, with the Yanks taking both. This time the Reds were the favorite.

What I remember most about this Series is that Pete Rose took a gamble that really paid off. Rivers, the Yankees' left-handed hitting lead-off man, liked to bunt down the third base line or slap hits to the left side of the field. Well, Rose positioned himself down the line so close to Rivers that it appeared that if Mickey swung he would hit Rose in the schnozz. If that happened the bat would have probably broken since Pete was such a "hardnosed" player. This maneuver took the Yankee table setter out of the Series - he was 3 for 18.

The Series opened in Cincy on Saturday and was the only day game. It was so cold for the remaining games, it seemed the games were being played in Alaska.

The NL MVP Morgan showed how the Series would be when he homered in the first inning. Nettles tied it with a sac-fly in the second but that was the only run they would be able to push across as Don Gullett went seven innings for the victory. The Big Red Machine scored 4 more times with triples by shortstop Dave Concepcion and Bench being the key hits. Cincy 5 – Yanks 1.

In game 2 Catfish got nailed for three runs in the second with Bench getting a big double. While Catfish kept the 'Machine scoreless, the Yanks tied it with one in the fourth and two in the seventh. Catfish deserved a better fate. With the game tied and two outs in the ninth the Yankees shortstop, Fred Stanley, made a throwing error allowing Griffey to reach second base. Catfish walked Morgan but Perez ruined the strategy with a game-winning RBI single. Cincy 4 – Yanks 3.

In game 3, Yankee Stadium looked like it was in Nome, Alaska. Since the game was in an AL park the DH was used and Cincy took advantage of it. The DH, Dan Driessen, had a single, double, homer and a walk. The Reds opened the scoring in the second on a Driessen single, a Foster double and singles by Bench and Concepcion for a 3-0 lead. Driessen's homer made it 4-0. The Yankees came back with one in the fifth and another in the seventh on a homer by the trivia question of who was the only Yankee to hit a homer in the '76 Series – it was Jim Mason, who matched his season total of one. The Reds salted the game away with two in the eighth on singles by Rose, Griffey and Foster and a double by Morgan. Pat Zachry pitched into the seventh inning (he was probably taken out so as not to get frostbite) for the win. Cincy 6 – Yanks 2.

The Yanks got a moral victory the next day. They didn't lose – it rained. But that only put off the inevitable. In game 4 the Yanks drew first blood in the first on a Munson single and a Chambliss double. Figueroa held the lead until the fourth when an RBI single by Foster was followed by a Bench 2-run homer for a 3-1 lead. Another Munson single made it 3-2 but the Reds ended any hopes the Yanks had when they scored 4 in the ninth with a Bench 3-run homer being the big blow. Nolan won the Series clincher battling the New York frigid weather going 6 2/3 innings. Cincy 7 – Yanks 2. The Big Red Machine buzz-sawed through the Series.

Poor Munson. He did his best to show the world he was the Majors' top catcher. After all he was 9 for 17 (an incredible .529) and set a record with 6 straight hits. But Bench was better - 8 for 15 (.533) with a double, triple and two homers, 4 runs scored and 6 RBIs.

The Boss was possibly musing "Where can I find a power hitter?"

1977 & 1978
Two Lost Years

As a Yankee Hater this two year period was very disheartening to me. This bought All-Star team (the Yankees) continued to win despite turmoil and chaos never before seen in a baseball organization. Boss Steinbrenner let the dollars fly as the Yanks had more stars than the Milky Way. Some of these top players were Reggie, "the Goose" (Gossage), Bucky Dent and Don Gullett. There was a managerial firing, players suspended, fights between players, and disputes with the Boss (the signature on this chaos was the Reggie/Billy Martin altercation in the dugout on national TV when team members had to restrain them from really hurting each other). The organization chemistry was such that these were known as the Bronx Zoo years. However, like the crazy A's of 1972 -74, they overcame these conditions (and probably thrived on it) to win. In 1977 there was a changing of the guard in NY baseball as the Mets traded their franchise, Tom Seaver, to Cincinnati in mid-season. (The Mets' glory days would not return until the mid '80's). He finished the season 21-6 (7-3 NY, 14-3 Cincy), and may have lost the Cy Young because of his split tenure. Carlton won the Cy Young Award (23-10) for the East champion Phillies.

This year (1977) the American League expanded as they put a team back in Seattle (Mariners) and one outside our borders in Toronto (Blue Jays).

In 1977 my younger son Chris became a Yankee fan. He was following his brother's path in becoming a Yankee fan, but I had hopes that since he was only five years old I could change his mind. During the summer sometime around his birthday we went to a game. There we were at the Stadium – Mike for the Yanks and Chris a quasi-Yankee fan. Naturally I was hoping if the Yankees lost, Chris would be a Yankee Hater. The reverse of my hopes occurred. The Yankees romped by a lot, and Reggie hit a monster home run.

This solidified him as a Yankee die-hard and Reggie fan. So now my household was two against me.

In 1978 my son Mike was eight years old was eligible for baseball. In our town of South Brunswick we were not Little League affiliated. Our town had the South Brunswick Athletic Association (SBAA). The SBAA had rules that made it more fun to play in than playing Little League. The rules that I thought made it more fun than Little League were that you played within your age group (not 8's with 12- year olds), the line-up had everyone batting (if twelve players were there all twelve batted), and the most important was that you had to play in the field every other inning. In the SBAA no one sat on the bench. The downside was we couldn't try for the Little League World Series in Williamsport, PA and through the years I was manager, I had some really good teams. Anyway, Mike opted not to play despite my encouragement. He was apprehensive thinking he was not good enough. He thought all dads played ball with their kids like I did.

So the town season started and he didn't play. But still we went out to the field to practice. I'd pitch and Mike and Chris would alternate hitting and fielding. On one of these occasions, an 8-year old team came over to practice. As we were leaving, the coach said Mike could join their practice. I don't know how good this team was but Mike was the best there, hitting shots over the outfielders and fielding like Willie Randolph. After the practice the coach asked me what team Mike was on. I told him he didn't sign up. He said "Why, he's one of the best I've seen". Mike heard this and was plenty mad about not signing up to play. From this point on Mike has never been apprehensive about anything.

On days we did not go to a field to practice, we'd do it at home. I would pitch a softball in the front yard while Mike and Chris would hit and play the field. The one in the field would play next to the curb on the opposite side of the street (we lived on a side street which had little traffic and cars didn't park there). The primary rule was any ball hit on a fly onto the yard across the street was a home run (our neighbor's there didn't mind - they had four older sons).

Mike had no problem accomplishing this, but Chris who was six couldn't do it. On occasion he'd get hold of one but Mike would glide right or left along the curb to snag them with his Fred Lynn model glove. Well Chris finally blasted a Reggie shot (Chris envisioned himself as a righty "Mr. October"). Mike and I watched the ball as it soared into the South Brunswick sky - while Chris was jumping up and down similar to Carlton Fisk in the '75 Series. However, his elation was suddenly squashed. As the ball was headed for a home run it slammed into a telephone wire and dropped right into Mike's Fred Lynn leather.

Chris' exasperation was too much as he had enough and went into the house as Mike and I were rolling on the lawn with laughter. This event ended with mom coming out of the house hollering at me and Mike to let Chris get his homer. Mike gave mom a proper response "Mom, you should be telling that to the telephone wire, not us."

Since Mike didn't play this year, I was asked to play for a Newark Post Office team, in an arc slow pitch softball league. I was naturally the third baseman. We didn't have a good arc pitcher so we didn't do so well, but I was one of the top hitters. A few times I took Mike to see me play. Kind of strange, I should have been watching him play. At our practice I observed some little league teams practicing on the adjacent fields. Some of these coaches were real idiots screaming at these kids. I thought that somehow I would have to get into coaching as I couldn't visualize my kids playing for these idiots.

The highlight of the season for me was a game that I went to that involved Pete Rose's 44-game hitting streak. Once Rose reached 30 games I saw that the Reds would soon be coming to Shea Stadium to play the Mets. If Pete kept the streak going to 36 games, a hit in the next game would tie the modern day National League record of 37 by the Braves Tommy Holmes in 1945 - the NL record is 44 games by Wee Willie Keeler in 1897. I made arrangements to attend this record tying game at Shea, if Rose kept his streak going. He did - so the day of the game, July 25, I put on a rose colored shirt and placed an artificial rose behind my ear – Josephine, naturally, opting not to go just shook her head at my get-up. With my sons in the car I made a stop in Belleville to pick up my sister Carole and her daughters Cheryl, Christine and Cathy, as they wanted to see this historic game. On the way to Shea I was explaining to my sons and nieces how Rose was going for the modern game NL record (post-1900), but there was still Wee Willie's NL record to go after. Before we even reached New York City I bored all five of the kids to sleep. I guess my sister had insomnia.

Even though Rose was facing the league's worst team, the Mets, he would be going against Craig Swan, who was the NL ERA leader in '78. With Tommy Holmes in attendance Pete tied the record in the third inning with a hit. Rose continued his streak for seven more games passing George Sisler's 40-game streak in 1922 and Ty Cobb's 41 in 1911. He wound up tying Wee Willie Keeler's NL 44-game batting streak record. Pete's streak was stopped in game 45, thus missing Joe DiMaggio's Major League record of 56 in 1941 by twelve games. This NL record-tying feat would just about make Rose an odds on favorite to be voted into the Hall of Fame in his first year of eligibility.

Editor's Note: The Dodgers once again became the Yankees whipping boys losing both the 1977 and 1978 Series. The '77 Series included Reggie's 3 homers in game 6.

During the 1978 season Ron "Gator" Guidry put on display one of the greatest pitching performances in the history of baseball. His Cy Young performance included an unbelievable 25-3 record (.893 winning %), 1.74 ERA, 248 Ks and 9 shutouts. As a result I patterned my pitching style after him even though I'm a righty.

The 1978 season saw the Yankees catch the Red Sox after being behind by 14 games in mid-season, go ahead by 6 in September, only to allow the Red Sox to catch them to force a one-game playoff highlighted by Bucky Dent's 3-run homer. (Bucky was a favorite of the teenage girls). The '78 Series was highlighted by Graig Nettles imitating Brooks Robinson in the field, Reggie (.391, 2 homers), Thurman Munson and Roy White (8 hits each), an unassuming Brian Doyle (.438 – replacing an injured Willie Randolph) and MVP Dent (.417, 10 hits, 7 RBIs).

1979
The Day the Playing Died

In February of 1959 rock singers Buddy Holly, Ritchie Valens and the Big Bopper died in a plane crash. The incident has been referred to as "The Day the Music Died". On August 2 of this year is what I refer to as "The Day the Playing Died". Yankee captain and catcher Thurman Munson died landing his jet in Ohio. Even a Yankee Hater like me was stunned and saddened by the event. I respected his total package as a ball player. I think if this tragedy hadn't happened, he would have compiled enough stats to get into the Hall of Fame. Despite this, I still think of what he accomplished during his time, and considering how his career ended, I think he should be in – I guess, sort of like Dizzy Dean and Sandy Koufax's whose careers were cut short due to injury. (Thurman was an All-Star in seven of his nine full seasons, won the Rookie of the Year in 1970, the AL MVP in 1976 and showed his defensive skills winning three Gold Gloves - he batted .292 lifetime and was clutch in six postseason series with a .357 mark - .373 in the Series). Any chance the Yanks had to come in first place was deflated by this tragedy, although at the time of it, it did not look like they would win the AL East flag.

I think The Boss figured the only reason the Yanks won the Series the past two years was because of his involvement - others would call it meddling. Being a shipbuilder, he acted like he was the captain of the Yankee Clipper, but in '79 the name of this ship was the Titanic. Actually the final results were not all that bad – the Yanks were in the wrong division. Their fourth place finish of 89-71 was better than the AL West division winning California Angels (88-74). The Yankees' problem started when with less than two weeks of the season played. Munson's back-up, Cliff Johnson, had a scrap with the Goose (Gossage) resulting in the ace reliever missing more than half the season.

The Orioles started the season strong, so with still a hundred or so games to go and the Yanks' chances not looking so good, Captain Steinbrenner fired manager Bob Lemon and hired back Billy Martin – this was a reversal from 1978 when Martin was fired and Lemon was brought in and brought home the bacon.

Part of the Yankee problems was on the mound. Catfish developed arm trouble and retired after his 2-9 record. Ed Figueroa was 4-6. The slack was taken up by the Boss' latest pick-ups Tommy John (20-9), Luis Tiant (13-8) and reliever Ron Davis (14-2, 9 saves). The Gator Guidry gave his usual good performance (18-8, 2.78 ERA). The Yankee offense was OK. Nettles had 20 homers, Chambliss 18, and Jim Spencer 23, in less than 300 at bats. Reggie, despite playing for his nemesis Martin, put up some good stats even though he missed 30 games (.297, 29 homers, 97 RBIs).

Baltimore won the AL East behind a pitching staff of six double digit winners including Cy Young Award winner Mike Flanagan (23-9) and Scott McGregor (13-6) while relievers Don Stanhouse and Tippy Martinez totaled 17 wins and 24 saves; and the hitting of Ken Singleton (.296, 35 homers, 111 RBIs) and future Famer Eddie Murray (.295, 25 homers, 99 RBIs).

One of the season's top performances was the extra base hitting of the KC Royals' third baseman George Brett who became the first player since the NY Giants' Willie Mays in '57 to reach the 20 mark in doubles (42), triples (20) and home runs (23) and only the fifth in Major League history – Chicago Cubs' Frank "Wildfire " Schulte in 1911, St. Louis Cardinals' "Sunny" Jim Bottomley in '28 and Cleveland Indians' Jeff Heath in '41 were the other three. However Brett was the only one to have over 200 hits while accomplishing this feat with an AL best of 212. He was ruuner-up in batting (.329) to Fred Lynn's .333. What would the Royals' King of Swing do for an encore next year? – Brett couldn't possibly improve on this year's performance.

California's road to the championship in the West was led by the league's top scoring team. Carrying the sticks for them were Rod Carew (.318), Bobby Grich (.294, 30 homers, 101 RBIs), Dan Ford (.290, 21 homers, 101 RBIs), Brian Downing (.326, 76 RBIs) and the AL MVP Don Baylor (.296, 36 homers and league leading 139 RBIs and 120 runs).

The Orioles took the Angels in four games but it wasn't easy as they won the opener in extra innings and followed that with a one run victory - they clinched it in game 4 behind McGregor's six-hit shutout 8-0. Murray (.417, 5 RBIs) and Singleton (.375) led the O's attack.

In late August I decided to take Mike and Chris to Shea to see baseball's emerging star pitcher, J.R. Richard of the Astros. He seemed to be on the road to the Hall of Fame. At 6' 8" he was a taller version of my old favorite Hoot Gibson of the Cards. For four straight years he won 18 games (20 in '76) and twice had over 300 Ks with a fastball that would sizzle like Nolan Ryan's. This year he would finish third in the Cy Young voting leading the NL in ERA and Ks. In 1980 he was contending for the award again with a 10-4 record and 1.89 ERA but on July 30 his season, career, and trek to Cooperstown was derailed after collapsing on the mound during a pre-game workout. His career was over at 30 years of age due to heart problems.

On the way to Shea I picked up my sister Carole and my nieces Cheryl, Christine and Cathy. During the drive the kids were playing with play-dough. It was a hot day so as soon as I parked the car all of us bolted out to the ticket booth. J.R. had a typical game as he just melted the Met bats with his blazing fastball. However, as good as he was he did not do as good a melting job as the sun did. You see, when we got to the game and bolted out of the car my kids left the play-dough on the dashboard – instead of a blue dashboard I now had one that was covered with melted green play-dough. For some unknown reason I even thought it was funny.

The Pirates won the NL East behind the lumber of Dave Parker (.310, 25 homers, 94 RBIS), NL Co-MVP Pops Stargell (32 homers, 82 RBIs), Phil "Scrap Iron" Garner (.293), Tim Foli (.291), Bill Robinson (24 homers), Omar Moreno (196 hits, 77 SBs, 110 runs) and mid-season acquisition Bill Madlock (.328, 44 RBIs). Pittsburgh's mound star was their bespectacled reliever with the stickman-type build, Kent Tekulve. With his wicked sidearm delivery he posted 10 victories and had 31 saves in his 94 appearances. It was a huge sigh of relief whenever he went in for Buc starters John "Candy Man" Candelaria (14-9), Bruce Kison (13-7), Jim Bibby (12-4), and the owner of the game's nastiest curveball Bert Blyleven (12-5). All year the Pirates played like a Family headed by its "Dad" manager Chuck Tanner (Stargell wasn't the only Pops on this team) – the Bucs won their division and gave

much of the credit to its theme song "We Are Family" by the group
Sister Sledge.

The Cardinals were managed by Ken Boyer, my boyhood idol
(along with Stan the Man), who took over during the 1978 season.
In his first full year as skipper he had St.Louis improve by 17 games
(86-76) from last season. My hopes of him leading the Cardinals to
a World Series title in the foreseeable future were ended when St.
Louis fired him after a slow start the following year and hired
Whitey "the White Rat" Herzog, who recently won three AL West
titles, 1976-78, with the in-state KC Royals.

Cincy was still decent, but they were now the Little Red
Machine. They were led by Johnny Bench (22 homers, 80 RBIs),
George Foster (.307, 30 homers, 98 RBIs), and Ray Knight (.318, 79
RBIs). On the mound their best hurlers were Tom Seaver (16-6) and
Mike LaCoss (14-8).

The Family swept Cincy in three, winning the first two in extra
innings and the final on a complete game by Bert Blyleven, who
scattered eight hits in the 7-1 victory. Pops Stargell (.455, 5 for 11, 2
homers, 6 RBIs) and Scrap Iron Garner (.417, 5 for 12, 4 runs)
provided the offense.

Pops and Scrap Iron couldn't be stopped in the Series either as
the Bucs rallied from a 3 games to 1 deficit to take the Series. In the
final three games the Orioles could only muster up three runs
against the Pirates' arms. Pops (.400, 12 for 30 with 4 doubles, 3
homers and 7 RBIs and 7 runs) and Scrap Iron (.500, 12 for 24, 4
doubles, 4 runs and 4 RBIs) were too much for the Orioles. In the
decisive seventh game Pops was the "Star"gell blasting a homer, 2
doubles and a single in the 4-1 victory. Omar Moreno (.333) added
11 hits while Tim Foli (.333) and Parker (.345) each contributed 10
to the Buc attack. Madlock also swung a hot Bucs' bat (.375, 9 for
25). Pittsburgh batted a scorching .323 for the Series. For the
Orioles the weak hitting shortstop Kiko Garcia (.400, 8 for 20, 6
RBIs – it was his only year as a full-time starter) and Singleton
(.357, 10 for 28) carried the offense, while Murray was a
disappointment (.154, 4 for 26). Kent Tekulve was his usual self
registering three Pirate saves. Willie Stargell had quite a year – he
was NL Co-MVP (with the Cards' Keith Hernandez) and was
named MVP for both, the NLCS and World Series. It is often said
that the family is the strength of the country – well this year Family
was the strength of the World Series Champions.

This was my son Mike's first year of playing ball and my first exposure to it. I told his manager I'd coach for him except on Saturday when I had to work. I helped run the practices. I could see Mike was one of the best on the team, but his coach didn't utilize him or some of the other players the way he should have. Sometimes Mike would be at short and sometimes in right field and sometimes he'd bat lead-off and the next game eleventh (everyone batted in the SBAA). Also, Mike pitched only sparingly and I worked with the pitchers and knew he was second best on the team. The team's .500 or so record should have been better. Another coach, Jim Clos, was also dissatisfied. His son, Jim, and my son, Mike were friends. Jim had another son, Tommy, who was the same age as my son Chris. They would be eligible to play next year when they were seven.

The funniest event of the year took place in the first week of April. Our team was having a pre-season scrimmage. I was working late so Josephine took Mike to the game. I went right to the field from work. It was a cold April day and snow flurries began around the fourth inning. In the middle of an inning, Josephine stopped the game and ran to Mike at shortstop and brought him his jacket. Mike was saved from embarrassment when the other mothers followed Josephine's lead onto the field and brought jackets to their sons.

When the season was over Jim approached me and said he was going to manage both of his son's teams next year, and since our sons were the same age and were friends would I coach with him. Jim was a good guy and was full of baseball knowledge so I told him OK.

During and after the Series my sons started playing soccer – a sport I knew zero about (my Italian in-laws are huge fans). Because the games were on Saturday, I couldn't see them play. They both won their division championships and Chris' team went undefeated.

At work, I started to look for a position that would allow me to see my kids play sports, and hopefully even coach them.

1980
Brett GOOSES the Yanks

As the year began, I transferred from the Newark Post Office to the one in New Brunswick. I saved 75 miles and over an hour a day on traveling and would be available to coach full-time. I called Jim who I would be coaching with as he was set up to manage both teams. Jim was a good baseball man having been coached by Bob Hooper, a former Major League pitcher. Youth baseball runs to the end of the school year, but those that make the tournament team play other towns in area tournaments during the summer months.

When I arrived in the New Brunswick postal facility for work I met Bob LeVay who was a baseball guy and a big Yankee fan. Bob would be my boss on and off for several years. Most people don't like to have meetings with their boss, but I didn't mind as most of them invariably would turn into baseball talk (sometimes to Bob's dismay). Bob's major achievement on the athletic field was in the early '60's when he was playing for the New Brunswick (NJ) High baseball team and got a couple of hits off of Trenton (NJ) High's future Yankee star Al Downing - I guess the Hammer (#715) and Ken Boyer ('64 Series Grand Slam) were not the only ones to connect against Trenton's finest. Bob's son, Bobby, was as old as my son Chris. Bob had the same problem raising him as I had raising my sons - like me, the Yankee Hater bringing up little Pinstripers, Bob, a Yankee die-hard had a George Brett fanatic as a son. I think maybe a Fritz Peterson/Mike Kekich type trade (for our sons) was in order. NAH! My General Manager (Josephine) would have squashed the deal as would have Bob's wife.

Mike's team was sponsored by a pet store and Chris' by a bank. Up until recently the SBAA did not have nicknames like Yankees or Mets – your team was the sponsor's name. At least I didn't have to worry about coaching a team named the Yankees.

199

Jim and I had our work cut out for us. Coaching the older team was easier because all of the players had experience. But the younger team was something else. For me and my son Chris it was an eye opening time. The primary reason for this was that our town of South Brunswick is one of diverse ethnic backgrounds and some of the kids on our team had fathers who knew nothing about baseball. My son and Jim's son were playing ball in the backyard from the time they could walk and thought that all dads did the same with their own sons. Also, this being the first level of playing in the SBAA, an adult would pitch – during the season Jim and I alternated the pitching. There were many humorous episodes connected to coaching kids that never saw a game. We had a player that just could not throw (he was throwing with his left hand). We discovered the reason why at a pre-season practice. While he was waiting for his turn to hit during batting practice, he picked up a foul ball with his right hand and threw it to me on a line (I was throwing the batting practice). As it turned out his parents were told he was right-handed so they bought him glove that went on his right hand, which happens to be a left-hander's glove, (I guess you can't blame them - they didn't know). Another incident was at our first practice when one player after hitting the ball ran toward third base instead of first base, and another came to the plate holding the bat upside down.

Coaching two teams was fun but time consuming. Before the season we'd have one team practice at 4:00 p.m. and the other at 6:00 p.m. Both of our teams did fair. Coaching the younger team was really interesting. Since Jim and I pitched, with some of the weaker hitters, we'd watch their swing and try to hit the bat with our pitch. With our sons being used to playing, we'd throw harder. Our sons were the standouts and each had at least a homer every other game, and both hit about .750. The usual scores were in the teens and sometimes the twenties. After the regular season both my sons tried out and made the tournament team – Mike with the 10's and Chris with the 8's.

Seeing Chris at the plate for the first time in actual competition I noticed that he had a batting stance and swing similar to the future Famer Paul Molitor, who was in his third season with the Milwaukee Brewers. Chris, like Molitor, used this batting form to hit laser shots all over the field throughout his ball playing days. Chris also showed signs of being cut from the Molitor mold when running the bases (very fast), and by having the versatility to play several positions with exceptional skill.

In the SBAA, the 8-year old tournament team is the initial level. That level has everyone new and someone has to volunteer to be manager. Before I could volunteer, someone beat me to it. At the tryouts there were about 17 kids trying out for 13 positions, I was hoping that Chris would make the team despite him being one of the smallest. He did well in the tryouts but so did most of the kids. What probably sealed the deal for him was his speed. Chris looked like an average 8-year old until he ran. He was a real burner, and I take the credit. You see, Chris inherited my anti-authority trait, and I, being the authority, spent three or four days a week chasing him all over the neighborhood (when he reached six years old I couldn't catch him so I had to hire Mike to corral him in). All the kids trying out were timed with a stop-watch going home to first. Chris surprised the coaches but not me, by having one of the best times going down the line. Once Chris made the team I became one of the coaches. Chris attributes his anti-authority trait for his baseball success – you see I taught him everything I knew (which took me about 22 seconds) and he did the opposite.

Since this was the first year for these kids, not all of their abilities were evident. I knew Chris could field (infield and outfield) as well as any of them. But he wasn't a starter until the manager went on vacation and the shortstop went to Norway for a family vacation. The other coaches took over the team and didn't know who to put at short. I told them put Chris there – they were oblivious to me as they asked me, do I think Chris can play short? I said sure. Chris went to short and did well. When the manager came back from vacation and he saw Chris do some picking he commented that he didn't know Chris could play short.

While the manager was gone I got to rapping with Burt, one of the coaches. He saw how I was into this coaching thing so he told me the manager would not be coaching the tournament team next year. He recommended I request to do it. Burt was also the President of the SBAA and prodded me to run for a Board of Directors position. So when the board opening nomination came, I was selected (and was on the board for 14 years). Another reason I hit it off with Burt is that he grew up being a "Brooklyn Boys of Summer" fan and was now a Met fan and, naturally, anti-Yankee.

Being involved with coaching my son's regular season and tournament teams, my attention to the Majors was somewhat reduced. However, I did know the Yanks made some big moves. The big one came about because of a marshmallow salesman and Billy Martin. Billy and the Marshmallow Man got into a brawl and Billy, being good with the fists hospitalized the man. I didn't think the Boss was too happy over this. Possibly this incident was one of the factors for Billy being fired - again. Dick Howser took over as skipper. The most positive affect of this move was on Reggie. Without harassment from Martin, he tied for the home run title (41) and for the only time in his career hit .300. He also drove in 111 runs and was runner-up to Brett for MVP.

Other moves were getting pitcher Tom Underwood (13-9) and catcher Rick Cerone, who was my former co-worker's son. Replacing Thurman was impossible, but Cerone did well hitting .277 with 18 homers and 85 RBIs (he finished seventh in the AL MVP voting). Another addition, Bob Watson hit .307. My sons had a good year rooting for the Yanks as their favorites excelled. Chris was a Reggie nut and Mike's Willie Randolph hit .294, led the league in walks (119), and scored 99 runs.

The Yankee pitching was again led by Tommy John (22-9), the Ragin' Cajun Guidry (17-10) and the Goose (6 wins and 33 saves). But the surprise was another newcomer, Rudy May, who was 15-5 leading the AL with a 2.46 ERA.

The Yanks, minus the Martin/Reggie bad vibes, won 103 games with Howser. It was a good thing too, as the Orioles chased them all the way to the end with 100 wins. The O's just couldn't match the Yankee run of 28-9 down the stretch.

The Yanks would again play the Kansas City Royals for the fourth time in five years in the AL playoffs. The Royal offense was led by another outstanding performance of hitting by George Brett, the AL MVP; who made a run at .400 finishing at .390 (in the middle of September he was still over .400). The Royals' third sacker also belted 24 homers while driving in 118 runs despite playing in only 117 games due to injury. Speedster (and NJ All-State great on the gridiron and diamond) Willie Wilson hit .326 and led the league in hits (230), runs (133), and stolen bases (79). Hal McRae hit .297 with 83 RBIs and Willie Aikens rapped out 20 homers with 94 RBIs. On the mound Dennis Leonard was 20-10 and former Yankee whipping boy, Larry Gura, was 18-10 and an AL

All-Star. The AL Fireman of the Year Dan "Quiz" Quisenberry, throwing his dazzling tough to hit submarine pitch, matched the Goose's 33 saves and also won 12. The Royals finished 14 games ahead of the runner-up A's, who were managed by the marshmallow man slugging Billy Martin.

The Yanks hoped to win the playoffs against KC since they beat them three in a row from '76-'78, but this year there was some concern as the Royals dominated them during the regular season.

In game one Guidry faced Gura. The Yanks always seemed to have Gura's number and it appeared they did again as the Yanks got homers from Piniella and Cerone in the second inning to put him in a 2-0 hole. But that was all the Yanks got. Gura went the distance while KC scored seven times to win 7-2. Brett homered and second baseman Frank White had 3 hits and 2 RBIs.

Game 2 had Dennis Leonard against Rudy May. May pitched well except for the third inning when a 2-run triple by Wilson and an RBI double by U.L. Washington gave KC a 3-0 lead. The Yanks cut the deficit to one with 2 runs in the fifth. Then in the eighth the Yankees postseason was determined. With two outs and Randolph on first Watson bounced a shot off the left field wall. Randolph was running on contact and was waved home by third base coach Mike Ferraro. The shot caromed right back to Wilson, who should have hit the cut-off man and they would have had Randolph at home. But no, he over threw him and it looked like a tie score. But headsy Brett was waiting behind the cut-off man and he threw a strike to nail Randolph at the plate.

Boss Steinbrenner was livid at the third base coach Mike Ferraro for sending in Willie. He blamed him for the loss. Speaking as a coach - with two outs you take a chance – and give Brett credit for anticipating the situation and making a good play. Ferraro was history.

Possibly Ferraro's job could have been saved if the Yanks could win three in a row. In game 3 they had hits by Cerone and Reggie to take a lead 2-1 in the sixth. But in the seventh with two outs, Wilson doubled and in came the Goose. U.L. Washington got on via an infield hit and up came the AL MVP, Brett. All year Gossage was the goose that laid the golden egg – this time he was the goose that just plain laid an egg. Brett hit a shot into the upper deck that would have made the Mick proud for a 3-run homer (my boss was no doubt unhappy about this turn of events; but hey, his son Bobby must have been Royally, oops I mean really happy). The Yankees had a chance in the ninth when they loaded the bags with none out, but Cerone lined into a double play to end the threat. The Yanks lost 4-2 and the Royals would face the Phillies in the Series.

Both of the National League Divisions went down to the wire. The Phils were led by MVP Mike Schmidt (another fav of my son Mike) with a league leading 48 homers and 121 RBIs – but it was his last that determined the NL East champions. The Montreal Expos and Phils were tied for the lead with three games to play – the Phils took the first game 2-1 then won the second clinching the NL East title behind Schmidt's 2-run homer in the eleventh inning.

The Phillies won despite their other slugger, Greg Luzinski, missing 56 games, but he did pole 19 homers driving in 56 runs. Leadership was provided by Pete Rose (.282, 95 runs,) while Bake McBride (.309) and Manny Trillo (.292) got on base for Schmidt. The Cy Young winner Lefty Carlton (24-9, 2.34 ERA and NL best 286 Ks), Dick Ruthven (17-10), and "You gotta believe" Tug McGraw (5 wins, 20 saves) led the mounds corp.

The Houston Astros made the postseason for the first time ever copping their first West title by winning a one game playoff over the Dodgers. Houston had a three game lead over LA with three to play but the Dodgers swept all three contests (all by one run) necessitating a playoff game. In the game for the NL West title the Astros' Joe Niekro (Phil's little brother) knuckled down to business and pitched Houston to a 7-1 Division winning victory becoming a 20-game winner for the second time in his career.

Houston won the West despite losing their ace J.R. Richard, who was 10-4 in mid-season when his season and career ended due to heart problems. Joe Niekro was their horse on the mound going 20-12. A not so powerful line-up featured Jose Cruz (.302, 91 RBIs), Cesar Cedeno (.309, 73 RBIs), and Terry Puhl (.282 and a team leading 13 homers).

The Phils beat Houston 3 games to 2 with the last four games going into extra innings. In the decisive game the Phils overcame a 5-2 Astro lead in the top of the eighth scoring 5 runs to go up 7-5 – Houston fought back scoring twice to knot it at 7 - the Phils finally won it in the tenth as Del Unser scored on a two-bagger by Garry Maddox – and Ruthven kept Houston scoreless in the bottom of the inning. Rose batted .400 (8 for 20) and Trillo .381 (8 for 21) to lead the Phillies, but both were outshined by the Astros' Puhl (.526, 10 for 19). It was Philadelphia's first pennant since 1950. The Royals and Phils never have won a World Series (of course the Royals were an expansion team).

The Majors' and two of baseball's best ever third basemen faced each other and each proved their worth (ironic note: both Brett and Schmidt had 1595 RBIs for their career). Brett, playing with a much publicized hemorrhoid condition, hit .375 (9 for 24 with 2 doubles, a triple and a homer – the round-tripper was pretty dramatic coming in his first at bat after surgery), but he was out done by Schmidt, the Series MVP, (.381, 8 for 21, a double, 2 homers, 7 RBIs). The Phils' catcher Bob Boone (.412) and shortstop Larry Bowa (.375) joined the Phils' future All-Century third baseman with some pop at the plate as the team put up a .290 average for the six games. The best hitter though was KC first baseman Willie Aikens with 2 multi-homer games (.400, 4 homers, a triple and 8 RBIs) but their center fielder Amos Otis wasn't far behind (.478, 11 for 23, 3 homers, 7 RBIs). The Royals even out hit the Phillies by four points ringing up a .294 average. The Phillies won their only World Series in 6 games with Lefty Carlton winning twice – he was 2-0 with a 2.40 ERA and 17 Ks in 15 innings. The Phils had something to "believe in" late in the games as relief ace McGraw had a victory, two saves and a 1.17 ERA in over 7 innings of work covering 4 games. The City of Brotherly Love finally had a World Series celebration after 50 years – their Athletics with their four future Famers Jimmy "Double X" Foxx, Lefty Grove, Mickey Cochrane and Al "Bucketfoot" Simmons defeated the St. Louis Cardinals in the 1930 Classic. Ring that Liberty Bell,

During the fall my sons played recreation soccer and both won championships. Chris' team was undefeated again. Mike was also playing on South BrunswicKs first traveling all-star team, the Stars, and was selected to be the captain. I helped out coaching and was starting to pick up this game called soccer. (This would be another excuse not to do yard work). Plus I parlayed this opportunity to put on my scouting hat for new talent for the upcoming baseball season.

As far as the Yanks' post-series, the Boss was seething. Supposedly Howser "resigned", as it would be tough for the Boss to fire a manager after a 103-win season. Howser just wasn't a Boss yes-man.

1981
The Series Turns Out to be a LEMON

In January, Baseball Digest had an article "These Greats Belong in the Hall of Fame." They had all the positions mentioned. I was anticipating Ken Boyer to be the third baseman mentioned. He wasn't – George Kell was selected, and he subsequently made the Hall. This angered me to the point that I responded to Baseball Digest with a letter that was published in the "The Fans Speak Out" section in their April 1981 issue. The letter is as follows:

Regarding the article "These Greats Belong in the Hall of Fame" I was not surprised to see no mention of Ken Boyer, a third baseman. He must be the most outstanding overlooked third baseman in the history of the game.

During his prime years, mid – 1950 to the mid – 1960's playing for St. Louis, Ken Boyer received his due recognition, constantly being a member of the NL All-Star team. But, now whenever great third basemen are written about, Ken Boyer always seems to be left out. Why? It is beyond my comprehension?

Consider his batting stats- .287 lifetime average, 2143 hits, 318 doubles, 287 homers, 1104 runs scored, 1141 RBIs. His overall hitting (average plus power) ranks him as one of the best hitting third baseman of all time.

Consider his defense. During his prime years he was regarded as the top fielding third baseman in the NL – 5 times winning the Gold Glove Award.

206

Consider his only World Series in 1964; he made several outstanding defensive plays. Although only hitting .222 he came through in the clutch. He won the 4th game with a grand slam, 4-3, and he led St. Louis to a 7-5 victory in the final 7th game over the Yanks. In that final game he went three for four with a single, double and homer sparking every St. Louis rally.

Ken Boyer's caliber of performance is worthy of "Hall of Fame" selection.

Gene R. Hutmaker
Kendall Park, NJ

During the winter months, I decided to coach youth basketball (Mike's team) run by our town. We did OK and Mike proved to be one of the better players. Also, it was another scouting opportunity to see who the good athletes were for when I drafted players for the baseball season.

Let's get back to the Majors. In December of '80, the Boss signed free agent Dave Winfield, the San Diego Padre star, to the biggest contract ever given to a baseball player. On June 12, baseball abruptly ended due to owner/players difference. At this time the Yanks were first in the AL East 34-22, two games ahead of Baltimore. Newcomer millionaire Dave Winfield led the way with a hot bat (over .300 with 40 RBIs) while Reggie was only at .199 with 24 RBIs. The strike ended August 8 and what the leagues decided to do is to split the season into two halves. The first half-winner would play the second half-winner in a division playoff then have their league playoffs. This scenario really short changed Cincy and St. Louis as both had the best overall record in their division, but neither came in first in either one of the half seasons. So in reality the NL's best teams weren't in postseason play.

As the Majors were striking, our town league (SBAA) was coming to a close and I was getting ready for tournament play. In our town league Jim and I did pretty well. Our older team came in second and our younger team won the championship of the 9-year old league. Mike pitched well and played short with Ozzie Smith flair. He was the starting pitcher in the All-Star game. In the 9-year old league, Chris and Jim's son, Tommy, were outstanding. In this league you can only pitch two innings a game. Out of their combined four innings they would usually get 10 of the 12 outs on strikeouts. They both would hit about .600 – only going hitless in one game. The season was only marred by a game early in the schedule. My dad was up from Florida and attended this game. His grandson, Chris, and Tommy got their fastballs rapped pretty hard as we lost 21-0. To make things worse, we were no-hit by their pitchers. My dad commented it looks like a long season. He was really surprised when I called a month or so later informing him that we won the championship and along the way defeated the team that he saw clobber us.

During the spring Mike and Chris also played for the traveling South Brunswick soccer teams, as did Jim's sons. I assisted with Chris' team, the Comets, which went undefeated again. (Just never could get to that yard work).

This was my first year of being the manager of Chris' tournament team. As a manager I was more like Walter Alston than Billy Martin, but with Casey Stengel type quips. Burt was like a co-manager and coached a great third base. I would have lost him if Steinbrenner knew of his ability – to replace Mike Ferraro. We lost in the semi-finals of two tournaments and had a fun season. Chris justified my having him bat lead-off hitting .333 with a .500 on base average and he also could pick it in the field. Mike was on the 11-year old tournament team and threw my dad a no-hitter as a birthday gift to him.

Back to the Yanks. In the second half of the season they could have gone like 5-51 and still be in the playoffs since they won the first half of the season. They were one game under .500 in the second half going 25-26. Leading the Yankee hitters for the season (both halves) were Winfield (.297, 13 homers, 68 RBIs), Jerry Mumphrey (.307), and Nettles (15 homers). Reggie came on strong in the second half to finish at .237 and tying Nettles with 15 homers to lead the team. Lefty Dave "Rags" Righetti was AL Rookie of the Year (8-4, 2.06 ERA) and Guidry was 11-5. Tommy John won 9 and the Goose had 20 saves.

However, the whole Yankee season ended with a strange twist (a Lemon twist at that). Gene Michael was picked to replace the resigned Howser. Michael was exasperated the whole season by having to put up with questions and second guessing by the Boss. Michael more or less told the Boss to fire him, which he did in September, less than a month before postseason play. The Boss, like in 1978, put Bob Lemon back at the helm and hoped to have the same results as in '78 – a World Series title.

In the division playoffs the Yankees faced the second half-winner, the Milwaukee Brewers. The Brewers were down 2 games to 0 but came back to force a fifth game. It didn't look good for the Yanks as Guidry was down 2-0 in the fourth when Reggie homered and Oscar Gamble followed with another. The Yanks put up two more in the inning and went on to win 7-3. Reggie was regaining his Mr. October form hitting .300 with 2 homers and 4 RBIs. Winfield hit .350 with 3 doubles.

The A's, led by manager Billy Martin, were ready for the Yankees, or so they thought. They swept the Royals in the AL West playoffs, only allowing two runs. But it wasn't going to happen as the Martin led A's played as soft as marshmallows - the Yanks swept them. Reggie got hurt in the second game and loaned Graig Nettles his Mr. October name – Nettles hit .500 (6 for 12) and drove in a record 9 runs. George Frazier impressed the Yanks with almost 6 innings of shutout ball in the middle game. He assured himself of some work during the World Series.

In the NL East, Montreal beat the Phils the hard way, besting Lefty Carlton twice. Steve Rogers won twice and Gary "The Kid" Carter hit .421 with 2 homers and 6 RBIs. The Dodgers took the NL West by beating Houston in five games also doing it the hard way - winning the final three games with superb pitching. Houston only scored two runs in those three games. Jerry Reuss had a zero ERA in 18 innings and Rookie of the Year and Cy Young winner Fernando Valenzuela had a 1.06 ERA in 17 innings and won game 4 by in a 2-1 nail biter. Reuss bested Nolan Ryan 4-0 in the finale. Steve Garvey led LA with 2 homers, 4 RBIs and a .368 average.

In the NL playoffs, the Dodgers' Rick Monday hit a ninth inning homer in game five to give Valenzuela a 2-1 victory. Burt Hooten won two games hurling over 14 innings without giving up a run. The Expos' Carter stayed hot at the plate hitting .438 but it wasn't enough as the Dodgers, for the 11th time, would meet the Yankees in the Series. Manager Tom Lasorda will be out to avenge his '77 and '78 losses to the Pinstripers. I wasn't too confident with the Dodgers' chances. I felt that the Yanks would have an easy time since the NL's best (Cincy and St. Louis) weren't even in the playoffs.

After two games my unhappiness was justified, as the Yankees won the first two. In game 1 the Yanks took the lead on a Bob Watson 3-run homer. Guidry and Gossage combined on the 5-3 victory, but the save belongs to Nettles and his glove that squashed a Dodger rally in the eighth. The Dodgers were thinking, "not him again" (Nettles vacuumed many Dodger shots in '77 and '78).

In game 2 the Yanks got a run off of Hooten in the fifth (breaking his 19 inning scoreless streak). It was all that was needed as Tommy John and Goose combined on a four-hit shutout. The Yanks won 3 – 0.

The Dodgers were down two-zip, but at least now they would be going home to get some West Coast cooking. The Dodgers had their rookie from Mexico ready to go to get them back in it. Valenzuela was the best thing to happen to baseball in this year of the mid-season strike. His pitching style of looking to heaven during his wind-up was very entertaining to watch. Anyway, Ron "The Penguin" Cey gave him a quick lead with a 3-run homer. (Cey's nickname was derived from his running form.) But the Yanks were thinking sweep, and rallied for 2 in the second and third to take a 4-3 lead. Pedro Guerrero tied it with a double and Mike Scioscia hit into a double play as the deciding run scored in the fifth. After the third inning, Valenzuela's looking to the heavens paid off as he held the Yanks scoreless despite throwing a countless amount of pitches. LA won 5-4 and enjoyed their first helping of home cooking. George Frazier was charged with the tough loss.

In game 4 the Yanks got off to a quick lead as the Dodger starter, Bob Welch, was taken out before he even got an out. It looked like a gloomy day for the Dodgers as the Yanks led 6-3 going into the bottom of the sixth. But then baseball's super flake, Jay Johnstone, was sent up to pinch-hit and crushed a 2-run homer. Davey Lopes then got on via a Reggie error and scored on a Bill Russell hit. The Dodgers put up 2 more in the seventh on a Steve Yeager sac-fly and a RBI hit by Lopes that gave them an 8-6 lead. Reggie, reminding people who Mr. October was, blasted one into the Pacific to cut the lead to one. But that's where the scoring ended as LA won 8-7. The Dodgers and Yanks were even at two. Again George Frazier was the loser.

Ron Guidry and Jerry Reuss, the Series opening game starters, met again in the fifth game. Both pitchers were outstanding as Guidry had a 1-0 lead until the seventh inning when Guerrero and Yeager both went yard to give LA a 2-1 lead that stood up. In the eighth Ron Cey proved how hard-headed he was when the Goose hit him in the head with a fastball. Initially the first reaction was, "Is he dead?" Nope! The Penguin's alive and kickin'. Dodgers went up 3 games to 2.

The Yankees were now the ones that couldn't wait for home cooking and the Boss couldn't wait to go home to New York elevators. After game 5 the Boss was all bruised. His response was that a couple of Dodger fans had bad-mouthed his Yankees while on an elevator. He felt it was necessary to uphold the Yankee honor and teach them a lesson. (To my knowledge, this version has never been authenticated).

In game 6, back at Yankee Stadium, it was Tommy John versus Burt Hooten. The score was tied in the fourth at one when Lemon took out John for a pinch-hitter that resulted in nothing. George Frazier went in and the Dodgers scored three times and scored four more in the fifth. They won 9-2. Guerrero had a homer and 5 RBIs to lead the attack and Ron Cey showed the Yanks he was alive and kickin' going 2 for 3. Frazier became the first pitcher since Claude "Lefty" Williams of the White/Black Sox of 1919 to lose three times in a World Series. The Dodgers had three players selected as MVP: The Penguin (coming back from the beaning) hit .350 with 6 RBIs, Pedro Guerrero (.333, 2 homers, 7 RBIs), and Steve Yeager (.286, 2 homers and played a great defense behind the plate). Steve Garvey was their leading hitter at .417 (10 for 24).

For the Yankees, Reggie was hurt most of the Series but hit .333 (4 for 12). The Boss' new Mr. October, Dave Winfield went 1 for 22 (.045).

This Series, which started off so promising, turned into one big Lemon. My sons were not too happy so I tried to console them by making them some lemonade – they said "No thanks, were not thirsty."

Boss Steinbrenner was so aggravated by his Yanks losing that he, via a press release, apologized to the fans of New York for the Yankees' embarrassing, poor performance in the Series. He should be the one to be embarrassed for making the apology, after all his team made it to the Series. No other owner would have reacted in such a negative way.

During the Series and the rest of autumn, I coached soccer (recreation league and traveling teams). Both of Mike's teams won the championships. Chris' teams also won championships and again both of his teams were undefeated. I heard him on the phone tell my sister Carole he never lost a soccer game in his life. I overheard this and told him not to lie. He told me, "Dad, I'm not lying my teams have never lost". I checked it out and he played in 47 games of soccer (recreation and traveling teams) and never lost. Chris was sorry he told me this. I let our town paper know and they did a human interest story on him. I was surprised when we got our weekly paper and they had a full page story and picture of Chris in the sports section. Boy was he mad!!! (But I don't think as mad as Boss Steinbrenner – he didn't issue a press release apologizing for his dad's part regarding this story).

Not knowing it then – this was the beginning of my Yankee Hating Golden Years Part 2. They wouldn't make the playoffs again until 1995, despite the $$$$$ they spent.

1982

The Postseason: Reggie YES – Yankees NO

As the year started, the Boss let Reggie go. In January Reggie signed with the Angels. I think Steinbrenner was making moves like someone who was on speed. He decided to go for speed on the team acquiring Cincy players Ken Griffey, who hit .277 in '81 and would steal about 20 bases a year, and Dave Collins, who hit .303 with 79 steals in 1980.

During the winter months I again coached basketball and was busy being President of one of the SBAA's baseball leagues which, as a member of the SBAA Board of Directors, was the position I usually held. The position consisted of getting the managers/coaches, umpires, making the schedule, and setting up a player draft. This was done in the winter months. I tried to run my league with an iron fist like Kennesaw Mountain Landis, Baseball's Commissioner after the Black Sox scandal from 1920-1944.

In March I read an article that really adversely affected me. My guy, Ken Boyer, was in bad shape with lung cancer. The article was about a benefit for him, and at the end of the story there was an address to mail to if you wanted to help. Billy Martin, the Yankee Hater nemesis, was the Chairman of the Ken Boyer fund, but despite that I still sent a contribution.

The Yankees had a miserable season. The defending champs came in fifth with a 79-83 record. Dave Winfield did all he could with his bat swatting 37 homers (second in the league) and was second in slugging % (.560). The new speed guys, Griffey (.277 with 10 steals) and Collins (.253 and 13 steals) didn't live up to expectations. Jerry Mumphrey hitting .300 was the only real help Winfield had in the line-up. On the mound, only the old reliables came through -- Guidry was 14-8 and the Goose had 30 saves.

Bob Lemon started out as the skipper, but having made the wrong decisions in last year's Series, the Boss had a sour taste in his mouth concerning how long Lemon would last. The Boss probably did Lemon a favor by firing him after only 14 games (6-8 record). The Boss' next victim was Gene Michael (like Michael didn't have enough of him last year). Michael was fired after a 44-42 record. Clyde King had the misfortune to finish out the season going 29-33.

To rub salt into the Yankees' wound, Reggie was the main attraction for the Angels, leading them to AL West title. He led the league smashing 39 homers and led the team with 101 RBIs. When the Angels came to New York and Reggie homered the Stadium went crazy. The Boss was one of the least liked people in New York. Met fans hated him and now even the Yankee fans hated him.

In the spring my sons were playing traveling soccer and SBAA baseball. Jim and I again coached both teams. We did so-so. Mike's team was sponsored by the South Brunswick Republicans. In the playoffs I tried to motivate them by saying President Reagan would be there for the finals. I guess I sounded convincing because a couple of my players were really upset when we lost in the semis because we wouldn't get to see the President.

Like I said, Chris' team wound up with an unimpressive record. My most memorable game was in the middle of the season when we were 2-4. During dinner Chris was telling Mike what a lousy team he was on. Mike commented that all the losses were when mom went to the game. Chris, half-kiddingly, said "Yeah! Mom you're a jinx." Josephine, not known for her sense of humor, went off on that comment and stated she promised not to go to any more of Chris' games.

Our next game was against a team with red uniforms (our team had green ones) and Josephine would not be there (yeah, right!). It was probably the fourth inning (games were six innings) and we were up 13-5 when all of a sudden I saw Josephine drive into our sports field complex. She parked away from our field so Chris and I wouldn't see the car. She then got out of the car and hid behind some of the shrubbery at the complex. Josephine, not having been in the Army, was not exactly well versed in the art of camouflage. With the shrubbery she picked to hide behind, Josephine would have been better off choosing a pane of glass for coverage. Chris easily spotted her and pointed her out to me. Jim saw her too and asked me what was going on. He laughed when I told him the situation. Chris said," Watch us blow this eight run lead." I told Chris "No way - but in any event don't let mom know we see her." Well, Chris proved to be right – the red team won 14-13 in the last inning and jumped up and down celebrating. As soon as they won, Josephine sped away so she would be home way before us.

On the drive home I told Chris to act like we didn't know she was there. When we went into the house Josephine was attempting to play it cool and asked who won. I winked to Chris as I was saying we won. She became startled and said, "Then why was the red team celebrating." Chris then asked mom "How'd you know the red team was celebrating?" Mom then stammered "Uh, uh, I think something's burning in the oven." Chris and I had to go outside so Josephine wouldn't see us laughing. Josephine didn't come to any more games – but we still lost a few despite her not being there.

During the SBAA All-Star Day (which was also trophy day), the SBAA always tried to get a New York Yankee to present them to the kids. This year we had the 1980 AL ERA leader pitcher Rudy May, who this year had 6 wins 3 saves and a 2.89 ERA. I reluctantly had a photo taken of him with me, my wife Josephine and my son Chris. Even as a 37-year old I still did not want to be in a photo with a Yankee, but I did it anyway.

Burt and I again ran the 10-year old tournament team. Chris batted lead-off and hit .429. With Burt waving runners home from his third base coaching box our team won the East Brunswick Coaches Tournament. The SBAA gave out jackets for any team that won a tournament. The team's parents were glad Burt and I were good coaches (it helps to have good players – ask Joe Torre).

On September 7, Ken Boyer succumbed to cancer and passed away at the age of 51. My wife could not understand how this affected me. She said it's not like family. I thought it would be a waste of time to explain it to her.

Back to the season. Harvey Kuenn took over the managerial reins of the Milwaukee Brewers (no he did not replace Rocky Colavito) after about 50 games and put a powerful line-up out there every day. Their offense became known as the "Harvey Wall Bangers". The Brewers hit 216 homers and hit .274. AL MVP Robin Yount (.331, 29 homers, 114 RBIs) was the big "Banger" and was joined by Paul Molitor (.302, 19 homers, 136 runs), Cecil Cooper (.313, 32 homers, 121 RBIs), Ben Oglivie (35 homers, 102 RBIs), Ted Simmons (23 homers, 97 RBIs), Gorman Thomas (tied for the league lead with 39 homers, 112 RBIs) and Jim Gantner (.295). Pitching was provided by Cy Young winner Pete Vuckovich

(18-6), Mike Caldwell (17-12) and Rollie Fingers (5 wins, 29 saves). The Brewers picked up future Famer Don Sutton just before the September 1 cut-off, and he went 4-1 including the last game of the season beating Jim Palmer and the Orioles for the AL East title by a 10-2 score. Yount made it easy for Sutton blasting two "Bangers" over the wall – I guess when you mention birds just one Rockin' Robin proved to be too much for this flock of Orioles. Possibly this loss was just too much for the Orioles skipper Earl Weaver as he retired after managing them since 1968.

The single major feat of the season was accomplished by the feet of Rickey Henderson who set a new Major League stolen base record with 130. Despite his base path exploits the Oakland A's wound up in fourth place with a dismal 68-94 record.

In the AL playoffs, the Angels won the first two and only needed to win one more as it appeared that their manager Gene Mauch would finally get into a World Series, but like his Phillies' collapse in '64 his Angels did the same losing the next three to Milwaukee. Cecil Cooper's 2-run single drove home the tying and winning runs in the seventh inning to win the decisive game 4-3. Overall Molitor led the "Bangers" (.316, 2 homers, 5 RBIs). For the Angels, Fred Lynn was on fire at the plate batting .611 (11 for 18). The disappointment was Reggie – he couldn't find his Mr. October handle, as he was 2 for 18 (.111).

The Brewers faced St. Louis in the Series. The Cardinals were making a special effort to win it all (because of Boyer). In the NL playoffs, they swept the surprising Braves, managed by the Red Birds' former MVP, Joe Torre. Atlanta took the West by only one game over the Dodgers as Joe Morgan, now playing for the Dodgers' eternal rival, the Giants, hit a 3-run dinger against them in a 5-3 season ending loss as LA tried to tie the Braves for the Division title. The Braves' war path to the West title was led by the batting of NL MVP Dale Murphy (.281, 36 homers, and also sharing the RBI crown with 109 tying the NL's batting champ, the Expos' Al Oliver who hit .331), Bob Horner (32 homers, 97 RBIs), Chris Chambliss (20 homers, 86 RBIs), and the knuckler of Phil Niekro (17-4).

The Cards were the exact opposite of the Brewers. Whitey Herzog was their manager so they played a style called "Whitey Ball". They only had 67 homers and George Hendrick had 19 of them. Lonnie Smith hit .307 and led the NL with 120 runs. Keith

Hernandez (.299) and Willie McGee (.296) provided more offense. A big reason they won the NL was do to newly acquired shortstop Ozzie Smith gobbling up anything hit on the left side of the infield, and future Hall of Famer "close the door" relief ace and master of the splitter, Bruce Sutter (9 wins and league leading 36 saves). Starters Joaquin Andujar (15-10) and Bob Forsch (15-9) were the top aces in this deck of Cards.

In the Series the Cards couldn't stop Yount (.414, 12 for 29) or Molitor (.355, 11 for 31), but down 3 games 2 Whitey Ball beat the Wall Bangers in the sixth game in a role reversal, wall-banging Milwaukee in a 13-1 rout to force a seventh game. In the finale, St. Louis overcame a 3-1 deficit in the sixth rallying for three runs to take the lead and went on to win 6-3 as Andujar and Sutter combined on a seven-hitter. Hernandez led the Cards with 8 RBIs while role player/DH Dane Iorg batted .529 (9 for 17) and Hendrick and Smith each went 9 for 28 (.321). On the mound Andujar was 2-0 with a 1.35 ERA (and should have been MVP) and the closer Sutter registered a victory with two saves. The Cards' catcher Darrell Porter (.286, 5 RBIs) was Series MVP capping a great postseason, as he was also MVP of the NLCS,

In December my wife, Josephine takes care of the Christmas cards. I'd come home from work and ask her who we got them from. One day I asked her and she said "Billy Martin sent you one". I said "What"? She gave it to me and it was signed Billy Martin, Chairman of the Ken Boyer Cancer Fund. (Billy was Chairman because he was close with Clete Boyer who was one of his coaches).

1983
Pine Tar is a ROYAL Pain in the - - - !

In '82 the A's fired Billy Martin as they finished fifth in the AL West. The Yanks let Clyde King go as he was only a stop gap remedy for them. Like magnets, the Boss couldn't help but rehire the Ken Boyer Cancer Fund Chairman. Despite some strange doings the Yanks improved to the point that they tied for the fourth best record in the Majors with a 91-71 record. Unfortunately, two of those teams were in the AL East (Baltimore was 98-64 and Detroit 92-70).

The Boss' bucks brought in hitters Don Baylor (24 homers, 93 RBIs in '82) and Steve Kemp (19 homers, 98 RBIs in '82). Baylor came through (.306, 21 homers 85 RBIs) but Kemp was injured and only played in 109 games with 12 homers and 49 RBIs. Griffey bounced back with a .303 average and Nettles had 20 homers. Rookie Don Mattingly in two-thirds of the season showed great promise at first and hit .283. But again, the star was Winfield (32 homers, 116 RBIs). Despite this he was in the Boss' dog house. When Steinbrenner signed Winfield to the 10-year contract it had a cost of living adjustment in it making the $16 million contract actually worth $23 million. The Boss attempted to have it restructured, but Winfield put his University of Minnesota education to good use and declined the offer. Until the end of Winfield's Yankee days this contract created animosity between them.

Guidry was the Ragin' Cajun on the mound reaching the 20-win mark again (21-9). Rags Righetti tossed a Fourth of July no-hitter (the first Yank no-no since Larsen) and finished 14-8. In relief, the Goose won 13 and saved 22.

The Yanks were a good team but couldn't catch the Orioles. On the mound the O's had Scott McGregor (18-7), Mike Boddicker (16-8), and in relief, they had my niece Vita's former heartthrob, Tippy Martinez (9 wins, 21 saves). (Vita was happily married by now).

218

The offense had Ken Singleton (15 homers, 84 RBIs), Eddie Murray (.306, 33 homers, 111 RBIs), and Cal Ripken, who made a joke of the sophomore jinx. The '82 Rookie of the Year was the '83 AL MVP putting up one of the best offensive shows ever for an AL shortstop (Yount was outstanding last year). Ripken led the AL in hits (211), doubles (47), extra base hits (76) and runs (121). He also had a .318 average with 27 homers and 102 RBIs. As a shortstop he was tall at 6'4", but could make the plays, eventually winning two Gold Gloves. He was also on his way to playing in a record 2632 consecutive games.

The Chicago White Sox managed by Tony La Russa put together a powerful offense that led the AL in runs to coast to the AL West title by 20 games. It would be their fist postseason since 1959. Leading the bat attack were Carlton Fisk (.289, 26 homers, 86 RBIs) who a few years ago changed his Sox from Red to White, Tom Paciorek (.307), Greg Luzinski (32 homers, 95 RBIs), Harold Baines (20 homers, 99 RBIs) and the AL Rookie of the Year Ron Kittle (35 homers, 100 RBIs). In the AL West you couldn't even say "Darn them Sox" since they had no holes as the arms of the Cy Young winner LaMarr Hoyt (24-10), Rich Dotson (22-8) and Floyd Bannister (16-10) anchored a deep talented staff.

On the local scene Jim and I coached together for the last time – they moved to the next town in '84. Our older team (Mike's) went 12-3 (second place) and lost in the finals. Chris' team went 14-1 (first place) but lost in the finals when Jim's son, Tommy, was ill and couldn't play.

Chris and Tommy were both dominating on the mound. In this league pitchers were limited to 3 innings. They would each pitch 3 innings getting 13-15 of the 18 outs on Ks (games were 6 innings). In the playoffs, without Tommy, we lost. In tournament play, Burt and I again did well with the 11-year old team, coming in third in the 32-team field in the Hamilton Tournament. We did the best out of 26 teams from NJ. The game I recall was against Pemberton, NJ. Their pitcher was Irv Smith, the future All-American tight end from Notre Dame and an NFLer for the New Orleans Saints. At 11-years old he was already over 6 ft. tall. He threw smoke and blasted the longest Little League home run that I ever saw, but despite that we won the game 4-2. Chris, who was about a foot shorter than Smith, connected with one of his fastballs and drove it over the right fielder's head for a triple. Two Pennsylvania teams met in the finals. Chris performed well from his lead-off spot hitting .375.

The Major Leagues' highlight was a bizarre comedy act by the Yankees and KC Royals. Nettles noticed the KC star George Brett had his bat covered with pine tar. There's a rule that pine tar or any substance can only be 18 inches up from the bat's knob. Nettles made this known to Martin who would pick the proper time to use this information.

The proper time came on July 24. The Yanks were still in the division race and were facing the Royals. The Yanks were ahead 4-3 in the ninth with two outs but KC had one on creating the match-up that was a re-enactment from the 1980 AL playoffs. It was The Goose versus Brett. Same result - "Boom"!! As Brett went into the dugout, Martin came out quoting the 18-inch rule. The umpire measured the bat against home plate which is 17 inches. The measuring showed the pine tar was over the 18 inches. The umpire had no choice but to call Brett out. Brett charged onto the field like he was shot out of a cannon toward the umpire. Brett was restrained and dragged back to his dugout. Since no one got hurt, this remains one of baseball's funniest happenings ever, always being shown on TV. Brett was tossed and manager Dick Howser, one the Boss' favorite people, filed a protest.

I, being an SBAA league President know a protest is hardly ever upheld, but this time AL President Lee MacPhail upheld it. Brett had his homer and the game would resume from the point after the homer. Steinbrenner and Martin were livid. On August 18, the game resumed and Martin made a mockery of it. He made appeal plays to each base and had Guidry play center field and left-handed Mattingly played second base. The Royals won the game 5-4. I guess my boss, Bob, wasn't too pleased by the outcome but at least his son Bobby, the Brett fanatic, was happy.

Another bizarre incident occurred in August as the Yankees were in Toronto. It was between innings and there was a seagull on the field. While warming up between innings, Dave Winfield, the Yankee left fielder threw the ball toward the bird. His intent was to scare the seagull off the field. Instead his throw mistakenly hit the bird, killing it. (Maybe he visualized the bird as the Boss). The Canadian police took him to jail (at least Winfield was used to wearing pinstripes). After posting bond the case was dropped. There were no intentions to hurt the bird.

The Audubon Society got satisfying revenge when the Orioles won the ALCS and World Series. Ripken hit .400 with 5 runs scored as the O's beat the Chisox, (who as a team scored two less runs than Ripken) in the ALCS in 4 games. The White Sox offense just had no sock in their bats. It was a quick exit for the Chisox who were in their first postseason in 24 years.

The O's would face the Phillies who's only threat at the plate was Mike Schmidt with 109 RBIs and a league leading 40 homers. The Phils had the Cy Young winner but it wasn't Lefty Carlton (15-16) – it was John Denny (19-6). The Phils beat LA in the NL playoffs in 4 games. Schmidt (.467, 5 runs) and Carlton (2-0, 0.66 ERA) were the Phils' leaders.

The Phils took the Series opener behind Denny but then the Orioles swept the next four games to win the Series as Mike Boddiker (one unearned run) and Scott McGregor (a five-hit shutout in the Series clincher) each tossed a complete game victory while Tippy Martinez registered saves in the other two wins. Schmidt was like Winfield in '81 (1 for 21), and Ripken wasn't much better at .167 (3 for 18). Former Yank farmhand, catcher Rick Dempsey was MVP (.385, 5 for 13, 4 doubles, a homer and a .923 slugging %). The Orioles' rookie manager Joe Altobelli had to be pretty happy as he replaced the legendary Earl Weaver and brought home the World Series title back to Baltimore; something Weaver could not do since 1970 despite the talent laden teams he had.

At the season's end the Boss got rid of Martin (again). In order to appease Yankee fans, he brought in one of their favorites, Yogi Berra. After all he did have two pennants to his credit.

1983
Errors in Cooperstown

It was just after the Orioles defeated the Phillies in the World Series when I suggested to Mike and Chris that it would be cool to go to the Baseball Hall of Fame in Cooperstown, New York. It would be a 250-300 mile drive from our house in central New Jersey. In early November, NJ parent/teacher conferences were held, thus the kids have no school. I had some vacation days to use so we made plans to go in early November. (Josephine said she'll pass on this trip). Her place was taken by Mike's friend Rob Klein, who I also coached in all sports.

We left central NJ about noon and arrived about 7 o'clock. We got our room, ate dinner and walked around the town. The next day we got up, had breakfast and opened up the museum.

A good reason to go during this time of the year was that there would not be big crowds to contend with. There were only 20 or so visitors this day. We started visiting the various displays, and I saw the All-Star Game section. While there I pointed out to my sons and Rob a large photo of my favorite, Ken Boyer, making one of his great diving catches in the '56 game.

We then walked into the World Series exhibit. They had a row of large six foot displays with the year on it and a brief description of the Series for that year. Well, the one that was 1934 stated that Dizzy Dean won 3 games as the St. Louis Cardinals defeated the Detroit Tigers 4 games to 3. Being a baseball history buff, especially when it involves the Cardinals, I knew that the Dean brothers, Dizzy and Paul (a.k.a. Daffy), each won 2 games. Someone who looked like he might have been the curator (he had on a suit, tie and a name tag) walked by and I told him of this error. He looked at it and said something like "Really, I'll check it out". It bothered me that someone who had this job had to check it out. A while later he came back disgusted saying "You're right, and this is a new display".

222

Later on we were in a room with a TV screen. When you push a button a film came on. We were watching it and they were showing the 1960 World Series. Being the Yankee Hater, I just loved reliving the World Series-winning Mazeroski homer. As we were watching it, I heard the audio part say that Hal Smith's 3-run homer tied it up at 9 apiece leading to Maz's blast. With a smirk on my face I said "I don't believe it". Mike, Chris and Rob said "Believe what?" I explained to them that Hal Smith's homer put the Pirates up 9-7 and the Yankees came back with 2 in the ninth – then the famous Maz' blast. They exclaimed, "Let's get the curator again". I replied "Forget it, this guy doesn't know anything about baseball and I already ruined his day".

I didn't see any other mistakes – but two were enough!

1984
Hold that TIGER: No Way

As the year began I was making plans to go to West Germany (Germany was split then). A parent of one of Mike's traveling soccer teammates was from West Germany and would go there, I think on business, a few times a year. To make a long story short, he arranged for our South Brunswick team to play in a tournament during Easter week (it wouldn't interfere with school). I helped out at practices and was hip with all the players. Our team was fortunate that our coach was Denis Mayer who was one of the top high school soccer coaches in the state (Piscataway High), and also a former Brooklyn Dodger fan so naturally he and I got along just fine. It also helped that his son Chris was quite a player and would go on to be the Middlesex County High School Player of the Year (St. Joseph's High - Metuchen) for soccer during his senior year in 1989.

I decided I'd go with Mike. As a Board Member of the SBAA, I brought a box of our baseball hats so our kids would have a gift to give to the player of the family they were staying with. Our players stayed with the families of players on the team of the host town (the town was Schwarzenbach). Mike stayed with a family that lived in a condo built in 1970 whereas I stayed in a hotel built in the 1400's – yes, it did have electricity and indoor plumbing.

When we arrived our kids gave them the South Brunswick hats. Nobody wore them until after our first two games - we routed the German teams 6 to 1 and 8 to 0 (Mike even had a goal in each game from his defensive sweeper position). The Germans found out we could play something else besides baseball. The hats became a hot item all over town; in fact I even gave mine away. We won four of the five games we played and outscored the German teams 23-10 as Chris Mayer ran the offense and Mike was the maestro of the defense (our only loss was to the Hof City region's top team – we had them tied at the half but our guys ran out of gas most likely due

224

to a 6:00 a.m. wake-up call for a trip to the East/West German border prior to the game). But we won the tournament defeating one of the area's other top teams – in fact they beat the team that we lost to. Mike played despite a sore hammie and gave a Spartan performance as the sweeper - keeping the opponents from scoring in the second half in the 4-1 victory.

Here is a little something about our trip to the East/West German border. I thought it would be a novel idea for Mike to take a picture of me with my arm in East German (Communist) air-space. Mike was looking at the East German machine gun towers that were across the fences of barbed wire that separated the borders and stated that he did not think it was a good idea (I guess at 14 years old he was already wiser than me). Since I grew up during the Krushchev/Cold War era and was an Army vet I said something like "Don't worry about them Commies." Anyway while Mike was taking the picture of me with my arm in East German air-space the East German soldiers in the machine gun tower seemed to be observing us with binoculars. All of a sudden an East German armored personnel carrier came upon the scene across the fences – to counter this a West German one came rolling in on our side of the fence and some soldiers emerged. With this going on our bus driver and guide said it would be a good time to leave. As I was entering the bus I was hoping that I did not start World War III (luckily I didn't).

I thought I lost valuable time practicing my SBAA team. In a way I lucked out. It rained in NJ the whole time we were away, so no teams could practice.

This was the first year I coached without Jim, and the first year against Burt. His team took first place but was upset in the first round of the playoffs on some questionable calls by the home plate umpire. My second place team then had an easy path to the championship, not having to face Burt's team, sweeping three games as Chris won two games in the playoffs only allowing only one run and batted .600 with seven RBIs. Burt and I then joined forces on the 12-year old SBAA Tournament team. Our team got jackets again as we won the South Plainfield Tournament. Chris batted .341 from his lead-off spot in the line-up. In the finals, Chris led the comeback from a 4-1 deficit with a double and then broke a 4-4 tie with a 3-run homer. We held on to win 7-6 in the jacket-winning game.

Let's get back to the Majors. After 40 games the Yankee season was over. Manager Yogi's "It ain't over 'til it's over" saying went down the drain. The Detroit Tigers started the season with a ROAR (35-5). The baseball adage "a team strong up the middle wins" was never truer. Catcher Lance Parrish (33 homers, 98 RBIs), shortstop Alan Trammell (.314, 85 runs), second baseman Lou Whitaker (.289, 90 runs), and center fielder Chet Lemon (20 homers, 76 RBIs) provided plenty of pop along with excellent defense. Former Michigan State football All-American Kirk Gibson's choice of baseball over football proved correct, as he hit 27 homers and drove in 91 runs. Manager Sparky Anderson must have thought he was back with his Big Red Machine teams the way the Tigers manufactured runs.

The pitching crew was Jack Morris (19-11), Dan Petry (18-8), Milt Wilcox (17-8), reliever Aurelio Lopez (10-1, 14 saves), and Cy Young and AL MVP Willie Hernandez (9-3, 32 saves 1.92 ERA).

The Yanks' season was marked by the batting race of Dave Winfield and Don Mattingly. Winfield put aside his differences with the Boss to hit 19 homers and drive in 100 runs. He was leading the AL going into the last game by 1 1/2 points, over Mattingly .341 to .3395. Winfield went 1 for 4, and Mattingly went 4 for 5 to take the crown - .343 to .340. Mattingly was another who for the first half of his career looked like another Stan the Man. He also led the league in hits (207), doubles (44), and was second in slugging % (.537). He also had 23 homers and 110 RBIs. Willie Randolph, steady as ever, hit .289 scoring 86 runs and Don Baylor led the team with 27 homers.

The Yanks really missed Graig Nettles and the Goose who both went west to the San Diego Padres leading them into their first World Series (was Winfield sorry he left San Diego?). Nettles hit 20 homers and played his usual great "D", while the Goose won 10 and saved 25 for the NL pennant winners.

The Yankee pitching was led by the ageless Famer Phil Niekro (16-8). Guidry had an injury filled year and was 10-11. Without the Goose, Rags Righetti was moved to the 'pen and won 5 and saved 31. But the Yanks didn't have a starter to take his spot. The Yankees came in third (87-75) finishing 17 games out.

The Yanks had other problems – the revived Mets. They went from last in '83 to second in '84. Rookie of the Year Doc Gooden (17-9), Ron Darling (12-9), and reliever Jesse Orosco (10 wins, 31 saves) led the charge. Darryl Strawberry clouted 26 homers and had

97 RBIs and Keith Hernandez hit .311 with 94 RBIs. The New York media swung back to the Mets. The Mets finished second to the Cubs mainly because of Rick Sutcliffe – the Cubs got him in June from Cleveland where he had a 4-5 record. The changing of leagues and the friendly confines of Wrigley Field must have really agreed with him as he was almost perfect posting 16 wins against only one loss – needless to say he won the NL Cy Young Award. The only Yank media was about a new Bronx Zoo. What really must have annoyed the Boss was that the Mets outdrew the Yanks (only by 20,000 but the Boss hated not being first, especially when it came to drawing fans).

Kansas City won the AL West flag, but in the playoffs the Big Tiger Striped Machine swept them as Gibson (.417) and Trammel (.364) royally thrashed their pitchers. But it was not as easy as it seemed as they won game 2 in the eleventh inning and the final 1-0 on a three-hitter by Wilcox (8 inn.) and Hernandez (1 inn.).

Detroit faced San Diego in the Series. The Padres route to the NL title was more difficult than the Tigers in the AL. In the NL playoffs the Cubs sparked by NL MVP Ryne Sandberg (.368, 7 for 19) were up 2-zip but then the "Billy Goat" curse came and the Padres led by Steve Garvey (.400, 7 RBIs – his ninth inning 2-run homer won game four 7-5) and Tony Gwynn (.368, 6 runs scored) won the next three. (In the 1945 Series a Chicago tavern owner put a hex on the Cubs that they'll never win another World Series. This was because the Cubs would not let his Billy goat into Wrigley Field even though he had bought it a ticket. I've also heard it was allowed into the park but during the game the Cubs' owner Phil Wrigley had the goat ejected because it smelled. After the Tigers beat the Cubs for the World Series the tavern owner sent Mr. Wrigley a telegram, "Who smells now"). The Tigers had no curse and took the Padres in 5 games for the World Series title. Trammell (.450, 2 homers, 6 RBIs) was MVP nosing out Gibson (.333, 2 homers, 7 RBIs) and Morris (2-0, 2.00 ERA).

On the local scene Mike entered South Brunswick High. He was captain of the freshman soccer team. In December he made the freshman basketball team and after five games became a starter, leading the team in steals. Naturally, I was able to attend all of the games. Don't worry Josephine; I'll get to the yard work.

1985
Mr. May & Co. Fall Short North of the Border

As the season began the Boss' bucks lured Rickey Henderson from the A's and Ed Whitson from the NL Champs, the San Diego Padres.

The Boss made comments, to the effect that Yogi would be the Yankee skipper for the whole year no matter what. No matter what didn't mean anything to Steinbrenner as he reneged and for Yogi it was over after 16 games (6-10 record). This lie affected Yogi so much he would have nothing to do with Steinbrenner and would not return to Yankee Stadium for 14 years, until 1999 when the Boss apologized. Who else was brought in? - Billy Martin for Round 4.

While the Yanks were hovering around .500, my sons were playing ball. Mike was one of the main guys on the freshman high school team until three quarters of the way through the season. Playing with the town's traveling soccer team he got kicked in the ankle, breaking it. Bob Cleffi, the freshman baseball coach, was sort of peeved with Mike breaking his ankle in the spring doing a fall sport (Mike and I weren't exactly too happy about it either).

I was managing Chris' team – it was his first year on the Major League size field, although I practiced with him on it last fall to get him accustomed to the difference. Every year my team would either come in first or win the playoffs. My sons attributed this to my Steinbrenner-like tendencies. Coaching basketball and soccer gives me an insight to who the good athletes were, whereas other coaches only did baseball. I was known for selecting soccer players – you know they can run, had stamina, and were usually good fielders.

Midway through the season one of the kids that went to Germany with us was one of my key players (he was my second baseman). He developed a stress fracture and would be out for the year. Even though half the season was over, I sweet-talked another soccer player, Henry Hunt (who also played with Mike in Germany)

228

to play. Henry quit baseball two years ago but I remember him being really good with the leather, especially at second or shortstop, plus he had a knack for getting on base and motoring around the bases (.500 on base % scoring 80 % of the times he got on base). His dad didn't want him to stop playing baseball in the first place so he was glad of his son's decision to play. Again, Burt's team came in first, but my team beat his in the playoff finals. Ironically, the final game went into extra innings as my team took a two run lead; but my bullpen was depleted (poor managing?). With the two run lead to protect I put in my soccer recruit to save the game, and he came through pitching a scoreless extra inning, leaving the bases loaded to give my team the title. That's how my sons tagged me the Steinbrenner of the SBAA.

Burt and I teamed up again to do the 13-year old tournament team. Two of our pitchers from last year's championship team didn't come out this year, so we were hurting for pitching. In two tournaments, we lost in the semis. Chris for the second year in a row hit .341.

Back in the Majors, the Yanks had a very good year because of a powerful offense. Don Mattingly was the AL MVP and again drew comparisons to Stan the Man. He led the league with 145 RBIs and 48 doubles. His 35 homers (fourth in the AL) and a .324 average (third in the AL) weren't too shabby either. The main reason for his RBI production was Rickey Henderson, who led the league with 146 runs and 80 steals. He also hit 24 homers to go with his .314 average (fourth in the league). Willie Randolph was the ideal #2 hitter; besides his .276 average, he had 85 walks. Third baseman Mike Pagliarulo had 19 homers and Don Baylor contributed 23 driving in 91 runs. Winfield's contribution to the Yankee offense was overlooked only by the Boss as he clubbed 26 homers and finished third in the AL with 114 RBIs. Steinbrenner was still miffed at Winfield for the contract which involved payment to the Winfield Foundation, a charity organization for the community's youth.

It was in September, Toronto came into the Stadium with a 2 1/2 game lead. The Yanks took the opener to cut the lead to 1 1/2, but the Blue Jays took the last three to leave with a 4 1/2 game lead. I believe it was after this "el foldo" that a frustrated Steinbrenner inferred that Winfield was a Mr. May (piling up his stats in the spring instead of the stretch run in the fall). I think Steinbrenner was singing his version of Simon and Garfunkle's "Mrs. Robinson" with the words "Where have you gone Mr. October?" (I know the lyrics say Joe DiMaggio).

Toronto had nowhere the offense the Yanks had. George Bell (29 homers, 95 RBIs) and Jesse Barfield (27 homers, 84 RBIs) couldn't compare to Mattingly and Mr. May. The Blue Jays had an edge on the mound with ex-Yankee flop Doyle Alexander (17-10), Jimmy Key (14-6), and Dave Stieb (14 wins, AL best 2.48 ERA). The Yanks countered with Guidry (22-6, Cy Young runner-up), Phil Niekro (16-12), and Rags Righetti (12 wins, 29 saves). Ed Whitson, who supposedly had problems on the big stage of NYC, was only 10-8 with a 4.88 ERA. Whitson was booed by the hometown fans whenever he pitched at the Stadium plus he was also under constant scrutiny by the Boss. He was really having a frustrating year, just like the Boss; but he showed how good he could be with his hands when a few games after the Toronto debacle he and Martin got into a bar room brawl. Whitson finally gave a good performance as Martin wound up with a broken arm and fractured rib.

Despite the chaotic year the Yanks were having, they still had a chance going north of the border to Toronto needing a sweep to tie the Jays. Things began promising as they took the first, but then ran into their cast-off Doyle Alexander (he was 2-9 as a Yank) who nailed shut the Yankee coffin. The Yanks' 97-64 record left them in second place two games behind the Blue Jays.

Toronto would meet the KC Royals in the playoffs. The Royals were managed by another Yank cast-off, Dick Howser. The West AL titlists were 91-71 – actually 6 games behind the Yanks. Guess the Yanks were in the wrong division – just another thing to frustrate the Boss. For the Royals, the Pine Tar Kid, George Brett, (using less of the stuff) continued to stick it to AL pitching to the tune of a .335 average, 30 homers and 112 RBIs. He led the AL with a .585 slugging %. And yet another former Yank cast-off Steve "Bye-Bye" Balboni helped Brett in the power department with 36 homers (third in the AL) and Frank White contributed 22. Twenty-one year old Bret Saberhagen (20-6) gave a regal show on the Royals' mound winning the Cy Young Award. Using his submarine delivery, their bullpen ace Dan Quisenberry continued to torpedo opponents late inning rallies. The AL line-ups had no answers for the "KC Quiz" (8 wins, 39 saves) as Dan was the AL Fireman of the Year for the fourth consecutive season. Charlie Liebrandt (17-9) and

Mark Gubicza and Danny Jackson with 14 wins each also performed well in the Royals' march to the throne.

The '85 playoffs was the first year for the best-of-seven game league championship series. This would be to the benefit of KC. Toronto had a 3 to 1 lead when KC pulled a Royal Flush and the Blue Jays went down the drain in three straight. Danny Jackson came up with the ALCS best pitching performance keeping KC alive in game 5 as they faced elimination blanking Toronto 2-0 scattering eight hits. Brett again led the KC attack hitting .348 with 3 homers.

In the NL the Mets proved to be a thorn to Steinbrenner. They, like the Yanks, won more games than the NL West winner, but their 98 wins were three less than the East winning Cardinals. The improvement was due to the hitting of newly acquired Gary "The Kid" Carter (32 homers, 100 RBIs), who joined Darryl Strawberry (29 homers, 79 RBIs in two-thirds of the season), and Keith Hernandez (.309, 91 RBIs) to provide runs for a tough pitching staff. Doc Gooden (24-4, 1.53 ERA) won the Cy Young, Ron Darling was 16-6, and Jesse Orosco and Roger McDowell combined for 14 wins and 34 saves. The Mets won the fan battle again outdrawing the Yanks by half a million.

A major historical baseball event took place on September 11 when Pete Rose singled for his 4,192 hit breaking the all-time record held by Ty Cobb. He went on to accumulate a career total of 4,256 hits. "Charlie Hustle" was one of the top players of his era but he pales in comparison to "The Georgia Peach" (one of the game's greatest all-time players). Cobb's lifetime average of .366 is the highest in baseball history as he won 12 batting crowns, constantly hitting 120 or so points above the league average. Pete's lifetime average was .303 with three batting titles. I am aware that Pete's fans would say that Rose overshadowed Cobb when it comes to postseason performances (Cobb's "TYgers" came up empty in three straight World Series tries, 1907-09, but Rose had three rings playing on better teams). In any event, at this time, would anyone now doubt Rose's entrance into The Baseball Hall of Fame on the first ballot? He was a sure bet.

The Cards, again playing Whitey Ball, were led by NL MVP Willie McGee who led the league in hitting (.355), hits (216), and triples (18). Tommy Herr (.302, 110 RBIs), Rookie of the Year Vince Coleman (110 SBs, 107 runs), and Jack Clark (22 homers, 87

RBIs) were other providers to the jack-rabbit offense. Of course, the Wizard of Oz (Smith) solidified the defense along with entertaining fans with his patented back flip before the game began. John Tudor (21-8, 1.93 ERA, 10 shutouts), Joaquin Andujar (21-12), and Danny Cox (18-9) gave the Cards three aces.

The Cards won the NL playoffs against the Dodgers the hard way – after losing the first two they swept the last four, winning the last two in dramatic fashion. Switch-hitter Ozzie Smith, who batted .435 (10 for 23), won game 5 breaking a 2-2 tie with a ninth inning homer (some timing as it was the first time he EVER hit a homer batting lefty). Jack Clark, who hit .381 (8 for 21), mimicked Smith in game 6 as his 3-run homer in the ninth erased a one run Dodger lead as the Cards won the clincher 7-5. Dodger reliever Tom Niedenfuer was not having a good postseason as he gave up both of them game deciding home runs. For LA, Bill Madlock, the former four-time NL batting champ, tried his best to get the Dodgers in the Series batting .333 with 3 homers and 7 RBIs but it was not enough. The Cards won the NL pennant, however for the Series their Whitey Ball style of running the bases suffered a severe setback when their rookie speedster, Vince Coleman, was almost devoured by the automated tarpaulin at Busch Stadium during pre-game warm-ups in game 4 of the NLCS – Coleman escaped with his life but injuries to his leg made him unavailable for the rest of the postseason.

In the Series the Cards had a 3 to 1 lead in this all-Missouri Final. The Royals stayed alive by winning the fifth game 6-1 behind the clutch pitching of Danny Jackson who duplicated what he did in the ALCS. The Cards were winning the sixth game 1-0 and needed three outs to take the Series. The lead-off batter, Jorge Orta, made the first out in the ninth, according to everyone in America except the one that counted. Umpire Don Denkinger missed the call and called Orta safe. This is now known as one of the worst calls ever in the history of all sports. The Cards should have sucked it up and concentrated on getting three outs – after all there was only a guy on first. Instead they imploded – a passed ball, a dropped foul and with the bases loaded, Dane Iorg (a former Red Bird) hit a 2-run single to give KC a 2-1 victory that deadlocked the Series at three apiece. The teams had their aces ready – the Cards' Tudor, who only yielded one run in his two victories versus Saberhagen, who allowed only one run in his one win.

Game 7 was a Royal rout, 11-0, behind Saberhagen. Tudor didn't have it lasting only a few innings. For the Series, Brett pine-tarred the ball at a .370 clip while Willie Wilson (.367), Lonnie Smith (.333), Frank White (homer, 3 doubles, 6 RBIs) and Bye-Bye Balboni (.320) made some Royal contributions. Saberhagen was the Series MVP at 2-0 with a 0.50 ERA. The Royals showed that they were masters of their own domain by coming back twice from 3-1 deficits in the same playoff season.

A couple weeks or so after the Series, Martin Chapter 4 ended – no doubt Whitson beating the heck out of him was a contributing factor. The Yanks hired former hero ('77 & '78 World Series Champs) Sweet Lou Piniella to be the new Zoo Keeper in the Bronx.

On the home front Mike was a sophomore and went out for the soccer team. Most sophomores play on the junior varsity (JV) team but Mike was selected to be a starter on varsity - playing the defensive stopper position.

1986
The Yanks' Worst KNIGHTmare:
A Mets/Red Sox World Series

This year had to be the Boss' most frustrating season yet. They gave it the old Yankee try but again came up short by finishing second. Being runner-up was bad enough, but to the Red Sox was unacceptable. To top it off, in the other league their cross-town rivals, the Mets, ran away with their division winning it by 21 1/2 games over the Phillies. Also, the Mets trounced the Yanks again in the fan battle by a half million.

Piniella put out a productive line-up hitting .271 and even outscored the division winning Red Sox. Mattingly was making the Musial comparison look good. He had great stats - .352 (second in the AL), 31 homers, 113 RBIs (third in the AL) and led the AL in hits (238) and doubles (53). Again he took the Gold Glove award (one of the nine he would eventually win). Mr. May (Winfield) put up his perennial good numbers (24 homers, 104 RBIs) and the table setters did their job - Rickey Henderson (24 homers, 130 runs, 87 SBs) and Willie Randolph (.276, 94 walks, .393 on base %). Mike Pagliarulo (28 homers) and new acquisition Mike Easler (.302, 78 RBIs) were other offensive assets. Also contributing was Dan Pasqua, in his second year, subbing for an injured Winfield he showed some real promise as he batted .293 swatting 16 homers and driving in 45 runs in only 280 at bats – hitting from the left side the Yanks envisioned Pasqua being another Roger Maris.

What really hurt the Yanks was their pitching staff. Dennis Rasmussen was the surprise going from 3-5 in '85 to be the only Yank to reach double figures (18-6). Guidry was a disappointment at 9-12. Righetti was the hero of the staff. He set a save record (46) and also had 8 wins. He was involved in 54 of the 90 Yankee victories.

The Yanks just could not catch their hated Red Sox rivals as they finished second 5 1/2 games out. The Red Sox hitting was on a par with the Yanks (both hit .271 and their season run total was separated by only three runs). Future Famer Wade Boggs led the AL in batting with a .357 average. Marty Barrett (.286, 94 runs), Bill Buckner (18 homers, 102 RBIs), Dwight "Dewey" Evans (26 homers 97 RBIs), ex-Yank Don Baylor (31 homers, 94 RBIs), and Jim Rice (.324, 20 homers, 110 RBIs) provided the rest of the hitting.

It was the pitching that gave the Bosox the edge over the Yanks. "Rocket" Roger Clemens was embarking on his All-Century Team career by leading the AL in wins (24-4), winning % (.857) and ERA (2.48) to win the Cy Young and MVP award (beating out Mattingly). Starters Dennis "Oil Can" Boyd (16-10) and Bruce Hurst (13-8) were also effective for the Red Sox staff while Bob Stanley, Joe Sambito and Calvin Schiraldi combined for 12 wins and 37 saves out of the bullpen.

The California Angels took the AL West by 5 games over the Texas Rangers. They also had a potent offense led by Wally Joyner (22 homers, 100 RBIs), Brian Downing (20 homers, 95 RBIs), and Doug DeCinces (26 homers, 96 RBIs). Just to frustrate the Boss even more, a 40-year old Reggie made the playoffs again contributing 18 homers and 58 RBIs. Mike Witt (18-10), Kirk McCaskill (17-10), and 41-year old Don Sutton (15-11) were their top hurlers.

On the local scene Burt and I joined forces for the first time during the regular season, and again, according to my sons, I pulled another Steinbrenner maneuver. In the SBAA, to ensure balance, team selection was based on rating players A – D, with A being best. Each team had two A-rated players. Well mid-way through the season, one of my A players injured his hip, putting him out for the season. Chris was then my only A-rated player, as we were hanging on to first. The solution to my problem then occurred. Jim Clos, who I used to coach with, was not satisfied with his new town's baseball program. Jim wanted his son, Tommy, to play on a South Brunswick tournament team and in order to do so you have to play in the regular season. It was mid-season and Tommy, who was an A-rated player, would upset the balance in the league. I politicked to the league president that since I only had one A-rated player, Tommy should be assigned to my team, and then all the teams would still have two A-rated players. It made sense to him. He was put on my team and he hit about .600. We won the first place and playoff trophies.

On the high school team, Mike started out on the JV team but was one of two sophomores moved up to the varsity after a few games. He even pitched a game – he lost but only gave up two earned runs. They would finish 3-18. Mike also played in the SBAA high school league leading his team to the championship, going 6-0 on the mound. I was also helping coach this team.

On the tournament scene Chris was on the 14/15-year old team. Burt and I were friends with the 14/15 year old team manager Steve Altamura, who was also on the SBAA Board of Directors, so we became coaches for him. Steve was a former Brooklyn Dodger fan and was not particularly fond of the Yankees. It was three Yankee haters running this team. Most of the starters were 15 including Steve's son Rich and nephew Paul Seifert, who both would go on to receive All-County honors for the South Brunswick high school team. Chris, who was 14, didn't play that much.

In the fall, Mike, a junior, was one of stars of the high school soccer team. Chris was a freshman and because of his soccer skills he was put on the JV team, bypassing the freshman team. On his fourth day in high school his JV team had a scrimmage. In the game, Chris, who had outstanding quickness, beat the opponent to the ball passing it to a teammate. The opponent, being late getting to the ball, kicked Chris in the shin. Despite the shin guard the impact fractured his tibia bone. What a way to start high school! Also, a week prior to school opening we moved into a new, larger house in South Brunswick. Our other house was a ranch; our new one is a colonial, so Chris had to sleep in the downstairs TV room until he was put in a leg cast since the bedrooms were on the second floor. I told him he should have broken his leg last year when we lived in the ranch house – Chris was in no mood for my humor. Chris' decided to hang up his soccer cleats for good.

I spent a lot of the Major League playoffs chauffeuring Chris back and forth to his doctor. Both playoffs went down to the wire. In the AL the Red Sox were down 3 games to 1 to the Angels and were losing 5-2 in the ninth in game 5. Some one in heaven has something against these Angels. Mike Witt pitched a fine 8 2/3 innings, but gave up a 2-run homer to Don Baylor. Manager Gene Mauch then made pitching changes that had as much luck as in 1964 when his moves caused the Phillies to blow the pennant. Reliever Gary Lucas hit a batter and Donnie Moore came in and promptly gave up a 2-run homer to Dave Henderson putting the Bosox up 6-5. To the Angels' credit they tied it in the bottom of the ninth but Henderson hit a sac-fly in the eleventh to win it. Hey, it wasn't all that bad. The Angels were still up 3 games to 2. But back in Fenway the Red Sox knocked their halos off - 10-4 in game 6, and Clemens put them away in game 7 in an 8-1 win. It seemed no matter what, he did Gene Mauch couldn't get in the Series. It looked like the Curse of the Bambino may be over. The Yankees organization and its fans had to be upset by the Red Sox being in the Series.

The Mets' runaway season was due to an NL best team batting average (.263) and ERA (3.11). The Mets' skipper, Davey Johnson, could have managed this team from a rocking chair. The Mets had a pitching rotation that was the darling of the New York media. All four starters were outstanding – Bob Ojeda (18-5), Doc Gooden (17-6), Sid "El Sid" Fernandez (16-6), and Ron Darling (15-6). Even their fifth starter was effective, Rick Aguilera (10-7). When they got in trouble they had relievers Roger McDowell (14 wins, 22 saves) and Jesse Orosco (8 wins, 21 saves) to put out the fire. The Mets line-up only had shortstop Rafael Santana (.218) as an easy out. The power guys were "The Kid" Gary Carter (24 homers, 105 RBIs – third in the NL) and Darryl Strawberry (24 homers, 93 RBIs). The other stick men were Keith Hernandez (.310), Wally Backman (.320), Ray Knight (.298), Mookie Wilson (.289), and Lenny "Nails" Dykstra (.295). With all this balance in their line-up the league MVP was won by the Phillies Mike Schmidt for the third time as he led the NL with 119 RBIs and 38 home runs (for an NL record setting eighth time).

Their playoff opponent was the Houston Astros. They, on paper, did not match up well with the Mets. On offense they had the runner-up for the NL home run crown Glenn Davis (31 homers, 101 RBIs) and Kevin Bass (.311, 20 homers). On the mound they had Cy Young winner Mike Scott (18-10, NL best 2.22 ERA), Bob Knepper (17-12), and a 39-year old Nolan Ryan (12-8).

The Mets were heavy favorites to launch the Astros into space. In game 1 the only thing the Mets could say was "Great Scott". Mike Scott pitched a shutout to beat Gooden 1-0 on a homer by Davis. The Mets took the next two, (game 3 on a game-winning 2-run homer by Nails Dykstra for a 6-5 victory). It was Great Scott winning again, 3-1, to even the series. Game 5 is the one I recall ferrying Chris to the orthopedic – I think the cast was coming off. Ryan pitched a two-hitter for nine innings, but one of the hits was a game-tying homer by Strawberry in the fifth. Carter broke a long slump by winning the game in the twelfth on an RBI hit. The Mets were up 3 games to 2 but if they lost game 6, looming in wait was Scott, who only gave up 1 run in 18 innings.

In game 6 the Astros tallied three in the first and made it stand until the ninth behind Knepper. The fear of facing Scott probably spurred them to score three in the ninth on a triple by Dykstra and RBIs by Mookie, Hernandez, and Knight to tie it. In the fourteenth the Mets took the lead on a RBI single by Backman, but Houston tied it on a homer by Billy Hatcher. The Mets again went ahead scoring three times in the sixteenth on hits by Strawberry, Knight and Dykstra and a couple of wild pitches giving them two very important insurance runs to lead 7-4. Orosco was in his third inning and was faltering. The Astros had cut the deficit to one and had two on but Orosco, I think, put himself in a fishing mode throwing some kind of sinker and Bass bit with a game-ending strikeout. With the victory and NL pennant, the Yankee-nation had their World Series interest sucked out of them. They probably hoped it would go into infinity. Both my sons rooted for the Mets to take the Series; as they do not wear Red Sox.

In the Series opener Boston lefty Bruce Hurst blanked the Mets 1-0 - the run scoring in the fifth on an error. In game 2, Doc and the Rocket met and most thought it would be another 1-0 game. But no, neither pitcher lasted five innings as Boston won 9-3 taking both games at Shea, and were thinking of not coming back. Well, at Fenway the Mets kept their heads up and came out of the gate with smoldering bats. Leading off Dykstra nailed one off of Oil Can and they scored three more to lead 4-0 before the Red Sox batted. The Kid Carter had 2 hits and 4 RBIs in the 7-1 win. The next day The Kid stayed hot banging out two homers and Dykstra one as the Mets evened the Series with a 6-2 win. Hurst, looking like a lefty Mike Scott, beat the Mets in game 5 by a 4-2 score.

The Series moved back to Shea for game 6. It would become one of the most famous games in Series history. Clemens was up 3-2 when he developed a blister in the seventh inning. There was much speculation to the move of the Rocket coming out of the game – whether he requested it or manager McNamara just took him out and brought in Calvin Schiraldi. The Mets tied it in the eighth on a lead-off pinch–hit by Lee Mazzilli, a miscue by Schiraldi and a sac-fly by Carter that scored Maz. In the tenth the Bambino's curse appeared to be over. Henderson, who hit the famous playoff homer, did it again with a blast and the Red Sox also tagged on an insurance run on a double by Boggs and RBI single by Barrett for a 5-3 lead. With two outs in the bottom of the tenth, the Red Sox clubhouse/locker room was ready for the champagne, and the scoreboard lit up a Congratulations Red Sox message.

Like the famous Yogi-ism "It ain't over 'til it's over" the Crimson Hose still had to get that third out – it would get ugly. With Schiraldi still in there and two outs The Kid refused to make that last out and singled; Kevin Mitchell also not wanting to end the game singled - not wanting to make that last out became contagious as Ray Knight then got a hit driving in Carter sending Mitchell to third. Bob Stanley, their top reliever then came in to face Mookie. Stanley had a 2-2 count and threw an inside pitch hoping Mookie, who you never knew what he'd swing at, would take a hack at it. But it was too inside and the catcher Rich Gedman couldn't block it. The wild pitch allowed Mitchell to score the tying run. Hold the champagne! Mookie, after what seemed like a hundred pitches, sent a nasty slow roller down to first. The first baseman Bill Buckner, who usually was out for defensive purposes late in games due to bad legs, was ready to field it but it went under his glove. Knight scored from second with the winning run. You know, when I talk to people today some of them think Buckner's error allowed the tying and winning runs to score. When Buckner made the error the score was already tied so if he made the play there's no guarantee Boston would have won. Also, seeing this play a million times, there's a slim chance Mookie, a real speedster, might have beaten Buckner to first that would have left Knight on third and Mookie on first.

The finale was delayed a day by rain. The Bosox were going with Hurst who only gave up four runs to the Mets in his two victories. It looked like Boston, Stanley, Schiraldi and Buckner may escape the game 6 blunders as homers by Evans and Gedman and an RBI hit by Boggs gave the Red Sox a 3-0 lead as Hurst was continuing his mastery over the Mets as he only gave up one hit in the first five innings. But in the sixth pinch-hitter Mazzilli came through again (like in game 6) as his lead-off single ignited a rally as Mookie singled, Tim Teufel drew a walk, Hernandez had a 2-RBI hit and The Kid had an RBI (it was Carter's ninth RBI of the Series) to knot the game at 3 apiece. In the seventh Knight had the key blow, a homer off of Schiraldi that ignited another 3-run inning (RBIs by Santana and Hernandez). Singles by Buckner (trying his best to avoid defeat) and Rice followed by Evans' 2-run double made it close at 6-5, but for dessert the Mets had a Strawberry homer and an Orosco RBI hit to make the final 8-5.

The Red Sox had some valiant efforts from several players – Barrett tied the Series hit record with 13 batting .433, Henderson (.400, 10 for 25, double, triple, 2 homers, 5 RBIs), Evans (.308, pair of doubles and homers, 9 RBIs), Rice (.333, 9 for 27, 6 runs scored) and on the hill Hurst (2-0, 1.96 ERA in 23 innings) – but it just wasn't enough. Even though the Yankee-nation could care less, it was Good KNIGHT Red Sox. Ray Knight was the Series MVP (.391, 9 for 23, 5 RBIs).

1987
The Yanks are in the WRONG Division, Again

For the fourth time in nine years the Yankees were in the wrong division. Like '79, '84 and '85, the Pinstripers had a better record than the AL West division champ. The Yanks were 89-73 while the Minnesota Twins at 85-77, won the West. Even so, the Blue Jays and Brewers felt worse as they too had a better record than the Twins and Yanks, finishing second and third respectively behind the AL East winning Tigers. I was surprised that that Boss didn't lobby to have the Yanks put in the West. After all the NL has Atlanta in the West, whereas the Chicago Cubs, Pittsburgh and St. Louis are in the East. (All further west than Atlanta)

Back at home Chris was one of the stars of the high school freshman baseball team hitting around, .400 and going 3-1 on the mound. Since I was the manager of this group for years, Bob Cleffi who was now the South Brunswick varsity baseball coach informed the freshman coach to consult with me as I would be at most of the games.

Mike was on varsity and was a back-up pitcher. Coach Cleffi had Mike pitch a JV game to get a line on him. He tossed a no-hitter and hit a homer in a 1-0 victory. It earned him a start on the mound in a varsity game. He was doing OK on the mound for three innings. Then at the plate he led off the fourth with a shot down the left field line. As he was rounding first he saw the back of the left fielder chasing the ball so he was thinking triple and put his running into high gear. But the ground gave and his feet went out from under him and as he fell he braced himself with his left arm. He then was grimacing in pain as he crawled back to first. He was taken out and I told him he had enough time to crawl to second. He said he was in too much pain. I took him to the hospital – he had a hyper-extended elbow and the remedy was to rest it and not to straighten it for a few weeks. Like his freshman season he was done for the rest of the year (at least this time it was a baseball related injury). The team showed a remarkable improvement from last year as it finished with a 12-12 record (Coach Cleffi was a drill master on fundamentals).

Our town's SBAA high school age league goes longer than the high school year. Burt and I had the team in first. Mike and Chris were two of the reasons as they were finally, age wise, able to be on the same team. Mike missed a few games due to his hyper-extended arm, thus we lost a couple of games and the other teams caught us for first place. We had a game for the league championship coming up. Mike said he wanted to pitch (it was two weeks since he injured the arm), Josephine had a fit, "No way" she said. It was a family argument. Mike convinced me that he would be able to throw and he'd bat lefty. Against Josephine and my better judgment I gave in to Mike. Burt asked me if I was sure it was OK to throw Mike. I told him Mike said he's OK and we'll see how it goes. In this league a pitcher is limited to 4 innings. Mike had his right arm rested for two weeks, so it was fresh. He was on, striking out 8 in his 4 innings, not allowing a run. He even got a key hit batting lefty. Chris then went in and K'd 5 in 3 innings. We clinched first place – Mike was OK and Josephine talked to me again (maybe my team should have lost).

Burt and I again got ready for the tournament season. The 14/15-year old team was the last year the SBAA sponsored a team. Steve, last year's manager, coached with us as his son Rich moved up to play Legion Ball but his nephew Paul stayed on the 14/15-year old team. We had one of the best teams in central NJ. We were entered in four tournaments and won three of them (North Edison, Monroe, and Middlesex County) and was runner-up in the other (East Brunswick). It was very satisfying to win the trophy in Monroe, the town where the judge there took away a certain serviceman's license for a month in 1967. Our team went 19-4, beat teams from five different counties, and defeated the teams that beat us. I felt like Casey Stengel, as just about all of our moves panned out – and Burt's arm almost fell off waving all our base runners home from his third base coaching box.

Our nemesis was a team from Hazlet, NJ. They were similar to our team and really could pound the ball. They had four players that would eventually be on the NJ All-State team. They beat us in the finals of the East Brunswick Tournament 17-16 (we missed the extra point). Hazlet had beaten us three times when we ran into them again, this time in the Monroe Tournament. Burt and I decided to start Darrell Sunkins. Darrell was a five tool player until he threw out his arm – as a four tool player he was still real good, and as my top slugger sent chills down the backs of opposing pitchers (he would go on to be an All-Division, All-County high school selection and had a tryout with the Phillies). On the mound Darrell, who use to be a flame throwing lefty, made an adjustment a la Frank Tanana and became a junk ball pitcher with three speeds (slow, slower and slowest). The Hazlet batters were so off stride they were seemingly screwing themselves into the ground when they swung at Sunkins' late arriving pitches. We finally got even with Hazlet, knocking them out of the tournament with a satisfying 10 to 1 victory. The path to the trophy was now in the bag. Chris again did well hitting .328 with an over .500 on base % and led the team in stolen bases and runs scored.

One of the strangest plays and calls by an umpire that involved my team occurred in the Monroe Tournament. In the middle of a game the opposing team's batter hit a long drive to left that bounced over the fence. My left fielder, Chris Cassese, vaulted the fence, and while retrieving the ball, saw the batter rounding second. Chris instinctively fired a throw to third. In a close play the umpire called the runner safe. As the play at third was being made I knew it was moot - safe or out the player would have to go back to second. (As all baseball people know, a fair ball that bounces over the fence is a ground-rule double). As play was about to resume I called time and told the umpire that the player had to go back to second since it was a ground-rule double. Burt and I were shocked that the ump said that my player made a throw to third and that's where the player would stay. I questioned the ump "Suppose he was called out at third?" his reply was "It doesn't matter, he was safe - Play ball". The other manager had his back to us as he was chuckling over this ruling. (This tournament had a no-protest rule – no matter what, whether it be a judge or umpire I just can't get a "just" call in this town). I don't recall if this runner scored or not since we won the game on our way to the Monroe Tournament crown. In any event when Chris came back to the dugout, I asked him about this play. He said "Mr. Hut, it's your fault, you always instruct us to follow through on a play, so when I saw him rounding second I instinctively threw to third - ya' know it's not over 'til it's over." I laughed as I said, "You're right and you probably pegged him out at third - just another thing the ump blew". Cassese would later use his athletic instincts quarterbacking our high school football team to its first winning season in many years.

Let's get back to the Yanks. During the spring and up to the All-Star game the Yanks dominated and were in first place. Winfield was carrying them with 20 homers and over 60 RBIs up to that point. The second half was not too good. Winfield's stats fell off - for the year he finished with 27 homers and 97 RBIs (missing his try for a sixth consecutive year of 100 RBIs). The team's record after the All-Star Game was five games under .500. Mattingly had a Stan the Man year (.330, 30 homers, 115 RBIs) and, for not being known as a home run hitter he tied the record for most consecutive games with a homer (8), and set one with Grand Slams (6) in a season. Also pacing the offense was Willie Randolph (.305, 96 runs) and Mike Pagliarulo (32 homers, 87 RBIs). Rickey Henderson missed a third of the season but hit .291 with 41 steals and 78 runs. The thought of Dan Pasqua being another Maris faded as he homered 17 times but only batted .233 with 99 Ks in 318 at bats. Rick Rhoden (16-10) and 44-year old Tommy John (13-8 with his 15-year old rebuilt arm) led the pitching staff aided by Rags Righetti in relief (31 saves, 8 wins). The Yanks finished 9 game behind the Tigers.

The season's highlight was the 39-game hitting streak by the Brewers' Paul Molitor. It was the longest in the AL since DiMaggio's 56 in 1941. The streak ended with Molitor in the on-deck circle in the tenth inning on August 26. Molitor batted .353 for the season finishing second to Wade Boggs' .363.

Detroit won the AL East because of a Blue Jay meltdown. Toronto lost their last seven games including the final three to the Tigers to lose the division. A potent line-up was the main reason Detroit was able to overtake Toronto; and it was led by Alan Trammel (.343, 28 homers, 105 RBIs), who should of been AL MVP. (Toronto's George Bell was selected as the AL MVP with .306, 47 homers, 134 RBIs, but I think a lot of voters sent in their ballots before the unexpected Blue Jay collapse). Trammel was joined by fellow Tigers Darrell Evans (34 homers, 99 RBIs), Kirk Gibson (24 homers, 79 RBIs), Matt Nokes (32 homers, 99 RBIs), and Chet Lemon (20 homers, 75 RBIs) in this "rip roaring" line-up. The Detroit mound aces were Jack Morris (18-11), Walt Terrell (17-10), and former Yank cast-off Doyle Alexander, who they picked up in August, had an unblemished 9-0 slate with a 1.53 ERA. Alexander was acquired from Atlanta for John Smoltz, a minor league pitcher of unknown ability.

The Twins had a similar offense to the Tigers. Future Famer Kirby Puckett (.332, 28 homers, 99 RBIs), Tom Brunansky (32 homers, 85 RBIs), Kent Hrbek (34 homers, 90 RBIs), and Gary Gaetti (31 homers, 109 RBIs) were the Twins lumber men. Frank Viola (17-10) and Bert Blyleven (15-12) were their only double figure winners. Reliever Jeff Reardon won 8 and saved 31. In the AL playoffs the Twins pulled another surprise caging the Tigers 4 games to 1. Brunansky (.412, 7 for 17, 2 homers, 7 RBIs) and Gaetti (.300, 2 homers, 5 RBIs) were Twins that the Detroit hurlers couldn't handle. Blyleven had two of the Twins victories.

On the home front Mike was a Captain and MVP of the South Brunswick high school soccer team. Academically he was on the Spanish, Math and National Honor Society. He was also elected Senior Class Treasurer.

In the NL the West was taken by the San Francisco Giants. Their stars were Will "The Thrill" Clark (.308, 35 homers, 91 RBIs), Chili Davis (24 homers 76 RBIs), Candy Maldonado (20 homers, 85 RBIs), and Jeff Leonard (19 homers).

Their foe would be the Whitey Ball Cards. The Mets were chasing the Cards when in September with a three run lead and two outs, one of the most infamous homers ever for the Mets occurred as Terry Pendleton tied it with a homer and the Mets lost the game, and also their heart as they finished in second place.

Like the Giants, St Louis' big star was a Clark (Jack) who hit 35 homers and drove in 106 runs. Whitey Ball was provided by Vince Coleman (109 SBs, 121 runs – and no doubt keeping his distance from automated tarpaulins), Willie McGee (.285, 105 RBIs) and, who I thought of who should have been NL MVP, the Wizard of Oz Smith, who besides his great leather, had great stats on the offensive side (.303, 40 doubles, 104 runs, 43 SBs). The last place Cubs' Andre Dawson (49 homers, 137 RBIs) was MVP. The Cards won their division despite having no hurler with more than 11 victories.

In the NL playoffs, St. Louis was down 3 games to 2 but took game 6 by a 1-0 score behind John Tudor and relievers and triumphed in the finale as Danny Cox whitewashed the Giants 6-0 scattering eight hits. Cardinal pitchers held the San Fran offense scoreless for the last 22 innings. The Giants' Jeff Leonard was the batting leader of the playoffs (.417, 10 for 24). He set a record with a home run in each of the first four games.

In the Series it was the AL's turn to have four home games if it goes seven games – that meant four games at the Metrodome. This stadium, when full, makes more noise than Josephine asking me to do some yard work. The Twins won the first two there, lost three in St. Louis and won the last two back at the Metrodome. Frank Viola won games 1 and 7 and was MVP and Kirby Puckett led the Twins with 10 hits batting .357.

After the Series it was time again for the Boss to play his favorite game – musical Yankee manager's chairs. Piniella wasn't a good yes-man and I think had a problem responding to phone calls. Lou was moved to the front office as the Boss' magnet Billy Martin was brought back for Round Five.

1988
Billy, Lou and Boston Make the Boss See Red (Sox)

In the early part of spring, Billy Ball had the Yanks playing at a .667 clip; but not all was good in the Bronx. In May, Martin got involved in a bar room brawl in Texas and was roughed up to the point that he might have had more stitches than a baseball. Maybe getting knocked around affected his brain as his antics became more pronounced. He had to serve a three-game suspension and was fined for tossing dirt on an umpire. The Yanks were winning but getting negative media, while the winning Mets continued to be the NY dailies favorites. Even though the Yanks set a Yankee Stadium attendance record (2.6 million), they still were beaten by the 3 million at Shea. Near the end of June, after the Tigers swept them, Billy Chapter 5 was over. It was time to recycle Lou Piniella (from the front office). Martin had the Yanks playing .588 ball (40-28) at the time of his removal – had he stayed and they played at that clip they would have won the division as the Red Sox took the AL East with a .549 winning %.

Back home, Mike was a senior and Chris a sophomore. During his senior season, Mike started at second, but his versatility gave Coach Cleffi options as Mike was able to fill in at the position of whoever was pitching. Chris would play JV and be his brother's back-up on varsity. Chris' role on varsity was usually pinch-running and late-inning defense. Chris was the big hitter for the JV team – there were condos behind left field and Chris bounced some off of their walls. Mike got off to a horrendous start at the plate, but his ability to walk kept his on base % respectable. Chris who was smashing the ball on the JV team felt he should have replaced his brother. The team was 13-1 and ranked in the top 20 in the state, so Coach Cleffi did not want to disrupt the winning line-up - and as the dad, I would rather see the senior play. (My sons really enjoyed playing for Coach Cleffi as he was also a Yankee die-hard).

One thing about Chris, the year before he went to a sophisticated hitting camp. Being a studious person, he absorbed it all and could tell what batters were doing wrong. I asked him to study Mike and give him some tips. Mike isn't stupid (glad he has a smart mom?) and was aware of Chris' batting instruction talent so he took his advice and finished out the season at a .400 clip – which was a factor in Mike being the recipient of the Viking Award (one of the three baseball awards presented after the completion of the season). South BrunswicKs moniker is the Vikings.

Our high school finished 18-3, winning the White Division Championship of the Greater Middlesex Conference (GMC), and Coach Cleffi was selected by the Newark Star-Ledger as the Middlesex County Coach of the Year. (The Conference was made up of about 30 high schools in Middlesex County NJ, split into four divisions based on enrollment – the divisions were designated by colors and South Brunswick was in the White Division). The Vikings' quest for the state crown was ended in the NJ State tournament sectional finals. Mike would finish his baseball varsity career with the Vikings having a .500 percentage (not bad considering how poor their record was his sophomore year). For his three years of varsity in both soccer and baseball, Mike received two of South Brunswick High's Scholar Athlete Awards.

Our central NJ newspaper, the Home News, sponsored a high school league after the regular season. The SBAA sponsored tournament teams only up to 15 years old. Being on the Board of Directors of the SBAA and having some other members of the board whose sons would be on the team, the SBAA agreed to sponsor a team in the Home News League.

The Home News League was composed of towns from Middlesex County. We were in the Southern Division. Burt and I again combined to coach the team. It was comprised of varsity and JV players. After a couple games, Chris had a problem bending for grounders. Since I had back surgery for a herniated disc in 1974, I surmised Chris inherited my back, and sure enough he had two herniated discs. The doctor said he could play if he felt like it. Again, like Mike playing last year against Mom's wishes, Chris wanted to play as he wasn't restricted from swinging a bat or running (he just couldn't bend). Since he was my only shortstop,

Mike was recruited to play as he was listed on the roster in case I needed him in an emergency (not having a shortstop could be called an emergency). Mike didn't forget Chris' batting tips and led the team in batting (.422). Chris wound up at .375 leading the team with three homers.

The final game of the regular season was for the Southern Division Championship against a team from Old Bridge, NJ. Both teams came on strong down the stretch, matching wins. We were facing their undefeated pitcher (5-0). Because of his back I had Chris bat ninth. He went 4 for 4 and Mike went 3 for 4 with 2 walks. The brothers combined for a 7 for 8 day with 7 runs scored and 4 RBIs. We were ahead 13-3 in the last inning but due to some sloppy defense and a bunch of hits the Old Bridge team made it 13-7. My pitcher than changed places with Mike and he got the final two outs. We won the Southern Division Championship of the Home News League. It was probably my most enjoyable and satisfying game. Our high school coach (Cleffi) was ecstatic as most of the team would be playing for him next year. For the most part it was Burt and my last year as a coaching tandem.

Here's something about Burt's son Jay. He personified the typical "Moneyball" hitter. Every year he would be one of the team's on base and walks leaders. He was similar to Phillie Hall of Famer Richie Ashburn, in that he just kept fouling pitches off until he got one he liked or walked (Jay once had a streak of ten straight times on base). He was exasperating for a lot of pitchers. More often than not, Jay would see at least six or more pitches per at bat. An opposing pitcher would probably have been better off plunking him with the first pitch to keep their pitch count down. Jay was always one of my smartest players. Two examples of his intelligence were becoming a graduate of Yale Law School and being a Met fan.

In the Majors, Piniella kept the Yanks in the race going into August, but had a miserable month losing 20, making the Boss feel the same way. They had one last gasp when they were 3 1/2 out facing first place Boston for three games. Boston took all three making the Boss see Red (Sox).

The Red Sox had better luck changing managers. Joe Morgan (not the Reds' Hall of Famer) took over for John McNamara and went 46-31, .597 winning %. Boston was led by MVP runner-up Mike Greenwell (.325, 22 homers, 119 RBIs), Dewey Evans (.293, 21 homers, 111 RBIs), and Wade Boggs (his .366 and 128 runs led

the AL). Bruce Hurst (18-6) and Rocket Clemens (18-12) with
reliever Lee Smith (4 wins, 29 saves) led the pitching corp. In a
close race they nosed out Detroit by 1, Milwaukee and Toronto by 2
and the Boss by 3 1/2. The Yanks ended with a 85-76 record.

The Yanks again provided a powerful offense. Dave Winfield
put up some good numbers as usual (.322, 25 homers, 107 RBIs)
and Mattingly gave another good show (.313, 18 homers, 88 RBIs).
The Boss' bucks picked up St. Louis slugger Jack Clark (27 homers,
93 RBIs) in an attempt to pulverize opponents. Also, adding to the
attack were Claudell Washington (.308) and speedster Rickey
Henderson (.305, 93 SBs, 118 runs). Pitching again was the
Pinstripers' downfall. Newcomers, former 20-game winners John
Candelaria (13-8) and Rich Dotson (12-9) were the top starters with
Rags Righetti (5 wins, 25 save) providing relief.

The Oakland A's easily took the West. Jose Canseco (.307, 42
homers, 124 RBIs) was the AL MVP showing arms that made
Popeye's look like mine. Canseco became the Majors' first 40/40
man (40 homers and 40 SBs). Dave Henderson (.304, 24 homers, 94
RBIs) and Mark McGwire (32 homers, 99 RBIs) brought in more
muscle. Dave Stewart (21-12), Bob Welch (17-9), and Storm Davis
(16-7), with lights out reliever future Famer Dennis Eckersley (4
wins, 45 saves), blew away their opponents. At least the Boss had
some satisfaction with the A's sweeping the Red Sox in four.
Canseco bashed three homers, and reliever Gene Nelson was 2-0 in
a scoreless 4 2/3 innings of work.

In the NL East, the Mets coasted to the delight of their 3 million
at Shea. Doc Gooden (19-8), David Cone (20-3), and Ron Darling
(17-9) were the mound aces. Roger McDowell and Randy Myers
combined for 12 wins and 42 saves. Darryl Strawberry (39 homers,
101 RBIs), Kevin McReynolds (.286, 27 homers, 99 RBIs), and
Howard Johnson (24 homers) provided the pop, while aging
veterans Gary Carter and Keith Hernandez provided leadership.

Somehow the Dodgers took the West, beating the Reds by
seven games. The Dodgers had only one real star in their attack,
their John Wayne-type leader Kirk Gibson (.290, 25 homers, 76
RBIs, 105 runs), who was the NL MVP. Outfielder Mike Marshall
did help out at the plate with 20 homers and 82 RBIs. But it was the
year of Orel "Bulldog" Hershiser that put LA over the top. He
looked like the second coming of Don Drysdale for the Dodgers. He
went 23-8 tossing six consecutive shutouts and a record 59 scoreless

innings (breaking Drysdale's record set in '68 by a third of an inning) to end the season. Actually Bulldog and Big D had similar won/loss records for their careers – Drysdale (209-166) and Hershiser (204-150). He was an easy pick for the Cy Young Award. Gibson (not nicknamed Hoot or Hondo) and Hershiser were LA's only marquee players.

Mike was in his first semester at Rutgers University in New Brunswick, NJ. Even though he was only 15 miles from home he lived at Rutgers, but he was only two miles from my work office.

As the NL playoffs were going on, Chris was having back surgery. He was concerned about his recovery time as he wanted to be ready for baseball in April as he was penciled in as a starter. The doctor said with an accelerated therapy program he might make it. The operation went fine and I spent time with him at the hospital watching the Mets succumb to the Dodgers

During the season the Mets beat the Dodgers 11 out of 12 and were expected to roll over them in the playoffs. And it looked that way as the Mets were up 4-2 in the ninth inning of game 4. This victory would put them up 3 games to 1. But Mike Scioscia (3 homers all year) hit a 2-run homer to tie it and LA won it in the eleventh to even the Series at two apiece. (This homer, like Pendleton's last year, remains one of the most infamous hits in Mets' history). The teams split the next two, but LA had Orel going in the finale so he predictably tossed a shutout as LA pulled the upset. Now they had to face the A's, who with their Bash Brothers (Canseco & McGwire), won 104 games during the regular season. They were heavy favorites to "dodge" an LA upset.

The first game was one of the most dramatic events in Major League history. The A's were up 4-3 via a Grand Slam bash by Canseco. If God was a reliever he would be Eckersley (considered the best ever - at least until Mariano Rivera came along). You could tell something was strange when the Eck-man walked Mike Davis in the ninth with two outs. So what! LA had no one available to do damage as their leader, Gibson, was so riddled with leg injuries he shouldn't even have been on the roster. Then, like Willis Reed for the Knicks years ago hobbling out hitting two baskets that psyched out Wilt the Stilt and his Lakers leading New York to the NBA title, out came Gibson. He was so hobbled that only a homer would do - even if he hit a gapper he might be thrown out at first. Somehow the count was full as Gibson hung in there fouling off the Eck-man's fastballs. Then the Eck-man got cute and tried to sneak a breaking pitch by him. It wasn't so cute as Gibby sent a blast into the right field stands in the now famous clip of him rounding the bases while pumping his arms (his adrenalin must have carried him around the 360 feet). LA won 5-4 and had Orel going the next day – naturally another shutout as LA went up 2 - zip.

The A's showed some life in game 3 as McGwire bashed a game-winning homer for a 2-1 win. The Dodgers came back in game 4 with a line-up that probably wouldn't have even been competitive in Triple A. Somehow they won to go up 3 games to 1 with Orel to try to wrap it up in game 5. He pitched badly (for his standards, anyway) as he gave up two runs, but LA prevailed 5-2 and were World Series Champs. The Dodgers' Mickey Hatcher (.368, 7 for 19, 5 RBIs and 5 runs scored) was the unlikely batting star of the Series – after only hitting one homer in 192 plate appearances he banged out two in the Series. Hershiser was easily selected the Series MVP (2-0, 1.00 ERA). He even went 3 for 3 at the plate while the Bash Brothers went a combined 2 for 36 (their homers in games 1 and 3).

In October a distraught Boss again played musical (manager) chairs. Sweet Lou Chapter 2 was over and in was a former World Series winner, Dallas Green (Phils' '80). Hey, the Yanks did well when they hired a former World Series winner, Johnny Keane. DIDN'T THEY?

1989
GREEN with Envy Doesn't Work

In October '88 the Yanks hired Dallas Green to be manager. He was sort of in the General Patton mold and won the Series in 1980 with the Phils. But as Major Houk found out in the late '60's/early'70's, you have to have good troops to lead. The Yanks were just plain lousy. Like my son Chris, Winfield was out for the year with a disc/back operation. The Boss would've loved a Mr. May, now. Mattlingly's average dropped to .303 but he still had pop (23 homers and 113 RBIs, second in the AL). Steve Sax was second in hits (205) and batted .315 while Roberto Kelly hit .305. The Yanks got the '86 home run leader (40) Jesse Barfield but he only hit 18. The moody Rickey Henderson made Green feel blue, so after 60 or so games he was traded to the A's solidifying their run to the World Series.

The Yanks' best pitcher was Ed Whitson, oops - wait, I forgot his 16-11, 2.66 ERA was done for the San Diego Padres showing the Boss his talents are more than just beating up Billy Martin. The Yank pitching ERA was 4.50 - next to last in the AL. Andy Hawkins was the only one to reach 10 wins (15-15) and Rags Righetti did his best, still being effective out of the 'pen (25 saves).

Similar to when General Patton didn't listen to Ike (Eisenhower) in WWII, Green didn't listen to the Boss. Since the interaction between them was not good and the Boss was most likely green with envy of the division leaders, he decided to put a dent into the losing. He got rid of Green and brought in former teeny-bopper homer hero ('78 playoff game) Bucky Dent to turn things around. I think he was chosen to bring back the former teeny-boppers to the Stadium. The team played at a worst clip for him than they did for Green. For the year their record was 74-87, finishing fifth 14 1/2 games behind their hated rivals from Boston.

Chris was doing his accelerated therapy surprising even the doctor at how he was progressing. Chris did his therapy religiously. Also, his class academic rankings came out and he was second (it's good to have a smart mom – Josephine always says that the kids have her brains; at least I know where they are...ha ha). Coach Cleffi was surprised that he joined the spring practice after only missing a couple of weeks. As the season started he was rounding into form. He was used as a pinch-hitter in the first couple of games, and then cracked the line-up as the DH, although he could have played the field. He started off like his brother the previous year and was like 0 for 10 but he hit some hard shots. After getting all the rust off and regaining his Paul Molitor batting form he finished out the year at a .333 pace. Like last year our high school team was ranked in the top 20 in the state and won the White Division Championship in the Greater Middlesex Conference. However, we also again came up short in the finals of the NJ State Tournament sectional finals. It was a tough 2-1 loss. Chris went 2 for 3 and was left on third base as the game ended.

Again, I coached the SBAA Home News League team. Burt helped out on occasion, but when he wasn't there I coached third and felt like Mike Ferraro of the '80 Yanks (but there was no Steinbrenner around to fire me). I sent them when I shouldn't have and vice versa. The team was new as most of my players from last year's team moved up to American Legion ball. Chris was a year younger so he didn't move up. This was a young team compared to our opponents. We came in fourth place, but since Chris only DH'd on varsity he had a chance to play short and was my best pitcher. For the year he was 3-2 on the mound and hit .434 out of the clean-up spot in the line-up.

Our season would have been worse if one of Chris' best friends Craig Swanson a.k.a. "Swanny" had decided not to play (it was the first time he played for my team). Swanny got some time at second base on the varsity during the high school year. Leading off for my Home News team he displayed great bat control, bunting, hit and run, etc. and batted .420. The following year he would bring his batting skills back to the high school team batting in the two slot in the line-up where his main job was to get Chris, who led off, into scoring position – which he did with great success having more sacrifices than an Aztec ritual. Swanny's unselfish hitting talents would be recognized next year as he received All-County mention as a second baseman for South Brunswick High.

Toronto took the AL East with 89 wins. Bad timing for the Yanks as four times ('83, '85, '86 & '87) they had as many wins and couldn't take the division. The Blue Jays were led by AL home run leader "Crime Dog" Fred McGriff, (36 homers), George Bell (.297, 18 homers, 104 RBIs), and Kelly Gruber (.290, 18 homers, 76 RBIs). Their pitching was no great shakes – Dave Stieb (17-8) was the only reliable starter. Relievers Tom Henke and Duane Ward were the backbone of the pitching staff combining for 12 wins and 35 saves.

The A's again showing a balance of power and pitching took the West again. Newcomer Dave Parker (22 homers, 97 RBIs) joined McGwire (33 homers, 95 RBIs), Canseco (17 homers, 57 RBIs, injured half the year), and Dave Henderson (15 homers, 80 RBIs) to provide a high-powered offense. Rickey Henderson escaped the Bronx Zoo and in only 85 games hit .294 with 52 steals and scored 72 runs. Carney Lansford chipped in with a .336 average. Their four starters on the mound were outstanding winning 76 games – Dave Stewart (21-9), Storm Davis (19-7), Mike Moore (19 -11), and Bob Welch (17-6). Of course when you have the Eck-man saving games it makes things easier. Rebounding from the Gibson homer Eckersley went 4-0 with 33 saves and a microscopic 1.56 ERA.

In the AL playoffs, the powerful A's took the Jays in five games as Rickey Henderson was outstanding (.400, 6 for 15, 2 homers, 5 RBIs, 8 runs). On the hill Stewart posted 2 victories and the Eck-man had 3 saves.

In the NL West the Giants won the flag behind the lumber of Will Clark (.333, 23 homers, 111 RBIs), NL MVP Kevin Mitchell (47 homers, 125 RBIs), and Matt Williams (18 homers). Rich Reuschel was their top hurler (17-8).

In the NL East the Mets made a run behind the bats of Strawberry (29 homers, 77 RBIs), Howard Johnson (36 homers, 101 RBIs), and Kevin McReynolds (22 homers, 85 RBIs). On the mound, Sid Fernandez, David Cone, and Ron Darling all posted 14 wins. But the Mets finished runner-up to the Cubs. The new Mr. Cub, Ryne Sandberg (.290, 30 homers, 76 RBIs, 104 runs) was joined by Mark Grace (.314, 79 RBIs) and Andre Dawson (21 homers, 77 RBIs) to give them a productive line-up. Greg Maddux

(19-12), Mike Bielecki (18-7), and Rick Sutcliffe (16-11) led the starters while the "Wild Thing" Mitch Williams picked up the pieces in the bullpen (36 saves).

In the NL playoffs, the curse of the Billy Goat reared its head again as the Giants took the series in five games. But there was quite a "thrilling" sideshow put on by the rival first basemen. Will Clark had Giant stats (.650, 13 for 20, 3 doubles, a triple and 2 homers with 8 RBIs and 8 runs scored). Not to be out done, Mark Grace kept pace with Clark (.647, 11 for 17 with 3 doubles, a triple, a homer and 8 RBIs).

The Series started in Oakland and the A's juggernaut took the two games easily. They figured to go to San Francisco and shake things up. Things were shaken up, but not by them - it was the San Andreas Fault shaking the whole area with a huge, tragic earthquake just before the start of game 3. The quake made people realize how inconsequential baseball is in the total scope of things.

The inconsequential Series resumed after a ten day grace period and the A's finished business by making it the longest four-game sweep in history. The A's line-up not having to face a Hershiser-type pitcher batted .301. Rickey Henderson (.474, 9 for 19, double, 2 triples, homer, 3 RBIs, 4 runs scored, 3 SBs) continued to have a smoldering postseason bat. Lansford (.438, 7 for 16, 4 RBIs, 5 runs scored), Canseco (.357, 5 for 14, 3 RBIs, 5 runs scored) and the other Henderson, Dave (.308, pair of doubles and homers, 4 RBIs, 6 runs scored) joined Rickey in pounding the Giants' staff. The Series MVP Dave Stewart (1.69 ERA) and Mike Moore (2.08 ERA) each posted two victories.

At the end of August Pete Rose, the Reds' manager, agreed to a lifetime ban with the chance to ask for reinstatement from Baseball Commissioner Bart Giamatti after a year for allegedly betting on baseball. An unfortunate tragic incident possibly relative to this Pete Rose case occurred when the Commissioner, Giamatti, who was approaching the completion of his first year on the job suffered a massive heart attack and died just eight days after the banishment of Pete Rose from baseball.

In any event the Cincinnati Reds now needed a new manager. Who would they get to lead them in '90? Sparky Anderson, their former Big Red Machine skipper who managed to get them two rings? – Nah! His Detroit Tigers lost 103 games this year and even drove him to take some time off during the season.

As the fall of '89 arrived, Mike was a sophomore at Rutgers U. and Chris was starting his senior year at South Brunswick High.

1990
Why is Sweet Lou Smiling So Much?

As the '90's began, the Yankees had to be glad to leave the '80's. During the decade the Yanks didn't win a World Series. It was the first time in six decades that they did not win at least one. Despite having baseball's best regular season record during the '80's, they only made the postseason twice (losing to KC in the '80 playoffs and to the Dodgers in the '81 World Series). The Glory Years Part 2 was rolling along quite well.

The Yanks started off their worst season since 1912 like that's what it would be. In May, Bucky Dent (18-31) was fired (the '90's teeny-boppers didn't know who Bucky Dent was and the ones from the late '70's were probably married and could care less). When I heard the Yanks hired Merrill to manage, I really thought the Boss lost it, hiring the opera star Robert Merrill who sings the National Anthem at the Stadium. My mistake - it was Stump Merrill, who had the Yanks improve (?) to .438 ball.

In January, Chris started getting some letters from college baseball coaches. Since Chris was ranked second in his class they were from the top academic schools - RPI, Wesleyan, Bucknell, Columbia, and Johns Hopkins. We went for visits to Johns Hopkins in Baltimore and Columbia in NYC at the request of their coaches. He really liked NYC and liked the idea of going to an Ivy League school. During the winter months he put on some real muscle – the old fashioned way - dedicating himself to an intense work out regimen. During the pre-season Coach Cleffi told Chris he was captain and would play third. Even though Chris was the best pitcher on the Home News team last year, the coach didn't want to risk him injuring his back pitching.

From the lead-off spot, Chris pounded the ball batting .408 (fourth highest on the 12-man All-County team as was his 27 runs scored) with a .620 slugging %. Despite being a step slower due to his back surgery and added muscle he was still one of the fastest on the team and had 10 stolen bases, only being caught once and that was on a questionable call. The Columbia coach came to one of the games. He garnered a truckload of honors being selected by the NJ papers as the All-Division, All-Conference, All-County, and All-Area third baseman, which culminated with a selection to the NJ All-State team. In addition, he finished third in his class and was South Brunswick High's Scholar Athlete recipient. He received three academic scholarships, but declined them all to go Ivy League (Columbia).

Chris would be attending Columbia University with his friend, Colby Bressler, who lives a couple of blocks from us. Colby played for my summer Home News League baseball team the past two years (he was my team's "heavy hitter"), but at the high school varsity level he decided to use his 6'5" 250 lbs. body to hit quarterbacks instead of a baseball as he received All-County honors as a lineman for South Brunswick High.

During the summer, Chris played American Legion ball. The South BrunswicKs Legion team also has players from nearby towns that did not have a Legion team (North Brunswick, Monroe and Franklin). The coach was there ever since I could remember. The coach, knowing I had been coaching eight of the players through the years asked me to be the stat-man for the team (I always did it for my teams). So I was officially listed as the statistician in the league office. Due to our ace being out for the season, we got off to a poor start. Knowing the team as I did, I offered some possible line-up changes. At the time the team was 7-9 and looked out of the county playoffs. At this point an incident occurred causing the coaching staff to be suspended. I wasn't listed as a coach, so our Legion contacted me to see if I was available to coach the remaining games. Being a member of our Legion and being familiar with the team, of course my answer was "Sure". Sorry Josephine I can't get to the yard work.

While I was the team's statistician, an unusual incident occurred that possibly can be viewed as comical. In baseball vernacular, umpires are called "Blue" (not for their mood) because of their uniforms. Over the past ten years I had the good fortune to manage/coach the Blue brothers – not Jake and Elwood - but George and Steve, who played good music on the diamond. George was 14 months older and was an All-Division first baseman for South

Brunswick HS. Steve was a two-time All-Division and All-County catcher with a cannon-like arm ala Johnny Bench, and could also swing a good bat (.370). Although George didn't pitch for the high school team, he was one of my summer tournament aces over the years. The Blue battery was my version of the Cooper brothers battery (Mort & Walker) of the 1942-44 championship Cardinal teams.

Anyway, throughout this particular game, our players and coaches felt we were getting squeezed by the umps resulting in much bickering between our team and Blue. In the last inning the umpire made a bad call against our team. Steve Blue was heading to the batter's box and taking some practice swings. As encouragement, I started to holler "Let's go Blue, let's go Blue". The umpire moved in front of Steve, threw daggers at me, and asked me what I said. Being respectful I repeated "Let's go Blue". The umpire threw up his arms and shouted to me "YOU'RE OUTTA HERE!" With the scorebook in hand and a stunned look on my face I answered "What for? I'm cheering on my player". I told Steve to tell him his name. He said with a suppressed smile "Steve Blue". I then pointed out his brother and said "There's his brother George Blue". The ump responded "I don't care. Go. you're outta here." As I turned to leave, I saw George and Steve's parents, Bob and Ruth, sitting on lawn chairs next to the dugout. While waking away, I spun around and gave a parting shot to the ump "There's Mr. and Mrs. Blue, say hello to them." With that he threw up his arms and proclaimed "THIS GAME IS OVER". This didn't have much impact on the outcome since we were losing by plenty. Later I did apologize to Steve for making him lose a chance to hit. After pleading my case to the league officials the next day, asking "Why can't I encourage my players just because their name is Blue?" They seemed a little embarrassed by the ump's decision. I even think they felt blue about it.

Taking over the reins, I made the line-up changes I suggested and our offense took off. Being short on pitching I had one of my pitchers from two years ago, George Blue, start and he won a game, and even though my son Chris didn't pitch since last summer, I knew he'd be good, so I asked him and he said OK. He proceeded to go out and toss a one-hit shutout with 7 Ks. We kept winning. One of the moves I made was putting our top pitcher, Jim Stoops, in the clean- up spot – he didn't hit that well his senior year, but last year I remember him clobbering the ball in the Home News League. This moved was fruitful as he became a major run producer. (Jim Stoops would make "The Show" in 1998, pitching in three games for the Colorado Rockies beating the Giants in extra innings. That loss forced the Giants to play a one-game playoff against the Cubs for the NL Wildcard spot - which they lost). Our team fooled everyone winning eight in a row forcing an extra game for the final playoff spot. In the play-in game we routed our opponent for our ninth win in a row earning the last spot in the league playoffs.

The most notable game of this winning streak happened against East Brunswick. Some people believe in Marxism, some in Confucius sayings, - I advocate Yogi-isms, (hey, he was a Met, too). Many of them make sense (I always take the fork when I come to it). The one I always practiced is "It's not over, 'til it's over". I know that Yogi said "ain't over" but my sons said that ain't is not proper grammar so I had to modify it. I never let my team get the equipment, bats, and gear packed, or take off their cleats until the last out is made. It doesn't matter what the score is. We were winning easily. In the dugout with me was Matt DeKok. For over a ten year period he was another one of my aces. In high school he was an All-County, All-Division pitcher (second in Middlesex County with a 1.23 ERA).

As the last inning began we were up 10-2. Matt was taking off his cleats and putting on his sneakers. I saw this and said "Hey, Matty." He knew what I meant and said "Mr. Hut, it's 10-2". I reluctantly shrugged an OK and went back to the game. Before you knew it, a couple of hits, walks, and miscues and it was 10-8. While the eighth run was crossing the plate, Matt hurriedly was changing back into his cleats saying, "Mr. Hut, I guess you want me to go out and get the last two outs?" I answered, "That would be a good idea." Matt went out and quickly retired the last two batters and finally IT was over.

In the playoffs we wound up facing Piscataway, NJ who beat us twice earlier in the season. Stoops pitched and we won the first game of the series. At work the people were reading the paper before I got in, and knowing my team won again – they were thinking maybe this guy really knows what he is doing. During this nine game winning streak Boss Steinbrenner was banned from baseball – some at work said that was too bad because he would have maybe checked on my availability to take over the Yankee reins. Anyway, my Midas touch disappeared as Piscataway squeaked out the next two games to knock us out of making the NJ state playoffs – but the team and I had a nice run. This season would be my coaching swan song.

Chris hit a point over his high school average (.409) and led the team in most hitting categories. He looked ready for the Columbia freshman team. Interestingly at the Legion All-Star game, a Princeton assistant coach asked me why my son didn't apply there. With his class ranking and baseball ability he would have been accepted. I replied "We are just down the road; you should've come and seen him play – the Columbia coach did."

Back to the Majors – Sweet Lou Piniella, the former Yankee hero who batted .300 (42 for 140) in 10 postseason series for them and recently managed in the Bronx, took over in Cincy. He got away from one strange Boss and was now manager for another, Marge Schott. But she didn't interfere like Steinbrenner. Cincinnati was desperately in need of some baseball success. They were West division runner-up in four of the five past seasons and their beloved hero Pete Rose was banned from baseball and also was headed to prison for tax problems.

Fate shined brightly for Cincy as Sweet Lou was smiling the whole year. The Reds started the season hot. Sweet Lou took Satchel Paige's advice and never looked back – they went wire to wire to snag the NL West. Their offense was not intimidating. Their double play combo, Mariano Duncan and Barry Larkin, both hit over .300 while Paul O'Neill (16 homers, 78 RBIs), Chris Sabo (25 homers), and Eric Davis (24 homers) supplied pop. Yank cast-off Hal Morris hit .340 in just over 300 bats. The main starters were Tom Browning (15-9) and ex-Yank Jose Rijos (14-8). But the heart of the team were the Nasty Boys, Rob Dibble, Randy Myers and Norm Charlton, who threw fear into NL batters to the tune of 24 wins and 44 saves. Piniella known for his explosive tantrums was actually quite sweet this season. Another major factor for Sweet Lou's smile was the chaotic conditions back in Yankeeland. The manager was fired and replaced by a singer - oops, scratch that, it wasn't the singer - and the team was going nowhere.

In one of baseball's more embarrassing episodes, Steinbrenner agreed to pay a worker of the Dave Winfield Foundation (a charitable organization) for damaging information concerning its operation. When the worker wanted more money Steinbrenner called in the Feds. The Boss, in his desire to defame Winfield ever since his contract fiasco in 1981, had his plan backfire on him. Baseball Commissioner Fay Vincent, "in the best interest of baseball" was going to suspend the Boss. At this time Steinbrenner was involved with the U.S. Olympic Committee and the stigma of the word suspension might not sit well with the Committee. Steinbrenner and Vincent decided to call the action against the Boss an agreement that he would be banned from baseball.

On the field, Sweet Lou had to be smiling about not being in Yankeeland. Their only offense came from Jesse Barfield (24 homers), Roberto Kelly (.285, 42 SBs) and rookie Kevin Maas, who gave the Yanks hope for the future smashing 21 homers in only half the season. Mattingly's bad back ended any Musial comparisons (.256, 42 RBIs in about 100 games). And the Yanks parted with Winfield after ten years, trading him appropriately in May, to the Angels. The Yankees only positive (besides the banning of the Boss) was Rags Righetti who saved 36 of the Yanks 67 victories. The Yankees at 67-95 were the AL East's cellar dwellers - 21 games in back of the penthouse Red Sox.

In the fall Josephine and I were now alone for the first time since 1970. Mike was a junior at Rutgers and Chris was a freshman at Columbia. When Chris got there he was in for a surprise – no freshman team. The Ivy League schools, in a budget cutting move, eliminated freshman baseball. There was only a varsity team and with their starters coming back he only saw limited action.

In the AL East, Boston won the East again behind Rocket Clemens (21-6) and Mike Boddicker (17-8). Their offense was only fair – Wade Boggs (.302), Jody Reed (.289), Mike Greenwell (.297), and Ellis Burks (.296, 21 homers, 89 RBIs). The Bosox went 88-74.

One of the season's highlights was in September when the Ken Griffeys (father and son) hit back to back homers – it was the first time in baseball history that a father and son were teammates (Tim Raines and his son Junior were the second dad and son teammates - for the Orioles in 2001). The Griffeys were both born in Donora, PA a small town in the vicinity of Pittsburgh. The reason I'm bringing this up is that my boyhood hero Stan Musial was also born there - and he and Junior share the same birthday, November 21, and both would go on to make The All-Century Team (a pretty good feat for such a small town). In fact Musial played high school basketball with Junior's grandfather (I once saw a picture of the team in, I think, Baseball Digest - Musial had a basketball scholarship to the University of Pittsburgh but he declined it to play baseball). Before Musial became Stan the Man his nickname was The Donora Greyhound.

The Oakland A's under Tony LaRussa, were still a juggernaut going 103-59 (15 games better then the East champs - the Red Sox). They coasted to the AL West title finishing 9 games ahead of the surprising White Sox (94-68) who improved from their last place 69-92 record of last year behind reliever Bobby Thigpen's Major League record 57 saves. Again the Bash Brothers, McGwire (39 homers, 108 RBIs) and Canseco (37 homers, 101 RBIs) were their power source. They finished runner-up and third for the AL home run crown that was won by the Tigers' Cecil Fielder, who had 51, becoming the first AL slugger to bang out more than 50 since the M&M boys of '61. They were joined by the Henderson guys, Dave (20 homers) and AL MVP Rickey (.325, 28 homers, 65 SBs, 119 runs). Yet, once again it was their pitching staff that made them so imposing. Bob Welch won the Cy Young Award with the most wins (27-6) since Lefty Carlton in 1972. Dave Stewart (22-11) and Scott Sanderson (17-11) were the other aces. But they were outshined by Dennis Eckersley (4 wins 48 saves and an unbelievable lowest ever ERA of 0.61). This staff only gave Boston a run a game making it a 4-game sweep in the AL playoffs as Stewart won twice and Eckersley saved two. Does the Bambino have an apartment in Oakland?

Cincy's opponent was the Pirates. The Pirates beat out the Mets by 4 games. I don't know how the Mets lost. They had offensive pop – Darryl Strawberry (37 homers, 108 RBIs), Kevin McReynolds (24 homers, 82 RBIs), Howard Johnson (23 homers, 90 RBIs), Dave Magadan (.328, third in NL), and Gregg Jeffries (.283, 96 runs). Frank Viola (20-12), Doc Gooden (19-10), and David Cone (14-10) with John Franco's 33 saves gave their pitching corp a good nucleus. However, former quality hurlers El Sid Fernandez, Ron Darling and Bob Ojeda were only a combined 23-29.

Pittsburgh overcame the Mets with their hard hitting outfielders - NL MVP (the first of many) Barry Bonds (32 homers, 120 RBIs), Bobby Bonilla (.301, 33 homers, 114 RBIs), and Andy Van Slyke (17 homers, 77 RBIs). Their mound ace was Cy Young winner Doug Drabek (22-6). In the NL playoffs, Sweet Lou must have had a nasty smile on his face as his "boys" Dibble, Myers and Charlton held the Bucs to only one run in 15 2/3 innings, with 20 Ks. Cincy beat the Bucs in 6 games with Paul O'Neill being their big stick (7 for 18, .471).

The A's were overwhelming favorites to win the Series. It was their third straight trip and they needed to win it to validate their claim as an all-time mini-dynasty. (But like the Orioles of '69–'71, they only won the middle one, being Oreo'd by two upset specials). Cincy looked like the juggernaut as they swept the A's behind the pitching of MVP Rijos (2-0, 0.59 ERA) and the nasty relieving of the "boys" who didn't give up an earned run in 8 2/3 innings. Billy Hatcher (9 for 12, .750, 4 doubles, a triple 6 runs), Chris Sabo (9 for 16, .563, 2 homers, 5 RBIs) and Barry Larkin (.353) blasted the vaunted A's staff.

Sweet Lou most likely was musing how great it must be to not be a Yankee.

1991

The Yanks are STUMPED: How Do You Go From Last to First? Ask the Braves and Twins.

As the '91 season was starting, last year's division winners were expected to do well but not too much was hoped for the four cellar dwellers – Yanks and Twins in the AL and the Braves and Cards in the NL. It was pretty much unthinkable of what actually transpired during the season.

The Twins improved their record by 21 games (74-88 to 95-57). They won the AL West by eight games over the Chisox. The A's probably never got over getting swept in the Series and came in fourth. In the NL West the Atlanta Braves went from last to first improving by 29 games (65 - 97 to 94 - 88). The Braves edged LA by one game – Cincy came nowhere near repeating as they were 14 games under .500. St. Louis made a big jump of 14 games to finish runner-up to the Pirates in the NL East. Now that leaves the Yanks. Well, they also improved - by 4 games to 71-91 finishing fifth instead of last – but again were 21 games out of first. The Yanks were stumped. How did these other teams improve so dramatically?

Minnesota had three new players that were instrumental in their rise to the top. Rookie of the Year second baseman Chuck Knoblauch hit .281 and solidified the infield (at this time he could still throw to first base). Chili Davis (29 homers, 93 RBIs) came over from the Angels, and free agent Jack Morris (18-12) decided to return to his home town. These three joined Kirby Puckett (.319, 15 homers, 89 RBIs), Kent Hrbek (20 homers, 89 RBIs), Shane Mack (.310, 18 homers, 74 RBIs), and Brian Harper (.311) to put the Twins on top. Also, Scott Erickson (20-8) and Kevin Tapani (16-9) improved on their performance from '90. Relief ace Rick Aguilera (4 wins, 42 saves) was a key factor in almost half the Twins victories.

The Braves' war path to the East title was marked by the maturity of three young pitchers and two additions to the line-up. Cy Young winner Tom Glavine (20-11), Steve Avery (18-8), John Smoltz (14 wins), and veteran Charlie Liebrandt (15 wins) formed a strong group of starters. At this time it wasn't that evident yet, but the success of the staff was due to Leo Mazzone who became the Braves' pitching coach in the middle of last year at the same time Bobby Cox was hired as the skipper and since they have been a tandem, every year the Braves won their Division title, basically because of their pitching staff. Mazzone, with his patented perpetual rocking motion on the dugout bench observing his "students" during the game is regarded as the Michelangelo of pitching coaches – and if anyone ever makes the Hall of Fame for coaching it would be him. On the offensive side Terry Pendleton (.319, 22 homers, 86 RBIs) signed as a free agent after a horrible .230 year in St. Louis. He led the league in hitting and in hits (187) and was the NL MVP. The other addition, Otis Nixon hit .297 with 71 steals and 81 runs scored. They combined with holdovers David Justice (21 homers, 87 RBIs) and Ron Gant (32 homers, 105 RBIs) to provide most of the Braves offense.

St. Louis made their improvement with mirrors. They only hit 68 homers and only Todd Zeile (11) reached double digits. There were no aces in this group of Cards that comprised the mound corps, but five pitchers had between 10 and 12 wins. Their success was attributed to Lee Smith (6 wins, 47 saves). They were 14 games behind the first place Pirates.

Like I said the Yanks were stumped. Their new addition for the year panned out well – Scott Sanderson (16-10) pitched well and the Yanks were hoping he'd bring some winning magic over from Oakland. Didn't happen! He was their only quality starter. The offense didn't fare much better. Steve Sax (.304, 198 hits), Mel Hall (.285, 19 homers, 80 RBIs), and Matt Nokes (24 homers, 77 RBIs) were the main hitters. Mattingly's back problems were evident. His .288 average was solid but he had no power stats (9 homers, 68 RBIs). Kevin Maas smacked 23 homers (but that was disappointing as it was only two more than he hit in half a season last year). Roberto Kelly missed a quarter of the season but still had 20 homers and 32 steals. Jesse Barfield had 17 homers but only played half the year. The only good thing about the Yanks' dismal season was that the Boss wasn't around to spread around his usual good cheer.

The big highlight of the season was the first day of May when Texas Ranger pitcher Nolan Ryan at 44 years old (2 years younger than me) fired a record seventh no-hitter (Sandy Koufax is second with four no-hitters). Nolan is Baseball's all-time top power pitcher. Blessed with an arm that should be at Cape Canaveral launching missiles, he is the holder of all the strikeout records. It is conceivable that this All-Century team pitcher could have won 400 games (he had 324) had he not been on so many mediocre teams throughout his career. Throwing his famed Ryan Express fastball, his record 5714 strikeouts ranks with Pete Rose's hit record and Cal Ripken's consecutive games played streak as being unreachable. Speaking of Ripken he had an outstanding year despite the Orioles' sixth place finish – he was the AL MVP (.323, 34 homers, 114 RBIs and league leading 85 extra base hits) and the All-Star Game MVP as his 3-run homer led the AL to a 4-2 victory.

On the local front Mike finished his junior year and in the fall started his last year at Rutgers. In the spring Columbia had most of its hitters back and Chris surmised he wouldn't see much time, and still battling the lingering effects of his back surgery decided to focus on academics - so much for Chris becoming the righty Lou Gehrig (or for that matter, Columbia's next major leaguer like current Twins' utility player Gene Larkin). Besides the reality of the situation, was he wasn't going to Columbia to be a Major League baseball player.

For me, it was the first time since 1979 that I would not be coaching. Now I could get to that yard work. But wait. As an SBAA board member my main job was serving as one of the league presidents. I decided I would be an on-site president – going to some of the games and also umpiring a few.

About three or four years earlier, I started umpiring games in my league when I wasn't coaching my sons. Basically I started doing it due to a shortage of umpires or filling in for last minute cancellations.

What qualified me as an umpire?

1. For over ten years I helped run our town umpiring clinic.
2. Three of my favorite singers are Ray Charles, Roy Orbison, and Stevie Wonder.
3. I was born with an innate ability to ignore.

4. I've been married over 20 years.
5. At work, I have to handle customer complaints about the Post Office.

I usually didn't involve myself in reacting to any taunts when I was umpiring – I'd take advantage of my ability to ignore. But one time someone yelled out "Somebody get that guy some glasses", I hollered back "Please have those glasses filled with Bud Lite". Everybody busted out laughing. Anyway, I did get some yard work done (though Josephine said raking the mound before games didn't count).

In the NL playoffs, the Pirates, who had the Majors' best record, were heavily favored and had no reservations to put these Braves back where they belong. Again, the Bucs' offense was powered by outfielders Barry Bonds (.292, 25 homers, 116 RBIs), Andy Van Slyke (17 homers, 83 RBIs), and Bobby Bonilla (.302, 18 homers, 100 RBIs). John Smiley (20-8), Zane Smith (16-10), and Doug Drabek (15 wins) were the Bucs' top starters. The Braves tomahawk chopped the Pirates to win the NL in seven games (the last two on shutouts). Steve Avery was 2-0 (both were 1-0 wins) and Smoltz also was 2-0 winning the finale with a six-hit whitewashing 4-0.

In the AL the Blue Jays were expected to put these upstart Twins in their nest. Leading the Jays' attack were Joe Carter (33 homers, 108 RBIs), Roberto Alomar (.295, 88 runs), Kelly Gruber (20 homers), and Devon White (17 homers, 110 runs). Jimmy Key (16 wins), Todd Stottlemyre (Mel's son) and David Wells (both 15 wins) led the pitching staff. The upstarts took the Jays in five for the AL pennant. Jack Morris was 2-0 and Rick Aguilera saved three. Kirby Puckett carried the Twins' big stick (.429, 9 for 23, 2 homers, 6 RBIs).

Amazingly two last place teams from 1990 are playing in the 1991 World Series. After three boring Series in a row, where none went past five games, this proved to be one of the best classics that the Yankees weren't a participant. The Twins again were fortunate this year with the AL having four games at home if it went seven. They just didn't lose at the Metrodome with its thunderous noise.

The Twins took the first two at their 'Dome home and the Braves took the next three at home. Game 6 was a classic and it's the game that showcased Puckett's talents to the whole country. He had an RBI triple and a sac-fly for two of his team's three runs, and had one of the great catches in Series history which thwarted an early Brave rally. The game was tied 3-3 going into extra innings because of him. It was only fitting he won the game with an eleventh inning home run.

Game 7 was a scoreless duel between Smoltz and Morris. Smoltz went deep into the game, but Morris - the hometown guy - stayed in for all 11 innings. He was the game 7 winner as former Columbia U. star Gene Larkin broke up the scoreless tie with a pinch-hit in the eleventh inning to win the Series for the Twins and give manager Tom Kelly his second World Series title (won it in '87). Morris was an easy selection as Series MVP (2-0, 1.17 ERA).

The Yanks were stumped as what to do for '92. They decided to fire Stump Merrill and hired Coach Buck Showalter. The Yanks were hoping the Buck stops here.

After the Series, my son Mike was playing quarterback in a fraternity intramural football game. Mike's style at this position is more Fran Tarkenton and Roger Staubach than Dan Marino. He was very elusive and as he was scrambling to his left, he threw a pass to his right. He felt something happen to his back. The next day he had difficulty getting out of bed. When he called me and explained what took place I had to apologize to him. Like his brother he inherited my back. He had a herniated disc. Since there's an 8-10 week recuperation period, and he was to graduate in May, he put the operation off until a week after graduation.

1992

Mr. May's October Hit Wins the World Series, For the Blue Jays.

As the season began, even without the Boss, the Yankee bucks were spent for the '91 AL slugging % (.593) leader Danny Tartabull (.316, 31 homers, 100 RBIs) of the KC Royals for $25 million for five years. You know I could never figure out why right-handed power hitters sign with the Yanks with their deep left field dimensions. Winfield probably lost about 10 or so homers a year during his Yankee tenure – the same for Jesse Barfield. The Yankee Stadium dimensions were never kind to the right-handed hitters. Before the new stadium configurations in 1976 it was even more difficult for the righties – left field was 402 ft. and the left-center power alley was 457 ft. Joe DiMaggio, the best ever Yankee righty hitter, would have most likely challenged the Babe's record of 60 if he played in any other park in the league. Tartabull did OK (.266, 25 homers, 85 RBIs in 123 games) but his slugging % dropped by over 100 points to .489.

Mattingly still had the bad back (I wonder if he's a distant cousin of the Hutmakers), but again hit .288 with an increase in power (14 homers, 40 doubles, 86 RBIs). Donnie Baseball led the Yanks in average, hits, doubles, runs and RBIs, and, despite the back problems, won his seventh Gold Glove. The other contributors to the attack were Mel Hall (.281, 15 homers, 80 RBIs), Charlie Hayes (18 homers), and Matt Nokes (22 homers). Their top pitcher was Melido Perez whose 13-16 slate belies his effectiveness. He had a 2.83 ERA, but the team's lumber seemed to have termites every time he started. The Yanks did lead the league in Kellys – (Roberto and second baseman Pat) and also in players suspended for drug situations - pitchers Steve Howe and Pascual Perez (Melido's brother). The Pinstripers improved by five games to 76-86 as they came in fourth 20 games behind the leader.

The Yanks got some good news, but some would disagree and consider it not good at all. Steinbrenner had law suits filed against the Baseball Commissioner, Fay Vincent, pertaining to his agreement of banishment. In July Vincent agreed to allow the Boss to take over the Yankees' reins in March of 1993 and, in return, all pending law suits would be dropped. Less then a month later Vincent, for whatever you want to call it, was kicked out as Baseball Commissioner. I figured letting the Boss back into the ring was probably one of factors as to why it was done.

In the NL West, the Braves showed their last to first jump was not a fluke as their war chant continued on to another division title under former Yankee player Bobby Cox. Pitching under the tutelage of coach Leo Mazzone again was their major asset. Tom Glavine (20-8) was Cy Young runner-up and Charlie Liebrandt and John Smoltz both posted 15 victories. On offense Terry Pendleton followed up his '91 MVP year finishing second this year (.311, 21 homers, 105 RBIs) while David Justice (21 homers) and Ron Gant (17 homers) supplied the pop.

In the NL East, the Pirates lost Bobby Bonilla to free agency so that left it up to Barry Bonds and Andy Van Slyke to carry the offense. Bonds (.311, 34 homers, 103 RBIs) was the NL MVP again while Van Slyke led the league in hits (199), doubles (45), was second in hitting (.324) and had 89 RBIs. Doug Drabek was their top starter at 15-11, while Randy Tomlin (14-9) and Bob Walk (10-6) were the only others to reach double figures in wins, but 15 other pitchers had at least one victory.

The NL playoffs were a true topsy-turvy event. The Braves were up 3 games to 1 when I don't know what happened - maybe they became woozy from smoking a peace pipe. The Pirates plundered the next 2 games to knot the series at 3, and had a 2-0 lead in the ninth inning of game 7. The Braves broke the peace pipe and loaded the bases. After scoring a run on a sac-fly, a walk reloaded the bases and with two outs their 25th roster player, Francisco Cabrera, came to the plate. He hit a single to Bonds in left. The runner on third scored easily, but Sid Bream, a Pirate in 1990 who had my speed, was trying to score lumbering around third heading home. He slid home to beat Bonds' throw and give Atlanta the NL flag.

In the spring Chris finished up his sophomore year at Columbia being a regular student. Mike graduated in May and then a week later had successful back surgery – now all three of the Hutmaker guys had the same back. In the fall Chris started his junior year at Columbia. Mike got a college administration job and was applying to graduate school. He was also looking for a graduate assistantship position, which would include room, tuition for a Masters Degree and a stipend. He received notification of acceptance at Clemson University in South Carolina. Josephine and I were happy that our son was going back to college for his Masters - but not our money. As for me I was still an SBAA league president umpiring here and there. I will get to that yard work.

In the AL West, Oakland dethroned the Twins taking their fourth division flag in five years. They won despite Rickey Henderson being out for a fourth of the season and trading slugger Jose Canseco in August. Mark McGwire (42 homers, 104 RBIs) carried the brunt of the offense. Mike Bordick hit .300 and Harold Baines hit 16 homers. Mike Moore (17-12), Ron Darling (15-10) and Jeff Parrett (9-1) led the starters while league MVP Dennis Eckersley was his usual self in relief (7-1, 51 saves, 1.91 ERA). The A's beat out the Twins by 6 games. The Twins really missed their World Series MVP Jack Morris, who signed with the Toronto Blue Jays.

In the AL East, the Blue Jays made two additions that really feathered their nest. They signed World Series MVP Jack Morris who turned out to be their ace at 21-6. He was joined on the mound by Juan Guzman (16-5) and Todd Stottlemyre and Jimmy key who combined for 25 wins. Dousing opponent's fire was relief ace Tom Henke (34 saves, 2.26 ERA). The other addition was former Yank, Mr. May, Dave Winfield. All he did was hit 26 homers and drove in 108 runs at the age of 40. (I don't know how many RBIs he got in May). His run production along with their mainstay slugger Joe Carter (34 homers, 119 RBIs), John Olerud (.284, 16 homers), and Roberto Alomar (.310, 109 runs) kept the Blue Jays flying above the rest of the flock.

In the AL playoffs, the A's were down 2 games to 1 and had a 6-1 lead going into the eighth inning. They were still leading 6-4 in the ninth with the Eck-man out there. But Roberto Alomar brought back memories of Kirk Gibson in '88 and hit a homer that tied it and the Blue Jays won it in the eleventh. The A's rebounded to take game 5, but it was just a tease as the Blue Jays took game 6 by a 9-2 score. The Yanks' former Mr. May did OK in October. Although only hitting .250 he banged out 2 homers and scored 7 times. The Blue Jays were Canada's first World Series representative. The average fan was probably pulling for the Braves to keep the championship in the States.

In the Series opener Morris pitched well except for a 3-run homer to Damon Berryhill. Glavine gave up only one run as Atlanta won 3-1. I missed watching this game as Josephine and I attended her cousin Louis Pascarella's wedding. Lou was a NJ All-State football player from Kenilworth who intimidated opponents on the gridiron with his high school teammate, former NFL star Tony Siragusa, who was a main factor in the Baltimore Ravens' 2000 Super Bowl win.

Game 2 started in turmoil. The Canadian flag was inadvertently hung upside down during the playing of the Canadian anthem O' Canada. The North of the Border team avenged this inadvertent mistake by winning the game on a two-run pinch-hit homer by Ed Sprague off Jeff Reardon, who was, at the time, the Majors' career leader in saves. The Blue Jays won 5-4 to even it at one.

In the first Series game on foreign soil Old Glory was not hung upside down – only the Braves. Early in the game Toronto center fielder, Devon White, made one of the most memorable catches in Series history and it became a double play when a Brave runner made a base running mistake. (Maybe he thought he was on a war path instead of a base path). The Braves still had a 2-1 lead in the eighth but Kelly Gruber tied it with a homer. The Blue Jays wound up with a sweet win when Candy Maldonado singled in the game-winner in the ninth for a 3-2 victory. Pitching was the key to the Blue Jays' third win in a row. Jimmy Key beat Tom Glavine in a 2-1 pitching duel.

Like last year Jack Morris was hoping to end the baseball season, but he gave up a Grand Slam to Lonnie Smith, and John Smoltz, who started against Morris last year, only gave up 2 runs. The Braves stayed alive, 7-2. In game 6 the Braves were down 2-1 with two outs in the ninth when an Otis Nixon single tied it. Toronto had two on in the eleventh with Mr. May coming up. Maybe Steinbrenner was right – Winfield is not clutch - so far he was a non-factor. Well this time a line shot into left field resulted in a two-run double. The Blue Jays went up 4-2. The two runs were necessary as the Braves scored one and had the tying run on third when Nixon tried a surprise drag bunt that didn't work ending the Series.

Mr. May's October double was the Series winning hit, probably to the dismay of his former Boss. I'm sure Winfield was probably forgiven by the Canadian Audubon Society for his seagull-killing incident in Toronto in 1983. After all, he won the Series for these Birds.

1993
The Yankees' KEY to Success is not Enough

Prior to 1993 (after the '92 Series), the Yankees made some moves that hopefully would be the key to a championship. With the Boss coming back in March the front office wanted to have everything in place for his return. They traded their All-Star game representative Roberto Kelly for Cincy's Paul O'Neill. The Reds' skipper Sweet Lou and O'Neill were not on the same page. Piniella never thought O'Neill would be able to handle southpaws. The Yanks always went for left-handed hitters throughout the years to take advantage of the friendly right field stands. The Yanks also traded for Jim Abbot, the well publicized one-handed pitcher who had a 2.77 ERA but a losing record. The Yanks also spent bucks for Showalter's team adding Wade Boggs, the Red Sox third baseman who hit below .300 for the first time and Toronto's Jimmy Key the World Series ace (2-0, 1.00 ERA).

The Yankees' key moves worked out well but it was not enough to put them over the top. Jimmy Key did his best (18-6 with a league leading .750 %), but the rest of the staff was mediocre. Abbott lost some mph off his fastball and only went 11-14, but he did throw a no-hitter in September as the Yanks tied Toronto for first place. It was hoped this feat would spur the Yanks to overtake the Blue Jays. Instead the opposite happened – the Blue Jays flew away from the other teams taking the flag by seven games over the runner-up frustrated Pinstripers (88-74).

The Yanks' lumber men put on a good show tying the Blue Jays with a .279 average. The new additions Boggs (back over .300 at .302) and O'Neill (.311, 20 homers, 75 RBIs, hey Lou he could hit lefties) did well. Mattingly, (again playing with the Hutmaker back), won another Gold Glove and hit well (.291, 17 homers, 86 RBIs). Tartabull, despite the far reaches of the left field power alley, led the team with 31 homers and 102 RBIs. Showalter's big move was replacing offensive minded Matt Nokes with defensive back-stopper Mike Stanley. All Stanley did was put up Yogi-type stats (.305, 26 homers, 84 RBIs). A young Bernie Williams hit .268 with 12 homers. The Yanks also got a lot of mileage out of their utility guys – Jim Leyritz (.309, 14 homers), Randy Velarde (.301), and Matt Nokes (10 homers, 35 RBIs).

Even though the Yanks hit the same as the Blue Jays, they scored 26 less runs. After the middle of July the Blue Jays never were out of the top spot (although tied on occasion). Their stick men were the main reason. They had the AL's three top hitters – John Olerud, (.363, 24 homers, 107 RBIs), DH Paul Molitor (.332, 22 homers, 111 RBIs), and Roberto Alomar (.326, 17 homers, 96 RBIs). As this wasn't enough they were supported by their perennial slugger Joe Carter (33 homers, 121 RBIs), Tony Fernandez (.306), and Devon White (.273, 15 homers, 116 runs).

You might think that Jack Morris the 21-game winner of 1992 would have another 20-win year with this offense, but no, he had a 7-12 record with an over 6.00 ERA. With Morris' bad year and Key gone to the Yanks, Pat Hentgen (19-9), Juan Guzman (14-3), Dave Stewart (12-8), Al Leiter (9-6), and Duane Ward (45 saves) all picked it up a notch to keep the Blue Jays ahead of the flock.

Chicago has not had a club in the Series since the Go-Go Sox of 1959, (the Cubs' last appearance was the Billy Goat hexed one of 1945). But this time there was hope in the Windy City as the White Sox took the AL West. There was balance on the mound and at the plate. Providing sock for the Sox were the catchy named Batman and Robin duo. Batman was AL MVP Frank Thomas (.317, 41 homers, 128 RBIs) and Robin was Ventura (22 homers, 105 RBIs). The other batmen were Lance Johnson (.311, 14 triples), Ellis Burks (14 homers, 74 RBIs), Tim Raines (.306), Ron Karkovice (20 homers), and Bo Jackson (16 touchdowns, oops, I mean home runs in half a season). The beneficiaries of these batmen were Cy Young winner Black Jack McDowell (22-10), Alex Fernandez (18-9), Wilson Alvarez (15-8), and reliever Roberto Hernandez (38 saves).

However, the White Sox hopes for Chicago to host a World Series blew away in the wind. Providing the wind was the swinging of the Blue Jays bats. As a team they hit .301. The real Batman wore Toronto on his uniform. He was DH Paul Molitor (.391, 9 for 23, 2 doubles, a triple, a homer, 5 RBIs and 5 runs). Devon White (.444, 12 for 27) and John Olerud (.348, 8 for 23) also smacked the ball around. Former A's playoff ace Dave Stewart was the ALCS MVP going 2-0 to raise his record to 8-0 in the playoffs.

This year the National League expanded putting franchises in Denver (Colorado Rockies) and in Miami (Florida Marlins). Now each league consisted of 14 teams.

In the NL West the Braves signed Greg Maddux who gave them a starting group of hurlers reminiscent of the 1950's Indians. Maddux (20-10) was joined by Tom Glavine (22-6), Steve Avery (18-6), and John Smoltz (15-10) giving the Braves 104 wins. They needed every one of them as they overcame a ten game lead by the San Fran Giants to win the flag by only one game. San Fran had a giant season from new addition Barry Bonds (.336, 46 homers, 123 RBIs), but winning 103 games wasn't enough. Igniting the Braves' second half run was the mid-season addition of the Crime Dog Fred McGriff (.310, 19 homers, 55 RBIs in half a year). In his first game as a Brave, there was a huge fire at Fulton County Stadium, a sign of his hot hitting to come. Also, helping the teepee uprising was second baseman Jeff Blauser (.305, 15 homers, 110 runs), Ron Gant (36 homers, 117 RBIs), Terry Pendleton (17 homers, 84 RBIs), and David Justice (40 homers, 120 RBIs).

The NL East went to a strange cast of mullet wearing characters from Philadelphia. Like the Braves and Twins in '91 they rose from last to first. Their offense was the principle reason for the elevator ride to the top. They led the league in hitting (.274) and runs (877). Scraggly looking West Virginian John Kruk (.316, 14 homers, 85 RBIs), catcher Darren Daulton (24 homers, 105 RBIs), Dave Hollins (18 homers, 93 RBIs), Pete Incaviglia (24 homers, 89 RBIs), and tough as nails lead-off man, NL MVP runner-up Lenny Dykstra (.305, 19 homers, 143 runs) provided a lot of thunder. Kevin Stocker (.324) came up at mid-season to stabilize the defense at short and Jim Eisenreich (.316), who battled Turette's Syndrome, were other positive factors for their success. Their starters Tommy Greene (16-4) and Curt Schilling (16-7) would be middle relievers on the Braves' staff – well, maybe not Schilling. Their other starters Ben Rivera, Terry Mulholland and Danny Jackson combined for 37 victories. They had the "Wild Thing" Mitch Williams (43 saves) for entertainment. Phillie fans went into cardiac arrest whenever he came in.

Most fans had reservations about this last to first place team to beat the 104 game winning Braves. But it was the Braves that had to go back to the reservation losing the playoffs in 6 games (three of the losses by 1 run and two of them in extra innings). Jackson, the KC Royals' hero in the '85 postseason, won game 4 as his single drove in the deciding run in the 2-1 win, and Dykstra's tenth inning dinger won the fifth game 4-3 after the Braves tied it in the ninth. Greene took care of Atlanta going seven innings in the game 6 clincher. The Wild Thing Williams put the Braves into cardiac arrest with his relief display – 2 wins and 2 saves.

In the World Series, the Blue Jays were up 2 games to 1 but were trailing 14-9 in the eighth inning of game 4. I fell asleep on the sofa at this point. I woke up at 3:00 a.m. and put on ESPN to see the final score. I was totally shocked to see that Toronto came up with 6 runs to win 15-14. I was also totally mad I dozed off missing this ridiculous, but historic game.

Schilling came back with a 2-0, five-hit victory to keep the Phils alive. In game 6 we were at a party in South Jersey (Phillies' terrain). The Phils were down 5-1 going into the seventh but all of the guys at the party suddenly were riveted to the TV when the Phils' scored five times to go up 6-5. The big hit was a 3-run blast by Dykstra, who had a great Series (.348, 4 homers, 8 RBIs, 9 runs scored). In the ninth the Wild Thing went in to protect the lead – and if he did so the Blue Jays would have to face Schilling again in game seven for all the marbles. A walk to Rickey Henderson and a Molitor hit had two on with the Blue Jays slugger Joe Carter up. With a 2-2 count he caught a Wild Thing pitch and blasted it for a World Series winning walk-off homer – the second in history (Maz's in '60 was the only other one). The catalyst for Toronto winning the championship was Series MVP, Paul Molitor. He continued his torrid postseason performance at the plate (.500, 12 for 24, a pair of doubles, triples, and homers, 10 runs and 8 RBIs and 1.000 slugging %). Alomar (.480, 12 for 25, 6 RBIs), Fernandez (.333, 7 for 21, 9 RBIs) and Carter (2 homers, 8 RBIs) complemented Molitor in the Toronto line-up that batted .311 for the Series. The Blue Jay manager Cito Gaston became the first skipper to win successive World Series titles since the Big Red Machine's Sparky Anderson did it in 1975 & '76.

After '93 all the baseball fans were looking forward to another exciting season.

On the local scene, Mike was still at Clemson working on his Masters. He also told me that Jim Stops, my player in Legion ball, was pitching well for Clemson's rival, the University of South Carolina. Chris finished his junior year and in the fall started his senior year at Columbia. As for me – I was umpiring in lieu of yard work.

1994
FEHR Strikes Out the Yankees

Back in the '50's there was a biography book and movie about Jimmy Piersall, the eccentric outfielder, who spent most of his career (seven years) with the Red Sox. Actor Tony Perkins portrayed him in the movie. The title was "Fear Strikes Out." Well the year 1994 can be titled "Fehr Strikes Out" – for the Yankees, and all of baseball. Donald Fehr was one of the head honchos of the players' union.

With contract negotiations on the horizon, the owners wanted implementation of revenue sharing and some sort of salary cap. This would create a semblance of parity and competitive balance. The baseball franchises then would be on a level playing field much like the other sports. Needless to say this would be adverse to the Yankees who had more money than anyone to spend. As I have stated before I really don't put much attention into non-field issues. I guess Mr. Fehr figured these proposals were to control player salaries, which is why he rejected them. Negotiations went nowhere and the players and Fehr would strike out the season on August 12.

It was a real shame that the season could not continue as 1994 was the first year with three divisions (East, Central and West) in each league. Also added was another playoff series with a Wild Card team added, so the playoffs would now have eight teams. When the strike happened, over half of the teams still were in the hunt for a playoff spot. In the AL Fehr's decision struck the Yankees the hardest. They had the best record in the league (70-43) and led their division by 6 1/2 games. It looked like my Glory Years Part 2 was going to come to an end, but Fehr kept it alive. Sorry Mr. Steinbrenner.

The Yanks had a big stick offense tying the Indians in batting (.290). These stats are based on the 113 games played before the strike. Paul O'Neill (.359 led the AL, 21 homers, 83 RBIs) was one of five regulars that hit the .300 mark. The others were Wade Boggs (.342, 11 homers), Mike Stanley (.300, 17 homers, 57 RBIs), free agent Luis Polonia (.311), and Donnie Baseball (.304, 51 RBIs). Tartabull (19 homers, 67 RBIs), Jim Leyritz (17 homers, 58 RBIs), and emerging star Bernie Williams (.289, 57 RBIs) completed the potent offense. Jimmy Key led the AL in wins (17) and winning % (.810), while Steve Howe (3-0, 15 saves) was the ace in the 'pen.

There was other news concerning the Yanks - it was on the TV sitcom Seinfeld, which is my all-time favorite program. The show had past baseball themes (i.e. Keith Hernandez with Elaine, Joe DiMaggio dunking his doughnuts), but this one took the cake. George Costanza, played by Jason Alexander, was hired by owner George Steinbrenner as the assistant to the traveling secretary. Costanza was given the position despite verbally tearing into Boss Steinbrenner for the terrible job he's done since 1978 (no World Series Championships) and mocking Steinbrenner's ego. Ironically, for the Yankee Hater (me), it was a "Sein"feld of things to come.

This year could have seen many offensive records fall. Many sluggers were having great years (and like noted these were done in 115 or so games). Chisox's Big Hurt, Frank Thomas (.353, 38 homers, 101 RBIs and AL MVP) and Cleveland's Albert Belle (.357, 36 homers, 101 RBIs) were battling for the Triple Crown. Ken Griffey, Jr. (Seattle) was chasing Maris with 40 homers and Kirby Puckett (Twins) led the AL with 112 RBIs. Toronto's Joe Carter also hit the century mark with 103 RBIs.

Montreal in the NL East had the best record in baseball (74-40) 3 1/2 games better than the Yanks. Their clout was supplied by Moises Alou (.339, 22 homers, 78 RBIs) and Larry Walker (.322, 19 homers, 86 RBIs). Ken Hill (16-5) led the NL in wins and Pedro Martinez (11-5) showed signs of great promise.

Jeff Bagwell (Astros) was NL MVP and got injured just before the strike and possibly would have missed the rest of the season. In 110 games his stats read - .363, 39 homers, 116 RBIs, .750 slugging %. The Giants' Matt Williams (43 homers, 96 RBIs) and Barry Bonds (37 homers, 81 RBIs) joined in the Maris chase. Other gaudy numbers in the NL were put up by the Braves' Crime Dog, Fred McGriff (.318, 34 homers, 94 RBIs), Reds' Kevin Mitchell (.326, 30 homers, 77 RBIs), Rockies' Andres Galarraga (.319, 31 homers, 85 RBIs) and Dante Bichette (.304, 27 homers, 95 RBIs), Cubs' Sammy Sosa (.300, 25 homers), and Dodgers' Mike Piazza (.319, 24 homers, 92 RBIs). Another reason it was a shame the season ended like it did was that the Majors' best hitter (average-wise), the Padres' Tony Gwynn was batting .394 and appeared to have a shot at being the first to bat .400 since Ted Williams in 1941.

It would have been interesting to see how the stats would have turned out if there had been a full season. One other note – the Orioles' Cal Ripken (.315, 75 RBIs) kept on playing (about 2000 games in a row) and I was hoping there was going to be a '95 season to see if he would break Lou Gehrig's 2130 consecutive game streak.

In closing, baseball, in my opinion, should have had some kind of World Series (i.e. like between the hated Yanks and Montreal, the best from each league). The profits could have gone to charity. This would have kept interest in the game. I thought the owners and the Fehr group must have a brain (together) the size of a pea not to have a World Series, with all the inroads the NBA and NFL are making with the country's fans, especially its youth. It was Fehr-ed that this strike could be the demise of the National Pastime.

Mike finished his Masters degree from Clemson. He would get a position in administration at St. John's University in Staten Island. Chris graduated cum laude from Columbia majoring in Economics and accepted an investment banking position on Wall Street.

1995
Sleepless in Seattle

The season that fans Fehr-ed would never start did - even if it was pushed back three weeks (it would be a 144 game schedule).

The Yankee family had two major losses in 1995. In the summer their Mighty Mick (Mantle) passed away. In September Cal Ripken played in his 2130 and 2131 consecutive game breaking Lou Gehrig's record. Ripken, who would later be selected as one of the shortstops (along with Honus Wagner) on the All-Century Team, hit a homer in each game. Cal ran his streak to 2632 consecutive games.

This was the first full year of three divisions and an extra round of playoffs. (There would be the Division winners and a Wild Card team in the playoffs).

The Yanks didn't do as well as last year and could not overtake Boston for the East title – they finished with a 79-65 record, 7 games out. However, this was the year of the Wild Card and the Yanks had a shot at it. As September began it seemed like a dismal year. But like in 1964, they won 22 of their last 28 to take the Wild Card spot by one game over the Angels. This would be another page in Yankee lore, as they became the first American League Wild Card team. The Angels still had a shot for the postseason but lost a one-game playoff for the West title to Seattle behind Randy Johnson (the Cy Young winner, 18-2 record).

The Yankee offense dropped 14 points from last year. Even though Paul O'Neill hit .300 (22 homers, 96 RBIs), it was 59 points below his league leading figure of '94. Bernie Williams continued to improve (.307, 18 homers, 82 RBIs), while Mike Stanley (18 homers, 83 RBIs), Wade Boggs (.324), and Donnie Baseball (.288), in his farewell season, provided the rest of the offense. Their former slugger Danny Tartabull had a power outage and was traded to Oakland.

The Yanks took a gamble and got the Chisox's Black Jack McDowell, who was a 20-game winner in '92 and '93, but 10-9 in '94. He was their ace at 15-10. During the summer they signed the '94 Cy Young winner David Cone and he came up big posting a 9-2 slate. Another integral addition was NL relief ace John Wetteland from Montreal – he saved 31 games. Called up from the minors were Andy Pettitte who went 12-9 and rookie Mariano Rivera, a middle reliever, who was 5-3.

It looks like my Glory Years Part 2 was coming to a close as the Yanks were getting ready to play the West champs - the Seattle Mariners. During the year Seattle defeated the Yanks six out of seven in their Kingdome Stadium and if the series goes five games three will be in Seattle.

With the Big Unit, Randy Johnson, being the only ace, it was a lot of lumber that carried the Mariners to the West flag. Even with young superstar Ken Griffey, Jr. (17 homers, 42 RBIs) out for half the year a powerful bat attack was led by former Yankee farmhands Mike Blowers (23 homers, 96 RBIs) and Jay Buhner (40 homers, 121 RBIs) and the non-brothers Martinez, Tino (.293, 31 homers, 111 RBIs) and Edgar, who led the AL in batting (.356), doubles (52), and runs (121), and had 29 homers driving in 113 runs.

The series started at Yankee Stadium and the Yanks initially lucked out because the Big Unit had to pitch the West playoff game against the Angels and wouldn't be ready until game 3 in Seattle. The Yanks felt the pressure of having to win the first two because of their record in Seattle. Without the Big Unit going, the Mariners pitching was suspect and the Yanks took the opener 9-6 behind 2-run homers by Boggs and Ruben Sierra. Cone went 8 innings and Wetteland 1 as the Yanks withstood two homers by Junior Griffey.

Game 2 was one for the books, much like the sixteen inning playoff game between the Mets and Astros in 1986. The game went fifteen innings, took 5 hours 13 minutes and ended at 1:22 a.m. I learned my lesson from the '93 Phillie/Blue Jay World Series game. I stayed up all the way to the horrible ending. The Mariners surprisingly had a 2-1 lead going into the sixth when Sierra hit a homer for the second day in a row and the Yankees mainstay Mattingly (in his first playoff) followed with another. But in the seventh Seattle tallied twice to go up 4-3, but that was short lived as O'Neill parked one in the bottom of the inning to deadlock it at 4.

In the twelfth, the Yankee stopper Wetteland was in his fourth inning of work and was probably tiring as Junior launched one to give the Mariners a 5-4 lead. But in the bottom of the inning with two outs Sierra kept up his hot hitting bouncing a double off the wall to deadlock it, again, at 5. Bernie Williams was thrown out at the plate on the play trying to end the game. The game goes on. Mariano Rivera, showing signs of his future, went in and shut down the Mariner attack for the remainder of the game – until Jim Leyritz cranked out a 2-run homer to end it in the fifteenth inning.

Sweet Lou Piniella, the Mariner skipper who escaped the Bronx Zoo a while ago and won a ring managing the '90 Reds, did not appear to seem to be concerned about being down 2-0 - he was going home. Back at the Kingdome, there would be a battle of recent Cy Young winners Randy Johnson and Black Jack McDowell. Johnson gave up two homers to Bernie Williams and one to Mike Stanley, but the Mariners prevailed 7-4. Tino Martinez hit a homer for the Mariners. Buck and the Yanks probably had a restless night back at the hotel. At least there would be no more Big Unit to face.

In game 4 it seemed the Yanks would take the series as they took a 5-0 lead after two innings. In the third, Edgar Martinez hit a 3-run homer as Seattle made it 5-4. Seattle got a run in the sixth and seventh but the Yanks tied it in the eighth. The see-sawing of the game was decided by another homer (a Grand Slam) by Edgar giving him 7 RBIs for the game. That made the score 10-6. The final was 11-8. The Mariners' attack also received homers from Buhner and Junior (his fourth). Back at their quarters, Yankees' insomnia was a possible happening.

In the finale, David Cone was pitching well into the eighth with a 4-2 lead courtesy of a bases loaded two-bagger by Donnie Baseball. A third run would have scored but the opposite field shot bounced into the stands for a ground-rule double forcing the runner to be stranded at third. (Maybe another page in the Mattingly curse?).

In the eighth, Cone was laboring. Junior put one out to cut the deficit to one. Cone was down but Showalter left him in even though he couldn't throw strikes. After walking in the tying run, Black Jack came in to get the last out. In the top of the ninth the prospects for a Yankee win looked good. A lead-off double and walk put two on with none out. Sweet Lou summoned the Big Unit who took care of the threat. It was again a battle of Cy Young winners, this time in relief. Johnson K'd the side in the tenth but in the eleventh the Yanks manufactured a run on Randy Velarde's RBI hit.

All Black Jack had to do was get out the side. Not so easy. Joey Cora bunted for a hit and Junior singled. Now it was Edgar's turn. He showed he owned the Yanks (the pitching staff anyway) more than Steinbrenner. He lasered a shot into the left field corner scoring Cora easily and also Junior who slid home with the winning run, Seattle won the division playoff. Why is Sweet Lou smiling again? At least now the Yanks could get some zzzzz's.

The Seattle lumber blasted Yankee pitching for a .315 average. The non-brothers Martinez, Edgar (.571, 12 for 21, 10 RBIs), Tino (.409, 9 for 22, 5 RBIs), Buhner (.458, 11 for 24), and Junior (.391, 9 for 23, 5 homers, 7 RBIs) were unstoppable. On the hill the Big Unit was 2-0 with 16 Ks in 10 innings.

For the Yanks, Bernie Williams (.429, 9 for 21, 2 homers, 8 runs), and Paul O'Neill (.333, 3 homers, 6 RBIs) also put up some good numbers in a losing cause. Mariano Rivera was outstanding out of the 'pen (zero ERA in 5 1/3 innings). For a moment I felt sad for Mattingly, his career ending like this − but that thought only lasted less than half a second. Donnie Baseball did leave on a positive note (.417, 10 for 24, 4 doubles, 6 RBIs).

Seattle would face Cleveland in the AL playoffs who swept the Red Sox in three games. Their offense was baseball's best (.291, 202 homers). In a curtailed season Albert Belle had over 100 extra base hits, blasting 50 homers and 52 doubles. He hit .317, had 126 RBIs and scored 121 times. Also, carrying Indian war clubs were Manny Ramirez (.308, 31 homers, 107 RBIs), Jim Thome (.314, 25 homers), Eddie Murray (.323, 21 homers), Kenny Lofton (.310), Carlos Baerga (.314, 90 RBIs), and Paul Sorrento (25 homers). Charles Nagy and Orel Hershiser, who were both 16-6, were the Chiefs of the Indians' staff. The Indians took Seattle in 6 games. Hershiser (2-0, 1.29 ERA) took the bats out the Mariners' hands as the Martinez tandem combined for a 5 for 45 series.

In the NL the Braves were the class of the league. They had an excellent balance of pitching and hitting. The Crime Dog McGriff (27 homers, 78 RBIs), Ryan Klesko (.310, 23 homers, 70 RBIs), Chipper Jones (23 homers, 86 RBIs), David Justice (24 homers, 78 RBIs), and Javy Lopez (.315, 15 homers) provided a deep line-up.

Greg Maddux (19-2 Cy Young winner), Tom Glavine (16-7), and John Smoltz (12-7) were the best threesome in the game. The Braves coasted through the playoffs, beating the Colorado Rockies 3 games to 1 and sweeping Cincy in 4 straight. The Braves teed off on the Rockies' pitchers batting .331 - Marquis Grissom (.524, 11 for 21, 3 homers), Klesko (.467, 7 for 15), Chipper (.389, 7 for 18, 2 homers) and the Crime Dog (.333, 2 homers). Colorado's Dante Bichette (.588, 10 for 17, 3 doubles, homer), Vinny Castilla (.467, 3 homers, 6 RBIs) and Eric Young (.438, 7 for 16) put up a valiant effort to match the Braves' war clubs. Against Cincy, Chipper and the Crime Dog stayed hot as each went 7 for 16 (.438).

That old baseball adage good pitching beats good hitting was never truer than the 1995 Series. The Braves held the Indians, who hit .291 for the year, to a .179 average, so it would only be justice for the Braves to win.

This was a repeat of the 1948 Series, when the Braves were in Boston. Cleveland won then in six games. This time the Braves returned the favor by winning in six games. Five of the contests were decided by one run. Tom Glavine, the Series MVP, (2-0, 1.29 ERA) and Mark Wohlers combined on a one-hitter to win the sixth game 1-0 on a sixth inning homer by David Justice. Grissom (.360, 8 for 25), Klesko (.313, 3 homers) and the Crime Dog (a pair of doubles and homers) led the Brave attack.

On the home front I was still umpiring youth games, but I did cut the grass. Mike was an Assistant to the Dean at St. John's and Chris was living in NYC working about 80-100 hours a week at his investment banking job on Wall Street.

1996
The 'ZEUS Wears Pinstripes' Theory

The season began with a lot of changes. Even though Buck Showalter got the Yankees into the postseason for the first time since '81 he was finished. Although not actually fired, he had a dispute with the Boss about one of his coaches and resigned. Also, General Manager Gene Michael gave up his Mylanta-required job to become a scout. Bob Watson, a former Yank who hit .500 in the '80 playoffs and .318 in the '81 World Series, took the GM position. As for manager, the surprise selection was Joe Torre. He was one of the guys I used to root for being an ex-Met and Cardinal and had near Hall of Fame stats from his playing days. His managerial stint was less successful as his record was under .500, but he did win a division title as the Braves' skipper in 1982. Basically his teams generally lacked the necessary talent to win.

The other two big changes were at first and catcher. Mike Stanley left for Boston, so the Yanks signed a defensive back-stopper, Joe Gerardi who also came alive with the bat (.294). During last year's loss to Seattle the Boss must have gotten tired of seeing Tino Martinez clobber his pitchers (.409), so to replace Mattingly the Boss' bucks brought in Tino. Replacing a Yankee legend wasn't easy but after a slow start Tino put up numbers that more than made up for the absence of Donny Baseball. The Yanks also brought up rookie shortstop Derek Jeter and he became Rookie of the Year. The Yank $$$$$ brought in whatever was needed during the year (i.e. Darryl Strawberry, Doc Gooden and Cecil Fielder).

This was not a good year for me. I usually watched the Mets, Braves or Phils on TV. But when I watched the Yanks, it seemed like there was divine intervention, and this carried into the postseason.

Some of these happenings included a kid interfering with an apparent fly ball out (which the whole country saw, except the umpire Rich Garcia) to give Yanks a game-tying homer in the ALCS. The

NY opponents in all three postseason series could not overcome this apparent outside intervention. There were ridiculous errors, fantastic plays by Yankee fielders that made it seem like a God was in the play (i.e. O'Neill's catch on a Polonia drive in this year's Series, no way his bad hammie runs that down). There is a saying in baseball that when things go your way, "the Baseball Gods are with you". I developed a more in depth theoretical explanation for this saying.

The "Zeus Wears Pinstripes" Theory

Zeus is the Greek God of Gods. Back in grade school, Greek mythology was one of my fun subjects; The Iliad written by a poet with the baseball name of Homer was what I remember most. Homer was blind and is thought by some to be the ancestors of many umpires (including me?). I could see where his bloodlines would extend to Rich Garcia.

The Iliad was a tale of a long war between the Greeks and the city of Troy. The war was over a salary cap and revenue sharing - oops, wrong war. It was over a woman, Helen. She was married to a Greek King but ran away and sailed to Troy with Paris, a Trojan Prince. The Greek King wasn't too happy about this, so he got a Greek army together to get her back.

In Greek mythology there are several gods and goddesses, but Zeus is the Top God. The gods/goddesses in Greek mythology interacted with the mortals on Earth. During this long war, some of the gods were interceding on the side of the Greeks and some on behalf of the Trojans. Zeus was taking all of this in, but eventually stepped in. Once the God of the Gods enters it's all over – I know this contradicts the Yogi-ism "It ain't over 'til it's over."

Zeus decided to have the Greeks win with their trick of a huge wooden horse full of their soldiers as a departing gift for the Trojans. Once pulled into Troy the hidden soldiers snuck out at night and opened the gates of Troy to let in their fellow soldiers who had doubled back. The walled city Troy was destroyed and now the word Trojans conjures up thoughts of Southern Cal (USC) athletes and birth control devices.

I felt that this year Zeus decided to take a look at baseball in his leisure time. He took a fancy to this team in pinstripes called the New York Yankees. All during the playoffs, I was ranting about this

Zeus theory. The baseball fans at work and my family were all aware of how my Zeus theory put the Yankees over the top.

It was probably a week after the Series when my son Mike came over for a visit – he only lived a few miles from us. He was in a used book store and came upon a book about Zeus. It was only a couple of bucks so as a laugh he bought it for me. I cracked a big smile when he told me the Yankees are in Chapter 10 (he was kidding). We decided to have some fun with the booKs cover of Zeus. We went through the newspapers and found photos of Yankees and got scissors and cut out the Yankee uniform and put it on Zeus. Then we found a bat and put it in Zeus hands over the thunderbolts he always carries with him. Zeus now had on his pinstripes.

I read a few of the fables and found them interesting. I found out that Zeus was very fond of women, goddesses and mortals alike, and was always on the prowl for the attractive ones. This behavior has to be constantly hidden from his wife, the goddess Hera. She was always chasing him down for his infidelities. Another distraction for him was the never ending squabbles among the other gods/goddesses that he has to mediate.

Hopefully, when baseball postseason comes, Zeus will be distracted by the aforementioned and be unable to focus on the Yanks' behalf.

Editor's Note: The Yankees made their first World Series appearance since 1981 and won their first since 1978. They were the AL Wild Card entrant and beat the Texas Rangers in the first round 3 games to 1 and in the ALCS took their AL East rivals the Baltimore Orioles in 5 games. This series was the one that showed that maybe my dad was right – Zeus wears Pinstripes – as a 12- year old from NJ reached over the wall in right field and interfered with an apparent out according to everyone but umpire Rich Garcia who ruled it a home run for Derek Jeter costing the Orioles the opening game. In the World Series the Bronx Bombers were down 2 games to 1 and losing game 4 by a 6-0 score when they rallied for 3 in the sixth, and tied it in the eight on a 3-run bomb by Jim Leyritz. The Yankees won it in the tenth inning. The Series was now deadlocked at two. The Pinstripers then went out and defeated Atlanta in two squeakers 1-0 and 3-2 as they won the last four games to become World Series Champs.

1997
Remember the ALOMAR

The defending World Series champs figured on a repeat in 1997. They did let the MVP of the World Series, John Wetteland, go, but they elevated Mariano Rivera to the closer role after being the seventh-eighth inning set-up man. The Yanks did add pitcher David Wells from Baltimore.

The one who was to keep the Yanks on top was Hideki Irabu, a supposed better pitcher than his Japanese countryman Hideo Nomo, who was so far a successful Major League pitcher. Naturally $$$$ was not a problem for Boss Steinbrenner. He had his front office do whatever it took to get him (the order was to get the rights from San Diego and give Irabu all the sushi he wants). Irabu's talents, if he had any, were left in Japan. He was a flop – after winning his first two games his stats were 5-4, 7.09 ERA. It seemed Hari-Kari may be in order for some Yankee brass or scouts. (Editor's Note: Although Irabu did not reach the expectations predicted for him, he did have a winning record of 29-20 in his three years with the Yankees).

The Yankees never could catch the high flying Orioles for the AL East flag. Baltimore had a big lead going into September, but the Yanks made a run at them but finished two games out. The O's finished at 98-64 and were led by Rafael Palmeiro (38 homers, 110 RBIs) and Cal Ripken (17 homers, 84 RBIs). On the mound Scott Erickson and Jimmy Key won 16 games, Mike Mussina won 15, and Randy Myers was nasty out of the 'pen with 45 saves.

The Yanks, at 96-66 had the AL second best record so they naturally were the Wild Card entry. The powerful Yankee offense was only behind the Red Sox in hitting .291 to .287 and second to the West winning Seattle Mariners in runs. Tino Martinez was making some say "Donnie Baseball who?" as he cranked out 44 homers to drive in 141 runs (second in the AL). There was a lot of

292

pop from outfielders Paul O'Neill (.324, 21 homers, 117 RBIs) and Bernie Williams (.328, 21 homers, 100 RBIs). Derek Jeter evaded the sophomore jinx (.291, 116 runs). Part-time players Wade Boggs (.292), Chad Curtis (.291), Luis Sojo (.307), Cecil Fielder (13 homers), and Tim Raines (.321) made for a potent line-up for opposing pitchers.

In the unreal world my favorite show Seinfeld had a riotous episode. George Costanza, in order to get a scouting job with the Mets first had to get fired from his position on the Yankees as assistant to the traveling secretary. To get Steinbrenner irked enough so he would get rid of him, he wiped his hands all over a Babe Ruth uniform and then tied one of the World Series Championship trophies to his car and dragged it around Yankee Stadium. No matter what he did Steinbrenner rationalized Costanza's actions and would find a reason not to fire him.

In 1997 the saying in Cleveland during the season was probably "Let there be Justice". The Indian offense was not something to overlook as they were only one point behind the Yanks and only scored 23 less runs. They even had more homers than the Yanks (220 to 161). David Justice, who beat the Indians in the '95 Series 1-0 in the sixth game with his homer, added average to his usual power stats finished third in the AL at .329. He belted 31 homers and had 101 RBIs. Also showing their Indian war clubs were Jim Thome (40 homers, 102 RBIs), Matt Williams (32 homers, 105 RBIs), Manny Ramirez (.328, 26 homers, 80 RBIs), Brian Giles (17 homers), and catcher Sandy Alomar, Jr. (.324, 21 homers, 83 RBIs). Sandy is the brother of the Orioles' Roberto, and they're the sons of Sandy, Sr., who was on the Yankee pennant winners of 1976.

Like the past two seasons, Cleveland's top starters were Charles Nagy 15-6 and Orel Hershiser 14-6. Rookie Jaret Wright, son of Clyde who once won 22 games for the Angels, was 8-3. But it was thier 'pen that was the backbone of the staff. Jose Mesa, Mike Jackson, and Paul Assenmacher combined for 36 saves and 13 wins. (Do you think maybe all the sell-outs Cleveland had been because the fans wanted to see Michael Jackson the singer)? The Tribe had the worst record of the four playoff teams, and was the only AL Central division team to be above .500 (86-75). The Yanks drew the Indians and the O's faced the Mariners in the AL playoffs.

On the home front, Mike was at St. John's working and taking classes for his Doctorate. In the fall of '97 Chris was accepted at the prestigious University of Pennsylvania Wharton School of Business, rated number one in the country. He really did not want to give up being in NYC for being in Philly. For him, Phillies or Yanks, it was no contest but you have to do what you have to do. I was still doing some umpiring in lieu of yard work. For fun Josephine would come to some of the games and holler "Kill the ump".

I was pretty happy in the first inning of the Yank/Indians playoff opener - the Tribe put up a five spot with Sandy Alomar's 3-run blast the big blow. The Yanks got one in the second to make it 5-1. They both tallied one in the fourth and the Yanks got one in the fifth. Cleveland still looked good at 6-3 but then the Teepee collapsed in the sixth. Boggs and Rey Sanchez singled and Tim Raines tied it with a 3-run homer. Jeter imitated him breaking the tie and O'Neill joined the fun with one of his own (3 dingers in a row), Yanks were up 8-6. The Indians loaded the bags in the seventh, but Jeff Nelson got Matt Williams to fly out. The final score was 8 -6.

In game 2 Cleveland was going with the Wright stuff but it didn't look like it in the Yanks' first – it looked like the wrong stuff. Three walks, a two-bagger by Tino, a sac-fly, and the Yanks were up 3-0. Pettitte lost it in the fourth. Four singles (Omar Vizquel, Justice, Alomar, Thome), a walk, and a double by Tony Fernandez put the Indians up 5-3. They added two in the fifth on a Vizquel hit and Matt William's 2-run homer. The Yanks got one in the eighth and ninth (Jeter's homer) to make the final 7-5. Jarret Wright got the victory.

At Jacobs Field in Cleveland the third game was All's Wells That Ends Wells. O'Neill put the Yanks up 1-0 with an RBI hit in the first. Cleveland tied it in the second on hits by Matt Williams and Justice and an RBI ground out. Jeter and Tino singled in the third to put the Yanks up 2-1. In the fourth, three walks and an O'Neill Grand Slam was all she wrote, Yanks won 6-1 as David Wells went the route. The Yankees were smiling as they were up 2 games to 1. I was thinking of ol' Zeus working his Pinstripe magic.

In game 4, two former Cy Youngers went at it and both showed how good they used to be (Orel Hershiser vs. Doc Gooden). The Bronx Bombers got to Orel in the first on doubles by Jeter and O'Neill and a single by Posada for a 2-0 lead. Justice cut it in half with a second inning homer, and there it stood until the Cleveland eighth. The Yanks got greedy and put in their all-world terminator, closer Mariano Rivera to close out the playoffs. When Rivera came in it was usually see you tomorrow – in this case next year. Anyway, Sandy Alomar, Jr. had other thoughts as he parked one to the opposite field to tie it. Ramiro Mendoza, who was credited with the opening game win, came in for the ninth. Marquis Grissom singled, was sacrificed to second, and scored the winning run on Vizquel's walk-off single.

The Tribe had the Wright stuff ready for the finale against Pettitte. The Indians took it to Andy in the third for three runs on hits by Grissom, Bip Roberts, a 2-run double by Manny Ramirez, and another hit by Matt Williams. An Alomar double and a sac-fly gave Wright a 4-0 lead. The Yankees halved the lead in their fifth on two walks and a hit by Bernie Williams, his only hit in the series in 17 at bats. A double by Mike Stanley and a RBI hit by Boggs in the sixth cut the deficit to one. Where was Zeus?? I thought for sure he'd show up as the Yanks threatened in the seventh but that ended on a double play. In the eighth Charlie Hayes and Boggs singled, but Posada grounded out to end the inning and in the ninth O'Neill hit a two-out double but never saw third base.

Tom-toms were beating as the Indians took the division playoff, 3-2, over the Zeus-less Yanks. Why didn't the Zeus Theory work for the Yanks? Don't forget the mythology – The Greek gods have faults - they are not like our all powerful, all knowing, all compassionate God. Possibly the clouds on Mount Olympus (Zeus' home) got in his way and when he saw Alomar Jr. at the plate he had flashbacks to his father, the former '76 Yankee, and thought Junior was also a Yankee so he put a thunderbolt in his bat. Alomar led the Tribe's attack (.316, 6 for 19, 2 homers, 5 RBIs). Vizquel hit .500 (9 for 18) and Jaret, the Wright stuff, was 2-0. For the Yanks, O'Neill hit .421 (8 for 19, 2 homers, 7 RBIs) and Jeter hit .333 (7 for 21, 6 runs).

In the other AL playoffs Baltimore faced Seattle who won the West by six games over the newly named Anaheim (changed from California) Angels. Seattle was led by a powerful bat attack leading the Majors with 925 runs - MVP Junior Griffey (.304, 56 homers, 147 RBIs), Edgar Martinez (.330, 28 homers, 108 RBIs), Jay Buhner (40 homers, 104 RBIs), ARod (.300, 23 homers) and Paul Sorrento (31 homers). Armed on the Mariners' mound were Randy "Big Unit" Johnson (20-4) and Jamie Moyer (17-5). However the Orioles short-circuited the Mariners' power, holding them to a .218

batting average and 11 runs as they took them 3 games to 1. Mussina posted two wins while Johnson suffered two losses.

Cleveland defeated Baltimore in six games with all of their victories decided by one run – they won game two 5-4 scoring 3 in the eighth, game three 2-1 in 12 innings, game four 8-7 scoring one in the ninth and game six (the clincher) 1-0 in 11 innings on a round-tripper by Tony Fernandez for the AL flag. They would face the Florida Marlins in the Fall Classic.

The Marlins were owned by H. Wayne Huizenga, who went the Steinbrenner route and bought a pennant by signing big name free agents. Three of them really produced - Bobby Bonilla (.297, 17 homers, 96 RBIs), Moises Alou (.292, 23 homers, 115 RBIs), and pitcher Alex Fernandez (17-12). Kevin Brown was their other ace at 16-8. The Marlins had an easy time in the playoffs as they swept San Fran and then took the Braves in 6 games. Brown and Livan Hernandez (NLCS MVP) each had two wins against the Braves. Hernandez was a media delight and made a good story having fled Cuba and was a half brother of the Yankees' Orlando "El Duque" Hernandez.

The Series would be the "old" (Cleveland Indians) versus the "new" (Florida Marlins). The Marlins took game 1 behind Hernandez 7-4. The Tribe rebounded winning game 2, 6-1. The teams left the Tropics to go to the deep freeze of northeast Ohio. In a game reminiscent of the 15-14 game in '93 between the Blue Jays and Phils, the Marlins scored 7 in the ninth to break a 7-up score. Cleveland came back with 4 but fell 3 short to lose 14-11. Despite the snow in game 4, the Indians won 10-3 to even the Series at two. In game 5, the Marlins were winning 8-4 in the ninth and held on as the Tribe put up 3 runs to fall 1 short.

Back in the Tropics, Cleveland stayed alive winning Game 6, 4-1. In the deciding game it looked like the Tribe would have their first World Series Championship since 1948 as they had a 2-1 lead going into the ninth, but the Marlins tied it on a sac-fly. In the eleventh the Indians botched a double play ball and the Marlins loaded the bases. With two outs Edgar Renteria hit a dinker into center for the winning run. Hernandez was selected Series MVP (2-0, 5.27 ERA) because in my opinion it made good copy. I really thought that Moises Alou (.321, 2 doubles, 3 homers, 9 RBIs, 6 runs) was more deserving.

Since the Marlins didn't have the revenue like the Yanks, they couldn't afford to keep their team together, so Huizenga had to cut his payroll. As a result, there was a Florida fire sale and the Marlins would lose 108 games in 1998. Maybe there's a need for some sort of salary cap?

1998 – 2000
The Focus from Mount Olympus

In '98, while sitting on his throne on Mount Olympus, Zeus was really annoyed with himself with his Sandy Alomar gaffe costing his favorite team the AL Division series last year. He would set up his itineraries so it wouldn't happen again. All of his focus in October would be for the Pinstripers. This would even include the signing of former Yankee nemesis, the hated Roger "Rocket" Clemens in 1999.

The baseball attendance was still way behind the pre-strike 1994 year. But in '98 the fan's interest was rekindled by a tremendous home run race by St. Louis slugger Mark McGwire and the Cubs' blaster Sammy Sosa. McGwire easily broke Roger Maris' record of 61 in '61 by smashing 70. Sammy banged out 66 and actually was ahead of McGwire for a couple of hours so technically McGwire broke Maris' and Sosa's record. Milwaukee's Greg Vaughn hit 50 dingers, but finished 20 behind the leader. This year the Milwaukee Brewers switched leagues in another realignment move by Baseball (from the AL Central to the NL Central).

One of the reasons the long ball effect became so prevalent in '98 was that Big League pitching became further diluted. The Majors expanded with two more teams putting one in the NL (Arizona Diamondbacks) and one in the AL (Tampa Bay Devil Rays) – where were the pitchers going to come from?

Swinging Sammy was the NL MVP, as he had an NL best 158 RBIs to go with his 66 homers. He probably beat out McGwire by virtue of his Cubs capturing the NL Wild Card spot. The Cubs had to beat San Fran in a one game playoff for the Wild Card spot as they finished with the same records. Jim Stoops, my Legion player in 1990, beat the Giants in relief which allowed the Cubs to tie them for the Wild Card spot. The National League was fun to watch. The Mets only missed the Wild Card by one game and that was due to trading for superstar Mike Piazza early in the season. Piazza got off to a slumping start and between the NY media and fans he seemed to be really pressing. I think it was July when Josephine called me at work saying someone at her place has two good seats for the Mets/Rockies doubleheader and could not go so not wanting them to go to waste asked her if her husband (me) could use them. I called my son, Mike, at St John's and we made arrangements to go. Piazza came up with the bags loaded and silenced the boooos with a bases-clearing shot to the wall. His slump was over as he hit .348 with 23 homers in his 109 games with the Mets, and made them postseason contenders.

In the AL, Ken Griffey, Jr. hit 56 homers, with 146 RBIs, but wasn't even MVP. That went to playoff-bound Texas Ranger, Juan Gonzalez (45 homers, 158 RBIs). In '98 with Zeus watching, the Pinstripers could not lose. It was a lousy year for me.

My poor son Chris - his favorite team set all kinds of records and he was stuck in Philly going to Wharton. I think it was W.C. Fields, the comic actor, who said something like "I'd rather be in Philadelphia" – well, Chris could tell you what to do with that saying.

In '99, Zeus kept his focus - so that's all I'll say about the American League. Well maybe not. Griffey hit 48 homers, the Red Sox's Nomar Garciaparra (.357) and Derek Jeter (.349) were the first shortstops to finish 1-2 in batting and Ivan Rodriguez (IRod), the Texas catcher, was AL MVP (.332, 35 homers, 111 RBIs).

In the NL, the Braves' Chipper Jones was MVP (.319, 45 homers, 110 RBIs). I thought Piazza should of captured it (.303, 40 homers, 124 RBIs) as he led the Mets to the '99 Wild Card. To get the Wild Card berth they had to face Cincinnati in a playoff game as they were tied when the season ended – the Mets prevailed 5-0 behind the 2-hit shutout tossed by Al Leiter. The Mets had pretty good stick men – Robin Ventura (.301, 32 homers, 120 RBIs), Edgardo Alfonzo (.304, 27 homers, 108 RBIs), John Olerud (.298, 19 homers, 96 RBIs), and Rickey Henderson (.315, 89 runs). This was balanced by arguably the best fielding infield in the history of baseball with Olerud at first, Alfonzo at second, Rey Ordonez at short and Ventura at third. In the postseason they beat Randy Johnson and the Arizona Diamondbacks 3 games to 1. The finale was won on an extra inning homer by Todd Pratt. Had the D'backs won, the Mets would have had to face the Big Unit again and that is never something to look forward to. In the battle for the NLCS, the Mets were on the verge of tying the series at three but blew leads in the eighth and tenth as Atlanta took it in six games.

This three year period encompassed the saga of John Rocker. Coming out of the 'pen for the Braves he was showing to have the talent to rival Mariano Rivera as Baseball's best fireman. In his rookie season of '98 his ERA was 2.19, and in '99 he had 38 saves striking out 104 batters while walking only 47 in 72 1/3 innings posting a 2.40 ERA. The following year he saved 24 games with a 2.89 ERA. In postseason he has the lowest ERA in baseball history for pitchers with over 20 innings – Rocker has a zero ERA in 20 2/3 innings with 26 Ks covering 20 games. However his communication skills did not match up with his pitching ability. During interviews Rocker would make disparaging remarks about various ethnic groups and just verbally ripped apart New York City. His comments appeared to show he was "off his rocker" – they also irritated his Atlanta teammates. Even the teaching genius of another "rocker", the Braves superb pitching coach Leo Mazzone, who is known for his rocking motion while watching the game, could not get Rocker to just focus on pitching. By 2003 his promising career was over.

Sosa and McGwire were in another home run derby, with Big Mac nosing him out 65 to 63. Poor Sammy - he hit over 60 homers twice and couldn't win a Sultan of Swat (home run) crown.

In '99 Chris became a graduate of Wharton. Naturally, Josephine, Mike and I attended the graduation ceremonies at Franklin Field (former home of the Eagles and Army/Navy games). Walking into the stadium I saw the building engraved <u>Franklin Field 1922</u>, so I commented to Josephine "Wow this stadium is one year older than Yankee Stadium". She shrugged her shoulders saying "So"! Here I am telling this to someone who, for the first eight years of her life, lived in the vicinity of the Roman Coliseum (2000 or so years old).

After graduating Wharton, Chris and three of his graduating buddies decided to backpack through Europe for over a month. They stopped in Rome and stayed with his Uncle Al, Josephine's brother, for three days. Chris' cousins showed them the hot spots that the tourists don't get to see. When he got back, he returned to his adopted city, NYC. No more Philly.

In 2000, the last year of the century, Zeus remained steadfast on keeping his October focus in NYC. In the AL, Nomar Garciaparra

hit .372 to become the first right-handed batter since Joe D in '39 &
'40 to win consecutive batting titles. He easily beat out Darin Erstad
(.355). Somehow Zeus watched a former Trojan (USC) star Troy
(isn't that a coincidence) Glaus take the home run title (47) – hard to
stop him, he was an Angel. The Boss' eyes were on AL MVP Jason
Giambi (.333, 43 homers, 137 RBIs) – he was most likely musing
"Gotta have him".

The NL was again entertaining to follow. The best hitter was
the Rockies' Todd Helton (.372) with the rare feat of over 100 extra
base hits (59 doubles, 42 homers) and 147 RBIs. With McGwire
retired, Sammy Sosa swung for 50 homers, 13 less than last year,
and finally won the home run title by one over Barry Bonds of San
Fran. The playoff Giants also had the NL MVP but it wasn't Barry –
it was second baseman Jeff Kent, who put up numbers like he was
related to Clark Kent because when he put on his uniform he hit like
Superman (.334, 33 homers, 125 RBIs).

The Mets again snagged the NL Wild Card going 94-68.
Piazza, as usual, was chief lumber man (.324, 38 homers, 113
RBIs). Also pounding the horsehide were Alfonzo (.324, 25 homers,
94 RBIS), Ventura (24 homers, 84 RBIs), Todd Zeile (22 homers,
79 RBIs), Jay Payton (.291, 17 homers), and Derek Bell (18
homers). The recipients of this offense were Mike Hampton (15-10)
and Al Leiter (16-8).

The Mets faced the former NYC residents, the Giants, in the
Division playoffs. After losing the opener they took the next two in
extra innings and took the finale 4-0 on a one-hitter by Bobby Jones.
The Met arms kept Barry homerless as he hit a paltry .176.

For the pennant my two favorite teams faced each other (Mets
& Cards). With the Piazza lumber (.412, 7 for 17, 2 homers, 4 RBIs)
and Hampton's arm (2-0, zero ERA in 16 innings), the Mets made
quick work of St. Louis in five games. However, the Mets lost in the
(Subway) World Series.

In the spring of 2000, my older son Mike finished his Doctorate
from St. John's. Combined my sons have five degrees. The only
degrees I attained were second degree burns from lying in the sun
too long.

Chris had such a good time last year in Europe that he decided
to return for another European excursion. To celebrate his
Doctorate, Mike decided to join him for the 16-day trip (is this
traveling to Europe after graduating an inherited gene - from

Gene?). I even wanted to join them but they cleverly said someone has to take care of mom - hmmmm.

Editor's Note: The Yankee dynasty was in full swing as they won three consecutive World Series championships (the first time a franchise won three straight since the '72-'74 A's). In 1998 they set a Major League record by winning 125 games (that included the postseason) and swept the San Diego Padres in the Series. In 1999, they had a rematch with Atlanta and swept them as well. The 2000 Series would be the first subway Series since the Dodgers and Giants went west, as the Mets represented the National League. This was great for me since I was pulling for the Yankees, but it wouldn't have been devastating if the underdog Mets won. The NY metropolitan area was a land divided. In game 1 the Mets missed a great opportunity to take a solid lead in the game because of some poor base running and lost due to shoddy relief pitching. As a result the opportunistic Yankees won in extra innings. The Mets would finally win Game 3 (breaking a record 14 consecutive World Series game streak by the Yankees). The Yankees would win the Series in 5 games. However the Series was extremely close as all the games were decided by 2 runs or less. This era of Yankee dominance would cause much debate on where they stood in the annals of Yankee and baseball history. The one negative about this Yankee run was that it gave my dad three years worth of illogical ranting and raving about his "Zeus Wears Pinstripes" theory.

2001
Snake Bitten

As the third century of baseball began, it was evident to me that the focus from Mount Olympus would continue to bring happiness to the Yankees and their fans. After being smiled upon for the past three years, why should this year be any different? With the addition of one of baseball's best pitchers, Mike Mussina, the balance of the American League East weighed heavily in favor of the Yanks.

The Yankees had a relatively easy time taking the East by 13 1/2 games over their rival Red Sox. All these years I cannot understand how the Yankee/Red Sox situation can be referred to as a rivalry (I know it has to do with the Babe for $$$$ trade). I always thought a rivalry involved two evenly matched foes where both teams won from time to time (i.e. the Army/Navy Football Game). The Yankees have destroyed the Red Sox, it seems, a 120 % of the time. To me this so-called rivalry is a creation of the New York media because of the Yankee dominance.

The Yanks finished 95-65, but it was only third best in the league. Seattle set an American League record with 116 wins (tying the Cubs of 1906, who did it in a 154 game schedule). In the West, Oakland A's won 102 games but still finished 14 games behind the Mariners. They took the Wild Card spot in the playoffs. Seattle had the league MVP and Rookie of Year, Japanese import Ichiro Suzuki. He had the most hits (242) and led the league in batting (.350), steals (56), and was second in runs (127). He also won a Gold Glove.

The Yanks had a well-balanced offense. Derek Jeter put together another stellar season (.311, 21 homers, 74 RBIs). His new keystone mate was Alfonso Soriano who looked like a budding star (.268, 18 homers, 73 RBIs). Paul O'Neill's average dropped in his farewell year but he put out 21 homers and 70 RBIs. Bernie Williams again hit over .300 (.307) with clout (26 homers, 94 RBIs,

107 runs). Jorge Posada was becoming one of the league's top hitting catchers (.277, 22 homers, 95 RBIs). But the main power supply came from Tino Martinez (34 homers, 113 RBIs). On the hill Rocket Clemens was 20-3 collected another Cy Young Award (some hobby) and Mussina earned the Boss' bucks (17-11, 3.15 ERA, second in AL). Andy Pettitte was his usual reliable self (15-10). Mariano Rivera had another "it's over when I come in" year (4 wins, 50 saves). For the Yanks, the regular season continued to be only a tune-up for the playoffs.

This year would also be Cal Ripken's last year. His scheduled last game was to be at Yankee Stadium on September 30. My sons knowing I was a Cal fan got tickets for the game as a Father's Day gift. I'd get to see Ripken's last Major League game.

On September 9 the Post Office was running a bus trip to the Stadium for a Yankee/Red Sox game. I signed up and went to the game. Going up the NJ Turnpike I took note of the NYC skyline especially the Twin Towers. The Yanks beat the Red Sox and as I was on the bus heading down the 'Pike I again glanced to look at the Towers. I never really saw this view of Manhattan since I was always driving food supplies (mom's lasagna and chicken parmigiana) to Chris and had to concentrate on the road.

On Tuesday 9/11, I was at work when I heard the employees in the break area watching the TV. It was just before 9:00 a.m. I went to see what the commotion was. I saw that an airliner had hit one of the Towers. Then another airliner hit the other Tower. My phone rang. It was my son, Chris, who worked on Wall Street about six blocks from the World Trade Center. He was at his desk when the first airliner hit one of the Towers. He then went outside to see what was happening; and was on the street as the second airliner crashed into the other Tower. After seeing both of the Towers spewing out smoke and flames, he instinctively dashed back to his building. Ironically I was scheduled at 10:00 a.m. to give a synopsis of an aviation security class I attended to some postal managers at another postal facility. I called my boss and told him my son was over there and to cancel my 10:00 a.m. meeting. He sensed that I was upset and told me to come over, anyway. I did and while driving there one of the Towers collapsed. When I got there I made phone contact with Chris, Mike and Josephine. Eventually Chris left his building after the second Tower went down. He walked the one mile or so back to his apartment. He had to walk all through the debris to get home. His roommate at Columbia University was killed in this tragedy. Mike didn't get home until 2:00 a.m. that night. He was one of a few administrators to make it in that day and needed to ensure that provisions and plans for the safety of his students at St. John's were in place. I, like the rest of the world was traumatized by this horrible act of terrorism. A short time later, we in the U.S. Post Office got hit with the anthrax terrorism – it occurred in a facility only 15 miles from our residence. What a year!!

To get back to the unreal world, baseball was pushed back a week, so I would not see Cal Ripken's last game – only his last game at Yankee Stadium. What a miserable game it turned out to be – it rained the whole time, went 15 innings, and was called with the score 1-1. Cal probably had one of his worst professional games, 0 for 8 with 5 Ks.

In the AL playoffs, NY was down 0-2 to the A's, but as usual won the next three to take the division series. Zeus obviously intervened, especially on the now famous Jeter relay to home plate. I guess Zeus slyly whispered to Jeremy Giambi not to slide. Their reward was to face the record setting Mariners managed by Sweet Lou Piniella. There was nothing sweet about the ALCS – the Yanks toyed with the Mariners and won it in five games.

In the NL it was again the year of Barry Bonds, (73 homers – so much for McGwire's home run record of 70 being unbreakable, 177 BB's, 137 RBIs, a record .863 slugging %). Sammy Sosa again hit over 60 homers (64) and had 160 RBIs but nobody really noticed. Neither the Giants nor the Cubs made the playoffs. The Colorado Rockies' Todd Helton became the first Major Leaguer to have over 100 extra base hits in consecutive seasons – 105 (49 homers, 54 doubles, 2 triples).

As a Yankee Hater I was pulling for the Arizona Diamondbacks to win the NL because of their pitchers – the best righty/lefty combo since the Dodgers' Koufax & Drysdale tandem in the 60's, - Randy "the Big Unit" Johnson (Cy Young winner 21-6, 2.49 ERA, 372 Ks) and Curt Schilling (22-6, 2.98 ERA, 293 Ks). They were easily the two best in the league. Byung-Hyun Kim (5 wins, 16 saves) was their guy in the 'pen.

Their offense was led by Luis Gonzalez (Gonzo) who in most years would have been league MVP (.325, 57 homers, 142 RBIs, 128 runs). Reggie Sanders (33 homers, 90 RBIs), Mark Grace (.298,

78 RBIs) and in two-thirds of the season Matt Williams (16 homers, 65 RBIs) were the other D'backs who rattled opposing pitchers.

In the NLDS playoffs, Schilling beat St. Louis 1-0 and 2-1 as the D'backs won in five games. In the NLCS Johnson won twice (2-0 and 3-2), while Schilling posted a victory as they constricted the Braves in five games. The team I wanted to face the Yanks was in, and I hoped they'd have the success the '63 Koufax/Drysdale Dodgers did (a sweep). I was only concerned about Zeus.

Some Yankee fans tried to get me to root for the Yanks in view of the 9/11 tragedy. Yeah, right. Would they root for the Mets if they were in it – I knew they wouldn't. One concern I had was that I was not a fan of the D'backs' manager Bob Brenly. I thought he was similar to Johnny Keane in '64 (hey, but he won the Series).

In the opener it was Schilling vs. Mussina. In the first Bernie Williams homered but Craig Counsell hit one in the bottom of the inning to tie it. In the third and fourth the D'backs rattled the Yanks for 4 runs. In the third Gonzo's 2-run homer was the big hit and in the fourth it was Grace's 2-run double. With Schilling on the mound, it was all over. Hiss, hiss, D'backs won 9-1 and had the Big Unit going next. In game 2 the Big Unit got a run to work with in the second on a Sanders hit and an RBI double by Dan Bautista. It was all he needed, even though Matt Williams 3-run homer in the seventh gave him a 4-0 cushion that stood up. Pettitte was the loser. D'backs were up 2-0 going to the Stadium.

At the Stadium the D'backs had to face Schilling's mentor, Rocket Clemens. Posada homered in the second to give the Yanks the lead. In the fourth a walk, a hit by Gonzo, and a sac-fly by Matt Williams tied it. The Yanks went ahead 2-1 in the sixth on hits by Bernie. Williams and Scott Brosius. The Rocket went seven innings only yielding three hits. Mariano came in for the last two innings (he K'd four of the six outs). Yanks won 2-1.

Game 4 was the game my son Mike, my nephew Frank, Mike's friend and high school teammate Kumar, and I would go to watch in the sports bar at the Hyatt Hotel in New Brunswick, NJ. Frank and Kumar, like my son, are die-hard Pinstripers. As a joke I brought along a copy of pinstriped Zeus. Since it was Halloween, I was hoping for a D'back treat. There was a lot said about Schilling going on three days rest (in the '50's that was the norm). He would be facing El Duque (Orlando Hernandez). They were both on their game. Shane Spencer put the Yanks up 1-0 in the third with a homer and Grace dittoed that to tie it in the fourth. Watching the game with these three Yankee-ites, we would argue about the close pitches and I'd bring up my pinstripe intimidation theory. With El Duque out of the game, the D'backs rattled for two runs on a Gonzo hit, an Erubiel Durazo double, and an RBI out by Matt Williams. I was ecstatic – Schilling with a 3-1 lead. Then the controversial part of the game occurred. Skipper Brenly supposedly asked Schilling how he felt. I think Schilling said he was gassed but he had another inning in him. Brenly took him out and looked smart because reliever Kim K'd the Yanks in the eighth. After this inning Kumar and my nephew decided to leave – they had to get up early in the morning. Frank was really shaken, his beloved Pinstripers, were going down. I showed him the copy of Zeus in pinstripes that I brought and said "You still got Zeus". With that he smirked and left.

There I was sitting there real happy while my son was sad. In the ninth I felt the horror of Zeus as O'Neill singled. With two outs Tino hit one deep into the New York night (3-3). I was glum, my son was happy. The game passed midnight, making it the first World Series game played in November. As Jeter came up, my son told me "Dad...right field stands". Boom - Zeus must have told my son. Hello Mr. November...it was a miserable ride home. The Series was now even at two. The next day at work I had to hear all the Yankee talk – I didn't read the newspaper or listen to the radio. My answer to Yankee fans was "Zeus Rules".

In game 5, the match-up favored the Yanks, Mussina vs. Miguel Batista. Both pitchers were hooked up in an old fashioned pitchers duel, except Mussina gave up homers in the fifth to Steve Finley and Rod Barajos (who had only 17 hits for the year). The score stood at 2-0 Snakes. In the ninth the skipper Brenly (no doubt a fan of déjà vu) put in his ace reliever Kim, who the previous day made Jeter "Mr. November". When I saw him come in my thoughts again went to Zeus - hoping some goddess was distracting him. Back to reality Posada doubled and Scott Brosius mimicked Tino of yesterday with a game tying 2-run homer. It seemed like the Yanks had a few Mr. Novembers. In the eleventh the Snakes had a threat but Sanders lined out. In the twelfth, Chuck Knoblauch singled and scored on a game-winning hit by Soriano. The Yanks won 3-2 and went up 3 games to 2 in the Series. And my most hated song became Ol' Blue Eyes' "New York, New York". The Yanks were anointed a "team of destiny" because of the 9/11 events. But I knew it was the meddling of Zeus.

With the Series moving back to Bank One Ball Park in Phoenix, I was hoping the D'backs would shed their skin and start anew.

At work I was talking about the Series with my boss (no, not Steinbrenner). He was from Queens, NYC and a Mets fan, so he was pulling for the D'backs to win. I explained to him my "Zeus Wears Pinstripes" theory. But since the Series was back in Arizona, I had a hunch that things would be fine. I explained to him that when Arizona played at home they would be wearing their home pinstriped uniforms and the Yanks would be wearing their road grays. So maybe Zeus would be distracted and would just aim his thunderbolts at the pinstriped uniforms. My boss laughed and said he hopes that scenario plays out.

In Game 6 the Snakes chances were pretty good since the Big Unit (Johnson) was going. The snake charmer for the Yanks was Pettitte, but as it turned out he was charming to them. Supposedly Pettitte was tipping off his pitches and the D'backs took advantage of it. It seemed like the whole state of Arizona got a hit as they banged out 22 hits and 15 runs. They scored one in the first, three in the second and eight in the third in which Matt Williams had two doubles. Tony Womack had 3 hits as did Dan Bautista (with 5 RBIs). Reggie Sanders had 4 hits. They tacked on three more runs in the fourth for a 15-0 lead. With the Big Unit going, you'd think Brenly would have taken him out after five innings (to get credit for the win) in order to use him in game 7 if needed. But no, Brenly left him in there for seven innings (I guess he felt with two innings to go a 15-2 lead was safe). Back when I was managing - Chris was my ace, and I took him out in the second inning of a playoff game after we scored 13 runs in the bottom of the first so I would have him available for the next game – maybe I should have been the D'backs manager.

Game 7 would be one of the classic match-ups – mentor, the Rocket vs. the student, Schilling. For five innings goose eggs were on the board. In the sixth Steve Finley singled and Bautista rapped one in the gap. Finley scored but Bautista was called out trying for a triple (I thought he was safe, I thought Homer, the blind Greek poet, was the third base umpire). That was the first out of the inning and one of the cardinal rules of base running is that you don't make the first out of an inning getting nailed at third. Still the D'backs were up 1-0. In the seventh Schilling gave up hits to Jeter, O'Neill, and Tino that tied it at one, and in the eighth Soriano blasted a shot over the left field wall giving the Yanks a 2 to 1 lead. The Big Unit then came into the game to finish the inning. In the bottom of the inning, Yankee skipper Torre sent in Mariano Rivera to seal the deal and he fanned three in the eighth.

After Mariano K'd the Snakes, I went upstairs to get ready for bed. Josephine heard me enter the bedroom and said "I don't hear you cursing; your team must have won". That egged me to come out with something like "no they didn't – that expletive Zeus". The Big Unit had a 1-2-3 ninth but I didn't watch that inning as I went to wash up and got into bed as the bottom of the ninth started. I told Josephine to shut off that expletive TV. Unknowing to me she pushed the mute bottom on the remote and was watching the game.

Mark Grace led off with a single to center; Josephine said "Oops there's a guy on first". I then turned over to see the TV and saw one of the worst sacrifice bunt attempts ever by Damien Miller – it went right back to Mariano Rivera, one of baseball's best fielding pitchers. Grace's pinch-runner would have been out by plenty, but Mariano threw his famed cutter to second and the ball sailed to the first base side of second, out of reach of Jeter's futile attempt to catch it. The next batter from Brenley's school of bunting, Jay Bell, tried to sacrifice the runners to second and third – but since Miller had such "excellent results" bunting it right to the pitcher, I guess Bell thought he'd try it too. Anyway, Mariano had better luck with Bell's bunt throwing to third for the force out. Tony Womack was up and laced a double to right tying the game and putting runners on second and third. My son Chris, to this day, says he couldn't believe Rivera let him (Womack) hit a pitch like that on a 0-2 count. When I saw WomacKs shot go into right field I jumped out of bed, hitting my head on our ceiling fan. My wife hollered at me, "How can you be so happy when your sons are so sad?" I replied that I didn't tell them to be Yankee fans. Mariano then hit Craig Counsell to load the bases for the Reptiles big stick, Gonzo. Everybody knows it's a no-brainer to play the infield in with the bags loaded and less than two outs. I think on TV it was announcer Tim McCarver (one of my Cardinal heroes in the '64 Series) brought up the point that with Mariano's pitches it may be a bad move because he jams many batters causing them to hit dinky flares.

McCarver was right as Gonzo, choking up, hit a little flare barely past the infield dirt behind second, but with Jeter playing in there was no chance for him to catch it.

I was ecstatic jumping up and down. I think the Arizona sound system started playing "New York, New York", but cut it short being in bad taste in view of 9/11. I never heard of a song "Arizona, Arizona". Maybe they could have played "Amazing GRACE". I was so glad to see these three-peaters run out of the dugout to their clubhouse.

Randy Johnson, who was 3-0, and Curt Schilling were voted Co-MVPs for the Series and later in the season garnered more honors being chosen Co-Sportsmen of the Year by Sports Illustrated magazine for derailing the Yankee Express.

I went downstairs and called my Yankee hating 87-year old Dad who lives in Florida. I think I stayed up until 4:00 a.m. watching interviews. I went to work at 7:00 a.m. and didn't say boo to the Yankee fans – but they saw me talking and laughing with the other Yankee Haters. My boss must have been thinking my Zeus theory worked. I was sure glad that Zeus let the pinstriped team win the World Series.

2002
Oh, What a HEAVENLY Playoff

This year is the last palindromatic year until 2112 and hopefully that will be the next time the Yankees win the Series. Anyway, the Yanks were determined to reverse last season's snake bitten World Series loss to the Arizona Diamondbacks. The Yanks made several additions to this year's team. After all last year Paul O'Neill and Scott Brosius retired and the Boss, showing his usual loyalty, opted not to re-sign Tino Martinez after he led the team in homers and RBIs last year. The reason Tino was expendable was that the A's Jason Giambi was a free agent and his numbers were better than Tino's. Also, $teinbrenner had the money to pay Giambi. To play third they had Robin Ventura and in the outfield they picked up Expo All-Star Rondell White. The additions to the mound were returnee David Wells and Indian ace reliever Steve Karsay, who would become a set-up man for the mighty Mariano.

Throughout the year the Yanks coasted. They tied the A's for the most wins in the AL (103) and took the East flag by 10 1/2 games. The Yanks should have won as they had six players on the All-Star team. They were Giambi (.314, 41 homers, 122 RBIs), Alfonso Soriano (.300, 39 homers, 102 RBIs and led the AL in hits (209) and runs (128), Robin Ventura (27 homers, 93 RBIs), Derek Jeter (.292, 18 homers, 124 runs), and Jorge Posada (20 homers, 98 RBIs). Mariano Rivera (28 saves, 2.74 ERA) was their mound pick. With the Yanks having that many All-Stars, there was no room for the league's third best hitter Bernie Williams (.333, 19 homers, 102 RBIs) to be on the AL squad. The Yankees also had many effective arms on the staff. The top starters were David Wells (19-7), Mike Mussina (18-10), Andy Pettitte (13-5), and the Rocket Clemens (13-6). It looked like the Yanks might have faltered with Mariano on the disabled list but Karsay, Mike Stanton, and Ramiro Mendoza picked up the slack to win 21 and save 22.

In the Division playoffs, the Yanks drew the Anaheim Angels. Incidentally, Josephine and I have a few shares of Disney who owned the Angels. The guys with the halos were the surprise team of baseball. They improved by 24 games from '01 winning 99 games to finish second in the West and captured the Wild Card by six games.

This match-up was seen by most as being a Yankee laugher. But actually the Angels' pitching staff had a lower ERA than the Yanks and their sticks had a better batting average. But the Yanks did outscore them by 46 runs over the course of the season. It was just that the Angel players were mostly unknowns. Compared to the Yankees they only had one All-Star, possibly the most underrated star in baseball, Garrett Anderson (.306, 29 homers, 123 RBIs and an AL best 56 doubles).

The team was solid all through the line-up. Bengie Molina was one of the top AL defensive catchers and was the only weak stick (.245). Their keystone combo performed well defensively and at the plate. At short was, appropriately, the Majors' shortest player Dave Eckstein who is listed at 5'6". However, he hit .293 scoring 107 runs and at second Adam Kennedy batted .312. At third Troy Glaus supplied power (30 homers, 111 RBIs). At first they had the son of a role player on my favorite team ('64 Cards), Ed Spiezio's kid, Scott, (.285, 82 RBIs). Darrin Erstad (.283, 99 runs) and Tim Salmon (.286, 22 homers, 88 RBIs) completed the outfield. The Halos on the hill were Jarrod Washburn (18-6), Kevin Appier (14-12), Ramon Ortiz (15-9), and rookie John Lackey (9-4). But it was the most complete bullpen in baseball led by relief ace Troy Percival (4 wins, 40 saves) and his set-up man Ben Weber (7 wins, 7 saves) who put them into postseason play. Oh, there was an August call-up, a 20-year old pitcher Francisco Rodriguez who got in just over 5 innings of work at the end of the year. My personal concern about this playoff was my Zeus theory. It just didn't seem like Zeus would let the Yanks lose to a team that had two of its key players named Troy (Percival and Glaus). We'll see!

The series opened at the Stadium, so the Yanks would not have to see the Rally Monkey. What is that?? Last year when the Angels were having a lousy season the scoreboard operator at Anaheim put on their big screen a spastic type monkey dancing and jumping around. The Angels would rally and win some games. The Rally Monkey would only be shown if the score was tied or the Angels were losing. Well in 2002 the Rally Monkey may have been more important than Percival. The Yanks only know of the Curse of the Bambino on the Red Sox. Rally Monkey bah! If it was true, I think that Steinbrenner would be a monkey's uncle.

Let the games begin. Jeter homered in the first to open the scoring. In the third an Erstad single, steal, and RBI hit by Salmon tied it at one. In the fourth Giambi hit a 2-run homer but in the fifth Anderson doubled home two to tie it at 3. But Rondell White put one over the wall for a 4-3 NY lead. Troy Glaus then belted homers in the sixth and eighth to give the Angels a 5-4 lead in the eighth. In the Yankee eighth, with two outs, my Zeus theory went to work. Two walks and an RBI hit by Giambi tied it at 5. Still the manager, Mike Scioscia, would not bring in Percival; he only entered a game in the ninth. Because Scioscia stuck to his plan, Bernie Williams cracked a 3-run homer. At the post-game conference, Scioscia was making light-hearted comments about his decision of not bringing in Percival - he had an air of not being worried. In '88 Scioscia broke the hearts of the borough of Queens with his homer off Doc Gooden that led the Dodgers over the Mets in the NL playoffs. Now he wanted to find a way to dishearten the fans in the borough of the Bronx.

You'd think the Angels would come into game 2 with their Halos hung low. Nope! They harped on Pettitte right off the bat. Salmon homered in the first and Spiezio in the second which was followed by three hits and another run. In the third, Anderson and Spiezio hits scored another for a 4-0 lead. A Jeter homer in the third and a 2-run double by Ruben Rivera put the Yanks down by only one.

In the sixth Francisco Rodriguez came in to pitch. The Yanks knew of hitting stars Ivan Rodriguez (IRod) and Alex Rodriguez (ARod), but not much of Angel pitcher Francisco Rodriguez (KRod). Soriano hit a 2-run homer and the Yanks finally erased the 4-0 Angel lead to go ahead 5-4. Holding the Halos at bay for four perfect innings was El Duque Hernandez. But in the eighth Anderson and Glaus smacked back to back dingers, followed by hits by Shawn Wooten and Molina as the Angels took a 7-5 lead.

The Yanks rallied in the eighth by loading the bags for Jeter. Scioscia deviated from his Percival rule and brought in Troy in the eighth - good move - he K'd Jeter. The Angels tacked on another run on hits by Anderson, Glaus and an RBI two-bagger by Spiezio.

The Yanks threatened in the ninth on hits by Giambi, Ventura, and Posada for one run but Nick Johnson K'd and Raul Mondesi popped out. The harps were playing as the Angels won 8-6.

Game 3 in Anaheim the Yanks forgot about blowing the lead and game in New York as they quickly gave Mike Mussina a three run lead in the first on hits by Jeter, Ventura's double and sac-fly by Posada. But the Angels were feisty. In the second Glaus got a hit, Spiezio doubled and Salmon's ground out scored Glaus to make it 3-1. The Yanks came back with another three in the third on a couple of walks and hits by Williams, Johnson and Ruben Rivera. They were now up 6-1 with Mussina going. But the Angels could hit - singles in the third by Kennedy, Erstad and a 2-run double by Salmon made it 6-3. A Kennedy homer in the fourth cut the gap to two.

Rally Monkey time was approaching. In the sixth Brad Fullmer got a hit and came around to score on a sac-fly to make it 6-5. KRod came on in the seventh and K'd three of the Yanks for an easy inning. In the Angel seventh, the Monkey was dancing like crazy, Anderson doubled and Spiezio drove him home to deadlock the score at 6. KRod again K'd two Yanks hurling a good eighth. In the bottom of the eighth Kennedy and Erstad rapped back to back doubles, followed by a Salmon blast for a 9-6 lead. Percival had a 1-2-3 ninth. KRod was the winning pitcher for the second game in a row. The Rally Monkey Rules! The Angels won and were now up 2 games to 1 with about a third of the salary the Boss paid. I think the Boss, maybe, put in a hurried call to the Bronx Zoo to check on the availability of any New York rally monkeys.

In game 4 the Yanks opened the scoring in the second on hits by Posada, Ron Coomer, and an RBI double by Ventura. But with runners on second and third and one out the Yanks couldn't score Coomer. The Angels tied it on hits by Wooten and Benji Gil. An error, a double by Soriano, and sac-fly by Jeter gave the Yanks a 2-1 lead. So far David Wells was doing well but in the fifth, like in the Bible when manna fell from the heavens for Moses, hits fell from heaven for the Angels – (hey, they had a direct line). Wooten started it with a homer, Gil singled, Eckstein singled, and then Erstad hit a Texas-leaguer that fell between right fielder Mondesi, second baseman Soriano, and center fielder Williams. Looking at Wells, I felt he was really angry someone didn't snag it - Bernie Williams was thought to have a chance to make the play. But it was a hit and the beat went on. Anderson singled, Glaus made the second out, but Spiezio and Wooten singled and Molina doubled. The manna resulted in eight runs for a 9-2 lead.

Posada homered in the sixth to make it 9-3. The Yanks rallied in the seventh, had a run in and the bases were loaded but KRod got Nick Johnson on a ground out. The score was now 9-4. In the eighth KRod had an easy inning with 2 Ks. The Yanks threatened in the ninth. Williams, Posada and Mondesi all hit safely for one run. But Nick Johnson grounded out to end the Yankee season. The Angels won the division playoff coming back in all three victories.

Why didn't my Zeus theory work, especially with two Troys on the Angels? Well when Zeus took a look at who his Pinstripers were playing I guess there were just too many Angels to beat. Plus the Angels sometimes wore pinstriped road uniforms.

The Angels won with their wood. As a team they hit .376, led by Erstad (.421), Anderson (.389), Spiezio (.400, 6 RBIs), Salmon (2 homers, 7 RBIs), Glaus (.312, 3 homers), and role players Wooten (6 for 9) and Gil (4 for 5). KRod with all of his five innings of experience was their best on the mound, pitching more innings than he did during the year (5 2/3 innings, 2-0, 3.18 ERA).

In the ALCS the Angels would be playing another surprise winner. The Minnesota Twins upset the Oakland A's, 3 games to 2. The two teams with over 100 wins were now just spectators. The Twins took the first game; then lost four in a row. In game 5 Adam Kennedy hit three homers and was MVP. The Angels' average fell to .280. Spiezio hit .353, Erstad .364, and Glaus .316. KRod again was the top pitcher (2-0, zero ERA, 4 1/3 innings). Percival had 2 saves and a zero ERA in 3 1/3 innings. The Angels World Series opponent would be like them – the Wild Card NL entrant, the San Francisco Giants.

Naturally the Giants were led by Barry Bonds, the league MVP, again. The league pitchers found a way to stop him, they walked him 198 times. He still batted .370, splashed many of his 46 homers into McCovey Cove, and drove home 110 runs. Barry had help in the line-up from Jeff Kent (.313, 37 homers, 108 RBIs), and last year's Series ring wearer with the D'backs Reggie Sanders (23 homers, 85 RBIs). Also David Bell (20 homers), 17-year veteran catcher Benito Santiago (.278, 16 homers, 74 RBIs) and Rich Aurilia (15 homers) provided more lumber support for Barry. The Giants five starters had between 12 and 14 wins and Robb Nen, (whose dad Dick, hit the big homer in 1963 for the Dodgers against my Cardinals), was the ace in the 'pen with 6 wins and 43 saves.

The Giants took the Braves 3 games to 2. Barry (.294, 3 homers, 4 RBIs), Benito Santiago (5 RBIs), and Rich Aurilia (2 homers, 7 RBIs) led the offense. On the mound Russ Ortiz was 2-0 and Nen had 2 saves. In the NLCS the Giants beat the Cards in five games. Barry (.273, homer, triple, 10 BB's, 6 RBIs), Bell (.412), Aurilia (.333, 2 homers, 6 RBIs) and Santiago (.300, 2 homers, 6 RBIs) provided the offense. On the mound Tim Worrell was 2-0 in relief and Robb Nen had 3 saves.

The World Series was a match-up of former Dodger teammates managing against each other, Angels' Mike Scioscia versus the Giants' Dusty Baker. In the opener Troy Glaus blasted two homers, but Barry, J.T. Snow, and Reggie Sanders connected for a San Fran 4-3 win. Game 2 was an old-fashioned lumber battle won by the Angels 11-10. Tim Salmon was 4 for 4 with a pair of 2-run homers including one that gave the Angels the lead in the eighth. Ho-hum, Barry also hit one for San Fran. KRod was the winning pitcher dousing the smoldering lumber of the Giants for three scoreless frames. Ironically another Rodriguez, Felix Rodriguez, was charged with the loss. Once again a major key to victory was the Rally Monkey.

A day off did not cool off the hot Angel sticks. In the third game they duplicated the second game total of 16 hits and again did in the Giants in their Pac Bell Park 10-4, despite Barry's daily homer. Game 4 I watched on the big screen at the Hyatt Hotel in New Brunswick, NJ with my son Mike, his friend Kumar, and my nephew, Frank. The game was a giant win for San Fran (4-3) as they even tagged the loss on KRod (even though the run off of him was unearned). The Angels had a moral victory not giving up a Barry blast (they gave him 3 intentional BB's). In game 5 the Giants scored three runs in the first and second innings as they pummeled the Angels with 16 hits in a 16-4 rout. Jeff Kent (a double, 2 homers, 4 RBIs) and Barry (single, 2 doubles, but no homers) led the offensive barrage.

The Giants were returning to Anaheim up 3 games to 2. Maybe the Giants figured enough about that damn spastic rally primate. And that's the way it looked as another Barry blast and a 2-run homer by Shawon Dunston helped San Fran to a 5-0 lead going into the bottom of the seventh. The Giants' locker room was being set up with plastic covers getting ready for the World Series champagne festivities (much like Boston in the '86 Series).

Enter the Rally Monkey – before you blinked, hits by Glaus and Brad Fullmer were followed by a Scott Spiezio 3-run rocket into the Angelic heavens. Where was Frank Buck (the famous Big Game Hunter) when you needed him? The Monkey kept dancing into the eighth as a Darin Erstad homer made it a one run deficit. Salmon and Garrett Anderson followed with hits and Glaus bounced a double off the wall to score them for a 6-5 Angel lead. Dusty Baker and the Giants just could not get the monkey off their back (or off the jumbo screen). Percival came in to blow the Giants away in the ninth, K'ing 2 of them. It would go down to a game seven with Angels' rookie John Lackey against '97 World Series MVP Livan Hernandez.

The Giants drew first blood in the second on hits by Benito Santiago, J.T. Snow and a sac-fly by Reggie Sanders. The Angels tied it in the bottom of the inning. In the third with the bases loaded Garrett Anderson cleared them with a double to give the Angels a 4-1 lead. Lackey went five innings and relievers Brendan Donnelly and KRod kept it that way until the ninth. Against Percival the Giants had the tying run at the plate – but the Giants had no Rally Monkey and Kenny Lofton flew out to give the Angels the World Series Championship.

As a team the Angels hit .310 and were led by Series MVP Troy Glaus (.385, 10 for 26, 3 homers, 8 RBIs), Tim Salmon (.346, 9 for 26, 2 homers, 5 RBIs), Dave Eckstein (.310, 9 hits, 6 runs), Darin Erstad (.300, 9 hits, 3 doubles, a homer, 6 runs), Garrett Anderson (6 RBIs), and Scott Spiezio (8 RBIs). Their mound stars were relievers KRod (1-1, 2.08 ERA, 13 Ks in 8 2/3 innings) and Percival (3 saves). Naturally, Barry, led the Giants (.471, 8 for 17, 13 BB's, 4 homers, 2 doubles, 8 runs, 6 RBIs), and finally shed the label of not being a clutch October player. J.T. Snow (.407, 11 for 27) and Jeff Kent (3 homers, 7 RBIs) also had some Giant stats.

In view of the fact Josephine and I had a couple of Disney shares, I felt we were World Series owners and suggested to her we should get World Series Rings. She nixed the idea. She said she had bad memories, the last time we got rings together – we got married. (I think she was kidding)?

2003
The Poseidon Adventure

For 2003 the Yankees had to make some changes. Boss Steinbrenner would not stand still after his $150 million dollar team lost to the $60 million dollar Angels in the Division playoffs.

The Boss, I guess, decided to go international. He went to Japan (the Boss probably forgot about his Irabu fiasco in '97) and landed Hideki Matsui, the best player in that country. His power hitting, there, earned him the nickname Godzilla. Interestingly, in the 1940's the Yankees had an All-Star outfielder Charlie (King Kong) Keller. (Maybe the Boss was trying to corner the market of movie monsters – is there a Frankenstein out there that could hit). This move helped solidify the Yankee outfield. Matsui was a center fielder but would play left in New York as Bernie Williams was in center. The other pick up was the best pitcher out of Cuba - Jose Contreras. He defected as soon as he could. He went from making a few bucks a month from the Castro regime to becoming an instant millionaire.

Most of the baseball teams try and get the make-up of their team to win enough to make the playoffs - not the Yankees; their make-up is to win the whole enchilada (The Series). For them, getting to the playoffs is a given (either as Division winner or as Wild Card entrant).

In the American League the East race was naturally between the Yanks and their rival (?) "whipping boys", the Red Sox. They played pretty even for the year, but the Yanks held a slight edge. Once again the Red Sox came up short finishing second to the 101-61 Yankees; but they did cop the Wild Card spot with a 95-67 record. In the Central whoever would win was given virtually no chance to make the Series. The Minnesota Twins came on strong at the end to beat out the Chicago White Sox and KC Royals. The West was the usual dog fight between Seattle and the Oakland A's. As a Yankee Hater, I always hoped they'll have to face Oakland as

they possess the three great young pitchers – lefties Barry Zito and
Mark Mulder and righty Tim Hudson. Anyway, Oakland held on to
hold off Seattle, despite losing Mulder, who came up lame in
August and would be out for the year.

The Yankee regular season was led by their pitching staff,
especially the starters - Andy Pettitte won 21 games, Mike Mussina
won 17, and David Wells 15. The relief terminator, Mariano Rivera
was his usual self despite missing some time due to injury. Roger
Clemens also won 17 including his 300th win (attended by my sons).
My son Mike tried to see the 300th game three previous times, and
almost missed the event this time as he and his brother went to the
milestone game (Clemens also was trying to join Nolan Ryan and
Lefty Carlton as the only pitchers with 4,000 strikeouts – he needed
four more). It was a weekday game and my son, Chris got tickets
through work contacts and called Mike. Mike would pick him up
and drive to the Stadium.

It was a rainy night and traffic was miserable. It got to the
point where Mike told Chris to get out of the car and run the half
mile or so to the Stadium so both of them would not miss the
Rocket's 4,000[th] strikeout. (Clemens K'd the side in the bottom of
the first and now only needed one more). While at a stop light, Chris
opportunistically jumped out of the car and sprinted to the Stadium
and got in just in time to see the Rocket fan the St. Louis Cardinals'
Edgar Renteria for his 4,000[th] career strikeout victim for the first out
in the bottom of the second - Clemens followed that by K'ing the
next two batters Tino Martinez and Mike Matheny for numbers
4,001and 4.002. The Stadium, minus my son Mike, was rocking for
the Rocket. (Mike heard it on the radio and did not get into the
Stadium until the fourth inning - he actually almost gave up and
turned around to go home but finally found a parking spot).
Naturally I wasn't happy that the Rocket got his 300th victory and
4,000[th] strikeout (as a Yankee, anyway), but since it was inevitable I
guess I was glad that my sons were able to be at this historic event.

Their offense was led by Captain Derek Jeter who got injured
in a freakish play sliding into third base on opening day and missed
five or six weeks, but came on strong to hit .324 and just missed
winning the batting title by two points. The Red Sox's Bill Mueller
snagged the batting title with .326, while the runner-up was his
teammate Manny Ramirez at .325. Alfonso Soriano, hit 38 homers
and drove in 91 runs in the lead-off spot. Jorge Posada tied Yogi

Berra's home run record for a Yankee catcher with 30 and had 101 RBIs. Jason Giambi despite hitting only .250 still had an on-base average of over .400 and hit 41 homers with 107 RBIs, while Godzilla was an All-Star and drove in 106 runs. The Yankees were like an American League All-Star Team.

The National League is always more fun to follow. You never know who is going to win except in the East where the Atlanta Braves seem to win every year (12 in a row). However, in all that time they only captured one World Series. As stated the Braves won in the East and the Florida Marlins reeled themselves ahead of the Phillies for second place, which would be enough to win the Wild Card spot.

In the Central, three teams, the St. Louis Cardinals, Chicago Cubs and Houston Astros all had a shot of winning. Albert Pujols led the Cards almost winning the Triple Crown hitting .359 with 43 homers and 124 RBIs, but it couldn't put them over the top. Houston did not win because their three B's Jeff Bagwell, Craig Biggio and Lance Berkman had average years (for them anyway) and their young stars on the mound Roy Oswalt and Wade Miller had injury plagued years. The Cubs with probably two of the best young arms in baseball, Mark Prior and Kerry Wood, won the Central. Sammy Sosa was most of their offense by slamming 40 homers – despite being suspended for bat-corking.

The West was won by the San Francisco Giants. In one word they were led by Barry Bonds and anybody else they put on the field. Barry hit .341 with 45 homers, 90 RBIs, 148 BB's and scored 111 runs. Ho-hum, he won another NL MVP award. The Los Angeles Dodgers gave a little bit of a fight. Their team was led by Eric Gagne, the Cy Young winner, who it seemed had a save every time they won. He blew only one save chance and it was not even in the regular season. It was in the All-Star Game when he gave up a homer to pinch-hitting Hank Blalock of Texas to win the game for the American League – thus giving the American League the home field advantage for the World Series. (For the first time home field advantage would be awarded to the league that won the All-Star Game – this was brilliant Bud's (Selig), the Baseball Commissioner, idea after last year's All-Star Game fiasco when the game was called because the teams ran out of pitchers with the score tied).

Both of this year's playoffs were to be remembered for the two Curses - one for the Boston Red Sox and the other for the Chicago

Cubs. The Boston Curse is the more famous – The Curse of the Bambino. In 1920 the Red Sox sold the best player in the game (Babe Ruth) to the New York Yankees for $125,000, supposedly, as legend has it, to finance the Broadway play "No No Nanette". It was evident that the Boston owner, a man named Harry Frazee had a greater interest in Broadway plays than baseball plays (surprisingly Frazee did not produce "No No Nanette" until 1925). From 1903-1918 the Red Box won five World Series championships. They have not won since 1918. They have lost four and missed out on pennants, and many of these misses were the results of unusual and freakish plays and circumstances that seemingly only a curse could cause. Harry Frazee is probably the most infamous name in Boston history - well maybe not more than the Boston Strangler.

The Cubs' curse was cast in the 1945 World Series by a Chicago tavern owner (See 1984 – wait, forget that, I'll repeat it here). For one of the games at Wrigley Field the tavern owner bought a ticket for himself and his pet Billy goat. The goat was not let in, or maybe it was as other accounts have the goat in the park and later thrown out during the game because it smelled as per the Cubs' owner Mr. Wrigley's orders. The tavern owner then put a hex on the Cubs (The Curse of the Billy Goat) – that the Cubs would never win another World Series. Supposedly the tavern owner took off the hex before he died, but it must have been irrevocable as the Cubs have not even been in a World Series since they were hexed in 1945.

Before the playoffs began the two teams given little chance to advance were the Twins in the American League and the Marlins in the National.

In the American League the Yanks gave us Yankee Haters a tease by losing the first game to the Twins, but it was short lived as they then took three in a row. Their opponent would be the Red Sox. It appeared the Curse may be over as the Red Sox rallied from a two game deficit to sweep the Oakland A's in the next three, to set up a Yankee/Red Sox ALCS playoff.

Their seven game series turned out to be one for the ages. The Yanks held a 3 games to 2 lead. At this point the series was marked by the team's bad blood between them. In game 3 a donnybrook occurred with Pedro Martinez and Roger Clemens coming too close to each others batters. The brawl was noted for 72-year old Yankee coach Don Zimmer, who was a former Red Sox manager, charging

Pedro and being pushed to the ground much like a matador with a bull. Anyway, the Red Sox came from behind to win game 6 forcing the Yankees to face arguably baseball's best pitcher, Pedro. Up until the eighth inning it looked like the Curse would be over. Five outs to go and Pedro had a 5-2 lead. But then the Bambino must have awoken. The Bombers strung together some hard hits against Pedro. The Boston manager Grady Little did not go to his bullpen, which during this series was unusually effective. He left Pedro in and he did not come through, although it was only a soft fly to short center field that tied the score. (The Curse had life). The game went into extra innings. The Yanks had their terminator in Mariano Rivera and the Red Sox countered with knuckleballer Tim Wakefield, who already registered two wins in the series. In the eleventh inning, Aaron Boone led off and blasted a long shot into the left field stands. You might say the Red Sox chances came up a Little bit short. The Bambino lives! Many speculate that Red Sox manager Grady Little was fired that winter because he did not take Pedro out in the eighth inning which resulted in the Yanks tying the game.

As a Yankee Hater, this was a simply horrible ending. At work, on the news, in the papers, everywhere this was said to be the greatest series ever – Blah, Blah, Blah. This torture included several after midnight phone calls from my sons...Josephine gleefully answered the phone despite being woken up. Even Boss Steinbrenner was making comments like winning is second to breathing and making quotes from one of the famous Generals - MacArthur or Patton.

No matter who would win the National League they would be given little chance of derailing the Yankees locomotive. In the NL the Cubs beat the Braves while the Marlins took the Giants. The Giants/Marlins series seemed to pick up interest with the nation's fans. The Marlins were very much unknown. They started so slow (10 games under .500 at one point) that they fired manager Jeff Torborg and hired 72-year old Jack McKeon. Picking someone so old was thought to be a joke, but as the saying goes "Who laughs last laughs best". The team started to play better and beat out the Phils for the Wild Card. Although, their players were not well known, they were fairly effective. They had good table setters. Juan Pierre had over 200 hits and Luis Castillo hit .314. To drive them home they had former AL All-Star catcher IRod (Ivan "Pudge"Rodriguez) who hit close to .300, All-Star third baseman

Mike Lowell (who hit 32 homers before getting hurt in August and would be questionable for postseason play), and Derrek Lee who hit 31 homers. A key to their winning was the pick up of Jeff Conine, a member of their 1997 World Series winner from Baltimore. It seemed to me he got big hit after big hit to lead the Marlins past the Phils' for the Wild Card spot.

The Marlins had IRod behind the plate controlling things as the young staff came of age. Despite not having AJ Burnett, possibly their best pitcher, all year, Brad Penny, Mark Redman and their May call-up, 21-year old phenom, 6'5" 240 lbs. Dontrelle "D-Train" Willis, the NL Rookie of the Year, all came through with 14 wins while Carl Pavano chalked up 12 and Josh Beckett posted 9 more. The rookie ace D-Train Willis (14-6 and NL All-Star) was a player with plenty of charisma as he had an entertaining high knee kick and unorthodox herky-jerky twisting motion of his body during his wind-up and delivery to the plate; and also as a pitcher swung a decent bat (.241, 14 for 54). In July they added American League relief ace Ugueth Urbina (33 games, 1.41 ERA) to join closer Braden Looper (6 wins 28 saves) in the 'pen.

In their series against the Giants, IRod's performance was put on the national stage showing why he was a perennial American League All-Star. With the series tied at a game apiece, the Giants led by a run in extra innings when IRod hit a sharp single into right scoring the tying and winning runs. In the next game the Giants were hoping to even it up. In the bottom of the eighth with the score tied, IRod was on second. On a base hit he was coming home, the catcher was waiting – with a hard slide he jarred the ball loose scoring the go ahead run. In fact the ball went far enough that another run crossed the plate giving the Marlins an important insurance run. The Giants came back with a run but lost when J.T. Snow tried to score on a hit from second much like IRod did, but IRod being a catcher knew how to absorb the collision and held onto the ball for the final out. The Marlins would be pitted against the Billy Goat hexed Cubs. The young Marlin staff continually kept Barry Bonds from being a factor in the series and was anticipating doing the same to the Cubs' Sammy Sosa in the NLCS.

The Giants' series appeared to take a lot out of the Marlins. The Billy Goat hex appeared to be over – the Cubs had a 3 to 1 game edge on the Marlins, when Josh Beckett their 23-year old right-hander tossed a shutout and Mike Lowell, who returned for the postseason, smashed two homers. This did not seem to phase any baseball followers as the Cubs still had a 3 to 2 game lead, were going home to Wrigley, and had their two aces rested and ready (Mark Prior and Kerry Wood). The fans of the friendly confines of the ballpark with the ivy covered walls in the north side of The Windy City were anticipating their first World Series since 1945 and maybe their first Title since 1908 when they beat the Detroit "Ty"gers behind their Hall of Fame double play combo with the famous poetic lyrics of "Tinker to Evers to Chance", and the pitching of Famer Mordecai 'Three Finger' Brown.

It appeared the hex was over, but like the Red Sox, with five outs to go and a 3-run lead the Billy Goat woke up. With one on, Luis Castillo hit a foul pop about a row deep down the left field line, Moises Alou, the Cubs' left fielder, reached into the stands, and probably would have caught the ball except for a fan getting in the way causing the ball not to be caught, thus giving Castillo life (he wound up walking). Rules say that a fan has every right to try for foul balls that are in the stands, but when you're in your home park, you hope the fans will clear the way for you to make the catch. The next batter hit a double play grounder that was botched by the shortstop Alex Gonzalez, who ironically had the fewest errors in the NL. This error led to a rally, giving the Marlins the win and forcing a game seven. The Marlins took an early 3-0 lead but the Cubs came back primarily on a big home run by pitcher Kerry Wood to lead 5-3. But Billy (the goat) had the last laugh (Baaaa!!!) as Wood could not hold the lead and Josh Beckett came in to throw four shut out innings. It would be a New York/Florida Series.

This match-up was total disappointment for most of the nation and the TV sponsors. It was hoped by them that there would be a Red Sox/Cub Series (The Red Sox have not won a World Series since 1918 when they ironically beat the Cubs as their southpaw Babe Ruth was outstanding on the mound with two victories and a 1.06 ERA; and the Cubs haven't won since 1908 when they defeated Ty Cobb's Tygers).

After beating the Red Sox in a tough seven games series, the Yankees and their fans thought the World Series would be a cakewalk. As a Yankee Hater, I had hopes that the Marlins could beat the big bad New Yorkers. There were the intangible factors – one was that the Marlins had no curses to be concerned about, secondly the state of Florida was having a good year (Tampa Bay won the Super Bowl and Miss Florida won the Miss America Contest), and thirdly the Marlins were given little chance to overtake the Phils for the Wild Card spot, or to beat the Giants and Cubs, but they showed they were genuine overachievers.

The Series opener had David Wells facing Brad Penny. This game proved the Florida Penny was better than the Boss' millions. Both my sons attended this game and were in contact with me during the contest via their cell phones. Most parents do not like to see their children sad; this includes me except when the Yanks lose. I was glad they did not enjoy their first World Series game. In my youth I was able to see about a half-dozen World Series games. If you total the amount of money I paid to see these half-dozen games it would not equal the price of one of their tickets. The score was knotted at one in the fifth when with runners on second and third, Pierre laced a single to left, one run scored easily, and the runner from second scored when the Yankees' playoff hero Aaron Boone cut off the throw home from Matsui. Replays showed the ball would have beaten the runner and there would have been a play at the plate. This run proved to be the winning run as Bernie Williams hit a sixth inning homer. The D-Train and Urbina kept the Yanks scoreless in the seventh, eighth and ninth. So much for the "fillet the fish" signs.

Game 2 was over in the first two innings. After the second inning the Yanks led 4-0 and Pettitte kept the Marlin bats quiet. The Yanks won 6-1. Game 3 was an exciting affair. Both mound's men were terrific. Mussina and Beckett were tied at one going into the eighth. Matsui got a 2-out RBI single in the eighth to put the Yanks up by one, and they scored four more in the ninth as the Yankees had consecutive 6-1 victories. With the Yanks up 2 games to 1 just about everyone in the New York area figured no way the Marlins could win. The newspapers, radio talk shows and all the fans thought the score could be mailed in.

Game 4 was the day when Michael, my nephew Frank, and I would watch our traditional game. For the past few years we would pick a World Series game and watch it at the Hyatt Hotel in New Brunswick, NJ at the sports bar with a large screen and several TVs. We were joined by a most unlikely family member, Josephine who just happened to be my wife, Mike's mom and FranKs aunt; and as you know could care less about our National Pastime (she would have rather been home watching "Murder She Wrote"). She was forced to go because we were at a seminar in New Brunswick and I convinced her to go from the seminar to the Hyatt instead of me having to drive her home then drive back to the sports bar. The seminar we were at ended about 8:30 p.m. and when we got to the Hyatt the game was in the third inning with the Marlins holding a 3-1 lead.

The starting pitchers were Roger Clemens and Carl Pavano. I was really sorry that I missed the first inning. Clemens, in most likely his last Major League performance, was hoping to put a huge nail in the Marlins' coffin by putting the Yanks up 3 games to 1. But in the first with one on, he faced Miguel Cabrera, who was the Marlins' new young star and was facing a pitcher twice his age (Clemens was 41 and Cabrera was 20). Clemens came in with his usual hard inside fast ball seemingly shaking up the youngster, or so he thought. Instead it was Clemens who was shaken up when Cabrera deposited an outside pitch into the right field stands for a 2-0 lead. Clemens, still shaken, gave up a few more hits as the Marlins tacked on another run. The Yanks came back with a run in the second and there the score stood as Pavano and Clemens, who regained his composure, threw up goose eggs. The sports bar was packed and I was probably the only one there who was happy with the Marlins holding a 3-1 lead into the ninth inning.

The Marlins put in their closer Ugueth Urbina to finish up. Naturally my son, nephew and my wife (all Yankee fans) were pretty down at this point. I told them I just hope my Zeus theory would not materialize. Urbina didn't have it. The Yanks had two on when Ruben Sierra was sent up to pinch-hit. After taking a couple of close strikes he fouled off a few then sent a laser shot into the right field corner for a game-tying 2-run triple. At least the Marlins kept Sierra at third as Aaron Boone made the final out. The sports bar erupted with high fives, while my thoughts went to that blankety-blank Zeus. We waited until the Marlins batted in the bottom of the ninth inning. They did not score and we all decided to leave as we all had to work the next day.

I would catch the extra innings on the car radio driving home (about a 20 minute drive). In the top of the eleventh inning Bernie Williams led off. I just can't stand the Yankee "homer" announcers and when they said that Bernie sent a shot into the right field area where Sierra hit his ninth-inning triple I clicked off the radio – my wife put it back on – I shut it off again stating that I do not want to hear those Yankee radio "homers" (no not ancient Greek poets) describing a Yankee victory. It was not a lead-off triple but a double. When we got home the Yanks had the bases loaded with one out. The match-up was Marlin reliever Braden Looper facing the playoff home run hero Aaron Boone. Looper was able to fan Boone and got John Flaherty, the Yankee back-up catcher, on a pop-up.

The Yanks then put in former Tiger All-Star, Jeff Weaver to pitch the eleventh, (had the Yanks scored the go-ahead run, their terminator reliever Mariano Rivera would have been in the game to close out the victory). Anyway, Weaver had an easy eleventh retiring the Marlins 1-2-3. Putting in Weaver was quite a gamble for Yankee Manager Joe Torre because Weaver did not pitch in a month or so and he was probably the least liked Yankee by the fans and possibly George Steinbrenner. The Yanks got him in a three-way trade with the A's and Tigers. With Detroit, the Majors' worst team, he was an effective pitcher. The Yankees (being a better offensive and defensive team than the Tigers) thought Weaver would be a 15 to 20-game winner. He just didn't have it with the Yanks while Ted Lilly who he replaced was very effective for the A's. In the eleventh Torre's gamble looked good. Now if only the Yanks could score in the twelfth then put in Mariano to close it. The Yanks did not score. Leading off in the twelfth for the Marlins was shortstop Alex Gonzalez. I was in bed watching not thinking too much would happen as Gonzalez was mired in a deep slump. All of a sudden he nailed a Weaver pitch - it was a rising line drive. I knew it would at least be a lead-off double but the ball held onto its height as it cleared the fence for a game-winning walk-off homer. I was so elated, I stayed up to watch all the post-game interviews. I think I got three hours of sleep before getting up for work (just like last year).

Despite the win the Series was tied up two games apiece and the Yanks would still have the final two games at the Stadium where supposedly the ghosts of Gehrig, Ruth, Mantle, etc. never let them lose. The New York area media roasted the Yanks for the game. You would think the Series was 3 games to 1 in favor of the Marlins instead of being knotted at two apiece. Fans and the talk shows were all over Aaron Boone, the ALCS hero only a week ago, for fanning with the bases loaded in the eleventh. Many thought Torre was brain-dead for putting Weaver in the eleventh instead of Mariano Rivera. Yankee fans were saying we get to play games 6 and 7 (if it goes that far) at the Stadium and that the team would win, but I seemed to sense a lump in their throat.

Game 5 was on Thursday with a re-match of the game one starters. Once again the Marlins' one-cent piece Brad Penny against the Boss' $$$$$$$. The Yanks would have David Wells to try and fillet the Fish. Yankee fans appeared to be confident as Wells has been one of the best postseason hurlers over the past few years. To me it appeared the Marlins got a break when two of the Yankee All-Stars were not starting. These two, Alfonso Soriano and Jason Giambi had a combined 79 homers for the year. The reason was Soriano was in a long postseason slump and Giambi had an injured knee. I think any pitcher would be very happy not to have to face those two.

The game did not start in a positive manner for the Fish. In the first inning I felt that Zeus was up to his old tricks. With the lead-off man on and no outs, Enrique Wilson, starting in Soriano's place, laid down a sacrifice bunt and Penny butchered it. With two on and no outs the Marlins got out of it with only one run scoring. Wells easily retired the Marlins in the first. Penny then put down the Yanks in the top of the second. The Fish got another break (maybe Zeus was taking a nap) when Wells could not take the mound in the second. His back problems (spasms or whatever) restricted his mobility. This situation was a real delight for a Yankee Hater. Not because he was injured (I never want to see anyone injured) but because of his comments of the previous day. The day before Wells was commenting on how strenuous workouts or any workouts were not necessary for pitchers. Yanks' hurlers Pettitte, Mussina and especially Clemens have intense work out routines. Wells' attitude is completely the opposite. He has his own methods and was saying how successful he has been (200 wins and his postseason stats attest to this). I don't know if his lack of conditioning caused him to leave the game, but it was very ironic happening the day after these comments. I think Boss Steinbrenner must have been livid when Wells could not continue. Anyway, Torre had to figure out who to put in. He or pitching coach Mel Stottlemyre selected their international pick-up Cuban Jose Contreras who had pitched two innings in yesterday's twelve-inning loss and maybe would be tired.

Contreras did not have it. In the bottom of the second the Marlins tied it and had runners on second and third with the pitcher Penny coming up. Not only did the Florida Penny prove his worth on the mound but proceeded to rap a 2-run single giving the Marlins and himself a 3-1 lead. Penny continued to throw goose eggs while his offense gave him another run in the fourth off of the Cuban millionaire. In the fifth inning the Marlins scored two more runs to make the score 6-1. The way Penny was pitching it seemed to be two meaningless runs, but in the end they proved to be the margin of victory. IRod led off with a double. The next batter, Jeff Conine, then hit a scorching grounder down the third base line (it looked like a sure RBI double). It was not to be as third baseman Aaron Boone made a great snag of the shot. IRod took off from second thinking it was going into the left field corner. Boone after catching the ball threw to Soriano's replacement, Enrique Wilson. As soon as Wilson caught Boone's throw he instantly threw to third not being aware that Boone or Jeter would be there to catch his throw. Boone was out of the play and could not get back to third and shortstop Jeter could not get there either. So IRod, who was thought to be a "dead fish" at third, was safe. No one caught it as it hit the wall. Instead of one out and a man on first, the Marlins had runners on second and third. Mike Lowell then hit a short fly to center that Bernie Williams had to field on a hop. Conine had a good read on the ball and even though not a fast runner scored behind IRod.

Penny gave up a run in the seventh to make it 6-2. I was hoping that Zeus would not wake up, but in the ninth he seemed to be opening up his eyes. Jason Giambi, benched because of his bad knee, hit a homer off of a Marlin reliever making the score 6-3. The Yanks got another run and had a runner on second with one out and Bernie Williams up (he already homered twice in the Series). As Bernie hit the ball my thoughts went to Zeus as it looked like a game-tying homer. Luckily the Marlin stadium dimensions are deeper then most of the other stadiums and the ball was caught in deep right field. Matsui was the Yanks' last hope. He hit a hard one-hopper that the National League Gold Glove first baseman Derrek Lee made an excellent play on to end the game 6-4. The Marlins won and I said, "Hey Mr. Steinbrenner, a PENNY for your thoughts".

The Series was going back to the Stadium. Being down 3 games to 2, Yankees fans and their media seemed to show a false sense of confidence. They had their ace Andy Pettitte ready to go while the Marlins starter was not yet decided according to the media. But the 72-year old Marlin skipper Jack McKeon knew he was going with Josh Beckett, who pitched so well in game 3. Beckett would be going on three days rest. Most of the media said this was a bad move as in recent times in big games, pitchers throwing on three days rest recorded 3 wins and 20 losses. However, McKeon is used to the old days when Gibson in '64 and Koufax in '65 won game 7's with only two days rest.

Game 6 started and for four innings both Pettitte and Beckett were outstanding. But in the fifth Pettitte ran into problems. After two were out, game 4 hero Gonzalez singled followed by a single by Pierre. Castillo was next and he was having a bad Series. The Yanks' hurlers fed him a steady diet of breaking balls and he couldn't handle them. However, this time he hung in there, fouled off some, and then hit a single to right. With two outs, Gonzalez was sent home. The throw from right fielder Karim Garcia was up the line a little but still it appeared Posada would tag him out. But Gonzalez made one of the most exciting and clever slides that I've seen in all my 50 years of watching the World Series. He slid by the plate reaching out and slapping the plate making Posada miss him. Marlins were up 1-0.

In the bottom of the fifth the Yanks put the tying run on second with one out, but Soriano popped up and Jeter fanned. Possibly Jeter took out to the field his failure at the plate because he made an error on a ball hit by Conine. Maybe this unnerved Pettitte as he walked Lowell. With two on and no outs Lee bunted, but it was a lousy bunt back to Pettitte. He had Conine out by 20 feet at third but he didn't hear Posada telling him to throw to third and instead threw to first. The botched bunt worked, and the Marlins made it 2-0 when Juan Encarnacion hit a sac-fly. Beckett stayed tough on the mound thwarting Yanks' chances. In the seventh Posada led off with a double but was left there. In the eighth Soriano led off with a single. Jeter then flew out. Soriano had 35 stolen bases for the season but being down by two runs he didn't try, especially against the IRod cannon. Nick Johnson then hit a hard grounder. At first I thought it was going into center for a hit, instead Castillo snared it and turned it into a double play.

Beckett seemed to be getting a little gassed in the ninth. Not wanting anyone on base maybe he put the ball too much over the plate as both Williams and Godzilla flew out to deep left field. Posada then grounded out to Beckett, who tagged him to end the game and give the Series to the Marlins 4 games to 2.

Ironically the stats do not tell the story. The Yanks out hit the Fish .261 to .232, outscored them 21 – 17, and had a better ERA 2.33 to 3.21. Beckett was named MVP of the Series which was OK with me, but I thought Brad Penny, with his two victories should have at least shared it, like Schilling and Johnson of the 2001 Diamondbacks.

This is my Zeus theory on this year's Series. Since Zeus has an eye for the women, one possibly caught his eye. After assuring the Yanks beat the Rest Sox in the ALCS, Zeus was to take care of business on Earth, so he delegated the World Series to his brother Poseidon, God of the Sea. No way was Poseidon going to let the Fish lose.

2003
The Yankee Shirt

On Christmas Day, Mike and Chris came over in the morning and Josephine and I joined them in opening gifts. We took turns opening them.

When my turn came, I opened the box and was disgusted when I saw that evil interlocking NY on a pinstriped shirt. I only had the box opened an eighth of the way before I closed it saying, "Right in the garbage with this".

My sons yelled at me "No, take it out". With a huge scowl on my face I re-opened the box and took out the shirt. I turned it to look at the back of it and fell over laughing.

There was no number, but there was an embroidered word - "ZEUS".

2004
Curse the of REVERSE

(Editor's Note: This is the longest Chapter. With the events of this year, I think you would be disappointed if my dad did not take advantage of this opportunity).

As the title suggests this year was such that the Yankees good fortune went into REVERSE quicker than you could say George Steinbrenner (well maybe not that fast).

The Boss must have been livid after last year's World Series loss to the Marlins – a team with less than a third of the Yankee payroll. Three years and no World Series championship - things had to change. This year he would continue his quest to have more stars than Old Glory.

Steinbrenner's first order of business was to trade for Curt Schilling of the Arizona Diamondbacks who was only 8-9 (because of a lack of run support) but had a 2.95 ERA which was fifth in the NL. However, Curt, who had a no-trade clause in his contract, gave George a set back. It was about 230 years ago when shillings gave a guy named George a set back in Boston. As I recall from my American history classes, King George III of England in 1773 raised the tax on tea for their American colonists. This would cause them to pay more shillings (a British monetary unit) for their tea. In a form of protest the colonists dressed as Indians (no, they weren't from Cleveland), boarded the English ships, and literally tossed the tea into the Boston Harbor. And now Curt Schilling figuratively tossed the "King" George of baseball into the Boston Harbor, as he OK'd a trade to the Boston Red Sox. Curt probably thought his place in baseball history would be better served if he could deliver the Boston Red Sox their first World Series Championship in 86 years, rather than just being another cog in the Yankee machine.

The reason "King" George went after Schilling so fervently was that the Yankee pitching staff of 2003 was pretty much depleted. They had to replace Rocket Clemens (retired) and Andy Pettitte and David Wells (both not re-signed) – they were a combined 53-24 last year. To replace them, the Boss got the Dodgers' Kevin Brown (14 – 9, 2.39 ERA second in the NL in '03) for $16 million and Javier Vazquez from Montreal for $9 million. In 2003 Vazquez was 13 – 12 with the Expos (not a quality team) and was considered a rising star. Also, they were counting on Jon Lieber to return to his 20-game win form of 2001 with the Cubs after having Tommy John surgery. They also signed free agent reliever Tom "Flash" Gordon primarily to be a set-up man for Mariano Rivera.

The Pinstripers' major offensive acquisition was perennial NL All-Star slugger Gary Sheffield (.330, 39 homers, 132 RBIs for the Braves last year) for right field. The Yankee brass was quite concerned about the hated Red Sox trading for 2003 AL MVP Alex Rodriguez (ARod). It appeared that the Red Sox line-up would have ARod at short and the Chisox All-Star Magglio Ordonez in left; Nomar Garciaparra would go to Chicago and Manny Ramirez to Texas. The ARod deal was agreed upon by the teams but the Player's Association would not approve to restructure his contract. Most Yankee haters were upset, but I wasn't, after all Manny and Nomar were potential Cooperstowners.

A strange turn of events soon took place to dishearten the country's Yankee haters. Aaron Boone, of the famous '03 playoff home run, injured his ankle playing in a pick-up basketball game and would be out for the season. The Yanks needed a third baseman. The Yankee GM contacted Texas - would ARod consider playing third base as the Yankee Captain Derek Jeter was at short? ARod wanted a ring so he said OK. ARod was traded for the Yankee All-Star second baseman Alfonso Soriano. As the Yankee Hater I was somewhat annoyed by this deal primarily because of what it did to Boston. But I always considered Soriano an offensive threat, so I didn't think the deal was all that one sided. Soriano was one of the reasons the Rangers improved so dramatically this year, winning 89 games and finishing three games out, as he batted .280 with 28 homers and 91 RBIs and was the AL All-Star second baseman.

As far as rooting for the Mets, their pre-season acquisitions were Mike Cameron, the Mariners' center fielder and shortstop Kaz

Matsui, a star in Japan. They went after Vladimir Guerrero of Montreal, but did not meet the Anaheim Angels offer because of a back injury he had during the year (hey, is he possibly related to the Hutmakers?). Vlad returned from that injury and pounded the ball until the season ended. All Vlad did this year was to become AL MVP (.337, 39 homers, 126 RBIs). He seemed to get the big hit game after game down the stretch, and in the last six games of the season he batted .467 (14 for 30) with 6 homers and 11 RBIs as the Angels overtook the A's to win the AL West by one game. The Mets somehow stayed in the NL East race until the All-Star Game, and then they collapsed. There was only one thing that went right for the Mets. After the All-Star game they called up their minor league All-Star third baseman that was knocking the cover off the ball for their Tidewater Triple A minor league team. He was David Wright and he brought his bat with him (.293, 14 homers, 40 RBIs in 69 games for the Mets) to the Majors.

In the NL the teams in the Central Division appeared the strongest. St. Louis easily won the division despite their pre-season pick of finishing third. They had the most feared line-up in baseball as they had the Majors' best record, 105-57. The middle of the batting order put up awesome numbers – first baseman Albert Pujols (.331, 46 homers, 123 RBIs), third baseman Scott Rolen (.314, 34 homers, 124 RBIs), and probably the all-time Web Gem leader on ESPN center fielder Jim Edmonds (.301, 42 homers, 111 RBIs). Edmonds won his seventh Gold Glove in eight years – he was injured in '99 the year he wasn't selected. Table setters second baseman Tony Womack (.307, 91 runs) and shortstop Edgar Renteria (.287, 84 runs) got on for the big boppers. If that wasn't enough, at the trading deadline they picked up .315 lifetime hitter Larry Walker from the Colorado Rockies. He had 11 homers in 44 games as a Red Bird. Benefiting from this offense were Jeff Suppan (16 wins), and Jason Marquis, Matt Morris and Chris Carpenter who all posted 15 wins. Carpenter may have been their best at 15-5 with a 3.46 ERA but he was shut down as the end of the season approached and was shelved for any postseason action. Jason Isringhausen had 4 wins and 47 saves out of the 'pen.

The Cubs looked like the favorite when they added future Famer Greg Maddux to join Mark Prior and Kerry Wood on the mound. He didn't disappoint as he won his 300th game, extended his consecutive year streak of 15 or more wins to 15 years, and he went

16-11. But Prior and Wood had injuries and only combined for a 14-13 slate. The Cubs' offense only sputtered a bit when Sosa sneezed injuring his back – in 126 games he parked 35 homers driving in 80 runs. Third baseman Aramis Ramirez (.318, 36 homers, 103 RBIs), outfielder Moises Alou (.293, 39 homers, 105 RBIs) and first baseman Derrek Lee (32 homers, 98 RBIs) all picked it up a notch as it looked like the Cubs would take the NL Wild Card coming down the stretch. But then the Billy Goat hex surfaced as the Cubs had some strange losses as their bullpen had a meltdown, and the batters could not get a clutch hit. Even the fading Mets beat them twice in the last week of the season.

The Houston Astros were the other NL favorite because of last year's Yankees – Rocket Clemens and Andy Pettitte. When the Yanks showed a lack of respect (so what else is new?) concerning keeping Pettitte, he signed with his hometown Astros, and then convinced fellow Texan, the Rocket, to unretire. Pettitte was hurt most of the year going 6-4, but the Rocket continued his hobby of collecting Cy Young awards (his seventh) going 18-4 with a 2.98 ERA. His mound partner Roy Oswalt was the only NL 20-game winner at 20-10. In the 'pen Brad Lidge became one of the Majors' top firemen with 6 wins, 29 saves and a 1.90 ERA. Again the 'Stros' attack was B'zzzzz (the Killer Bees) Lance Berkman (.316, 30 homers, 106 RBIs), Jeff Bagwell (27 homers, 89 RBIs), Craig Biggio (24 homers, 100 runs), and mid-season acquisition Carlos Beltran (23 homers, 53 RBIs in 90 games). A non-B, Jeff Kent (.289, 27 homers, 107 RBIs) added more buzz to the attack. Killer Bees Inc. was going nowhere at the mid-season point hovering around the .500 mark so Houston fired manager Jimy Williams and hired Phil Garner. Houston then took off like an Astro-naut, going 36-10 down the stretch to take the NL Wild Card.

The Braves had an easy time in taking the NL East, again, for the 13th year in a row. J.D. Drew finally had an injury-free year showing his talent (.318, 31 homers, 91 RBIs), and the Jones guys Andruw (29 homers, 91 RBIs) and Chipper (30 homers, 96 RBIs) provided their usual power. John Smoltz was the Braves' chief on the mound with a 2.76 ERA and 44 saves. Bobby Cox was voted NL Manager of the Year.

In the NL West the Dodgers held off the Giants and even cost them the Wild Card spot in the final weekend. In the dramatic next to last game of the season, LA scored seven runs in the ninth inning to win 7-3 (Steve Finley's Grand Slam capped the scoring) to finish off their long time rival. Barry Bonds again led the San Fran team with another Giant year. He was selected as NL MVP for the fourth straight year and seventh overall. (He collects these awards like Roger Clemens collects Cy Young Awards. Hey, but Roger is one up on him as he has an MVP trophy to go with his seven Cy Young Awards. Maybe next year Barry will win the Cy Young Award). Bonds had an incredible Major League record 232 walks to go with his 45 homers, 101 RBIs and 129 runs scored while leading the league in batting (.362), on base % (.609, a Major League record) and slugging % (.812). Like Bonds, Adrian Beltre carried the Dodgers' offense leading the NL with 48 homers tying Mike Schmidt's home run record for third baseman. He also batted .334 driving home 121 runs. He was the NL runner-up MVP. Shawn Green helped him with 28 homers and 86 RBIs and Finley cracked 13 homers in a third of the season after being acquired from the D'backs. The other Dodger marquee player was again lights out reliever Eric Gagne – 2.19 ERA, 44 saves.

On the issue of Barry being better than the Bambino - Those in support of Barry say that the Babe only was selected MVP once (1923) while Barry has seven (and is still not done). There is a reason for this that some are not aware of. During Ruth's time there were no MVP selections until 1922, (In 1920 Ruth's 54 homers were more than every other Major League team except the Phillies) plus the American League had a rule that a player was limited to only one MVP award, thus Ruth was not eligible for it after he won it in 1923. Looking back at the records of that era it is conceivable that the Babe could have been MVP from seven to ten times. Also if there was a Cy Young Award in his day, Ruth would of most likely won it in 1916 (23-12, leading the AL with 9 shutouts and a 1.75 ERA). NEWSFLASH – In December Barry Bonds admitted to possibly using steroids, although he admits if he did, he did it unknowingly. This should now put to rest any comparisons of him to the Babe or Hammerin' Hank.

As stated earlier, Anaheim rolled down the stretch to nose out Oakland as their three aces Barry Zito, Tim Hudson and Mark Mulder all failed in September. The Angels made their stretch run without their number two run producer Jose Guillen (.294, 27 homers, 104 RBIs) – he was suspended for the rest of the season including postseason (if they made it) by manager Mike Scioscia on

September 25 for having a tirade after being taken out for a pinch-runner – and supposedly that was the straw that broke the Angels' wings as this was supposedly one of several of his attitude episodes. In the AL Central, the division that didn't have a dominant representative since the 1997 Indians, the Minnesota Twins won easily with only two batters with 80 RBIs – Torii Hunter (81) and Jacques Jones (80). The Twins did have the Cy Young winner Johan Santana (20-6, 13 in a row after the All-Star game and an AL best 2.61 ERA) and a relief ace Joe Nathan (44 saves, 1.62 ERA and fifth in the Cy Young voting).

The AL East was again hotly contested by the Yanks and Red Sox. They met early in the season and Boston took five of six as the Yanks started out at 8-11. Captain Derek Jeter had the worst start of his career. There was some speculation that he was intimidated by playing along side his former shortstop rival ARod who was at third. Jeter had an unheard of 0 for 32 streak and was hitting under the Mendoza line (.200) for much of the early part of the season. Yankee haters were in their glory, but I knew it was only a matter of time before he'd get it together. Jeter turned it around becoming again one of the most feared lead-off men in the game as he finished strong (.291, 23 homers, 111 runs).

The Bombers earned their nickname and led the AL with 242 homers (two more than their '61 M & M team). They had five position players on the AL All-Star team. Joining Jeter were MVP runner-up Sheffield (.290, 36 homers, 121 RBIs), ARod (.286, 36 homers, 106 RBIs), Godzilla Matsui (.298, 31 homers, 108 RBIs), and Jason Giambi, who was an undeserving pick as his stats showed only .208, 12 homers, 40 RBIs in about half the season. Giambi was an enigma as he picked up a parasite, possibly in the opening series in Japan (along with Kevin Brown), then had a benign tumor, plus his name was mentioned whenever news stories came out with regards to steroids. BULLETIN: The enigma was solved as in December leaks from grand jury transcripts showed Giambi admitted to using steroids.

Their non-All-Stars also came through with good years. Jorge Posada, again one of the League's top hitting catchers, had 21 homers driving in 81 runs, and Bernie Williams cracked 22 homers scoring 105 runs. Miguel Cairo did a fine job replacing Soriano at second base batting .292. Also, role players Tony Clark (15 homers) and Ruben Sierra (17 homers) kept opposing pitchers jittery.

The Yanks had an unusual mound corps. They were the first team to win over 100 games and not have a pitcher with 15 victories. Jon Lieber (14-8), All-Star Javier Vazquez (14-10), Mike Mussina (12-9) and Kevin Brown (10-6) were their double digit winners. Their former old reliable Orlando Hernandez (El Duque) was picked up in mid-season after all the other teams passed on him and all he did was be their best pitcher down the stretch going 8-2. All-Star middle man Tom Gordon was 9-4 with 4 saves and a 2.21 ERA in 80 games. Naturally, the best closer ever, Mariano Rivera won 4, saved 53, had a 1.94 ERA, and finished third in the Cy Young voting. However the Red Sox weren't afraid of him, having beaten him twice during the season.

You know all year I heard about all the comeback Yankee victories (over 60 of them). Well, you don't have to be a Sherlock Holmes to figure out if your offense is an AL All-Star line-up, and you have Flash Gordon and Mariano in the 'pen, it just might be a little bit easier to stage a come from behind victory.

The Red Sox were a strange cast of characters – much like the 1993 pennant winning Phillies – who also had Curt Schilling as their ace. Schilling was the Cy Young runner-up leading the AL with 21 wins and was second in ERA (3.26). He took over as leader of the Red Sox mound's men passing Pedro Martinez. Pedro was still one of the league's top pitchers at 16-9, but he just couldn't beat the Yanks; in fact after losing to them in September, he was quoted as saying "I guess the Yankees are my daddy". The New York media had a ball with that one. The Bosox had three other double digit winners – Derek Lowe 14-12, knuckler Tim Wakefield 12-10, and Bronson Arroyo 10-9. Newly acquired fireman Keith Foulke (5 wins, 32 saves, 2.17 ERA) supplied them the missing piece from last year's team.

The Red Sox line-up was a self-proclaimed "bunch of idiots". Their spark was ignited by Johnny Damon, whose appearance was such that he could have been a model for the cover of Caveman Monthly. He showed he could use the club, rivaling Jeter as the best lead-off man in the game (.304, 20 homers, 94 RBIs, 123 runs). The two slot probably had the most unique one in baseball history in Mark Bellhorn. He had more missed swings with the bat then boxers of the '60 & '70's had trying to hit Ali. He went to the plate 265 times without making contact (177 Ks and 88 BB's). However, he had a .373 on base %, 18 homers, 82 RBIs and scored 93 runs. Their heavy hitters were Manny Ramirez (.308, league leading 43 homers, 130 RBIs) and David "Papi" Ortiz (.301, 41 homers, 139 RBIs – second in the AL to the Orioles' Miguel Tejada's 150). Any team in baseball could have had Manny, as the Bosox put him on waivers to reduce their payroll (lucky for them there were no takers). Papi, to me anyway, is a Willie "Pops" Stargell clone in build and in his terrifying hitting style. Catcher Jason Varitek (.296, 18 homers, 73 RBIs) and Kevin Millar (.297, 18 homers, 74 RBIs) were other productive "idiots".

In one of the Yankee/Red Sox games (July 1) Derek Jeter was out-playing his Bosox rival Nomar Garciaparra. It was quite easy to do so as Nomar was sitting this one out nursing his oft injured ankle, while Jeter went swan diving into the stands headfirst after he made a running catch and then emerged from the stands with a bruised and bloodied face. The Yanks won in extra innings while the TV cameras kept showing Nomar sitting in the dugout. Nomar despite his .321 average had to go. The Red Sox were involved in a three team deal at the trading deadline – the Cubs got Nomar, while Boston got Orlando Cabrera from the Expos, a .246 hitter with Gold Glove ability. For Boston he retained his fielding prowess while finding a batting stroke (.294, 31 RBIs in 59 games).

The Red Sox and Yanks met 19 times with Boston holding an 11-8 edge even though the Yankee payroll was $60 million or so higher. They went at each other pretty hard and on July 24 an old fashioned rumble broke out when Arroyo hit ARod with an inside pitch. ARod took exception to this and was mouthing off to Arroyo when Varitek stepped in to look out for his pitcher. At this point ARod went after Varitek - not very bright going after someone with a mask and equipment on - and the melee ensued. After play resumed the Red Sox overcame a 9-4 deficit to eventually win 11-10 on a ninth inning homer by Bill Mueller off of Mariano Rivera. This incident and game was the spark that turned around the season for Boston, who up to this point was playing a rather lethargic brand of ball. The Crimson Hose then took the next one from the Yanks and went on to play at a .700 clip the rest of the year, including winning 20 out of 22 games down the stretch. Although the Red Sox couldn't catch the Yanks, who won the AL East (101-61), they did have the second best record in the AL (98-64) to capture the Wild Card spot.

On the home front my son Mike, applied for a Dean's position at Polytechnic University in Brooklyn. I informed him that Yankee fans aren't welcome in Brooklyn. He laughed saying the Dodgers left almost fifty years ago. I told him it doesn't matter they still don't especially care for the Yanks. I told Mike that "Since you also pull for the Mets – just tell anyone that asks about your baseball affiliation that you root for the Mets – omit your Yankee interests". In any event I guess the baseball question didn't come up as Mike got the Dean position in Brooklyn. To celebrate he recruited his brother for another trip to Europe. I can't understand it – again I wasn't invited to join them.

Mike had vacation time to use from St. John's, so he suggested going to a day game in Baltimore as both of us always wanted to see Camden Yards at Oriole Park (about a 200 mile trip from central Jersey). We left early on August 9, a Monday. We arrived early enough to see everything and ate lunch at Boog Powell's place in the right field walk way. We really didn't care who won, we were there to see the stadium. Baltimore beat Texas 7-3 as Melvin Mora banged out two homers and Larry Bigbie one. Alfonso Soriano and Dave Dellucci cracked homers for the Rangers. We had great seats behind the dugout and we called Chris who was working on Wall Street telling him what a beautiful day we were having. Mike noticed on the scoreboard that there was only a few games scheduled and that one of them was the Colorado Rockies at Philadelphia. Mike and I decided to explore the possibility on stopping in Philadelphia on the drive home (it's on the way) and see Citizen Park, the Phils' new stadium. We called Josephine to check on the time. The game was at seven so we would give it a shot.

We arrived at Citizen Park just before six so we had time to purchase tickets and check out the stadium and have some of them famous Philly cheesesteaks in the concourse. As the game started we called Chris again who was still at work. Somehow he didn't think it was fair – Mike and I see a doubleheader in two different cities, Baltimore and Philadelphia, while he's working. Josephine thought we were crazy (hey, but she always does). The Colorado Rockies beat the Phils 4-2 as Vinny Castilla drove in two of his league leading 131 RBIs in the eighth inning breaking up a 2-2 tie. It was a great day and night for Mike and me.

Some of the season's major highlights were Junior Griffey getting his 500th home run, the Big Unit Randy Johnson tossing a perfect game, Barry Bonds joining the Hammer and Babe in the 700 home run club, and Ichiro Suzuki breaking the Major League record for hits in season held by George Sisler (257 in 1920). Randy and Junior had hard-luck seasons. Junior appeared to be over his injury jinx (he missed 234 games over the past three years) as he belted 20 homers at the season's mid-point, but then that jinx popped up again as he got injured ending his season – his home run total is now at 501. The Big Unit led the NL in Ks (290) and was second in ERA (2.60). His record was 16-14 for the worst team in baseball – the Arizona Diamondbacks (51-111). However he was the runner-up for the NL Cy Young Award despite being only two games over .500. The Yanks tried to get Randy at the trading deadline but their minor league prospects weren't talented enough to sway the D'backs to make the trade. It was Johnson's fault, as he exercised his no-trade clause stating he'd only accept a trade to the Yanks. I was elated when Johnson stayed in Arizona. Barry finished the year with 703 homers, but some of the luster was taken away by his name cropping up whenever the use of steroids situation surfaced in the news.

I think though that Ichiro breaking Sisler's record of 257 in 1920 was the top single achievement this year. And literally that's what it was (a singles record) as he also set a singles record (225). Ichiro stroked 262 hits surpassing Sisler's record by five. One thing this accomplishment did was bring Sisler's name to the forefront. When people heard of Sisler they may have been thinking "Yeah, the guy that won the pennant for the Phillies in 1950 with a pennant winning homer in the tenth inning of the season's final game" – no that was George's son Dick. Ichiro is a great table setter hitter and led the AL with a .372 average but he's not in George Sisler's class as a batter. Sisler is the St. Louis Browns' all-time best player making the Hall of Fame in its fourth year of selections in 1939 (overall he was the sixth position player elected to the Hall). His lifetime average was .340. In 1920, the year he set the hit record, he led the AL in batting (.407 - 124 points higher than the league average) and was second to the Babe in homers (19) and RBIs (122). Sisler, like Ichiro, had great athleticism leading the AL in stolen bases four times – plus he came up as a pitcher (like Ruth and Musial) – he was 4-4 with a 2.83 ERA in his rookie year (1915) and in a memorable game out dueled the "Big Train" Walter Johnson in a 2-1 nail biter. He was then moved back to first base full-time and began his Hall of Fame career. He was selected AL MVP in 1922 when he batted .420.

There was one other highlight that made Yankee haters all over the USA happy (even if it was only for one day). On August 31 Cleveland routed the Yankees 22-0 - it was the Pinstripers' all-time worst loss.

In the NL Division playoffs, St. Louis took the Dodgers in four games as Renteria (.455, 4 RBIs), and Pujols and Walker each hit two homers while batting .333. The Cardinal pitching held Adrian Beltre to four singles. In the other NL series, the sound was B'zzzzz as the Houston Killer Bees stung the Atlanta pitchers. Beltran had one of baseball's best ever playoffs (.455, 10 for 22, 4 homers, 9 RBIs and 9 runs). Berkman (.409), Biggio (.400) and Bagwell (.318, 2 homers, 5 RBIs) provided the rest of the stinging bats. The Rocket and Oswalt each posted a win. Despite this, the Braves took the Astros to five games behind the hitting of Andruw Jones (.526, 10 for 19, 2 homers, 5 RBIs) and Rafael Furcal (.381, 2 homers, 4 RBIs). Houston routed Atlanta 12-3 in the deciding game to win their first ever postseason series.

In the AL Division series Boston took the first two games from Anaheim behind Schilling and Pedro (there was no Rally Monkey or Jose Guillen), and was on the verge to sweep the Angels as they led 6-1 in the eighth inning. The Angels then tied it with a five run inning capped by Vlad Guerrero's Grand Slam. However, in the tenth with two outs Papi Ortiz launched a 2-run shot over the Green Monster that put the Red Sox into the ALCS. Papi hit .545 (6 for 11) while Caveman Damon (.467, 7 for 15) and Manny (.385, homer, 7 RBIs) were the other Red Sox sockers. Darin Erstad (.500, 5 for 10) and Troy Glaus (.364, a pair of doubles and homers) both hit well in the losing cause for Anaheim.

In the other AL Division playoff the Yanks faced off against the AL's usual sacrificial lamb, the Central Division winner, the Minnesota Twins. The Twins took the first game 2-0 behind the AL's best pitcher Johan Santana. The Yankee batters helped out the Twin pitchers by hitting into five double plays. The second game was attended by my son Chris (he was in the upper deck behind home plate). The Yanks had the game well in hand, 5-3, when the Twins tied it in the eighth off of Rivera. Corey Koskie tied it with a ground-rule double (if the ball stayed in play another run would have scored). As it was there was one out with runners on second and third. The Twins manager Ron Gardenhire elected to let Jason Kubel hit (he did bat .300, but in only 60 at bats), instead of sending up Lew Ford who hit .299 for the year. Kubel was K'd and the game went into extra innings. In the top of the twelfth I called Chris on his cell phone. We each claimed the other team was lucky. The time of the call was around midnight. As I hung up the phone I almost dropped it as I watched Torii Hunter smack a homer to put the Twins up 6-5, and I was full of elation. In the bottom of the inning Gardenhire left his relief ace Joe Nathan in there even though it would be his longest stint of the year (he already threw two scoreless innings). After getting one out, he walked Cairo and Jeter, which was followed by an ARod double that tied it at six. Jeter then scored the winning run on a sac-fly by Sheffield. Chris called me when he arrived home at 1:30 in the morning – he was full of elation.

Kevin Brown started game 3. He appeared to be recovered from his fractured wrist that he injured when he angrily, and not very intelligently, punched a wall after a poor performance in the beginning of September resulting in him missing three weeks. He gave up one run in six innings as the Yanks won 8-4. Santana started the next game and the Twins had a 5-1 lead in the eight – and it looked like the series would go to a decisive fifth game. But it all unraveled for Minnesota in the eighth as the Yanks tied it with Sierra's 3-run titanic homer being the big blow. The Yanks won it in the eleventh, 6-5, when ARod doubled, stole third and scored on a sac-fly – finally he was starting to come through in the clutch. For the losing Twins, Mike Cuddyer (.467, 7 for 15) and Torii Hunter (.353) led the offense, while Santana was 1-0 with a 0.75 ERA in twelve innings.

It looked like the Yanks had an easy time winning this series 3 game to 1, but I knew that wasn't true since Minnesota lost two games in extra innings that they probably should have won. I thought my 'Zeus Wears Pinstripes' theory had something to do with the outcome of this series. My sons told me to get real and not to be a bad sport – me and my Zeus stuff.

I read all about the Yanks back-slapping each other – how great ARod was, how Sierra comes through the whole year, blah, blah, blah, etc. ARod hit .421 (8 for 19) and Godzilla Matsui had a monster series (.412) while Captain Jeter (.316, homer, 4 RBIs) steered the Enterprise. Mariano had a zero ERA in over five innings.

The Yanks and Red Sox would meet each other again in the ALCS. How could it possibly be better than last year's series won by Aaron Boone's game seven extra inning homer?

I'll go over the NLCS first. It was an exciting affair. Naturally I was pulling for St. Louis. The Cardinals won the first two at home, but Houston took the next three at their home. Game four was dramatic as Beltran broke a 5-5 tie with an eighth inning homer. He homered in a record five straight postseason games and tied another record by homering in the first four games of a postseason series. In game 5 Brandon Backe had a no-hitter until Womack singled in the sixth. It was the Cards only hit in the game. Jeff Kent won the game for the 'Stros with a 3-run walk-off homer. Jim Edmonds countered that in the sixth game with a twelfth inning walk-off homer to deadlock the series at three apiece. In the deciding game the Rocket Clemens had a 2-1 lead in the sixth when Pujols doubled in a run to tie it and Rolen then lined a 2-run homer. The Cards won 5-2 to take the NLCS.

Houston had its stars – Berkman (.292, 3 homers, 9 RBIs), Kent (3 homers, 7 RBIs) and Beltran (.417, 10 for 24, 4 homers, 5 RBIs). Beltran was to be a free agent and the NY media has the Yanks opening their vaults to acquire him. (He would be heading to NY in 2005 as he did sign a lucrative contract - with the Mets). Three years ago I told people the Mets should do whatever to get him from the KC Royals - now they have him. For the two playoff series Beltran was 20 for 46 (.435) with 8 homers and 14 RBIs in 12 games. On the mound Brad Lidge won a game had two saves and a zero ERA in eight innings of relief.

The Cards' Pujols even out did Beltran hitting .500 (14 for 28) with 4 homers and 9 RBIs (sorry Boss, the Cards' have him signed for a few more years). Rolen shook his 1 for 12 funk against LA and hit .310 with 3 homers and 6 RBIs. Edmonds had 2 homers and 7 RBIs and Walker chipped in with 2 homers and 5 RBIs.

The ALCS overshadowed the NLCS simply because it was the Red Sox against the Yankees. The media was having a blast with the Curse of the Bambino, and the Yankee fans with their mocking chants of "1918" (the Red Sox last World Series Championship). It made good copy. Hey there's other curses – the city of Chicago with two teams haven't had a World Series winner since the White Sox in 1917 – the White Sox must have a Shoeless Joe Jackson/Black

Sox curse of 1919 (when they threw the Series) and we know of the Cubs Billy Goat Hex.

I had some optimism that the Red Sox could beat the Yanks for three reasons. First was that the Las Vegas people made Boston the favorite as the odds-makers don't care about curses; secondly, the New England Patriots won the Super Bowl and last year the state of Florida won the Super Bowl (Tampa Bay) and World Series (Marlins) so this year its Massachusetts turn to win both; and thirdly, the Yanks hired Don Mattingly as its batting coach this year and it seems there just may be a Mattingly Curse, as his fingers are ring-less (baseball wise, anyway).

Game 1 had Schilling versus Mussina. A problem with Schilling's ankle tendon, which was aggravated in the Division series against Anaheim, made Curt ineffective. The Yanks pounded him and had an 8-0 lead. Mussina had a perfect game for six innings, then the Red Sox bats erupted and they just missed tying it when an Ortiz shot just missed being a homer, hitting the top of the wall (I think Matsui had a shot at catching it). Papi wound up with a triple. Rivera came to the rescue in a heroic way. He just returned from a funeral in Panama as two of his wife's relatives were killed in an accident at his home. He quelled the Bosox uprising as the Yanks won 10-7. The Red Sox lost the game, and maybe their ace, Schilling. For Game 2 Pedro was facing Lieber. Yankee Stadium was a full blown chorus of "Who's your daddy?" My son Chris was there and was part of the chorus (I didn't know he could sing). Pedro pitched well but gave up a 2-run homer to John Olerud (Giambi's replacement) in the sixth. But the usual good hitting of the "idiot" Bosox line-up could not do anything with Lieber, who left in the eighth only having given up one run, three hits and a walk. Flash Gordon and Mariano kept the Red Sox scoreless in the final two innings. The Yanks won 3-1 and beat the two Bosox aces. The Red Sox were glad they were going back to Fenway.

My son Chris left me a phone message, "Who's your daddy?" I returned this call stating "I know who my daddy is and I know who your daddy is – and don't you forget it, boy". His response was his mockingly patented laugh that he inherited from his mother.

In the third game it was Arroyo and Brown. This game looked like the batters for both teams were hitting off of a tee instead of hitting a thrown ball. The score was tied at six after three innings. The Sox could have taken the lead 7-6 in the third, but Bill Mueller was thrown out at the plate. In the fourth the Yanks put up a five spot to lead 11-6. The final was 19-8. The Yanks had 22 hits – Godzilla (5 for 5, 5 RBIs, 5 runs), Sheffield (4 hits, 4 RBIs), Bernie (4 hits, 3 RBIs), and ARod (3 hits, 3 RBIs, 5 runs) all were hitting shots like they had thunderbolts in their bats. The Sox 8 runs and 15 hits are usually enough to win most games but for this game it was dwarfed by the explosion of the "Pinstriped" bats. Caveman Damon who stated before the ALCS began that the Sox were the better team admitted now it doesn't look good unless we play four very good games – No duh! Who says they're idiots???

The Yanks were up three games to none and only twice in the history of the major sports has a team come back from that kind of deficit to win four in a row and that was in the National Hockey League - a sport I know little about.

The next day was Sunday and Josephine and I were taking her sister Mickey (Michelina) and her husband Lou to the St. Gerard feast at St. Lucy's church in Newark, NJ. Mickey is like a second mother to Josephine as she was married before Josephine was born (they're 21 years apart). Lou, like my dad, was four years old the last time the Red Sox won the Series. He is 90 years old and grew up rooting for the Babe, Gehrig, DiMaggio, Mantle, etc. Growing up in Newark maybe he even sat next to my mom at some of them Newark Bear games back in the late '30's. (By the way, St. Lucy's is in the vicinity of Sacred Heart Cathedral where Josephine and I said our "I Do's" back in 1968 – she didn't appear too enthralled when we drove past it).

While we were at the church service, I was silently saying "Lord, I know you have a lot more to do than determine who wins a baseball game but how about the Red Sox winning a couple of games." Hey, the Yanks have Zeus on their side.

Prior to this ALCS most of the media was saying it was Boston's year – now down 0-3 they naturally said it was over as never has a baseball team come back from that kind of deficit. In Yankeeland this series was over – they were probably more concerned about seeing who they'll be playing next – St. Louis or Houston. Plus, how could the Sox skipper Terry Francona match-up against the four-time Series winner Joe Torre, who has been known to make better moves than chess player Bobby Fischer. The Yankee players completely thought it was in the bag and in a comment he denied making (he said he was misquoted), Gary Sheffield stated the Sox were a walking disaster - a bunch of characters.

Derek Lowe was hoping to keep the Sox alive against former Yank postseason star El Duque Hernandez. ARod still had a thunderbolt in his bat as he gave the Yanks a quick lead in the third with a 2-run homer. El Duque lost his control in the fifth as two walks, an RBI hit by Cabrera, another walk, and a 2-RBI hit by Ortiz put the Sox up 3-2. However, the Yanks retook the lead in the top of the sixth on a Godzilla triple, an RBI hit by Bernie, a walk, and hits by Sierra and Tony Clark. The Yanks were up 4-3 and there it stood until the ninth with Mariano needing only three outs for the Yankee sweep and keep the Curse alive. But wait, Mariano uncharacteristically walked the lead-off batter Millar. Speedster Dave Roberts pinch-ran and promptly stole second. Bill Mueller singled to center easily scoring Roberts to tie it at four apiece. From Connecticut to Maine there was one big SIGH of relief.

The scored stayed at four apiece until the bottom of the twelfth. Bosox relievers (Foulke, Alan Embree and Curtis Leskanic) kept the Yanks scoreless for 5 2/3 innings as their bats seemed to lose their thunderbolts. In the bottom of the twelfth Manny led off with a single, Ortiz, the hero for the Division series, came up and nailed a pitch from Paul Quantrill sending it into the old Yankee bullpen in right field for a walk-off 6-4 Red Sox win. This must have really rankled the Boss. Last year he wanted his GM Brian Cashman to get Papi Ortiz when Minnesota didn't re-sign him. The Yanks had Giambi and a potential star coming up in Nick Johnson (Larry Bowa's nephew) as DH/first baseman, so in reality there was no place for Ortiz on the Yankee roster. This game ended after 1:00 a.m. (it was five hours and two minutes long). Game five was scheduled at 5:10 p.m. the next day, oops I mean the same day. The Red Sox would probably sleep well – but the Yanks, I don't know??

Hey the Yanks were still up 3 games to 1 but you could almost see by their body language that they were worried. The Sox had "Who's your daddy" Pedro going against Mussina in the fifth game. Boston scored in the first on an RBI hit by that guy Papi and a bases loaded walk by Mussina. Bernie countered with a dinger off Pedro to make it 2-1. In the sixth came a pivotal point in the game. Jeter hit a base loaded triple to make the score 4-2 Yanks. A hit batsman, and walk, reloaded the bags. Matsui than hit a liner to right but Trot Nixon made a fine play charging in to snag it to end the inning, saving at least two runs. In the seventh Flash Gordon came in to stop a Sox threat getting Manny to hit into a double play. The Yanks missed a chance to increase the lead to three in the eighth when Cairo led off with a double was bunted to third, but ARod, with one out failed to get Cairo in when Mike Timlin fanned him. A Godzilla fly out ended the inning. Papi led off the Sox eighth and rocked one deep into the New England darkness over the Green Monster to cut the Yank lead to one. Millar then drew a walk and was pinch-run for by the speedy Roberts who was able to speed to third on a single by Nixon. Mariano came in an attempt to thwart the Sox from tying it, but Varitek came through with a sac-fly that evened the score at four.

In the Yankee ninth the Sox lucked out as Clark doubled to deep right with two outs and Sierra on first via a walk. Sierra would have easily scored the go ahead run but the ball hit the top of the wall and bounced into the stands for a ground-rule double forcing Sierra to go back to third, where he was stranded as Cairo popped out to first.

The game went into extra innings and neither team scored in four of them as the game went to the bottom of the fourteenth, as the Yanks' trading deadline acquisition, AL All-Star Esteban Loaiza, and the Sox Wakefield both tossed three scoreless innings. Both teams had runners in scoring position in the extra innings, but failed to deliver. Papi came up with two outs and two on as Loaiza issued two walks. After fouling off what seemed like a hundred pitches, he blooped a hit into center easily scoring the Caveman, Damon, with the winning run, as this Boston marathon finally ended after fourteen innings. For the second day in a row the contest went over five hours. Since the Yanks lost the previous game after midnight this defeat had them with two losses in one day. I guess the Boss wasn't getting too much for his $180 plus million. Ortiz had the walk-off hit in consecutive games and was responsible for three of the Sox runs in this game. My thought to Yankeeland was "Who's your Papi"?

The Yanks were still up 3 games to 2 but they looked defeated as they went back home. The question was would they have to face Schilling with his good stuff, as he had some kind of special footwear made for his tendon/ankle problem.

My son Chris was at game six to see game 2 winner Lieber go against Schilling. In the second, Lieber got Mark Bellhorn, the Sox second baseman, to ground into an inning ending double play with the bases loaded. Bellhorn was having a lousy series, 3 for 21. In the fourth with two down, Millar doubled and Varitek singled him in. Cabrera then got a hit and Bellhorn came up. Many thought that Pokey Reese should have been playing second base because of Bellhorn's poor performance. Well, Bellhorn made Francona look good as he slammed a shot to left field. The ball went into the stands and bounced off a fan and back onto the field as the umpire ruled it a double. I thought the umpire must have been Rich Garcia (who gave Jeter a homer in the '96 playoffs when a kid reached out and interfered with an apparent out). Nope, the umpire was Jim Joyce. The umpires got together, corrected the call, and ruled it a homer giving Bellhorn a 3-run homer and a 4-0 Sox lead. Things looked bleak for the Yanks.

Schilling discarded the new footwear as the team doctor had sutures made to keep his tendon from moving. Curt was literally a Red Sox pitcher as his sock became red with blood as it seeped through the sutures. Schilling, known as a money pitcher, went seven innings only giving up a dinger to Bernie Williams, and he left with a 4-1 lead. Outside of Bellhorn's blast, Lieber kept the Bosox scoreless thus keeping the Yanks in the game.

Arroyo came in to pitch the eighth. With one down the Yanks mounted a threat. Cairo doubled and Jeter singled him in. ARod came up as the tying run. ARod hit a slow bouncer that Arroyo fielded and as he went to tag him, ARod, looking as if he was auditioning for a part in a Karate Kid movie, gave a chop (I might add that he would have never gotten the part as it was a rather wimpy chop) at Arroyo's arm. (ARod and Arroyo were main participants in the July 24 brawl). The first base umpire was blocked from view as ARod's action knocked the ball loose and it rolled into foul territory in right field. As the play continued Jeter scored and ARod was on second with Sheffield coming up as the go ahead run. Francona came out appealing to the other umpires' eyesight (that seems like a hopeless endeavor). The Stadium looked like a football game as the umpires called for a huddle. Miraculously, they got it right as the Karate Kid (ARod) was ruled out for interference and Jeter had to go back to first as per the official rule. The martial arts master Mr. Miyagi would not have approved of ARod's actions. With Foulke on the mound in the ninth, Godzilla and Sierra both walked but Clark was K'd ending the game 4-2. The Red Sox tied

the Yanks at three apiece. Hey, the Yanks got a moral victory by
having Ortiz go for the collar – 0 for 4.

The seven innings Schilling pitched will go down in baseball
lore as one of the gutsiest performances in postseason play. Not
since Kirk Gibson's homer off of Eckersley in the 1988 Series has
this type of gutsy performance been given so much coverage. (Well,
maybe George Brett belting a homer in his first at bat in game 3 of
the '80 Series after hemorrhoid surgery the previous day was fairly
gutsy, butt don't mention that to Brett).

For the first time ever in baseball history a team has come back
from a 0-3 deficit to deadlock the series at three apiece. Could the
back pedaling Yanks recover and stop this Red Sox stampede from
making them the biggest chokers in Major League history in
tomorrow's decisive seventh game? One of the major reasons the
Yanks lost the three straight, besides the Bosox pitching, was the
lack of thunderbolts in their bats. In the 35 innings in the three
games they lost, they only scored nine runs (less than three a game),
and their one through five batters in the line-up were hitting only
.178 (13 for 73).

For one of baseball's most historic games it was a Brown/Lowe
match-up. The New York media was saying no way the Yanks
could lose on Mickey Mantle's birthday. In the afternoon Chris
called me and said he had a ticket by the 314 ft. sign in right field.
Chris and I had a short discussion about the game. He was griping
of the lack of thunderbolts in the Yankee bats while my concern was
of the Caveman's (Damon) 3 for 29 performance and Manny's zero
RBIs despite batting .320. I also talked to my Yankee hating
brother-in-law, Tom, about Damon's lousy performance, but maybe
he was reading tea leaves or something because he assured me the
Caveman was going to come up big in the finale.

The Sox jumped on Brown quickly as Damon singled and stole
second. Manny singled with one out and it appeared he'd get his
first RBI. Nope, Damon hesitated and was thrown out at home on a
relay peg by Jeter. The next batter, Papi, dispelled any thought of
going for another collar clobbering Brown's first pitch into the right
field stands for a 2-0 lead. In the second Brown continued his dismal
performance as Millar singled and Brown couldn't find the plate and
walked two, loading the bags with one down. Vazquez then came in
to face the Caveman. I'd hate to be the clubhouse wall as Brown
entered. Not even two innings old and the Yanks had about $25

million on the mound (just a little less than the Milwaukee Brewers' entire team's payroll). Vasquez delivered his first pitch but the Caveman used his club well, blasting it into the first row by the right field 314 ft. sign for a Grand Slam and a 6-0 Sox lead. The air was sucked out of the Stadium. A few minutes later the phone rang – it was Chris who asked me if I saw him try for Damon's homer. He was there trying to snag it when another fan ran in front, caught it and threw it back onto in the field. Chris sounded so dejected - not just for failing to catch Damon's homer, but for the score – I told him to hang in there, maybe Boston will put Pedro in there.

In the bottom of the third Jeter got an RBI hit to make it 6-1. However, the Caveman answered again using apparently a bigger club as he slammed a mammoth shot into the upper deck with one on to make the score 8-1. This seemingly sent all of Yankeeland back to the Stone Age (and this has nothing to do with Mick Jagger).

Meanwhile the Yanks couldn't do anything with Lowe. In six innings he yielded only one hit and one run. As Pedro came in to start the seventh he promptly got rocked for two doubles and a single as the Stadium was in full vocal harmony of "Who's your daddy?" He finally got out of the inning on a hard fly out by Cairo. It was now 8-3 and hey, the Giants blew a five run lead to Angels in the 2002 Series. Anyway, Bellhorn made it 9-3 with a homer off Gordon and the Sox got another in the ninth for a 10-3 lead and since the Yanks' bats had no thunderbolts in them, the Bosox relievers kept the Yanks from scoring. Red Sox won 10-3 in baseball's greatest comeback ever in a seven game series. I called my brother-in law Tom and we ecstatically high-fived each other over the phone. However, the Curse is still there as they had to win the Series against St. Louis, who beat Houston the following day.

My sons were not too happy about this. I tried to console Chris by telling him he was at one of baseball's most historic games. Hey, but my 90-year old Yankee hating dad was plenty happy that the Red Sox won the Series, after all he couldn't remember their last World Series Championship when he was four years old in 1918. I was real happy for the Boston execs, owner John Henry, GM Theo Epstein, and CEO Larry Lucchino who nicknamed the Yanks "The Evil Empire" (I heard he was now known as LUKEchino Skywalker). I wondered how Sheffield must have felt losing to such a walking disaster group of characters.

The Red Sox had many heroes. With the bats they had the ALCS MVP, Papi (.387, 12 for 31, 3 homers, 11 RBIs), Cabrera (.379, 11 for 29, 5 RBIs, 5 runs), Manny (.300, 9 for 30), the legs of Dave Roberts, and Bellhorn and Damon with their heroics in games 6 and 7 respectively. On the hill, Schilling and Lowe for games 6 and 7, and the relief corp headed by Foulke (5 games, zero ERA). And of course do not forget Francona, the Sox skipper (who had to overcome a lot of second guessing) for making moves that would be the envy of Bobby Fischer.

The Yanks' batting leaders (although mostly done in the first three games) were Godzilla (.412, 14 for 34, 2 homers, 10 RBIs), Bernie (.306, 11 for 36, 2 homers, 10 RBIs), and Sheffield (.333, 10 for 30, homer 5 RBIs). The Boston pitchers held Jeter to a .200 average although he had 6 RBIs. Mariano despite not getting the job done in games 3 and 4 had 2 saves and a 1.29 ERA in 5 games.

My take on why my "Zeus wears Pinstripes" theory did not work for the Yanks this time is as follows. After the Yanks were up two games to none, Zeus decided he had to step in on the Bush/Kerry Presidential race as the Greek gods and goddesses were taking sides much like they did in the Trojan War. I heard that Senator Kerry of Massachusetts (in a possible attempt to impress the nation's sports fans that he knew his baseball) referred to his favorite Red Sox player as being Manny Ortiz. I think what may have possibly happened was that one of the gods or goddesses (probably Eris, Goddess of Discord) whispered to him that the Red Sox's best players were Manny and Ortiz and he misunderstood it and thought it was one player. Maybe this mix up of his home state players' names may have been one of the reasons (small as it might be) that caused him to lose the election, as some voters throughout the nation were concerned he might mess up the country like he did these names (hey, look that's just my spin on it). Anyway, after the Yanks were up 2 to zip Zeus left the baseball arena, but before departing he gave the Yankee bats some of his thunderbolts he always carries around with him. He told them to use them wisely. Well the Yankee batters looked as if they were trying to out do each other as they used up the thunderbolts in the game 3, 19-8, 22 hit blow-out. They had virtually no thunderbolts left in their bats for the remaining games.

After two such dramatic League Championship series, the World Series would be hard pressed to match them. Boston still had the Curse of the Bambino to deal with. All four of the Boston World Series appearances since their last win in 1918, has ended in a game seven loss (St. Louis in '46 and '67, Reds in '75, and Mets in '86). You know if the Cardinals, who I rooted for since 1953, lost it would not bother me that much since it would be the Red Sox (the 2004 Yankee slayers) who beat them. If any Yankee fans still had any baseball interest left in them they'd be pulling for the Cardinals to take the Series. The main questions were - could Schilling give the Sox anything with his sutured tendon in his ankle, and of course, could the Red Sox beat the Curse?

The opener had Woody Williams, coming off his seven innings of shutout ball against the Astros in game 5 of the NLCS, facing the knuckler Wakefield. Neither lasted long. The Sox struck in the first with Papi blasting a 3-run homer as they took a 4-0 lead. Both starters were faltering as Wakefield could not hold a 7-2 lead as the Cards scored three in the fourth and the two off of Arroyo in fifth to make it 7-up. Boston went back in front scoring twice in the seventh but St. Louis countered with two of their own to tie it at nine. The Cards looked like they would take the lead, but with the bases loaded and one out, the Cards' big sticks didn't get it done. Rolen popped out and Edmonds K'd (it was a called strike that was nowhere near the strike zone). In the Sox eighth Varitek got on via a Renteria error. Bellhorn then hit a high fly down the line. It sounded with a big clang as it crashed into the Pesky pole for a 2-run homer (it was the third straight game that Bellhorn had homered in) and an 11-9 lead that held up as Foulke put down the Cards in the ninth. The Cards wasted a great game by Walker (a single, 2 doubles, and a homer). But the surprising fact was that the Cards scored nine runs despite their big three (Pujols, Rolen and Edmonds) only showing a bunt hit in twelve at bats. Another strange happening was that the Red Sox made four errors and still won.

In game 2 it looked like Schilling was in too much pain to pitch. When he arrived at the park the source of the pain was discovered. One of the sutures holding the ankle tendon hit a nerve, so once it was removed he would be able to pitch – even with the blood soaked red sock. Schilling again showed what a big game performer he is only giving up four hits and an unearned run in his six innings of work. He left with a 6-1 lead. (Back in 1895 there was a famous book written by Stephen Crane about the soldiers in the Civil War titled "The Red Badge of Courage" – when I was in high school it was mandatory reading. Look, I know that you can't really equate baseball with war – but this year baseball's postseason could be titled "The Red Sox of Courage"). The Sox hitters came through in the clutch with three two out hits providing the six runs (Varitek, 2-run triple in the first – Bellhorn 2-run double, in the fourth – Cabrera, 2-run double in the sixth). Boston won 6-2 as Foulke again ended the game with 1 1/3 innings of scoreless pitching. Naturally Schilling was credited with the win making him the first pitcher ever to post a World Series victory for three different teams - '93 Phils, '01 Diamondbacks and this year. Again the oddity of the game was another four errors by Boston (three by third baseman Mueller), but, hey they won.

You know birds go south for the winter and that's what it looked like the Cardinals were doing, at least their bats, anyway. In game 2, without Pujols' three hits, the rest of the line-up only got two hits. The Cards were going home now, where they hadn't lost in six postseason games.

Boston again struck in the first inning in game 3 as Manny parked one and then in the bottom of the first threw out Walker trying to score on a fly to shallow left field. Then in the third the Cards' pitcher, Jeff Suppan (a member of last year's Red Sox team), was on third when a grounder was hit to second. Boston was giving up the tying run but to the astonishment of the country, Suppan went back to third. Ortiz, who was playing first base, took the throw from Bellhorn then nailed Suppan attempting to get back to third. The Cardinal pitcher really made a bird brain move – it was the worst base running blunder that I ever saw in my 50 years of watching the Series. Maybe this affected Suppan as he gave up an RBI hit to Nixon in the fourth and RBI hits to Mueller and Manny in the fifth. The way Pedro was pitching it didn't matter, after the blown chances the Cards had, Pedro retired the last 14 batters he faced. The Cards only reached Martinez for three hits in seven innings. Timlin pitched a scoreless eighth and Foulke pitched the ninth, finally being scored on as Walker homered to keep St. Louis from being shutout. The Bosox triumphed 4-1.

The Sox were up 3 - zip. Can St. Louis do what the Sox did to the Yanks and take the next four? Keeping our annual tradition, this was the game my son Mike and nephew Frank went to watch at the Hyatt Hotel sports bar in New Brunswick, NJ. The Sox had Lowe going to try for the sweep. Lowe despite being in the Red Sox doghouse won the clinching games in the Division series against the Angels and in the ALCS against the Yanks and now he was attempting to do it for the World Series (never before has any pitcher won all three clinching games).

Even before I had a taste of my Bud Lite, the Caveman (Damon) clubbed a line shot into the right field stands off of the Cards' starter Jason Marquis. (My son Chris wasn't there to try to catch it). It was all that was needed as Lowe looked as good as he was against the Yanks, only yielding three hits in seven innings. Arroyo and Embree pitched the eighth and Foulke got another save blanking St. Louis in the ninth – to win the Series and END the CURSE. Terry Francona took four straight from the Midas-touch Torre and now four straight from the lawyer/manager LaRussa (these eight straight wins in postseason is a record). Bring on Bobby Fischer.

You have to hand it to Schilling as he accomplished what he set out to do – he made a decision to come to Boston to get the Red Sox a World Series Championship for the first time in 86 years, something his mentor Roger Clemens could not do. For his efforts (24-7 regular & postseason) Schilling was honored by being chosen the Major League Player of the Year by Sports Illustrated magazine. Curt now has a 184-123 lifetime record but will probably still need a few more good seasons in order to have a plaque in Cooperstown.

Like I previously stated the Cards' bats flew south. Hey, don't bats fly – oh wait, that's the flying mammal variety. The St. Louis offense mustered only three runs in the last three games. But you gotta tip your hats to the Red Sox staff, three great starts by Schilling, Pedro and Lowe, and terrific relief headed by Foulke (a win, a save, 1.80 ERA in all four games). They held Rolen and Edmonds to one hit (a bunt) in 30 at bats and Pujols' .333 average didn't produce an RBI. Only Walker came through (.357, 2 homers, 3 RBIs). For the Sox, the Series MVP Manny Ramirez (.412, 7 for 17, homer, 4 RBIs), Mueller (.429, 6 for 14), Nixon (.357, 3 RBIs), and Ortiz (.308, homer, 4 RBIs) provided the offense to knock the Cardinal hurlers off their perch. For the Red Sox, Papi Ortiz compiled one of the best stats in the short history of the three series format – 22 for 55 (.400), 5 homers (all clutch) and 19 RBIs in just 14 games. For St. Louis, Albert Pujols also put together some pretty hefty stats of his own in the Cards' three series – 24 for 58 (.414), 6 homers, 14 RBIs in just 15 games.

As the season ended I was pretty much satisfied with it as a whole. I feel the Yankee payroll will probably easily surpass $200 million, since $180 million plus couldn't get it done this year – they'll naturally go for the Big Unit (Johnson), Carl Pavano (18-8) and Beltran and who knows who else. Editor's Note: The Yankees signed Pavano and Johnson for '05, but Beltran inked with the Mets

And by the way, some more accolades were thrown this "idiotic" Boston Red Sox team's way - for their unprecedented outstanding achievements - Sports Illustrated magazine selected them as the 2004 Sportsmen of the Year. Since this century actually began in the year 2001 (not 2000), it is great knowing the Boston Red Sox are one up on the New York Yankees in World Series Championships for this century - that's just some information for Mr. Steinbrenner and everyone else in Yankeeland to think about throughout this winter.

2005
Angels in the Outfield

The baseball season began on an ominous note on March 17 (St. PatricKs Day) when Congress held hearings on steroids use in baseball. The highlights were the congressman from Kentucky and Hall of Fame pitcher Jim Bunning coming down like a ton of bricks on the illegal use of the performance enhancers, Mark McGwire losing the nation's respect by being evasive on answering questions on his use of them, and Rafael Palmeiro's demonstrative claim of NEVER having used the drug.

The team in the Bronx headed by the Boss George Steinbrenner was spending more $$$ to erase the past year's embarrassing choke job in the ALCS losing to their hated Red Sox rivals. They acquired three of baseballs top pitchers from last year - The Big Unit, Randy Johnson who was the NL Cy Young runner-up, Carl Pavano (18-8 with Florida) and Jaret Wright (15-8 with Atlanta). Some of Pinstriper's fans preferred they re-sign their 14-game winner Jon Lieber rather than Wright. On the offensive side they signed the Cardinals second baseman Tony Womack who batted over .300 for last year's NL champs. Would any team be able to derail this New York money train - their payroll was over $208 million – an $85 million advantage over the runner-up Red Sox who had the next highest at $123 million?

As the season was in its infancy the Bronx Bombers were getting blasted on the field and by the media. The situation was getting chaotic as they were 11-19. Another off season acquisition was their former postseason star Tino Martinez in case Jason Giambi could not recover from his ills (benign tumor, parasite, steroids?). Well, Tino carried the Bombers using a bat that seemed like it was loaded with steroids as he blasted 8 homers in 8 days sparking his team to a 16-4 record to get them back in the race. It should be noted that their re-entry into the race most likely kept Mr.

Steinbrenner from really losing it as he was the owner of Bellamy Road, who was the huge favorite to win the Kentucky Derby – alas the Boss' colt came in seventh place as the long shot Giacamo won The Race for the Roses (to the glue factory for Bellamy Road?). Meanwhile, Giambi was in a huge slump and was asked to get himself together in the minors but he refused saying he would work through it with hitting coach Don Mattingly. When Tino's bat lost its muscle Giambi went back in the line-up and became his old self as he hit 32 homers, driving in 87 runs and leading the AL in BB's (108) and on base % (.440).

Another set back early in the season was the play of Womack at second base, so to rectify this they called up Robinson Cano. All he did was become one of the league's top rookies (.297, 14 homers, 78 runs). He joined an All-Star type line-up – Giambi at first, at third the AL MVP ARod (.321, 130 RBIs and AL best 48 homers and 124 runs), at short Derek Jeter (.309, 19 homers, 122 runs), in left Godzilla Matsui (.305, 23 homers, 116 RBIs), in right Gary Sheffield (.291, 34 homers, 123 RBIs) and catcher Jorge Posada (19 homers, 71 RBIs). Only in center was the line-up weak as Bernie Williams was starting to feel the aging process (.249, 12 homers, 64 RBIs).

With this All-Star type line-up you'd think all the starters would be 20-game winners. But the Yanks' staff was a mess in the beginning. Carl Pavano was 4-6 then was injured for the remainder of the year. Wright was injured throughout the year and was 5-5. Mike Mussina was 13-8 but missed time during the year, and Randy Johnson was off his usual dominating performances but finished strong (17-8, 5-0 vs. Boston). Rookie Chien-Ming Wang came through early in the season (8-5) but he also got hurt. The GM Brian Cashman then went to the scrap heap and got Aaron Small from who knows where and all Small did was turn into Orel Hershiser of 1988 going 10-0. Cashman then rescued Shawn Chacon (7-3) from baseball Siberia (Colorado Rockies) where he was 1-7. Chacon and Small saved the Yankees' year as they combined for a 17-3 slate – it was like a miracle or divine intervention (ZEUS).

Naturally, the relief tandem of set-up man Tom Gordon (2.57 ERA) and best ever closer Cy Young runner-up Mariano Rivera (7 wins/43 saves, 1.38 ERA) was outstanding.

The Yankees went 95-67 and won the AL East beating the Red Sox in the next to last game of the season behind the Big Unit.

Boston won the final game behind Curt Schilling to tie New York with the same record; however the Yanks were awarded the AL East title by virtue of their 10-9 slate against the Red Sox.

Boston was led by one of the most intimidating 3 & 4 slot in the line-up since Ruth and Gehrig - Manny Ramirez (.292, 45 homers, 144 RBIs) and David "Papi" Ortiz (.300, 47 homers, AL best 148 RBIs). All-Star catcher Jason Varitek smacked 22 homers driving in 70 runs while Johnny Damon, still looking like a resident of the Neantherdal Age with his flowing locks and facial hair, continued to be one of the game's best lead-off men (.316, 117 runs, 75 RBIs).

The Red Sox staff was a puzzle. Curt Schilling never recovered from last year's ankle/tendon problem and was used as a closer when last year's ace fireman Keith Foulke was shelved for the year. Schilling finished up as a starter and beat the Yanks twice late in the season including the season's final game which gave them the Wild Card spot. Knuckler Tim Wakefield was 16-12, David Wells 15-7, Bronson Arroyo 14-10 and Matt Clement 13-6 (although he was never the same after getting hit in the head in mid-season by a line drive).

Baltimore had a terrible season despite a fast start. Early in the season the Orioles held first place as the Yankees stumbled out of the gate. Then they went into a tailspin. In the middle of the season their manager Lee Mazzilli was fired; and Rafael Palmeiro after joining the 3000 hit club was suspended for using some kind of steroid drug that was on the banned substance list - and, naturally, he stated he did it unknowingly. The Orioles' horrible season continued as their All-Star second baseman Brian Roberts (.314, 18 homers) broke his arm in September when he was run into by Yankee Bubba Crosby while covering first base on a bunt attempt by the Yankee center fielder.

In the AL Central the Chicago White Sox went wire to wire winning 99 games, best in the AL. Their pitching staff with four quality starting put them over the top - Jon Garland (18-10), Mark Buehrle (16-8), Jose Contreras (15-7) and Freddy Garcia (14-8). Dustin Hermanson saved 42 and had a 2.04 ERA out of the 'pen. Their much maligned offense (why? - they belted out 200 home runs) was led by Paul Konerko (40 homers, 100 RBIs), Jermaine Dye (31 homers, 86 RBIs), Carl Everett (23 homers, 87 RBIs) Joe Crede (22 homers) and speedster Scott Podsednik (.290, 59 SBs).

Rookie Japanese import second baseman Tadahito Iguchi (.274, 15 homers 71 RBIs) solidified the infield.

The Chisox had a 15 game lead on August 1 but then played .500 ball as the Cleveland Indians got hot and came within an eyelash of overtaking them. But the Chisox regrouped behind the genius of their manager Ozzie Guillen (the former White Sox shortstop who was Rookie of the Year and a three time All-Star) and beat the Indians the final three games of the season to knock them out of the Wild Card spot – the Chisox won their final five games. Guillen was a media delight (he had the best quips since Yogi) and as the Indians put the pressure on down the stretch he stated he might quit if his White Sox won the World Series. Guillen was voted the AL Manager of the Year.

The Angels did not relocate but their name did – to the Los Angeles Angels of Anaheim. It didn't matter as they repeated as AL West champs beating the Oakland A's who put on a rush after a horrendous start. Vlad Guerrero, last year AL MVP put up big numbers again (.317, 32 homers, 108 RBIs in 141 games). Garret Anderson (17 homers, 96 RBIs), Chone Figgins (.290, 116 runs, 62 SBs), Adam Kennedy (.300) and Bengie Molina (.295, 15 homers) helped out with the bats. Bengie's brother Jose was his back-up behind the plate. The AL Cy Young Award winner Bartolo Colon (21-8), John Lackey (14-5), and Paul Byrd and rookie Ervin Santana with 12 wins each led the starters while Francisco Rodriquez a.k.a. KRod had a 2.67 ERA saving 45 games.

Seattle's Ichiro Suzuki set a Major League record with 200 or more hits in his first five seasons. He amassed 206, but his .303 average was 69 points lower than his league leading .372 of last year. The Mariners had another terrible season (69-93) finishing last for the second year in a row after posting over 90 wins the previous four years (2000-03).

The big news in the NL was that Barry Bonds would be out for the season due to knee surgeries. However, in September he came back and had 5 homers and 10 RBIs in 14 games as the San Francisco Giants hoped to overtake the San Diego Padres; but the Padres held on to win the NL West with the worst record (82-80) of any team to ever make the playoffs. San Diego was led by Jake Peavy (13-7, 2.88 ERA, and NL best 216 Ks in 203 innings) and Brain Giles (.301, 15 homers, 83 RBIs).

In the NL Central the Cardinals had the best record in baseball 100-62. Albert Pujols had his fifth great year in a row and was the NL MVP (.330, 41 homers, 117 RBIs and NL best 129 runs). He carried the St. Louis attack as Scott Rolen missed most of the year and Larry Walker (.288, 15 homers) and Reggie Sanders (21 homers) also missed significant time. Jim Edmonds, (29 homers, 89 RBIs) and the new double play combination of the St. Louis mighty mite 5'6" Dave Eckstein (.294, 90 runs; and his .373 was the Majors' best average with runners in scoring position), and Mark Grudzielanek (.294) contributed to the Red Bird attack. Cy Young winner Chris Carpenter (21-5, 2.83 ERA), Mark Mulder (16-8), Jeff Suppan (16-10) and Matt Morris (14-10) gave the Cards four aces while Jason Isringhausen (39 saves, 2.14 ERA) was king of the 'pen even though Ray King was in the most games (77 with a 3.38 ERA).

The Cards coasted to the NL Central title, but Houston won the Wild Card for the second year in a row on the last day of the season. As the season began the Astros' offense lost Jeff Bagwell (injured most of the season), Carlos Beltran and Jeff Kent (signed with other team) and Lance Berkman (injured the first 30 games). The Killer Bees had no buzz and were 15 games under .500. Berkman (.293, 24 homers, 83 RBIs) came back, Morgan Ensberg (.283, 36 homers, 101 RBIs) emerged as a star, Jason Lane (26 homers, 78 RBIs) got hot, rookie speedster Willy Taveras (.291) piled up a slew of bunts and infield hits while lead-off hitter Craig Biggio (26 homers, 94 runs) provided hitting and leadership as Houston got back their buzz to finish with a 89-73 record. Additional buzz was created by the leagues best threesome on the mound – Roy Oswalt (20-12) and the ex-Pinstriper aces Andy Pettitte (17-9, 2.39 ERA) and the Rocket Clemens (13-8, NL best 1.83 ERA) who should have won at least 20 games but the 'Stros didn't score when he pitched (shut out 9 times when he started). Brad Lidge was arguably the NL's best fireman (42 saves, 2.29 ERA).

The hopes of Cub-nation were again dashed by a pitching staff full of potential. Kerry Wood again was injured most of the season, Mark Prior was 11-7 and Greg Maddux had his first losing season (13-15) in many moons. Derrek Lee tried his best to pick up the offense with the loss of Moises Alou and Sammy Sosa putting up Triple Crown type stats leading the league in batting .335, and was runner-up with 46 homers and drove home 107 runs. The Cubs' third-sacker Aramis Ramirez again had a good year at the plate (.302, 31 homers, 92 RBIs).

In the NL East the Atlanta Braves won again – for the 14th straight year. The Braves looked like they were in a rookie league as they had so many of them – at one time they had 15 of them on the roster. The best was Jeff Francoeur, an Atlanta hometown high school legend (.300, 14 homers, 45 RBIs in 70 games). He also displayed a rocket arm from right field and was among the leaders in assists despite the limited amount of games he played. Andruw Jones led the league with 51 homers and 128 RBIs. Chipper Jones only played 109 games but still hit 21 homers with 72 RBIs. The double play combo of Marcus Giles (.291, 104 runs scored) and Rafael Furcal (.294, 100 runs scored) set the table for the Jones guys. On the hill John Smoltz (14-7), Jorge Sosa (13-3) and Tim Hudson (14-9) were three of 26 pitchers the Braves had on their roster this year. Winning with this constantly changing roster skipper Bobby Cox was an easy choice as NL Manager of the Year.

The other NL East teams were all in the Wild Card race going into September – even the Washington Nationals (by way of Montreal) managed by Frank Robinson. They came in last but finished at .500 (81-81). The Phils missed the Wild Card spot by only one game as Jimmy Rollins (.290, 196 hits, 115 runs) led them down the stretch finishing the season with a 36-game hitting streak. Chase Utley (105), Pat Burrell (117) and Bobby Abreu (102) all hit the century mark in RBIs while Ryan Howard the NL Rookie of the Year (22 homers, 63 RBIs in 88 games) filled in nicely for an injured Jim Thome. Jon Lieber (17-13), who the Yanks opted not to sign and flame throwing relief ace Billy Wagner (38 saves, 1.51 ERA) led the mound corps.

The Mets (now led by Willie Randolph) continued moving in the (w)right direction as the left side of the infield led them to a better record than the NL West winning Padres (83-79) – it was David Wright at third (.306, 27 homers, 102 RBIs) and Jose Reyes at short (196 hits, 99 runs, 61 SBs). Cliff Floyd hit 34 homers with 94 RBIs, but their big free agent signee Carlos Beltran (.266, 16 homers, 78 RBIs) was a disappointment. Their other major addition, Pedro Martinez, was as good as advertised (15-8, 2.82 ERA) and would have been a 20-game winner had not the Mets' bullpen blown a bunch of leads for him.

The Florida Marlins had a shot for the Wild Card but also faded down the stretch. The new NL star Miguel Cabrera (.323, 33 homers, 116 RBIs) and Carlos Delgado (.301, 33 homers, 115 RBIs) led the offense while Cy Young runner-up D-Train Willis led the league in wins (22-10) and shutouts (5). Dontrelle also batted seventh (.261 average) on occasion in the Marlins' line-up.

On a sad personal note, my dad, who was in relatively decent health had a heart attack in June and passed on a few days later just months before his 91st birthday. At least he was able to see his favorite American League team, the Red Sox, win a World Series. In other personal news, my son Mike sold his house in South Brunswick to move to the City (NYC) in order to reduce his commute to Polytechnic University in Brooklyn. He's also helping me complete this book. Chris, when not working 10/12 hours a day on Wall Street provided us with some input on some of the chapters.

On a much happier note, in July, I retired from the Post Office after 42 years of service. With so much free time now my sons suggested that I go back to school so I took a position as a security aide at our high school (I really don't know if that's what my sons meant). The high school is less than a mile from our house.

Back to baseball – in the NL Division playoffs the Padres did not have a prayer against the Cardinals as they were swept in three games never having had a lead in any of them. Three of the Cards' aces - Carpenter, Mulder and Morris posted victories while the bat attack was led by Pujols (.556, 5 for 9), Eckstein (.385) and Sanders (.333 and a record 10 RBIs).

The other NL playoffs showcased the longest postseason game in baseball history as the Astros outlasted the Braves 7-6 in 18 innings on a home run by Chris Burke (another Killer Bee?). Despite their 14th straight appearance in the playoffs Atlanta failed for the fourth straight year to make it through the first round. Atlanta was down 2 games to 1 and was on the verge of tying up the series leading 6-1 in the eighth inning – but then a Berkman Grand Slam made it 6-5 and a last chance two out homer by Brad Ausmus tied it at six in the ninth. Clemens threw the last three innings for the win. Oswalt and Pettitte picked up the other Astro wins. John Smoltz won the only Atlanta game increasing his Major League postseason win record to 15. Andruw Jones who batted .526 in last year's playoffs again powered the Braves attack (.471, 8 for 17, 5 RBIs).

For Houston Berkman and the rookie Taveras both were 5 for 14 (.357) and Ensberg had 7 RBIs.

In the AL Division playoffs it was White over Red in the battle of the Sox. The Red Sox quest to repeat as World Series Champs was quickly ended in three straight. Chicago pummeled Boston 14-2 in the opener – won the second 5-3 when Tony Graffanino made an error on a potential double play ball that went through his legs and Tadahito Iguchi followed with a 3-run homer (it was sayonara Red Sox) - and won the third 5-3 overcoming two homers by Manny and one by Papi. The Red Sox had a chance with a bases loaded no outs situation and down by one run but El Duque Hernandez, the ex-Pinstriper, came in to get two pop ups and K'd Damon on a full count checked swing that would have been ball four and tie the game.

The other AL playoffs had the Yankees in a 2002 rematch with the newly named LA Angels of Anaheim. Back in 1994 there was a remake of a 1951 movie "Angels in the Outfield" – it starred Danny Glover as the manager of the last place Angels who won the World Series when real angels intervened on their namesake's behalf. That's what this series reminded me of. In the opener some of the sports media personnel may have thought there was no outfielder in left for the Angels as in the first inning Robinson Cano hit a bases loaded double clearing the bases to give the Yanks a quick three run lead. Some of the media though Garrett Anderson could have caught it but he got a bad jump on the ball – if he caught the deep drive I thought it would have been a great catch. In any event the runs were all that was needed as the Pinstripers won 4-2 behind Mussina. The Angels' Cy Young winner Colon was the loser.

In game 2 the Yanks seemed to be on their way to victory. In the second Matsui and Cano hit back to back two-baggers for a run and in the fifth an ARod walk, a double by Giambi and a force out gave then another – the inning ended when Figgins playing the hot corner made a great diving stop on a sizzling grounder by Godzilla that would have scored Giambi from third. Former Yank Juan Rivera got that back with a homer in the bottom of the inning. In the sixth strange things began to happen. (Here comes the Rally Monkey). Orlando Cabrera, who helped beat the Yankees last year with Boston got on by an error by ARod. After reaching second he scored this unearned run to tie the score at two on a hit by Bengie Molina. Again in the seventh misfortune hit the Bombers as Rivera led off with a headfirst slide into first for an infield hit. Steve Finley was safe on pitcher Wang's throwing error. (It seemed real angels were more than just in the outfield). A sacrifice moved them to second and third but Wang looked like he might escape this jam as he got Figgins on a short fly to center, but Cabrera came through with a line single to center making the score 4-2. Rival catchers Bengie Molina (8th inn) and Posada (9th inn) had solo homers making the final score 5-3. Kelvim Escobar with a scoreless two innings got the win and KRod got the save.

After a day of rest the series came back to the House that Ruth built, and the Pinstripers had the Big Unit Johnson ready to show why the Boss signed him for these October occasions. Johnson, the former postseason Yankee Killer (5-0) again appeared trying to kill the Yanks as all 6'10" of him got rocked. In the first with two outs Guererro and Bengie Molina singles were followed by a 3-run blast into the right field stands by Anderson. My son Chris was sitting in the left field stands as rain fell throughout the game – besides the miserable weather the first inning added to his misery as his Yanks were down 3-0 before they even batted. In the third Johnson was getting pelted by rain and also by Cabrera (a double) and Bengie Molina (a 2-run homer). Note that a few days before Johnson bad mouthed the Yankee fans - all four million of them that came to the Stadium this year as he said that they weren't enthusiastic as the Arizona fans – he'd even welcome boos. The Angels were now up 5-0 and when the Big Unit (Big?) gave up two hits to the first two batters in the fourth he was Yanked to a full wet Stadium chorus of boos – I really do not think that he welcomed them.

However, like throughout the year the Steinbrenner star-studded line-up came through and erased the 5-0 deficit taking a 6-5 lead getting Johnson off the hook. In the fourth Godzilla homered, Cano, Bernie and Jeter singled, ARod walked and Giambi singled - the inning was good for four runs, and it would have been more had not Figgins, now playing in center field made a spectacular diving catch on a liner by Sheffield. In the fifth Godzilla led off with a walk, Cano doubled, Matsui scored on an error and Bernie hit a sac-fly scoring Cano for the lead - my son didn't care about getting wet.

The Yankees had their undefeated ace Aaron Small replace Johnson and Joe Torre must have felt comfortable as Small has been their good luck charm all year. But not today – in the sixth he gave up a double to Rivera and singles to Erstad, Kennedy and Figgins as the Angles scored twice to regain the lead 7-6; and again my son was miserable and wet. The Angels continued to pound the Yankee 'pen scoring two in the seventh and eighth. The final was 11-7 as the Angel relievers Scot Shields, Escobar and KRod only gave up one run (a Jeter homer). After Bernie's sac-fly in the fourth it appeared to me like something strange was happening – Johnson looks like Bob Friend for the Pirates in the 1960 Series, the Angels blew a 5-0 lead but rebound with a fury to win it - it just did not seem right.

The rain continued in The Big Apple so the Saturday game was postponed giving the sports media another day to roast the Yankees supposed October savior – The Big Unit.

The game 4 starters Lackey and the other Yankee good luck charm Chacon matched zeros for five innings. The Halo Caps opened the scoring in the sixth on a walk to Rivera and two out doubles by Figgins and Cabrera. In the bottom of the inning the Yanks got one back on a walk to ARod who moved to second on a ground out and scored on a hit by Sheffield. In the seventh the Yanks took the lead on what I refer to as Zeus happenings. Cano led off with a broken bat infield hit – with one out Posada walked – pinch-hitter Ruben Sierra singled in Cano who evaded a tag by Bengie Molina after a strong throw by the rocket arm of Guererro. Posada went to third and scored on a chopper by Jeter that Figgins fielded but hurriedly and awkwardly threw home a short-hopper to Molina as the Yankees took a 3-2 lead that stood as Mariano went in for the last two innings closing the deal. The teams now had to fly back to West Coast for the deciding game – not fair the Angels have wings (ha, ha).

For the finale it would be Mussina and Colon. After a scoreless first, Colon had to leave the game in the second inning due to a shoulder injury with a full count on Cano. The rookie Santana came in and finished the walk to Cano, but he was thrown out trying to steal second. The Yankees were smiling as the rookie looked like he also would not last as he walked Bernie and Posada and gave up an RBI hit to Bubba Crosby. Jeter then hit a sac-fly as the Angels were down 2-0, but as least Santana left the mound on a good note K'ing ARod with Crosby on second.

Before Mr. Steinbrenner could start writing his victory comments he was most likely startled by the Angels' lead-off hitter in the second as Anderson smashed a homer into the right field seats. Ben Molina then singled but Mussina got two out but walked Finley on a full count. Then the pivotal part of the series and game occurred. Kennedy drove a Mussina pitch to deep right-center. Crosby, who less than a month ago collided with the Orioles' Brian Roberts at fist base, was in center and Sheffield was in right as they both raced for the drive and either one appeared to have been able to snare it; but neither one, was aware of the other. As they both reached for the ball they had a huge collision and the ball bounced off of Sheffield's glove for a 2-run triple for Kennedy giving LA of Anaheim a 3-2 lead. (Hmm, were there Angels in the outfield?).

In the third the Boss thoughts maybe went to the nature of a congratulatory message to the Angels as they tacked on two more runs on hits by Cabrera and Guererro, a sac-fly by Anderson, a hit by Bengie Molina and a fielders choice by Darin Erstad. Randy Johnson came in with two on and got Finley on a ground out to end the inning. The Big Unit kept the Angles scoreless for four more innings as Yankeeland was thinking why he didn't do that in game 3. Meanwhile the Yanks who thought the game was in the bag with Santana out there found out that was a bad thought as he regained his composure shutting down the Yanks for four innings until Jeter reached him for a homer in the seventh. The Yanks did have a threat in the fifth when ARod was hit with a pitch, Giambi singled but Sheffield flew out and Matusi popped out – Cano struck out but the ball got away from Molina who threw to first striking Cano in the back as the ball rolled into right field but the umpire called Cano out for running out of the base path (the call was correct but it is one that is not usually called). After Jeter's homer Santana got ARod out then was replaced by Escobar who kept the Yanks off the board for 1 1/3 innings and was replaced by KRod.

KRod had an interesting ninth – Jeter led off with a hit to left, but ARod came through killing a potential rally hitting into a double play. Giambi singled and Sheffield followed with an infield hit. Matsui then hit a sharp grounder that Erstad (last year's Gold Glover) at first made a diving stop of and tossed to KRod for the Division series clinching out.

The Angels had a bunch of heroes – at the plate – Bengie Molina (.444, 8 for 18, 3 homers, 5 RBIs), Rivera (.353), Guererro (.333, 5 runs), Anderson (2 homers, 7 RBIs) – on the hill KRod (2.70, 2 saves), Escobar (a win, 1.29 ERA, 7 inn. covering 4 games), and Santana (a clutch win). And a lot of credit has to go to the skipper Mike Scioscia whose managerial moves sent Joe Torre & Co. back to "Wait 'til next year" (for the second time in four years).

For the Yanks, Giambi (.421, 8 for 19) and Jeter (.333, 2 homers, 5 RBIs) led the offense. Matsui was 4 for 20 (.200) and left an army on base. ARod was horrible (.133, 2 for 15). The Pinstriped sluggers - ARod, Godzilla and Sheffield combined for a total of 3 RBIs.

Here's my spin on why the 'Zeus Wears Pinstripes' theory once again did not pan out. Zeus, after assuring the Yankees of a game 5 decided to head to Chicago where the ALCS would start the next day. Before going he had to choose a god to guarantee a Yankee victory in the deciding fifth game of the Division playoffs. Zeus felt sad for Atlas for having the burden of carrying the world on his shoulders forever. Zeus also felt sad that ARod has no rings so prior to leaving he told Atlas to make sure that ARod's team wins and that he is a major factor in the victory. Atlas' hearing was not so good listening to all the world's conflicts for centuries so he replied "Oh, KRod's team." Zeus interpreted this reply as "OK ARod's team" and said "Yes." As Zeus left Atlas said "See you later Boss." The Greek God of Gods shot back "Don't call me Steinbrenner, I'm Zeus" as he departed for the Windy City knowing a Yankee victory is in the bag.

Once the Angels knocked out the Yankees there was little time to party as they had to catch a flight to Chicago to play the White Sox the next day in the ALCS. The fatigue factor did not come into play as the Angels took the opener 3-2. (Note that their ace Cy Young winner Bartolo Colon was not on the roster due to his injured shoulder). But that was it for the Angels as all they could say was "Darn them Sox and umpires" while losing the next four.

In the second contest one of the most controversial plays in postseason history took place. With the score tied at one in the ninth the White Sox catcher A.J. Piercynski swung and missed a low pitch for strike three and the third out. Replays appeared to show to some that the catcher Josh Paul (the Angels third string catcher) caught the pitch cleanly (although league officials said the replays were inconclusive). A.J. took a step toward the dugout then ran for first. The home plate umpire Doug Eddings threw up his fist like it was the third out. Seeing the fist in the air the catcher rolled the ball back to the mound. A.J. was called safe at first as all hell (not a good place for Angels) broke loose. Eddings said that his fist in the air

was his strike three call not his out call. Pablo Ozuna pinch-ran for
A.J. and stole second and then scored on a game-winning double by
Joe Crede.

With a day off for travel this strike out call was scrutinized to
no end by the media. The next two games in Anaheim, Paul
Konerko blasted homers in the first inning to set the stage for the
two Pale Hose victories (along with more missed umpire calls).
Facing elimination in game 5 the Rally Monkey showed up as the
Angels took a 3-2 lead. It did not last as Crede homered to tie it and
then put the Sox ahead for good with an infield single that scored a
runner from second base.

However, the main reason the White Sox won was the faith
their skipper Ozzie Guillen had in his starting pitchers Mark
Buehrle, Jon Garland, Freddy Garcia and Jose Contreras who tossed
four straight complete game victories – a feat not done in postseason
since the 1907 World Series when the White Sox' cross-town rivals,
the Cubs, had four different pitchers hurl four consecutive complete
game victories against the Detroit Tigers. I wonder what Hall of
Fame manager Sparky "Captain Hook" Anderson would say about
that.

For Chicago most of the socks were supplied by the ALCS
MVP Konerko (2 homers, 7 RBIs) and Crede (.368, 2 homers, 7
RBIs). The Angels only batted .175 and their big bat Vlad Guererro
was a woeful 1 for 20 (.050).

Chicago had its first World Series participant since 1959 when I
was 14 years old and was hoping to bring the Windy City its first
World Series title since 1917. The heck with Joe Jackson and the
1919 Black Sox!

As the NLCS was about to begin the Astros were out to show
their .628 winning % over their last 117 games (74-43) was not a
fluke as they were out to reverse last year's NLCS results against
their Central Division rivals, the Cardinals. In order to do so they'd
have to overcome one of the most potentially famous postseason
home runs.

After Carpenter pitched St. Louis to a 5-3 win in the opener
Houston took the next three behind the arms of Oswalt, Clemens,
Lidge and others.

In game 5 Houston was up 4-2 in the ninth with the NL
terminator Brad Lidge on the hill. After K'ing the first two batters
Eckstein singled and Edmonds walked. The NL's best hitter Pujols

was up and some thought Lidge should have walked him even if it put the tying run in scoring position – but Lidge was the NL's best reliever and would face the Pujols challenge. Well Albert put the Astros' pitch into orbit for a 5-4 Cardinal victory. The clubhouse personnel had hurriedly taken down the plastic curtains they put up for the seemingly sure Houston champagne celebration.

All of a sudden it was deja vu (all over again?) as the 'Stros had to go back to St. Louis up 3 games to 2 - like in 2004. Many thought that the 'Stros would not be able to recover from such a devastating loss – but they had Oswalt (20 wins and 2 in postseason). The Cards' only threat came in the fifth but it was thwarted by an umpire. The Cards' would have had the bases loaded and none out but the umpire called out Yadier Molina (brother of the Angels' Bengie and Jose) on a phantom tag at second base – it was not a good year for umpires in postseason. They did score one run, but who knows what would have happened if the right call was made. In any event Oswalt showed why he won 59 games over the past three years only giving up one run in seven innings. Astros win 5-1 and Houston finally gets into its first World Series. Oswalt was easily the NLCS MVP (2-0, 1.92 ERA). Biggio and Bagwell, the Astro legends, finally get into a World Series.

The Astros and the White Sox, the World Series participants have a combined payroll of $151 million over $50 million less than the sit at home Yankees get. At least Yankeeland could watch former Bronx residents Rocket Clemens and Jose Contreras start the opening game of the '05 Series.

Ironically two of the games top first baseman over the past 15 years, the Astros' Jeff Bagwell and the Chisox's "Big Hurt" Frank Thomas finally see their teams get into the Fall Classic without much contribution from them – Bagwell, who had surgery and could not throw, only played sparingly hit 3 homers in a 100 at bats while Thomas had 12 in a 105 but was out for the year after early season surgery. More irony is they were both born the same day May 27, 1968, they both were League MVPs the same year (1994), and only one home run separates them: Bags (449) - The Big Hurt (448). Will they go to Cooperstown together?

In the opener the Rocket was down 3-1 and had to leave after a strained hammie after two innings. The Astros buzzed back to tie it at three but Crede hit a homer to take back the lead 4-3 and then thwarted the 'Stros from scoring with two clutch fielding plays ala

Brooks Robinson. The 'Stros mounted a threat in the eighth with runners on the corners with no outs but relievers Neal Cotts and Bobby Jenks K'd three straight. Contreras, the former Bronxite, was the winning pitcher – so what do you think Mr. Steinbrenner?

I could only watch the last few innings of the game as my Post Office co-workers threw me a surprise retirement party. As I entered the room to my surprised astonishment they all had on Yankee shirts – but in view of the Yankee current status I did not mind – in fact I found it to be quite amusing.

In game 2 Pettitte had Houston up 4-2 but left after 6 innings. Houston's reliever Dan Wheeler had two on and two out when Dye was awarded first base because the umpire said the pitch hit his arm instead of the bat as replays appeared to show (was Homer, the Greek poet, the umpire?). The bags were loaded and Chad Qualls came in to face the Sox's power guy, Konerko. Well his pitch went zooming into the left field stands for a Grand Slam and a 6-4 Chisox lead. However, in the ninth with two outs and runners on second and third, Jose Vizcaino stroked a clutch two-RBI hit to deadlock it at six.

Lidge took the hill for the first time since the Pujols homer and with one down was facing Podsednik. Lidge must have been thinking no way can he park one as for the season in over 500 at bats he had none. (However he did hit one in the Division series against Boston). Lidge made the pitch too fat as Podsednik sent it over the right field fence for a game-winning walk-off homer.

Before game 3 began, Commissioner Bud Selig took away Houston's right to have its roof opened or closed (it is usually the home team's call). Houston wanted it closed as they were so dominate when it was closed. Selig ruled for it to be open. It didn't seem to matter as Oswalt had a 4-0 lead going into the fifth – but then he gave up a lead-off homer to Crede and the Pale Hose then batted around putting up a five spot to take a one run lead.

Lane hit an RBI double to tie it up at five and then the game dragged on to the fourteenth inning. In the extra frames Houston had seven runners on, but none made it home.

In the fourteenth Ensberg made a great play and turned it into a double play. Up next was a former Astro and the Chisox's July 31 trade deadline pick-up Geoff Blum. In 95 at bats he had only one homer and 5 RBIs – so not too much was expected. As unlikely as PodsedniKs game-winning homer was two days ago – so was this drive into the right field stands by Blum to put the Sox up 6-5 – and they tacked on another to make it 7-5. In the bottom of the inning Houston had the tying runs on base – but true to form they never made it home.

This contest tied the Series record for innings (14) and length of time 5 hours and 41 minutes.

In game 4 the roof caved in on the Astros (even though it was opened) as Garcia shut them out for seven innings and his relievers for two more. In the eighth, pinch-hitter Willie Harris had a lead-off single, wound up on third and scored the Series winning run on the Series MVP Jermaine Dye's (.438, 7 for 16) single through the middle off of Lidge. Houston's Brandon Backe's outstanding pitching kept the Pale Hose scoreless for seven innings but it was wasted as the Astros offense had no buzz to get him any runs. The Sox won the clincher 1-0. The Chicago White Sox are World Series champs and I don't think manager Ozzie Guillen has any thoughts of quitting.

In the past two games of 23 innings the Astros left 24 runners on base as they seemed to be zero for infinity for the Series with runners in scoring position. Berkman (.385, 6 RBIs) was the only Astro with buzz, but the Sox hurlers would pitch around him whenever possible walking him five times. With this four game sweep the White Sox finished out the season on fire winning 15 of their last 16 games – not bad for a team with only a $75 million or so pay roll - the Yankee brass would probably agree - Nah!

Well, last year the Red Sox ended their Curse of the Bambino (1918) and this year the White Sox ended their Joe Jackson/Black Sox Curse of 1919. Since the Red SOX ('04) and the White SOX ('05) won the last two World Series maybe Mr. Steinbrenner will change the name of the New York Yankees to the New York Pinstriped SOX.

Epilogue

Because I am the Yankee Hater, some of their fans say things like I should "get a life" and "stop being a negative fan" (root for a team to win instead of one to lose). Personally I feel that my baseball rooting interests are quite contrary to that viewpoint. First, I do pull for the Mets to win (also St. Louis). Take the question - is the glass of water half full or half empty? (If it was Bud Lite it'd be empty). Like how the glass is viewed, I root for the Yanks' opponent to win with the by-product of that being the Yanks lose.

As a kid growing up in the 1950's, there were three symbols of "evil" I learned to hate – the swastika, the hammer & sickle, and the interlocking NY of the New York Yankees. Just so you know I realized the first two were trying to do in the American Way of Life, whereas the interlocking NY of the Yankees was just trying to do in the American Pastime (my viewpoint). Just think how would you have liked to been an American League fan in any city but NYC from 1949-1964. Only twice were the Yankees not in the World Series (1954 & 1959). Meanwhile during this same 16 year period, 7 of the 8 original National League teams (the only one being the Billy Goat hexed Cubs) were in at least one World Series.

One thing I can't understand is why most Yankee fans just don't get it (not all of them, i.e. my sons). My son Chris who bleeds pinstripes, like Tom Lasorda bleeds Dodger Blue, is a Dallas Cowboy fan (Tony Dorsett was his guy) and would be ecstatic if their owner Jerry Jones paid for an All-Pro team to play for the Cowboys – like the Boss does for the Yanks. But he can't because of the salary cap system that keeps NFL teams competing on a level playing field.

The present system for baseball is tilted for the Yanks to win (I know it's not the Boss' fault, it's the system). The good small market teams just can't keep their team together because their revenue doesn't give them that option (i.e. the 1997 World

Champion Marlins had to dismantle their team in '98 and also after their 2003 championship). Also, the Oakland A's playoff teams lost Johnny Damon, Miguel Tejada and Jason Giambi to free agency because they couldn't afford them. Ever since the Yanks were the only team rich enough to buy the Babe in 1920, their money kept them ahead of the competition. From the 1920's through the 1960's, they had the resources ($$$$$) to have the biggest scouting system to acquire the country's best talent and stockpile them in their minor league system until they were needed, (i.e. when the Yanks were winning four straight Series from 1936-39, the second best baseball team wasn't even in the Majors – it was the Yanks' top minor league team, the Newark Bears).

In the 1940's and 1950's, the Yanks $$$$ would pick up aging veteran stars (i.e. Mize, Sain) to keep them on top as the other teams could not afford to keep them. The player depot in the 1950's was their Kissin' Cousin Athletics that let them have whatever they needed (i.e. Maris).

In the '60's baseball derailed the Yanks from signing all the young talent by implementing a draft system with teams selecting in inverse order. This was one of the reasons the Yankees only won the World Series twice from 1965 to 1995 (in '77 & '78). Free agency was established in the 1970's and the Boss' vaults were opened, but only until recent years has it brought home the bacon.

Another thing Yankee fans think (boy, is that an oxymoron) is that the purchasing of free agents has to be done smartly (No duh!!). They cite the spending sprees of the Orioles, Mets and Dodgers that produced little results as being poor management. The Yankee fan says the Yankee brass has the smarts for wise spending. Well, where were their brains from '79 – '95?

Under this present system (no salary cap), the Yankees will be in the hunt every year for the title. In 2005 their payroll was $208 or so million while the second highest is in the $123 million range. It should be the best team that $$$ can buy. Hey, look! Even the Yankees' General Manager's name is Cashman.

Look, since I've followed baseball (1954 to present) the Yanks are 10-9 in the World Series and probably in these 19 Series they were probably the favorite in 17 of them (I know the '76 Big Red Machine and '96 Braves were favored). Also, the Yanks failed six times in the playoffs to make the Series, so I'd say for the Yankee Hater the past 50 plus years have been OK.

Enemies of the Evil Empire

The following is a compilation of what I consider the top 100+ or so Enemies of the Evil Empire (the Yankee Organization). This list is in alphabetical order and is basically from the years I began following baseball (1954) to now.

Also, included are two World Series that were played before I was born – the World Series of 1926 and 1942 when my St. Louis Red Birds upset the mighty Yanks on both occasions. Since this is based on my recollections, I am truly sorry to anyone (i.e. my fellow Yankee Haters) who feels that I omitted one of their favorite "Enemies" that they feel should be on the list.

Aaron, Hank Milwaukee Braves '57 WS Atlanta Braves 1974	Hammered the Yanks in '57 to the tune of .393, 11 for 28, 3 homers, 7 RBIs - In '74 took the top spot as all-time home run leader hammering his 715th - Sorry Babe.
Alexander, Grover Cleveland St. Louis '26 WS	Ol' Pete at 39 was 2-0 with a save, a 1.33 ERA and 17 Ks in 20 1/3 innings. Saved game 7 after winning game 6 the day before by fanning Tony Lazzeri with the bags loaded in the 7th inning.
Alomar, Sandy Jr. Cleveland '97 ALDS	Hit .316 (6 for 19) 2 homers/5 RBIs. His 8th inning homer off Mariano Rivera in game 4 tied the game giving the Indians the momentum to win the game and the series.
Amoros, Sandy Brooklyn '55 WS	His spectacular catch in the 6th inning saved the Series for the Dodgers. He even turned Yogi's possible 2-run double into a double play preserving Brooklyn's 2-0 lead. As a role player hit .333 (4 for 12, homer, 3 RBIs).

Anderson, Garrett Anaheim '02 ALDS LAA Angels '05 ALDS	In '02 contributed to the Angels lumber attack - .389 (7 for 18). In '05 powered the Angels' offense - 2 homers and 7 RBIs.
Audubon Society Canada '83	Dave Winfield, trying to shoo a sea gull off the field, threw a ball that fatally hit the bird. Ironically they were playing the Birds (Toronto Blue Jays). Charges were filed but then dropped. Toronto fans gave the Yanks the "bird".
Bar Patrons Texas '88	Billy Martin was in a Texas bar and his usual persona got him in a brawl. Martin lost and got so many stitches he looked like a baseball. The incident would lead to his firing.
Beazley, Johnny St. Louis '42 WS	The Cardinal rookie capped his 21-win season beating the Yanks twice with a 2.50 ERA.
Beckett, Josh Florida '03 WS	His 2-0 win in game 6 gave the Marlins the Series. His ERA was 1.10 and he was MVP.
Bell, Les St. Louis '26 WS	It was more Bell than the Yankees wanted to hear - his 6 RBIs led the Cards in the '26 Series.
Bellhorn, Mark Red Sox '04 ALCS	His 3-run homer was the margin of victory in the 4-2 game six victory – also put his mark on the finale with a home run.
Bench, Johnny Cincinnati '76 WS	The Series MVP went 8 for 15 (.533, 2 homers, 6 RBIs) in the 4 game sweep (Thurman, who?)
Bottomley, Jim St. Louis '26 WS	The future Famer went 10 for 29, .345 and had 5 RBIs. It was "Bottoms Up"
Boyer, Ken St. Louis '64 WS	Oh Boy(er)! His Grand Slam won game 4 (4-3) and his single, double and home run were responsible for 4 runs in the 7-5 victory in the finale.

Brett, George KC '80 ALCS KC '83	A Royal pain in the butt for the Yanks. With NY up 2-1, Gossage came in to face Brett in the 8th with 2 on - Brett hit it far into the NY night for a 4-2 lead. In '83 he blasted Gossage in the famous Pine Tar incident (See McPhail).
Brock, Lou St. Louis '64 WS	Lou rocked Yankee pitching for a .300 average - 9 for 30, 2 doubles, a homer and 5 RBIs.
Buhner, Jay Seattle '95 ALDS	The former Yankee farmhand went 11 for 24 (.458) with a homer and 3 RBIs.
Burdette, Lew Milwaukee '57 WS	Had the saliva working as his "spitter" gave him the 2nd best pitching performance in Series history (behind Christy Mathewson's 3 shutouts in '05). He won 3 games finishing up with 24 consecutive scoreless innings. He was naturally MVP and his ERA was 0.67.
Cabrera, Orlando Red Sox '04 ALCS LAA Angels '05 ALDS	In '02 exceeded expectations as Nomar's replacement besides his "leather" display - batted .379 (11 for 29) with 5 RBIs and 5 runs scored. In '05 his clutch two out 2 RBI hit won game 2.
Campanella, Roy Brooklyn '55 WS	Campy had a single, double and homer in games 3 and 4 to even the Series. In the finale he scored the Dodgers 1st run after doubling.
CBS '65 - '73	The Columbia Broadcasting System (CBS) did what no one else could do - keep the Yanks from winning. During their reign they were playoffless, but they were a good TV sitcom.
Cey, Ron Dodgers '81 WS	The Dodgers' version of the Cey Hey Kid - a.k.a. the Penguin - showed he was quite a 'Batman' hitting .350 (7 for 20), 6 RBIs and was a Tri-MVP. He showed how hard headed he was surviving a Goose beaning in game 5. It looked like he was dead- but it was the Yanks who were dead, as he returned for game 6 going 2 for 3 in the 9-2 Series clincher.

Clemente, Roberto Pittsburgh '60 WS	Went 9 for 29 (.310) but it was his speed giving him an infield hit in the 5 run 8th in the 7th game that kept the inning going.
Concepcion, Davey Cincinnati '76 WS	The shortstop provided some punch with a double, triple and a .357 average (5 for 14).
Conine, Jeff Florida '03 WS	The Barbarian clubbed Yank pitching for a 333 average (7 for 21, 4 runs).
Cooper, Walker St. Louis '42 WS	The Cardinal catcher put the finishing touches (in game 5) for the Red Birds' coup in '42 - his lead off hit preceded Kurowski's 9th inning homer giving the Cards a 4-2 lead - in the bottom of the inning he picked off of second base Joe "Flash" Gordon (the AL MVP) and the Yanks' final threat was over in a "flash". Walker had 6 hits and 4 RBIs in the 5 games.
Copacabana Club NYC '57	In May Billy Martin's 29th birthday celebration at the Copa with a bunch of Yanks was disrupted by another group resulting in an altercation that made all the news. The Yanks' brass was embarrassed and soon after Billy was given a belated gift - a trade to the Yanks' Kissin' Cousins, the KC Athletics.
Covington, Wes Milwaukee '57 WS	Not known for his defense, the Yanks would disagree. He made 2 leaping catches (one would have been for extra bases, the other a homer) in games 2 and 5 to keep Lew Burdette from being scored upon.
Craig, Roger Brooklyn '55 WS St. Louis '64 WS	A rookie in '55 he won game 3 for the Dodgers' - in '64 he relieved in the 1st inning with the Cards down by 3. He went 4 2/3 scoreless innings with 8 Ks (his big play was picking the Mick off 2nd) He was credited with the victory.
Damon, Johnny Red Sox '04 ALCS	The Neanderthal man look-alike clubbed the Yanks into next year with a Grand Slam and 2-run homer in the decisive seventh game (Note: my son Chris narrowly missed snaring the 'Slam).

Davis, Tommy Dodgers '63 WS	Hit .400 (6 for 15) with a record tying 2 triples in one game.
Drain Cover Yankee Stadium '51 - '68	This began two years before I knew anything about baseball, but lasted long after it. In the '51 Series Wil!ie Mays hit a fly to right/center. Mickey Mantle, the right fielder was running for the ball when Joe DiMaggio called for it. The Mick put on the brakes and he tore up his knee stepping on a drain cover. His knee was an albatross his whole career. The Mick was great but what if ? We will never know.
Drysdale, Don Dodgers '63 WS	The Dodgers' offense got him a run in the 1st and he made it stand up in a 1-0, 3-hitter with 9 Ks.
Driessen, Dan Cincinnati '76 WS	The Reds DH hit .357 (5 for 14) with 2 doubles and a homer scoring 4 runs in the Series sweep.
Elevator Guys Anonymous '81 WS	After showing up bruised with a swollen lip and a cast on his hand, Steinbrenner explained that he was defending the Yankees' honor when two anti-Yankee guys were saying "bad things" about the Yanks. The Boss "thrashed" them pretty good - Never authenticated.
Epstein, Theo Red Sox '04 ALCS	The Bosox GM put together the team and laid to rest the Curse of the Bambino.
Erstad, Darin Anaheim '02 ALDS LAA Angels '05 ALDS	In '02 tagged the Yankee pitching (.421, 8 for 19) and scored 4 runs. In '05 batted .300 and the first baseman Gold Glover's diving stop with 2 Yanks on was the final out of the series.
Escobar,Kelvim LAA Angels '05 ALDS	The Angels former starter was 1-0 with a 1.27 era in 7 innings of work out of the 'pen covering four games.
Face, El Roy Pittsburgh '60 WS	The Yanks hated to Face the little fork-baller as he chalked up 3 saves.

Fehr, Donald Players Union '94	It looked like no one could stop the Yanks as they were headed for postseason play for the 1st time since '81. But Don Fehr did it without throwing a pitch - but he did "throw" a strike (work stoppage) ending the season for the AL's best team.
Figgins, Chone LAA Angels '05 ALDS	His spectacular diving catches at the hot corner in game 2, and in center in game 3 thwarted Yankee rallies in both of these Angels victories.
Finley, Steve Arizona '01 WS	The D'back hit .368 (7 for 19) and scored 5 runs.
Foster, George Cincinnati '76 WS	His "Black Beauty" bat produced a .429 average and 4 RBIs in the sweep.
Foulke, Keith Red Sox '04 ALCS	The Red Sox closer out did Mariano as he had a 0.00 ERA in 5 games and 6 innings.
Furillo, Carl Brooklyn '55 WS	The Boys of Summer right fielder, the "Reading Rifle" hit .296 (8 for 27) with a homer and 3 RBIs.
Garvey, Steve Dodgers '81 WS	Was the leading hitter for LA going 10 for 24 (.417).
Gibson, Bob St. Louis '64 WS	Hoot was MVP - won 2 games with his bat, fielding and intimidating the Yanks with his fastball - set a Series record with 31 Ks.
Glaus, Troy Anaheim '02 ALDS	Despite having the name of the city Zeus hates, the Angel hit .312 (5 for 16) and socked 3 homers into the heavens.
Gonzalez, Alex Florida '03 WS	His 12th inning homer won game 4 - in game 6 he scored the 1st of the Marlins 2 runs with one of the best slides in Series history.
Gonzalez, Luis Arizona '01 WS	Gonzo was 7 for 27 but it was his last - a blooper over a drawn in infield in the 9th off of Rivera that gave the D'backs the title.

Grace, Mark Arizona '01 WS	The leader in hits for the '90's was 5 for 19 but his last was a lead-off hit to center off the invincible Mariano Rivera that ignited the Series winning rally. The Yanks went down Gracefully.
Griffey, Jr., Ken Seattle '95 ALDS	One of the best postseasons ever - 9 for 23 (.391) with 5 homers, 7 RBIs and 9 runs scored.
Groat, Dick Pittsburgh '60 WS St. Louis '64 WS	In '60 got a big RBI hit in the Bucs 5 run 8th in the historic game 7, in '64 Groat uses the Throat to make the Mick Gloat then a Goat - in game 4 he was telling the Mick about his game winning homer the previous day Mick was gloating when Groat snuck in to pick him off to end a Yank rally - the Cards won by 1 run.
Guerrero, Pedro Dodgers '81 WS	A Tri-MVP he hit .333 (7 for 21) with 2 homers and 7 RBIs (5 in the last game).
Guerrero, Vladimir LAA Angels '05 ALDS	Although not driving in a run, he batted.333 scoring 5 times.
Gura, Larry KC '80 ALCS	A former Yankee whipping boy - whipped the Yanks going all the way in a 7-2 victory in the opener.
Haddix, Harvey Pittsburgh '60 WS	The "Kitten" was purring as he started and won game 5 and won game 7 in relief - the crafty lefty was 2-0 with a 2.45 ERA.
Haines, Jesse St. Louis '26 WS	Pop was 2-0 with a 1.08 ERA - hit a homer in his 4-0 game 3 win - but it was his blister that he is remembered for - in game 7 with a 3-2 lead it broke and Ol' Pete (see Alexander) had to come in and "blistered" the Yankee lumber.
Henry, John Red Sox '04 ALCS	The owner of the World Series Champions Boston Red Sox - Hope he doesn't get interested in financing/producing Broadway plays.
Hodges, Gil Brooklyn '55 WS	Was 7 for 24 (.292) with a homer and 5 RBIs - had the 2 RBIs in the Dodgers 2-0 win in the finale.

Hooten, Burt Dodgers '81 WS	Was the winning pitcher in game 6 giving LA the Series.
Hornsby, Rogers St. Louis '26 WS	The Cardinal player-manager only hit .250 with 4 RBIs, but he did 'manage' to win the Series - he ended the Series tagging out the Babe on a surprise steal attempt.
Howard, Frank Dodgers '63 WS	Hondo probably hit the 2 hardest shots ever off of Whitey Ford - in game 1 his double hit the 408' sign and bounced all the way back to second base - in game 4 his homer landed in the seats where Bob Uecker sits.
Hutmaker, Gene 1945 - Present	Author of "Banned in the Bronx - The Yankee Hater Memoirs, 1953-2005".
Jackson, Michael Cleveland '97 ALDS	The Indian middle reliever told the Yankees to "Beat It" - he didn't give up a run in 4 1/3 innings (in 4 games) plus was the winning pitcher in game 4.
Johnson, Randy Seattle '95 ALDS Arizona '01 WS	The Big Unit won games 3 and 5 (in relief) for the Mariners - in '01 he won games 2 and 6 then relieved in game 7 for a third win (he was 3-0, 1.04 ERA) - he was Co-MVP with Schilling. He's 5-0 in postseason vs. the Yanks.
Johnstone, Jay Dodgers '81 WS	Flakier than cereal, his 2-run pinch-hit homer was the big blow in the Dodgers come from behind victory 8-7 to even the Series at 2 games.
Jones, Nippy Milwaukee '57 WS	Helped polish off the Yanks in game 4. While pinch-hitting in the 10th behind by a run, a pitch hit him on his polished cleats, the ump didn't believe it until shown the polish on the ball. He was awarded 1st base and the Braves winning rally was started.
Koufax, Sandy Dodgers '63 WS	The Yanks were no match for the games greatest pitcher - he was 2-0, 1.50 ERA with 23 Ks in 18 innings. In game 1 he set a Series record 15 Ks.

Kuhn, Bowie MLB Commissioner '74	Suspended the Boss for 2 years for improper political contributions.
Kurowski, Whitey St. Louis '42 WS	The rookie third sacker led the Cards with 5 RBIs - his 9th inning 2-run homer in game 5 won the Series for the Cards.
Labine, Clem Brooklyn '55 WS	In 4 games, 9 1/3 innings had a 2.89 ERA and won game 4.
Law, Vernon Pittsburgh '60 WS	The Yanks had trouble with the Law - he won games 1 and 4 and was headed for a 3rd victory but the Buc relievers failed to hold the lead. In game 4 he was 2 for 3 with an RBI and scored a run in a 3-2 win.
Leonard, Dennis KC '80 ALCS	Menaced the Yanks, winning game 2 of the 3 game sweep by a 3-2 score.
Lowe, Derek Red Sox '04 ALCS	Came out of the Red Sox doghouse barking in game seven as he put the bite on the Yanks, yielding one hit and one run in his six innings of work.
Lucchino, Larry Red Sox '04 ALCS	The Boston CEO/President coined the "Evil Empire" moniker on the Yanks. In keeping with the Star Wars theme this year he was known as LUCchino Skywalker.
Marshmallow Salesman '79	Billy Martin beat him up to the point of hospitalizing him - but it was Billy who got roasted when the Boss fired him (again).
Martinez, Edgar Seattle '95 ALDS	He's been 1-hour Martinezing the Pinstriped uniforms for years. This series he hit .571 (12 for 21, 3 doubles, 2 homers, 10 RBIs) plus his shot into left field in the 11th won the series.
Martinez, Tino Seattle '95 ALDS	During his pre-Yankee tenure, he joined his non-brother Edgar with the lumber (9 for 22, .409, homer, 5 RBIs).
Mathews, Eddie Milwaukee '57 WS	His 2-run 10th inning homer in game 4 turned around the series in the Braves' favor.

Mazeroski, Bill Pittsburgh '60 WS	This defensive specialist led the Buc stick men (.320, 8 for 25, 2 doubles, 2 homers, 5 RBIs). Oh yeah, one of the homers was pretty dramatic.
McCarver, Tim St. Louis '64 WS	The future top announcer carved up Yankee hurlers (.478, 11 for 23, double, triple, 5 RBIs and a homer over the Yankee right field canyon in the 10th inning that won game 5).
McGwire, Mark St. Louis '98	Graciously broke Yankee Roger Maris' 37 year old home run record of 61 (some Yankee fans could care less…they never took to Roger). McGwire finished with 70.
McPhail, Lee AL Commissioner '83	"Stuck" it to the Yankee nation by upholding the Kansas City protest and let George Brett's Pine Tar homer count with the game resuming from that point. The Royals won the resumed game.
Molina, Bengie Anaheim '02 ALDS LAA Angels '05 ALDS	IN '02 the back-stopper hit .267 and controlled the mounds corps especially the rookie KRod. In '05 he was the Angels big bopper (.444, 8 for 18, 3 homers. 5 RBIs) along with his usual excellent defense.
Monroe, Marilyn 1954-1962	It wasn't Bob Feller's curve that made Joe DiMaggio go weak in the knees (it was her curves).
Morgan, Joe Cincinnati '76 WS	The NL MVP went 5 for 15 (.333) hitting for the cycle in the 4 game sweep.
Musial, Stan "The Man" St. Louis '42 WS	The Man was only a 21-year old "kid" and in his rookie year when his 8th inning hit won game 2 (4-3) and his catch robbed a Yank of a homer in game 3's (2-0) victory.
O'Farrell, Bob St. Louis '26 WS	The Cards' back-stopper was NL MVP and hit .304 (7 for 27); and ended the Series when he gunned down the Babe trying to steal second.

Ortiz, David (Papi) Red Sox '04 ALCS	Yanks knew "who their Papi was" (.387, 12 for 31, 3 homers, 11 RBIs); won game 4 with a 12th inning homer, game 5 with a 14th inning single and hit a first inning 2-run homer in the decisive seventh game.
Penny, Brad Florida '03 WS	What a penny will buy - 2 victories and a 2.19 ERA - thought he should have been at least Co-MVP with Beckett.
Percival, Troy Anaheim '02 ALDS	This Troy evaded Zeus to save 2 of the 3 Angels' wins.
Peterson, Fritz Yankee '73	Embarrassed the Yankee organization with baseball's most outrageous trade - his family (pets included) for teammate Mike Kekich's family - I didn't think it was all that bad - back in the '50's, I wanted to be traded to TV's Ozzie & Harriet's' family for Ricky Nelson (but I never could carry a tune).
Pierre, Juan Florida '03 WS	The speedster kept the Yank defense on edge- went 7 for 21 (.333) - his hit won the opener.
Podres, Johnny Brooklyn '55 WS LA Dodgers '63 WS	Brought Brooklyn its only title winning game 7, 2-0 (was 2-0, 1.00 ERA. & MVP). He had so much fun he befuddled the Yanks again in '63 by a 4-1 score.
Quisenberry, Dan KC '80 ALCS	Yanks failed the Kansas City Quiz - he was 1-0, a save and a 0.00 ERA in 4 2/3 innings.
Rally Monkey Anaheim '02 ALDS LAA Angels '05 ALDS	'02 the animated scoreboard primate would appear whenever the Angels were behind or tied in the 5th inning. In game 4 he appeared with the Angels down 6-4; naturally they won 9-6. Yanks couldn't get the monkey off their back as the Angels won the series the next day. In '05 his scoreboard screen antics put the fans in a frenzy cheering the Angels to a game 2 victory.
Ramirez, Manny Red Sox '04 ALCS	Although not having an RBI, batted .300 (9 for 30).

Reese, Pee Wee Brooklyn '55 WS	The Dodger shortstop hit .296 (8 for 27) with 5 runs scored including the second run in the Dodgers 2-0 win in the finale.
Reuss, Jerry Dodgers '81 WS	With the Series tied at 2 he bested Ron Guidry for a 2-1 victory in pivotal game 5.
Ripken, Cal Baltimore '95	The All-Century shortstop broke the hearts of the Yankee nation by breaking one of their most cherished records - Lou (the Iron Horse) Gehrig's 2130 consecutive game record. Cal went on to reach 2632 game before a well deserved rest.
Rivera, Juan LAA Angels '05 ALDS	The former Pinstriper batted .353 and in game 2 had a big home run and a headfirst slide into first base for a lead-off infield hit that led to a run in the 4-2 win.
Robinson, Jackie Brooklyn '55 WS	The All-Century second baseman steal of home made Yogi hopping mad - Yanks won this game but not the Series.
Rodriguez, Francisco Anaheim '02 ALDS LAA Angels '05 ALDS	In '02 K-Rod only pitched 5 2/3 innings all year and duplicated that in the series going 5 2/3 innings. He showed up in all 3 wins, getting credit for 2 victories and his fastball K'd 8 Yanks - Mariano who? In '05 KRod did in the Yankees like in '02 – 2.70 ERA, 2 saves.
Rodriguez, Ivan Florida '03 WS	IRod the perennial All-Star's bat cooled off from his hot NL playoffs but he still hit .273 (6 for 22) with 2 doubles. But his defense controlling the young Marlin arms was instrumental in the Fish winning the Series.
Rose, Pete Cincinnati '76 WS	The Yankee offense went through lead-off man Mickey Rivers. Pete, the third baseman this year, psyched out Mickey by playing right on top of him when Rivers batted, (so close he seemed to suck the air right out of him). The Yank offense never could get into gear with this maneuver by Charlie Hustle as Rivers went 3 for 18 (.167).

Russo, Chris 660 WFAN New York 1990-present	Probably the best known Yankee Hater on the NYC air-waves. Known as Mad Dog, he co-hosts a daily afternoon radio show, and is always growling whenever the Yanks have success.
Salmon, Tim Anaheim '02 ALDS	A main cog in the Angels "upstream" battle Salmon led them with 7 RBIs (4 in game 3).
Santana, Ervin LAA Angels '05 ALDS	In the deciding game in the second inning the rookie had to go in after Colon couldn't go on due to his bad shoulder – after a shaky start he stumped the Yanks into the seventh inning before being relieved. He was the winning pitcher in the 5-2 finale.
Schilling, Curt Arizona '01 WS Red Sox '04 ALCS	In '01, he was outstanding in his 3 games (1-0, 1.69) ERA. He was Co- MVP with the Big Unit for the Series. In '04 he gave one of the Series most heroic performances - won game 6 pitching with a sutured ankle - was literally a 'Red Socks' pitcher as his socks were red with blood oozing through the sutures - in six innings he only gave up 4 hits and one run.
Scioscia, Mike Manager Anaheim '02 ALDS LAA Angels '05 ALDS	The Big Apple's nemesis, the Angels skipper, sent Joe Torre's pinstriped teams home twice in four years in the ALDS.
Shannon, Mike St. Louis '64 WS	Moon Man's orbit shot was the big blow in the Cards opening game win. His rocket arm cut down the Mick trying to stretch a hit into a double in game 4 stopping a Yank rally. He only had 6 hits but made them count as he led the Cards with 6 runs scored.
Skowron, Bill Dodgers '63 WS	Moose had a poor season after the Yanks traded him to the Dodgers. Seeing his former Pinstripers in the Series woke him up. He was LA's big stick (.385, 5 for 13, homer and 3 RBIs) in the 4 game sweep.

Slaughter, "Country" St. Louis '42 WS	Enos was part of the Cardinal slaughter (4 games to 1) - in game 2 he doubled in the 8th and scored the winning run, then rifle-armed out the tying run at third - in game 3 robbed King Kong Keller of a homer in a 2-0 win - in game 5 final he tied the score at 1 with a homer and then his single led to a run to tie it at 2, setting the stage for winning the title in the 9th on Kurowski's homer.
Smith, Hal Pittsburgh '60 WS	It looked like he'd be the Series hero with his 3-run round tripper in the 8th inning of game 7 that put the Bucs up 9-7. The Yanks tied it setting the stage for the Maz homer. Anyway he should get the award for best supporting hero.
Snider, Duke Brooklyn '55 WS	The Duke of Flatbush flattened Yankee pitching (.320, 8 for 20, NL record 4 homers, 7 RBIs).
Southworth, Billy St. Louis '26 WS and '42 WS	In '26 belted Yank pitchers (.345, 10 for 29, double, triple, homer, 4 RBIs, 6 runs). In '42 was Cards' Manager in the big upset of the "invincible" Yanks in 5 games.
Spahn, Warren Milwaukee '57 WS	Won the only game that Lew Burdette didn't. It was a 5-4 10 inning white knuckler.
Spiezio, Scott Anaheim '02 ALDS	Ed's ('64 Cardinals) kid went 6 for 15 (.400) and drove in 6 runs.
Taylor, Ron St. Louis '64 WS	His near tailor made perfect relief performance (4 innings with only a BB to the Mick) was big in Cards 4-3 win in game 4.
Thevenow, Tommy St. Louis '26 WS	The Cards SS had the lowest average of the regulars during the season (.256) but hit like his player manager, Hornsby, during the Series leading the Red Birds batters (.417, 10 for 24, 4 RBIs, 5 runs).
Uecker, Bob St. Louis '64 WS	Without playing the back-up catcher loosened up any tension the Cards may have had by shagging fly balls with a tuba before game 1 (he knew then that his talents lie elsewhere).

Umpires '04 ALCS	Reversed the calls, after huddling together, in game six getting them right - Bellhorn's homer and ARod's karate chop being called interference.
Valenzuela, Fernando Dodgers '81 WS	With LA down 2 zip, the NL Cy Young winner and Rookie of the Year pitched a gutsy game throwing seemingly a thousand pitches to beat the Yanks 5-4.
Varitek, Jason Red Sox '04 ALCS	Besides handling the staff the catcher hit .321 with 2 homers and 7 RBIs. Also in July got involved in a fight with ARod which awakened the Red Sox from their season-long lethargic play.
Vincent, Fay MLB Commissioner '90	Had the Boss agree to a ban from baseball due to his hiring an alleged gambler to get "dirt" on Dave Winfield - to avoid lawsuits the Boss was exiled until '93.
Virdon, Bill Pittsburgh '60 WS	He made two great catches saving 2 games, had clutch hits (5 RBIs), and is remembered for his hard hit grounder that looked like a sure double play that bounced into Tony KubeKs throat (almost killing him). This was the main ingredient in the Bucs' 5 run 8th in game 7, which ultimately led to the Bucs' Title.
Vizquel, Omar Cleveland '97 ALDS	Besides his usual Gold Glove leather show, he was the Indians top hitter at .500 (9 for 18 with 3 runs scored) and his hit in the 9th inning won game 4.
Warwick, Carl St. Louis '64 WS	The Yanks must of grimaced every time they saw Warwick with his stick whenever the Cards needed a pinch-hitter - he was 3 for 4 with a BB and 2 of the pinch-hits were very key in winning games 1 and 4.
White, Ernie St. Louis '42 WS	Whitewashed the Yanks with a 6-hitter winning game 3 by 2-0 score.

White, Frank KC '80 ALCS	To be perfectly frank, he was a Yank nightmare or (Whitemare) .545, 6 for 11, 2 doubles, homer, 3 runs, 3 RBIs in the 3 game sweep.
Whitson, Ed Yankees '85	One of the Boss' big buys that didn't pan out - he and Billy Martin never hit it off so Whitson hit Martin in a bar room tiff breaking his arm, cracking his ribs and bloodying his nose - it was bye, bye Billy (again).
Williams, Matt Cleveland '97 ALDS Arizona '01 WS	1997 had a big 2- run homer in a 7-5 win in game 2 and an RBI hit in the 4-3 finale, 2001 was 7 for 23 (.304), with a homer and 7 RBIs.
Wilson, Willie KC '80 ALCS	The speedster was 4 for 13 with a double, triple and 4 RBIs in the Royals 3 game sweep.
Womack, Tony Arizona '01 WS	Had 8 hits but it was his double to right off the "great" Mariano that tied the score at 2 setting up Gonzo's winning hit - my son Chris still can't believe it was an 0-2 count.
Wooten, Shawn Anaheim '01 ALDS	The Angels role player was on a roll (6 for 9, .667, 4 runs and 2 RBIs).
Wright, Jaret Cleveland '97 ALDS	Indians had the Wright stuff on the hill as he posted 2 victories.
Yeager, Steve Dodgers '81 WS	A Tri-MVP, the LA catcher was 4 for 14 with 2 homers and 4 RBIs. In game 5 he followed Guerrero's homer with his own in beating Ron Guidry 2-1.
ZEUS Greek God of Gods '97, '01,'02, '03, '04, '05	Let the Pinstripers down - inattentive, inability to focus, poor delegating, etc. kept the Yankee fingers ring-less during these years.

Printed in the United States
50120LVS00004B/76-255